MIDDLE VOICE VERBS IN THE NEW TESTAMENT

STUDIES IN PAULINE USAGE

MIDDLE VOICE VERBS IN THE NEW TESTAMENT

STUDIES IN PAULINE USAGE

Susan E. Kmetko

GLOSSAHOUSE DISSERTATION SERIES 13

GLOSSAHOUSE
WILMORE, KY
www.glossahouse.com

Middle Voice Verbs in the New Testament: Studies in Pauline Usage

© GlossaHouse, 2022

All rights reserved. No part of this book may be reproduced or transmitted in any form or by any means, electronic or mechanical, including photocopying or recording, or by means of any information storage or retrieval system, except as may be expressly permitted by the 1976 Copyright Act or in writing from the publisher. Requests for permission should be addressed in writing to the following:

GlossaHouse, LLC
110 Callis Circle
Wilmore, KY 40309
www.GlossaHouse.com

Kmetko, Susan E.
 middle voice verbs in the new testament: studies in Pauline usage / Susan E. Kmetko — Wilmore, KY: GlossaHouse © 2022

  xxvi, 334p. 15.24cm. —
  (GlossaHouse Dissertation Series; Ref.)
  A revision of the author's Ph.D. dissertation, Australian Catholic University, 2018

  ISBN-13: 978-1-63663-0304

  Library of Congress Control Number: 2022948667

Cover design by T. Michael W. Halcomb

Text layout and book design by Andrew J. Coutras and Fredrick J. Long

Volume Editing by Andrew J. Coutras and Fredrick J. Long

The fonts used to create this work are available from www.linguistsoftware.com/lgku.htm

I dedicate this work to the risen Lord, Jesus Christ,

ὅτι ἐξ αὐτοῦ καὶ δι' αὐτοῦ καὶ εἰς αὐτὸν τὰ πάντα·
αὐτῷ ἡ δόξα εἰς τοὺς αἰῶνας, ἀμήν.
(Rom 11:36)

GlossaHouse Dissertation Series (GDS)

Series Editors

Fredrick J. Long ◆ T. Michael W. Halcomb
Carl S. Sweatman ◆ Andrew J. Coutras

Volume Editors

Andrew J. Coutras ◆ Fredrick J. Long

GLOSSAHOUSE DISSERTATION SERIES

The purpose of GlossaHouse Dissertation Series is to publish innovative, affordable, and cutting-edge scholarly research in the field of Biblical Studies that treat ancient and modern texts and languages.

ACKNOWLEDGEMENTS

I wish to gratefully acknowledge the following:

- ◊ Australian Catholic University for the opportunity to undertake this project.
- ◊ The expertise and guidance of my principal supervisor, Dr. Michael Theophilos, and that of my co-supervisors Dr. Stephen C. Carlson and formerly, Dr. Alan Cadwallader.
- ◊ Stirling Theological College for generous access and use of facilities during this project.
- ◊ The patience and support of my husband, Mike Kmetko, throughout the project.
- ◊ My daughter, Michaela, for assistance with formatting the original thesis.

Table of Contents

List of Figures — xiii

List of Tables — xiv

Abbreviations — xv

Chapter 1
   Introduction — 1

Chapter 2
   Survey of Literature on the Middle Voice — 7

Chapter 3
   The Middle Voice in First Thessalonians — 74

Chapter 4
   Present Middle Verbs in First Thessalonians — 119

Chapter 5
   Middle Verbs in Second Corinthians — 171

Chapter 6
   Selected Middle Verb Studies in Second Corinthians — 208

Chapter 7
   Exegetical Significance: Sample Studies from Galatians — 245

Chapter 8
   Conclusion — 301

Appendix: Middle Verb Forms in 2 Corinthians — 307

BIBLIOGRAPHY	309
INDICES	327
AUTHOR INDEX	325
SUBJECT INDEX	329
INDEX OF EXEGETICAL CASE STUDIES	332
INDEX OF MIDDLE VERBS EXAMINED	333

LIST OF FIGURES

2.2 Diagrammatic Representation of Voice Form	41
3.1 Percentage of Middle Verbs per NT Book	75
6.1 Frequency of Middle Verbs per Chapter in 2 Corinthians	209
6.2 Number of Occurrences of καυχάομαι in the NT	219
7.1 Conceptual Diagram of Galatians 3:3	271
7.2 Conceptual Diagram of Galatians 4:10–11	288

LIST OF TABLES

3.1 Properties of Aorist Middle Verb Forms in 1 Thessalonians	117
4.1 Possible Readings of 1 Thessalonians 2:13	143
4.2 Properties of Present Middle Verb Forms in 1 Thessalonians	168
5.1 Properties of Middle Verb Forms in 2 Corinthians	207
6.1 Properties of Selected Middle Verbs in 2 Corinthians	244
7.1 Further Present and Aorist Middle Verbs from Galatians	247
7.2 Stages of Salvation History in Galatians 3	261
7.3 Possible Translations of Galatians 3:3b	268

ABBREVIATIONS

General

AB	Anchor Bible
ABD	Freedman, David Noel, ed. *Anchor Bible Dictionary*. 6 vols. New York: Doubleday, 1992
ALGNT	Friberg, Timothy, Barbara Friberg and Neva F. Miller. *Analytical Lexicon of the Greek New Testament*. Victoria, BC: Trafford, 2005
ANTC	Abingdon New Testament Commentaries
BAGD	Bauer, Walter, William F. Arndt, F. Wilbur Gingrich, and Frederick W. Danker. *Greek-English Lexicon of the New Testament and Other Early Christian Literature*, 2nd ed. Chicago: University of Chicago Press, 1979
BDAG	Danker, Frederick W., Walter Bauer, William F. Arndt, and F. Wilbur Gingrich. *Greek-English Lexicon of the New Testament and Other Early Christian Literature*. 3rd ed. Chicago: University of Chicago Press, 2000
BDF	Blass, Friedrich, Albert Debrunner, and Robert W. Funk. *A Greek Grammar of the New Testament and Other Early Christian Literature*. Chicago: University of Chicago Press, 1961
BECNT	Baker Exegetical Commentary on the New Testament
BGNT	Baker's Greek New Testament Library
BNTC	Black's New Testament Commentaries
BTS	Biblical Tools and Studies
CNTTS	Center for New Testament Textual Studies
CSL	Cambridge Studies in Linguistics

EFN	Estudios de filología neotestamentaria
GE	Montanari, Franco. *The Brill Dictionary of Ancient Greek*. English Edition. Edited by Madeleine Goh and Chad Schroeder. Leiden: Brill, 2015
GELNT	Thayer, Joseph Henry. *A Greek-English Lexicon of the New Testament*, corrected ed. New York: American Book Company, 1889
HUTh	Hermeneutische Untersuchungen zur Theologie
ICC	International Critical Commentary
JAAR	*Journal of the American Academy of Religion*
L&N	Louw, Johannes P., and Eugene A. Nida, eds. *Greek-English Lexicon of the New Testament: Based on Semantic Domains*. 2nd ed. New York: United Bible Societies, 1989
LCL	Loeb Classical Library
LEC	Library of Early Christianity
LSJ	Liddell, Henry George, Robert Scott, and Henry Stuart Jones. *A Greek-English Lexicon*. 9th ed. with revised supplement. Oxford: Clarendon, 1996
MLS	Miami Linguistic Series
MM	Moulton, James H., and George Milligan. *Vocabulary of the Greek New Testament*. London: Hodder & Stoughton, 1930
MNTC	*Moffatt New Testament Commentary*
NAGL	Perschbacher, Wesley J. *The New Analytical Greek Lexicon*. Peabody, MA: Hendrickson, 1990

NICNT	New International Commentary on the New Testament
NIDNTTE	*New International Dictionary of New Testament Theology and Exegesis.* Edited by Moisés Silva. 5 vols. Grand Rapids: Zondervan, 2014
NIGTC	New International Greek Testament Commentary
NovT	*Novum Testamentum*
NT	New Testament
NTL	New Testament Library
NTM	New Testament Monographs
NTS	*New Testament Studies*
OT	Old Testament
PNTC	Pillar New Testament Commentary
SBL	Society of Biblical Literature
SiHoLS	Studies in the History of the Language Sciences
SNTSMS	Society for New Testament Studies Monograph Series
SP	Sacra Pagina
TDNT	Kittel, Gerhard, and Gerhard Friedrich, eds., *Theological Dictionary of the New Testament.* Translated by Geoffrey W. Bromily. 10 vols. Grand Rapids: Eerdmans, 1964–1976
TiLSM	Trends in Linguistics. Studies and Monographs
TNTC	Tyndale New Testament Commentaries
TSL	Typological Studies in Language
WBC	Word Biblical Commentary
WUNT	Wissenschaftliche Untersuchungen zum Neuen Testament

Bible Editions

ASV	American Standard Version (1901)
Brenton	Brenton, Lancelot C. L. *The Septuagint with Apocrypha: Greek and English* London: Samuel Bagster and Sons, 1851
CEB	Common English Bible (2011)
CJB	The Complete Jewish Bible (1998)
DRA	The Douay-Rheims American Edition (1899)
ERV	English Revised Version (1885)
ESV	English Standard Version (2016)
GNV	Geneva Bible (1599)
KJV	King James Version (1611)
LXX	Rahlfs, Alfred, ed. *Septuaginta*. Stuttgart: Deutsche Bibelgesellschaft, 1935
NA^{28}	Aland, Barbara, and Kurt Aland, Johannes Karavidopoulos, Carlo M. Martini, Bruce M. Metzger, eds., *Novum Testamentum Graece*, 28th rev. ed. Stuttgart: Deutsche Bibelgesellschaft, 2012
NAB	The New American Bible (2011)
NAS	The New American Standard Bible (1977)
NAU	The New American Standard Bible (1995)
NEB	The New English Bible (1970)
NET	New English Translation (2005)
NETS	Pietersma, Albert, and Benjamin G. Wright, eds., *A New English Translation of the Septuagint*. New York: Oxford University Press, 2007
NIV	New International Version (2011)
NJB	The New Jerusalem Bible (1985)
NKJV	New King James Version (1982)
NLT	New Living Translation (1996)

NRSV	New Revised Standard Version (1989)
RSV	Revised Standard Version (1952)
TNT	Tyndale's New Testament (1534)
WH	Westcott, B. F., and F. J. A. Hort, eds. *The New Testament in the Original Greek*, 2 vols. London: Macmillan, 1881

Ancient Greek Works
Aeschines
Ctes.	*In Ctesiphonem*

Diodorus Siculus
Bibl. Hist.	*Bibliotheca historica*

Clement
Quis div.	*Quis dives salvetur*

Epictetus
Diatr.	*Dissertationes ab Arriano digestae*

Euripides
Iph. aul.	*Iphigenia aulidensis*

Josephus
A.J.	*Antiquitates judaicae*
B.J.	*Bellum judaicum*
C.Ap.	*Contra Apionem*

Luccian
Jupp.trag.	*Juppiter tragoedus*

Philo
Abr.	*De Abrahamo*
Conf.	*De confusione linguarum*
Det.	*Quod deterius potiori insidari soleat*
Her.	*Quis rerum divinarum heres sit*
Leg.	*Legum allegoriae*

Legat.	*Legatio ad Gaium*
Migr.	*De migratione Abrahami*
Mos. 1, 2	*De vita Mosis I, II*

Plutarch

Adul. amic.	*Quomodo adulator ab amico internoscatur*
Aem.	*Aemilius Paullus*
Cons. Apoll.	*Consolatio ad Apollonium*
De laude	*De laude ipsius*
Luc.	*Lucullus*
Praec.ger.rei.publ.	*Praecepta gerendae rei publicae*
Superst.	*De superstitione*
Vit. aere al.	*De Vitando aere alieno*

Xenophon

Apol.	*Apologia Socratis*

Papyri

Abbreviations as per: *Checklist of Editions of Greek, Latin, Demotic, and Coptic Papyri, Ostraca, and Tablets.* Founding Editors: John F. Oates and William H. Willis. https://papyri.info/docs/checklist

BGU 1–4	*Aegyptische Urkunden aus den Königlichen* (later, *Staatlichen*) *Museen zu Berlin, Griechische Urkunden.* Berlin. Vol. I, 1895; vol. II, 1898; vol. III, 1903; vol. IV, 1912.
O.Berenike 2	*Documents from Berenike.* Vol. II, Texts from the 1999–2001 Seasons, ed. R. S. Bagnall, C. Helms and A. M. F. W. Verhoogt. Brussels, 2005.
P.Amh. 2	*The Amherst Papyri, Being an Account of the Greek Papyri in the Collection of the Right Hon. Lord Amherst of Hackney, F.S.A. at Didlington*

	Hall, Norfolk, ed. B.P. Grenfell and A.S. Hunt. Vol. II, Classical Fragments and Documents of the Ptolemaic, Roman and Byzantine Periods. London, 1901.
P.Bad. 4	*Veröffentlichungen aus den badischen Papyrus-Sammlungen*. Vol. IV, Griechische Papyri, ed. F. Bilabel. Heidelberg, 1924.
P.Cair.Zen. 3	*Zenon Papyri, Catalogue général des antiquités égyptiennes du Musée du Caire*, ed. C.C. Edgar. Vol. III. Cairo. 1928.
P.Col. 3	*Columbia Papyri*. Vol. III. Zenon Papyri: Business Papers of the Third Century BC dealing with Palestine and Egypt I, ed. W. L. Westermann and E. S. Hasenoehrl. New York, 1934.
P.Fouad	*Les Papyrus Fouad I*, ed. A. Bataille, O. Guéraud, P. Jouguet, N. Lewis, H. Marrou, J. Scherer and W.G. Waddel, Cairo, 1939. (Publ. Soc. Fouad III).
P.Giss.	*Griechische Papyri im Museum des oberhessischen Geschichtsvereins zu Giessen*, ed. O. Eger, E. Kornemann, and P.M. Meyer. Leipzig-Berlin, 1910–1912.
P.Harr. 2	*The Rendel Harris Papyri of Woodbrooke College, Birmingham*. Vol. II, ed. R.A. Coles, M. Manfredi, P.J. Sijpesteijn, A.S. Brown et al. Zutphen, 1985. (Stud. Amst. XXVI).
P.Lond. 6	*Greek Papyri in the British Museum*. Vol. VI, Jews and Christians in Egypt; The Jewish Troubles in Alexandria and the Athanasian Controversy, ed. H.I. Bell and W.E Crum. London, 1924.

P.Mich. 3	*Michigan Papyri*. Vol. III, Miscellaneous Papyri, ed. J.G. Winter et al., Ann Arbor, 1936. (Univ. of Mich. Studies, Humanistic Series 40).
P.Mich. 5	*Michigan Papyri*. Vol. V, Papyri from Tebtunis, Part II, ed. E.M. Husselman, A. E. R. Boak, and W. F. Edgerton. Ann Arbor, 1944. (Univ. of Mich. Studies, Humanistic Series 29).
P.Mich. 8	*Michigan Papyri*. Vol. VIII, Papyri and Ostraca from Karanis, Second Series, ed. H. C. Youtie and J. G. Winter. Ann Arbor, 1951. (Univ. of Mich. Studies, Humanistic Series 50).
P.Oslo 2	*Papyri Osloenses*. Vol. II, ed. S. Eitrem and L. Amundsen. Oslo, 1931.
P.Oxy. 1	*The Oxyrhynchus Papyri*. Published by the Egypt Exploration Society in Graeco-Roman Memoirs. Vol. I, ed. B. P. Grenfell and A. S. Hunt. London, 1898.
P.Oxy. 3	*The Oxyrhynchus Papyri*. Published by the Egypt Exploration Society in Graeco-Roman Memoirs. Vol. III, ed. B. P. Grenfell and A. S. Hunt. London, 1903.
P.Oxy. 6	*The Oxyrhynchus Papyri*. Published by the Egypt Exploration Society in Graeco-Roman Memoirs. Vol. VI, ed. B. P. Grenfell and A. S. Hunt. London, 1908.
P.Oxy. 8	*The Oxyrhynchus Papyri*. Published by the Egypt Exploration Society in Graeco-Roman Memoirs. Vol. VIII, ed. A. S. Hunt. London, 1911.
P.Oxy. 10	*The Oxyrhynchus Papyri*. Published by the Egypt Exploration Society in Graeco-Roman

	Memoirs. Vol. X, ed. B.P. Grenfell and A.S. Hunt. London, 1914.
P.Oxy. 42	*The Oxyrhynchus Papyri.* Published by the Egypt Exploration Society in Graeco-Roman Memoirs. Vol. XLII, ed. P. J. Parsons. London, 1974.
P.Ryl. 2	*Catalogue of the Greek and Latin Papyri in the John Rylands Library, Manchester.* Vol. II, Documents of the Ptolemaic and Roman Periods, ed. J. de M. Johnson, V. Martin, and A. S. Hunt. Manchester, 1915.
P.Ryl. 4	*Catalogue of the Greek and Latin Papyri in the John Rylands Library, Manchester.* Vol. IV, Documents of the Ptolemaic, Roman and Byzantine Periods, ed. C. H. Roberts and E. G. Turner. Manchester, 1952.
PSI 4	*Papiri greci e latini.* (Pubblicazioni della Società Italiana per la ricerca dei papiri greci e latini in Egitto). Vol. IV, edited under the general direction of G. Vitelli and M. Norsa. Florence, 1917.
P.Sorb. 3	*Papyrus de la Sorbonne.* Vol. III, ed. H. Cadell, W. Clarysse, and K. Robic. Paris, 2011.
P.Tebt. 1	*The Tebtunis Papyri.* Vol. I, ed. B. P. Grenfell, A. S. Hunt and J. G. Smyly. London, 1902. (Univ. of California Publications, Graeco-Roman Archaeology I; Egypt Exploration Society, Graeco-Roman Memoirs 4).
P.Tebt. 2	*The Tebtunis Papyri.* Vol. II, ed. B. P. Grenfell and A. S. Hunt. London, 1907. (Univ. of California Publications, Graeco-Roman

	Archaeology II). Reprint 1970. (Egypt Exploration Society, Graeco-Roman Memoirs 52).
P.Wash.Univ. 1	*Washington University Papyri.* Vol. I, ed. V.B. Schuman. Missoula, 1980. (Am. Stud. Pap. XVII).
P.Zen.Pestm.	*Greek and Demotic Texts from the Zenon Archive,* ed. under the general direction of P. W. Pestman. Leiden, 1980.
SB 1	*Sammelbuch griescher Urkunden aus Aegypten.* (A collection of papyri, ostraca, inscriptions, mummy tablets and related texts published in journals or unindexed catalogues. Begun by F. Preisigke in 1915, continued by F. Bilabel, E. Kiessling, and H.-A. Rupprecht). Vol. I, Strassburg and Berlin, 1913–1915
SB 5	*Sammelbuch griescher Urkunden aus Aegypten.* (A collection of documentary papyri, ostraca, inscriptions, mummy tablets and related texts published in journals or unindexed catalogues. Begun by F. Preisigke in 1915, continued by F. Bilabel, E. Kiessling, and H.-A. Rupprecht). Vol. V, Heidelberg and Wiesbaden, 1934–1955.
SB 6	*Sammelbuch griescher Urkunden aus Aegypten.* (A collection of documentary papyri, ostraca, inscriptions, mummy tablets and related texts published in journals or unindexed catalogues. Begun by F. Preisigke in 1915, continued by F. Bilabel, E. Kiessling, and H.-A. Rupprecht). Vol. VI, Wiesbaden, 1958–1963.

SB 18	*Sammelbuch griescher Urkunden aus Aegypten.* (A collection of documentary papyri, ostraca, inscriptions, mummy tablets and related texts published in journals or unindexed catalogues. Begun by F. Preisigke in 1915, continued by F. Bilabel, E. Kiessling, and H.-A. Rupprecht). Vol. XVIII, Wiesbaden, 1993.
UPZ 1	*Urkunden der Ptolemäerzeit (ältere Funde)*, ed. U. Wilcken. Vol. I, Papyri aus Unterägypten. Berlin-Leipzig, 1927.

Symbols

[ ]	Indicates text added for clarity or reconstructed by editor in the case of papyri.
<αβγ>	Characters erroneously omitted by scribe, added by modern editor

Electronic resources

BibleWorks 10	Software for Biblical Exegesis and Research, version 10. BibleWorks, LLC. Norfolk, VA.
DDbDP	Sosin J., et al., eds. *Duke Databank of Documentary Papyri*, www.papyri.info
TLG	Pantelia, Maria C., ed. Thesaurus Linguae Graecae® Digital Library. University of California, Irvine. http://www.tlg.uci.edu

CHAPTER 1
INTRODUCTION

1.1 RATIONALE AND STATEMENT OF THESIS

This thesis challenges the general lack of attention traditionally afforded to the 3,726 middle verb forms that appear in the Greek New Testament.[1] Contrary to certain modern languages such as English that only distinguish between active and passive voice, in the Koine Greek of the New Testament era, three voices were recognized: active, passive, and middle. While the distinction between active and passive may be readily recognized, the one between active and middle, which was the fundamental opposition in early Greek, is less clearly defined and less well recognized in the Greek of the New Testament.

Greek middle verbs typically become active with translation into languages such as English that do not have a morphological middle voice; hence the middle sense is often lost or obscured in translation. This applies to both *media tantum* verbs (existing only in middle form) and oppositional middles (those having both active and middle forms). Hence, for example, the middle-only verb ῥύομαι becomes *I rescue* in English, appearing active to the English reader. Likewise, the distinction between the active παύω and the middle παύομαι becomes a lexical variation in translation, for παύω is rendered *I stop* and παύομαι *I pause*.[2] These both appear active in English, although one is actually a middle verb in Greek.

---

[1] This is the total number of inflected middle forms of various lexemes. Morphological data throughout this work is obtained from Bible Works 10, BNM database for NA28. It distinguishes between middle and passive according to context when forms are identical.

[2] Unless noted as citations, translations of Greek text are those of the author.

Relevant to this study is the fact that the majority of middle verbs in the New Testament are *media tantum* and have customarily been considered "deponent" (middle in form but active in function).[3] Applying this concept therefore reduces very many NT middle verbs to actives. However, the notion of deponency has come under considerable scrutiny in recent times. It is not innate to Greek; it was imported when Latin grammatical concepts were applied to Greek during the Renaissance.[4] In fact, the 2010 SBL panel for Biblical Greek Language and Linguistics rejected deponency as a valid category for Greek verbs.[5] Hence, if the *media tantum* verbs are not deponent, (not active) they must be regarded as middle. This consequently calls for a better understanding of the middle voice itself in the Greek New Testament.

In response to the above need, this thesis explores the meaning of the Greek middle voice and contends that middle morphology does indeed signify an ascertainable middle function for both *media tantum* and oppositional middle verbs in the Greek New Testament. Consequently, the exegetical implications of the middle function of the significant number of middle verbs warrant due consideration in the process of interpretation of the text.

1.2 ASSUMPTIONS AND PARAMETERS

The primary ground of this study is the language of the New Testament as it appears in the text of NA^{28}. Textual variants are not normally considered unless there is relevance for this study. The investigation proceeds based on three considerations regarding this language:

First, it is understood that the language of the New Testament can be viewed as a sub-set of the Koine Greek of the Hellenistic era (300

---

[3] Grammars often state that the majority of middle verbs in the New Testament are "deponent;" e.g., William D. Mounce, *Basics of Biblical Greek Grammar*, 2nd ed. (Grand Rapids: Zondervan, 2003), 152. See further below, §2.1.5.

[4] See n19, §2.2.3 and §2.2.4.

[5] As noted by Constantine R. Campbell, *Advances in the Study of Greek: New Insights for Reading the New Testament* (Grand Rapids: Zondervan, 2015), 98.

BCE–300 CE).[6] Therefore, use of the middle voice in contemporaneous literary works within and beyond the Judeo-Christian tradition, as well as non-literary samples of the language from documentary papyri or inscriptions is pertinent to this inquiry.[7] Second, it is recognized that the style of writing in the New Testament is not homogeneous, some being more literary than others.[8] Since this factor may affect the use of the middle voice, the samples of verbs for investigation are taken from one author, namely Paul.

Finally, although the Greek language has evolved through various stages, it is nevertheless understood to be a continuum, hence, the language of the preceding classical era can inform the study of Koine Greek.[9] While it is recognized that the use of the middle voice was

---

[6] Dates adopted for the stages of the language are Epic (e.g., Homer) 800 BCE–500 BCE; Classical (mostly Attic) 500–300 BCE; Hellenistic 300 BCE–300 CE (Chrys C. Caragounis, *The Development of Greek and the New Testament: Morphology, Syntax, Phonology, and Textual Transmission* [Tübingen: Mohr Siebeck, 2004], xx). James Hope Moulton refers to the work by Deissmann relating to evidence from papyri and inscriptions (discussed further below) which, he claims, "preserve for us the Hellenistic vernacular," noting that the New Testament writings can be aligned with the range of literary standards represented by these (*Prolegomena*, vol.1 of *A Grammar of New Testament Greek* [Edinburgh: T&T Clark, 1908–1976], 4–5). See similarly BDF, §§2–3 and Geoffrey Horrocks, *Greek: A History of the Language and its Speakers*, 2nd ed (Malden, MA: Wiley-Blackwell, 2014), 147.

[7] Accordingly, Albert Wifstrand comments that both "ordinary everyday language" and "Hellenistic literary style" are represented in the New Testament ("Language and Style of the New Testament" in *Epochs and Styles: Selected Writings on the New Testament, Greek Language and Greek Culture in the Post-Classical Era*, ed. Lars Rydbeck and Stanley E. Porter, trans. Denis Searby [Tübingen: Mohr Siebeck, 2005], 71–77).

[8] For comments on the various levels of literary style in the NT, see A. T. Robertson, *A Grammar of the New Testament in the Light of Historical Research* (London: Hodder & Stoughton, 1914), 76–139; also, BDF §3.

[9] Regarding changes in the language within the classical Attic period, see A. N. Jannaris, *An Historical Greek Grammar Chiefly of the Attic Dialect* (London: Macmillan, 1897) 6–8, 362–63. Francis Thomas Gignac identifies morphological trends through the Koine period which are evident from the papyri (*Morphology*, vol. 2 of *A Grammar of the Greek Papyri of the Roman and Byzantine Period*, Testi e Documenti per lo Studio Dell'Antichita [Milan: Cisalpino-La Goliardica, 1981], 321–27). Nevertheless, there is

declining in the Hellenistic period, a morphological examination of the NA^{28} text identifies 13.5 percent of all verbs in the New Testament as middle in form.[10] Accordingly, the extent to which the function of the middle voice still applies in the language of the New Testament and the consequent implications for interpretation of the text generate the particular focus of this project.

1.3 METHOD

The method adopted for this study is driven by the following questions:

1. How may the function of the middle voice be described?
2. Do middle form verbs in the NT typically exhibit middle function?
3. If so, what may be the exegetical and interpretive implications?

In chapter 2, a survey of the relevant literature reveals that there have been various descriptions and interpretations of the function of the middle voice over time. As will be shown (§2.1 below), Classical and New Testament grammars generally speak of subjects acting either on themselves (direct reflexive) or in their own interest (indirect reflexive) such that the subject is either a direct or indirect object of the middle verb. Some also refer to reciprocal actions and to subjects acting out of their own intrinsic resources. Although nomenclature varies between grammars, these functions may be summarized to say that "the subject acts on, for or by reference to itself[.]"[11] This is henceforth referred to as the 'grammatical sense'.

---

continuity in the language itself, as highlighted by Chrys C. Caragounis, *New Testament Language and Exegesis: A Diachronic Approach*, WUNT 323 (Tübingen: Mohr Siebeck, 2014), 2–3. Likewise, Horrocks discusses Koine as an extension of the Attic (*Greek*, 80–83).

[10] Statistical data obtained from *BibleWorks 10* NT morphological data base (BNM) for NA^{28}.

[11] Robert W. Funk, *A Beginning-Intermediate Grammar of Hellenistic Greek*, 3rd ed. (Salem, OR: Polebridge, 2013), 157.

Another perspective has developed from linguistic studies over the past century, generating the understanding that "subject-affectedness" is the distinctive characteristic of the middle voice.[12] Accordingly, Rutger J. Allan has written a well-received monograph on the middle voice in Ancient Greek based on this notion.[13] He identifies eleven sub-categories of subject-affectedness and demonstrates their connectedness by means of a network model.[14] Although Allan's findings are derived from Homeric and Classical Greek, his insight into the situation types represented by Greek middle verbs may fruitfully be applied to Koine Greek usage.

An alternative understanding of the Greek middle voice is offered by Philippe Eberhard who draws on the work of French linguist Emile Benveniste.[15] Benveniste asserts that middle *diathesis* (voice) designates that the subject is internal to the process of which it is an agent. Eberhard takes this to mean that the subject is conceptually placed within the sphere of the verb; it is acting medially within a process that encompasses it, rather like a player in a game. The emphasis is on the event, and the subject is functioning *within* the process described by the verb, not controlling it from the outside. Eberhard refers to this function as "medial."[16]

These three descriptors, namely the grammatical, subject-affected, and medial, serve as the analytical categories for this study. In chapters 3–6 they are applied to middle form verbs from 1 Thessalonians and 2 Corinthians as they appear in the text. The semantic sense of the verb is derived from lexica, biblical, and contemporaneous extra-biblical usage, while commentaries are consulted to illuminate the context under

---

[12] See §2.2.1.1 and §2.2.4 below.

[13] Rutger J. Allan, *The Middle Voice in Ancient Greek: A Study in Polysemy*, Amsterdam Studies in Classical Philology vol. 11 (Amsterdam: J. C. Gieben, 2003).

[14] Allan, *Polysemy*, 118–19.

[15] Philippe Eberhard, *The Middle Voice in Gadamer's Hermeneutics: A Basic Interpretation with Some Theological Implications* HUTh 45 (Tübingen: Mohr Siebeck, 2004), 15; Emile Benveniste, "Actif et moyen dans le verbe," in *Problèmes de linguistique générale*, vol.1 (Paris: Gallimard, 1966), 168–75. See §2.3 below.

[16] Eberhard, *Middle Voice*, 1.

examination, with any reference to the middle voice being noted. The syntactic function of each middle verb in context is then examined and compared with the three descriptors of middle voice to discover the extent to which middle function may be evident.

In total, ninety-two middle forms of forty-one different lexemes are explored in this manner, with an analysis of results presented in summary form at the conclusion of chapters 3, 4, 5, and 6. The correlation ascertained between form and function is then applied to a further ten middle verbs in Galatians (chapter 7) to explore the exegetical implications of reading these as verbs exhibiting true middle function. Each successive sample throughout the investigation deals with lexemes not previously studied in order to obtain the largest possible sample of middle verbs which may be meaningfully explored.

Chapter 2
Survey of Literature on the Middle Voice

Grammatical voice refers to the relation between subject and verb and is marked morphologically in the suffix of the verb. In Koine Greek, while three voices were recognized, these were not pervasively demarcated by unique morphology; hence, for example, as is well-known, middle and passive voices share the same form in the present tense, yet even in the aorist, some middle verbs exhibit the -ϑ(η)- morphology which is more typical of the passive, such as ἀπεκρίϑην: I answered.[1] Therefore, we must be mindful whether voice *per se* or voice morphology is the matter under discussion in any instance.

Further, there is a common perception that the middle voice is less widely used in the Koine language of NT times than it was in Classical Greek.[2] Nevertheless, it is not always clear whether such comments refer to a less frequent occurrence of the middle form or that the force of

---

[1] The fundamental distinction in voice in early Greek was between active and middle; the emergence of distinct passive suffixes is discussed by Nikolaos Lavidas, "Passives in the History of Greek: Evidence for the Role of the Passive Suffix," *Folia Linguistica Historica* 33 (2012): 87–121. Koine Greek represents a stage in the development of the language in which all three voices were recognized, as indicated in §2.1.1 and §2.1.2 below.

[2] Such statements are particularly evident in introductory grammars, e.g., "The middle voice was not as common in biblical Greek as it was in classical" (N. Clayton Croy, *A Primer of Biblical Greek* [Grand Rapids: Eerdmans, 1999], 47). Similarly, "the middle voice is on the decline in Hellenistic Greek and true middles are rare" (Funk, *Grammar of Hellenistic Greek*, 286). C. F. D. Moule claims that the distinction between active and middle had "become blurred" by the NT period (*An Idiom Book of New Testament Greek*, 2nd ed. [Cambridge: Cambridge University Press, 1960], 25). See also Daniel B. Wallace, *Greek Grammar Beyond the Basics: An Exegetical Syntax of the New Testament* (Grand Rapids: Zondervan, 1996), 415n17 and Jannaris, *Historical Greek Grammar*, 362–63.

the middle voice was less apparent, less understood, or perhaps all of these.³ Whichever the case, there has generally been a concomitant lack of clarity regarding the middle voice in New Testament grammars, particularly at the introductory level.⁴ It is pertinent therefore to consider the grammars and linguistic studies pertaining to earlier stages of the language, particularly the Attic of the classical era, in addition to those of Koine Greek, to search for an understanding of the middle voice as distinct from the active and passive. In short, what is the middle voice and how is it expressed?

In order to address this question, the following survey deals with accounts of the middle voice appearing in general Greek grammars before turning to more specific studies of the Greek middle voice.

2.1 THE MIDDLE VOICE IN GRAMMARS

We begin with two works written close to the period of the New Testament: The *Techné Grammatiké* of Dionysius Thrax and the *Syntax* of Apollonius Dyscolus. These consistently appear as foundational works in historical treatments of grammar or linguistics.⁵ Therefore, while this is not an historical study as such, it is nevertheless pertinent to observe the comments of these grammarians at the outset.

---

³ This is likely due to the evolution of the language from the Attic of the classical era, with a corresponding greater explicitness and loss of nuance, as discussed by Jannaris, *Historical Greek Grammar*, 6–8; see also Wallace, *Exegetical Syntax*, 15–19 and Horrocks, *Greek*, 79–159.

⁴ This is illustrated with examples below.

⁵ E.g., John Lyons, *Introduction to Theoretical Linguistics* (Cambridge: Cambridge University Press, 1968), 12; R. H. Robins, *The Byzantine Grammarians: Their Place in History*, TiLSM 70 (New York: Mouton de Gruyter, 1993), 41. Robins devotes ch. 4 to the *Techné Grammatiké*, also mentioning Apollonius Dyscolus, noting that his *Syntax* was highly regarded and formed a model for the renowned Latin Grammar by Priscian (ca. 500 CE) (*Byzantine Grammarians*, 15, 41).

2.1.1 Dionysius Thrax (ca. 100 BCE)

The *Techné Grammatiké* (also known as *Ars Grammatica*) by Dionysius Thrax has been described as the "the first attempt at a systematic grammar made in the Western World[.]"[6] A small concise booklet, it defines the parts of speech upon which later works are based.[7] In relation to the verb (περὶ ῥήματος) he states that "a verb is a word not inflected for case, but admitting tense, person and number and indicating an activity or being acted upon."[8] For what grammarians today speak of as the voice of a verb, Dionysius uses the term διάθεσις (disposition) and simply states that there are three, with brief examples, as below:[9]

| Διαθέσεις εἰσὶ τρεῖς, ἐνέργεια, πάθος, μεσότης· ἐνέργεια μὲν οἷον τύπτω, πάθος δὲ οἷον τύπτομαι, μεσότης δὲ ἡ ποτὲ μὲν ἐνέργειαν ποτὲ δὲ πάθος παριστᾶσα, οἷον πέπηγα διέφθορα ἐποιησάμην ἐγραψάμην. | There are three voices: active, passive, and middle: active like τύπτω 'I hit', passive like τύπτομαι 'I am hit', and middle, which sometimes designates an action and sometimes an experience, like πέποιθα διέφθορα ἐποιησάμην ἐγραψάμην.[10] |

---

[6] Thomas Davidson, *The Grammar of Dionysios Thrax* (St. Louis: R.P. Studley, 1874), 3. Dionysius, born 166 BCE, was known to teach in Alexandria; however, there has been some controversy regarding the authorship of the extant version of *Techné Grammatiké*. Robins concludes that it most likely consists of the original work together with some later redactions, hence some attribute a later date to the extant work. For discussion, see Robins, *Byzantine Grammarians*, 42–44. For the Greek text, see Dionysius Thrax, *Ars grammatica* in G. Uhlig, *Grammatici Graeci*, vol. 1.1 (Leipzig: Teubner, 1883; repr. Hildesheim: Olms, 1965), 5–100.

[7] Davidson's translation noted above occupies only 18 pages.

[8] Robins, *Byzantine Grammarians*, 69.

[9] Uhlig, *Grammatici Graeci*, 1.48.1–1.49.3. Davidson notes the 'unfortunate' rendition of διάθεσις as *Vox* in the transition to Latin, and hence to 'voice' in English (*Dionysios Thrax*, 12). Certainly 'disposition' would appear to be a better signifier for the relationship between subject and verb.

[10] Translation after Robins, *Byzantine Grammarians*, 69.

His examples of active and passive conform to the conventional understanding; however, his examples of the μεσότης (middle) voice are of interest.¹¹ Thus, "ἐποιησάμην (I became)" and "ἐγραψάμην (I registered)" exhibit the commonly recognized sigmatic aorist middle form; however, πέποιθα (or πέπηγα) and διέφθορα have the form currently recognized as perfect actives.¹² This implies that Dionysius is referring to the voice itself rather than morphology. Thus πέπηγα (I become fixed) or πέποιθα (I obey; I have been persuaded) and διέφθορα (I waste, decay) may be seen to reflect a change of state which is a characteristic of the middle voice recognized by more recent scholars.¹³ He gives no further explanation of the middle voice, nor does he mention deponents.

2.1.2 Apollonius Dyscolus (2nd Century CE)

The *Syntax of Apollonius Dyscolus* is a far more extensive work than that of Dionysius Thrax, focusing on construction of sentences rather than on parts of speech.¹⁴ Apollonius also refers to three voices, as shown below:¹⁵

Ἴδιον οὖν ῥήματός ἐστιν ἐν ἰδίοις   The essential features (*idion*) of a

---

¹¹ Notably, Robins and Davidson have πέποιθα where Uhlig has πέπηγα, from πήγνυμι (I fix or set) (Robins, *Byzantine Grammarians*, 69; Davidson, *Dionysios Thrax*, 12; Uhlig, *Grammatici Graeci*, 1.49.2).

¹² Translations according to Davidson, *Dionysios Thrax*, 12. Robins offers different translations, viz., "I did it for myself" and "I wrote for myself", respectively (*Byzantine Grammarians*, 69). Moulton notes that there are cases for which the "strong" perfect active is used for otherwise middle verbs, or reflects the intransitive middle, when "the rest of the active is transitive," noting, e.g., ἐλήλυθα from ἔρχομαι and γέγονα from γίνομαι (*Prolegomena*, 154).

¹³ See §2.2.1 and §2.2.7 below.

¹⁴ The work of Apollonius is duly recognized by Andreas U. Schmidhauser, "The Birth of Grammar in Greece" in *A Companion to the Ancient Greek Language*, ed. Egbert J. Bekker (Chichester: Wiley-Blackwell, 2010), 499–511.

¹⁵ Apollonius Dyscolus *De constructione*, 1–497 in G. Uhlig, *Grammatici Graeci*, vol. 2.2 (Leipzig: Teubner, 1910; repr., Hildesheim: Olms, 1965), 2.2.325 *ll*. 12–14.

μετασχηματισμοῖς διάφορος χρόνος διάθεσίς τε ἡ ἐνεργητικὴ καὶ παθητικὴ καὶ ἔτι ἡ μέση·

verb lie in the special inflections for different tenses and for voice—active, passive, middle.[16]

In reference to the general syntax of the verb, Apollonius refers to the middle (μέση) falling between the active and passive but not complying with either (καὶ ἡ μεταξὺ τούτων πεπτωκυῖα μέση, οὐ προσχωροῦσα οὐδετέρᾳ).[17] This notion is compatible with modern descriptions of the middle voice representing both activity (subject as agent) and passivity or affectedness. This more so if, being cautious of anachronism, it is not assumed that what is meant by πάθος or παθητικὴ is precisely what is meant today by passive voice; rather it may in fact simply refer to affectedness, without further accretions.[18]

Although this is not a diachronic study, it is pertinent to note that subsequent grammarians continued the above tradition regarding voice without significantly enhancing it.[19] It is appropriate therefore to glean from these early works that three voices were recognized in the New Testament era. One of these was considered neither active nor passive, but middle. Bearing this in mind, a survey of grammars from more recent times that are written to explain ancient Greek to non-native speakers, will now be examined. These are addressed broadly in chronological sequence in order to see the way that our understanding of the Greek

---

[16] Fred W. Householder, ed., *The Syntax of Apollonius Dyscolus*, SiHoLS 23 (Amsterdam: John Benjamins, 1981), 178.

[17] Uhlig, *Grammatici Graeci*, 2.2.319.7–8. Householder, *Apollonius Dyscolus*, 175.

[18] That is, in reference, e.g., to transitivity or number of participants. See §2.2.7 below.

[19] As noted by Juan Signes-Codoñer, "The Definitions of the Greek Middle Voice between Apollonius Dyscolus and Constantinus Lascaris," *Historiographia Linguistica* 32 (2005): 1–33. He demonstrates that there were no significant developments regarding the function of the middle voice until the time of the Renaissance when Latin grammar became influential. Hence, e.g., Constantine Lascaris (fifteenth c.) adopts the notion of deponency from Latin, adding it as an extra voice. See Signes-Codoñer, "Definitions," 15. Bernard A. Taylor makes a similar observation regarding deponency; see § 2.2.3 below.

middle voice has developed to its present state.

2.1.3 D. B. Monro (1882)

Written in the late nineteenth century is a grammar of the much earlier Homeric dialect by D. B. Monro. [20] This may be instructive since the middle voice was more widely used at this stage of the language than in later Greek. Monro describes the "original force" of the middle inflection to be "Reflexive" where the "action of the verb is directed towards the agent."[21] He then briefly describes five "chief" uses:

1. The agent is also the indirect object of the action that is done for or toward himself or in his own interest, e.g., δέχομαι: I take to myself.
2. The agent is the direct object of the action, e.g., λούομαι: I wash myself.
3. The intransitive use, in which the action centers in the agent and "the reflexive sense is faint," e.g., ἔρχομαι: I come; βούλομαι: I wish.
4. The reciprocal use, e.g., ἀμειβόμενος: taking his turn.
5. The passive use, e.g., ἔχεται: is possessed.[22]

Notably, the passive is but one use of the middle. This is evident also in his table of person-endings, which supplies only two sets of forms; that is, active and middle.[23]

---

[20] D. B. Monro, *A Grammar of the Homeric Dialect* (Oxford: Clarendon, 1882), 7, cited by Robertson, *Grammar*, 803.
[21] Monro, *Homeric Dialect*, 7.
[22] Monro, *Homeric Dialect*, 7.
[23] Monro, *Homeric Dialect*, 3.

2.1.4 A. N. Jannaris (1897)

Primarily discussing the Attic dialect, A. N. Jannaris states that the middle voice "represents the subject as acting *on, for* or *of itself.*"[24] He distinguishes between the two main categories of direct and indirect middle. The former are the less common reflexives, conceptually having an accusative (direct) object, while the second group signify a more indirect reflexive relation, effectively having 'self' as an indirect object, so that the action is done in the interest of oneself (*to* or *for* oneself).[25] As a further sub-class of the latter, he distinguishes a dynamic sense signifying that the action is done *of, from or through* self; that is, "with its own means and powers," giving as examples αἱρέομαι (I choose for myself), πορίζομαι (I provide for myself) and ἄγομαι γυναῖκα (I take a wife to myself).[26]

Jannaris identifies deponents as middle or passive forms with active meaning, labelled according to their aorist and future forms.[27] That is, if the aorist (and future) is a middle form with active meaning, it is classified as a middle deponent, similarly for the passive deponents. Significantly, he notes that there was a degree of flux as to which verbs fitted this category over time; some that were deponents in the classical period became active in the post classical. For example, δωρέομαι changed to δωρέω and even the reverse occurred, as in the case of χαίρω being "extruded" by χαίρομαι.[28]

2.1.5 Introductory Grammars of the Twentieth Century

There tends to be little discussion of the middle voice in introductory Grammars. Hence, for example, J. W. Wenham states: "No attempt will

---

[24] Jannaris, *Historical Greek Grammar*, 360 (italics original).
[25] Jannaris, *Historical Greek Grammar*, 360–61.
[26] Jannaris, *Historical Greek Grammar*, 360.
[27] Jannaris, *Historical Greek Grammar*, 179.
[28] Jannaris, *Historical Greek Grammar*, 284. Note, however, that the aorist middle form ἐδωρήσατο occurs in Mark 15:45.

be made to give any generalized explanation of the meaning of the Middle, which must be left for more advanced text-books."[29] Whereas the more rigorous and extensive grammars say more about the middle voice than the sub-category of deponents, the inverse tends to apply in the New Testament introductory grammars. Thus, for instance, Jeremy Duff states: "The vast majority of the time when you see a middle it is a deponent verb conveying an active meaning."[30] Mounce endorses this proportion, noting that deponents make up approximately 75 percent of all middle forms in the NT.[31] Such remarks suggest that the middle form is not particularly significant, a position which this work sets out to challenge.

Most works surveyed supply the standard explanation that deponent verbs are middle or passive in form but active in meaning (as Jannaris, above), noting also that they have "laid aside" their active forms.[32] Some, however, do not mention the absence of the active.[33] Further, remarks are made which appear confusing, especially to the beginning student. For instance, the widely used Grammar by Jeremy Duff indicates that deponents are "simply a second group of verbs," distinguished from "normal verbs" (those in the active voice) by a different set of endings.[34] He does not introduce the middle voice until several chapters later. Such attempts to oversimplify grammatical concepts reflect the challenges posed for condensed introductory works.

---

[29] J. W. Wenham, *The Elements of New Testament Greek* (Cambridge: Cambridge University Press, 1970), 92.

[30] Jeremy Duff, The *Elements of New Testament Greek* (Cambridge: Cambridge University Press, 2005), 174. Duff's grammar is a revision of the work by the same name by Wenham (1965, repr. 1970) and fits logically in this section.

[31] William D. Mounce, *Basics of Biblical Greek: Grammar*, 2nd ed. (Grand Rapids: Zondervan, 1993, 2003), 152.

[32] For example, Croy, *Primer*, 49; David Durie, *Greek Grammar: A Concise Grammar of New Testament Greek*, 4th ed. (Macquarie, A.C.T.: Zoe, 1989), 296; Eric G. Jay, *New Testament Greek: An Introductory Grammar* (London: SPCK, 1961), 85–86.

[33] For example, Wenham, *Elements*, 93; Watson E. Mills, *New Testament Greek: An Introductory Grammar* (Lewiston, NY: Mellen, 1985), 44; Mounce, *Basics*, 150.

[34] Duff, *Elements*, 92–93.

At variance with the common explanation, however, William Hersey Davis equates deponent verbs with defective verbs, preferring the latter term for verbs used in the middle or passive but not in the active.[35] He considers that the so-called deponent verbs of middle form do in fact express personal interest. That is, although they lack an active form (defective), they do not substitute the middle for the active.

While Mounce refers to the "self-interest" nuance of the middle voice in the classical tongue, he admonishes students not to assume that the middle verbs in the New Testament are used in the same way.[36] He asserts that the middle is not normally directly reflexive, and that "the force of the middle is so subtle that it is scarcely discernible" in most cases, so that *"the middle has the same meaning as the active."*[37] Importantly, however, he does point out that this equivalence relates to the English way of thinking. "Either they are deponents, or their middle meaning is active to the English mind."[38] Such a comment illustrates the difficulty of translating writings from one culture to the language of another. However, it also points to the importance of understanding the possible nuances of the middle voice in order to render it as accurately as possible in translation.

---

[35] William Hersey Davis, *Beginner's Grammar of the New Testament* (San Francisco: Harper & Row, 1923), 69. Robertson points out that defective verbs do not exhibit every voice in every tense (*Grammar*, 799); however, while the term "defective" tends to suggest that every verb *should* have every voice in every tense, this is not borne out in the actual use of the language.

[36] Mounce, *Basics*, 230–31. He cites the example of παυσόνται (1 Cor 13:8), which he considers to be problematic if interpreted in the middle sense, for it would suggest that tongues will cease by themselves. He firmly asserts that it is a deponent verb, to be understood as an active, i.e., they will cease.

[37] Mounce, *Basics*, 231 (italics original).

[38] Mounce, *Basics*, 231. Some other introductory grammars also note this distinction between active meaning and active translation, e.g., Durie notes that the "English equivalents" are active (*Grammar*, 310); see also A. W. Argyle, *An Introductory Grammar of New Testament Greek* (London: Hodder and Stoughton, 1965) 78 and Jay, *New Testament Greek*, 84.

Overall, the introductory New Testament grammars lack detailed explanation of the middle voice, subordinating it to deponency. Therefore, more substantial works will now be considered to ascertain a better understanding of the meaning and use of the middle voice in the New Testament era.

2.1.6 Intermediate and Advanced Grammars of the Twentieth Century

2.1.6.1 James Hope Moulton (1906)

Writing of New Testament Greek in a rather conversational tone, James Hope Moulton states that the essence of the middle "lies in its calling attention to the agent as in some way closely concerned with the action."[39] He also asserts that if the verb is transitive in the active, "the middle indicates that the action goes no further than the subject himself[.]"[40] Thus, νίπτομαι without an object would mean 'I wash *myself*,' whereas νίπτομαι τὰς χεῖρας means I wash *my* hands.[41] Rather than classifying the different uses of the middle voice, his discussion is largely descriptive and primarily focuses on the distinctive force of the middle voice compared to the active. As an overall distinction, he notes that the active draws attention to the action, whereas the middle draws attention to the subject; for example, ἀφίεται could be read "*He* pardoneth" emphasizing the source, whereas ἀφίησι (active) would be read "He *pardoneth*" emphasizing the pardon itself.[42]

Moulton does, however, identify some different types of applications, stating that the "most practical equivalent" of the middle is the active with the dative of the reflexive pronoun. Hence, for example, προσέχετε ἑαυτοῖς: "pay attention *for yourselves*" (Luke 12:1) is

---

[39] Moulton, *Prolegomena*, 153.
[40] Moulton, *Prolegomena*, 156.
[41] Moulton, *Prolegomena*, 156.
[42] Moulton, *Prolegomena*, 152 (italics original). The first use is reminiscent of what Jannaris refers to as the dynamic middle.

essentially equivalent to φυλάσσεσθε: "be on your guard" (Luke 12:15).⁴³ Similarly, he comments that the middle may parallel the use of the possessive genitive with the active, for instance, σπασάμενος τὴν μάχαιραν (Mark 14:47) is parallel to ἀπέσπασεν τὴν μάχαιραν αὐτοῦ: he drew *his* sword (Matt 26:51). A further function recognized is the reciprocal middle, such as συνεβούλευσαντο: they counselled one another (Matt 26:4).⁴⁴

For verbs in which the middle force is difficult to define, even "useless" to try to interpret, he adopts the term "Dynamic" middle; yet he still considers that the middle morphology emphasizes the part taken by the subject in the action of the verb in some manner.⁴⁵ He concludes that the middle does not always have a clearly identifiable meaning and comments: "We have in fact to vary the exact relation of the reflexive perpetually if we are to represent the middle in the form appropriate to the particular example."⁴⁶ He does not see this lack of clarity to be peculiar to the New Testament corpus, whose writers, he contends, were "perfectly capable of preserving the distinction between active and middle" noting that there were also "plenty of middles" that were hard to define in the Attic and even in Homer.⁴⁷

One further observation, which he considers to be an "abnormality" is the number of active verbs with middle forms in the future tense, such as ὄψομαι, -βήσομαι, γνώσομαι, φάγομαι, ἀποθανοῦμαι, κομίσομαι, κομιοῦμαι, λήμψομαι, πίομαι, πεσοῦμαι, τέξομαι, φεύξομαι. This phenomenon, he asserts, is less prominent in Hellenistic than in Classical Greek, indicating a levelling effect (i.e., a trend to remove the abnormality) noting that some verbs such as ἀκούω have

---

⁴³ Moulton, *Prolegomena*, 157. This is an instance of what Jannaris calls the indirect middle, above.
⁴⁴ Moulton, *Prolegomena*, 157.
⁴⁵ Moulton, *Prolegomena*, 158.
⁴⁶ Moulton, *Prolegomena*, 157.
⁴⁷ Moulton, *Prolegomena*, 158–59.

both active and middle future forms, consistent with a transitional stage in the language.[48]

Moulton gives little space to deponent verbs, which he deems an unsatisfactory name for verbs which are found only in the active or only in the middle, noting νέομαι, ἕπομαι, μαίνομαι, μητίομαι, κάθημαι, κεῖμαι as examples of the latter.[49] This is significantly different from the lists of deponents typically given in more recent grammars.[50] Notably, he does not include ἔρχομαι, but rather refers to it as a defective verb, since the present tense uses the middle voice but the aorist has an active form (ἦλθον).[51] Thus it appears that Moulton considers that middle form does indicate middle function, even if this is difficult to discern, and suggests that middle "deponent" verbs may simply be middle-only verbs.

2.1.6.2 A. T. Robertson (1914)

In his extensive work on New Testament grammar, A. T. Robertson states that the middle is exceedingly broad in its scope, being "essentially the voice of personal interest somewhat like the dative case."[52] Therefore, he asserts that the only difference between the active and the middle voice is that the middle calls special attention to the subject, which is "acting in relation to himself somehow."[53] The precise relation must come from the context or from the significance of the verb itself. Sometimes, he notes, "the variation from the active is too minute for translation into English."[54] Thus, for example, αἰτεῖσθε and αἰτεῖτε

---

[48] Moulton, *Prolegomena*, 154–55. Monro also notes this phenomenon (*Homeric Dialect*, 42–43).

[49] Moulton, *Prolegomena*, 153.

[50] Moulton, *Prolegomena*, 154. In contrast, see Duff, *Elements*, 97; Mounce, *Basics*, 153; and Wallace, *Exegetical Syntax*, 430.

[51] Moulton, *Prolegomena*, 154.

[52] Robertson, *Grammar*, 806.

[53] Robertson, *Grammar*, 803, 804.

[54] Robertson, *Grammar*, 804.

Middle Voice Verbs in the New Testament

are both translated as 'you ask' (Jas 4:2–3).⁵⁵ Alternatively, the difference may be acute when the force of the middle generates a meaning different from that of the same verb in the active, such as αἱρέω (I take) and αἱρέομαι (I take to myself, I choose).⁵⁶ He also notes that some verbs, such as φαίνω: I bring to light, are transitive in the active but intransitive in the middle (φαίνομαι: I appear.) Nevertheless, the middle is not intransitive of itself.⁵⁷ Transitive verbs, he asserts, may belong to any voice, as may intransitive, for transitivity is a property of the verb stem, not the voice in which it is expressed.⁵⁸

Regarding different types of middle uses, Robertson cautions against over-classifying, noting that "the divisions made by the grammarians are more or less arbitrary and unsatisfactory" and points out that the ancient Greeks themselves had no such divisions.⁵⁹ He does, however, discuss the use of middle verbs under the following sub-headings:

1. Direct Middle (direct reflexive)
2. Causative or Permissive Middle
3. Indirect Middle
4. Reciprocal Middle
5. Redundant Middle
6. Dynamic (Deponent) Middle.

---

⁵⁵ Robertson notes that the use of both forms side by side draws attention to the distinction (*Grammar*, 805).

⁵⁶ Robertson, *Grammar*, 804. Robertson cites many other instances, e.g., ἀναμιμνήσκω (I remind), ἀναμιμνήσκομαι (I remind myself, i.e., remember); ἀπέχω (I hold off), ἀπέχομαι (I hold myself off, i.e., abstain); βουλεύω (I counsel), βουλεύομαι (I take counsel); γεύω (I give to taste), γεύομαι (I taste); πείθω (I persuade), πείθομαι (I obey); φαίνω (I show), φαίνομαι (I appear); φοβέω (I frighten), φοβέομαι (I fear).

⁵⁷ Robertson, *Grammar*, 806. He cites four examples from Mark to illustrate this: ἥψαντο (Mark 6:56) νίψωνται (Mark 7:3) are used transitively, whereas ἐξίσταντο (Mark 6:51) εἰσεπορεύετο (Mark 6:56) are intransitive.

⁵⁸ Robertson, *Grammar*, 806.

⁵⁹ Robertson, *Grammar*, 806.

Robertson identifies several instances of the direct reflexive middle in the New Testament, for example, θερμαινόμενος: "warming himself" (Mark 14:54) and παρασκευάσεται: "prepare himself" (1 Cor 14:8).[60] He treats the causative and permissive functions as one category.[61] The causative use, he asserts, may occur with both the direct and indirect middle. For instance, in βάπτισαι καὶ ἀπόλουσαι τὰς ἁμαρτίας σου (Acts 22:16) he considers βάπτισαι to be acting directly on the subject but ἀπόλουσαι to be indirect, done in the interest of the subject, so renders this: "get yourself baptized and get your sins washed away."[62] As an example of the permissive middle which he states is "closely allied to the causative and approaches the passive," Robertson cites εἰ δὲ αἰσχρὸν γυναικὶ τὸ κείρασθαι ἢ ξυρᾶσθαι (1 Cor 11:6) which could therefore be translated: if permitting her hair to be cut off or shaved is shameful for a woman.[63]

Like Jannaris, Robertson identifies the indirect middle function, in which the subject acts "for, to or by himself" asserting that this occurs abundantly in the New Testament, although the exact nuance must be determined by the particular verb and its context.[64] He discerns in

---

[60] Further examples he proffers are 2 Pet 2:22; 1 Cor 6:11; Luke 7:6; Acts 12:8; Mark 8:22; Phil 3:13; Acts 20:27; Rom 13:2; Luke 12:15; Eph 4:2; Acts 15:29; 1 Pet 5:5. Possible or probable examples include Col 2:20; Col 3:18; Matt 6:29; Matt 26:45; Acts 18:5. Robertson states that, although the list is not a large one, "the idiom is clearly not obsolete in the N.T." He also states that there was a resurgence of this application of the middle as the indirect uses waned, such that it is "nearly the sole use" of the middle in Modern Greek. See Robertson, *Grammar*, 807–8.

[61] Robertson contends that the causative function is not a distinctive feature of the middle because active verbs may also be used in this way (*Grammar*, 808).

[62] Robertson, *Grammar*, 808. Conversely, "be baptized and wash your sins away" (NIV) translates ἀπόλουσαι as an active rather than as a middle imperative and βάπτισαι as a passive. This is in accord with Robertson's comments that the permissive approaches the passive (*Grammar*, 809).

[63] Robertson, *Grammar*, 809. Whereas the NIV translation: "if it is a disgrace for a woman to have her hair cut off or her head shaved" suggests that the verbs are read as causative middles or even passives.

[64] Robertson, *Grammar*, 809.

αἰωνίαν λύτρωσιν εὑράμενος (Heb. 9:12) an example of the subject acting *by* himself (i.e., Jesus securing eternal redemption of his own accord).⁶⁵ In προσλαβόμενος αὐτὸν ὁ Πέτρος (Matt 16:22) he notes that Peter takes Jesus *to* himself⁶⁶ and he discerns action *for* the subject in τί αἱρήσομαι οὐ γνωρίζω: what I will take for myself (choose) I do not know (Phil 1:22). Robertson comments: "No fixed rule can be laid down for the translation of this or any other use of the middle"; he does, however, give a helpful list of examples together with his interpretation of their meaning.⁶⁷

As also identified by others above, Robertson's fourth observation is the reciprocal middle use, for instance, συνεβουλεύσαντο: "they counselled with one another" (Matt 26:4).⁶⁸ He also comments on the redundant middle use, where a personal pronoun is used in addition to the middle form, citing the example οἱ μάρτυρες ἀπέθεντο τὰ ἱμάτια αὐτῶν: "the witnesses laid down their garments" (Acts 7:58, NRSV).⁶⁹ Interestingly, Robertson comments that most of the New Testament instances of middle forms occur with verbs that do not appear in the active.⁷⁰

---

⁶⁵ Robertson, *Grammar*, 809–10 for these examples.

⁶⁶ It could be argued that this sense is inherent in the lexeme. Nevertheless, the implication of acting in one's own interest is clear. Other similar compounds in Robertson's examples include: προσκαλεσάμενος: calling to himself (Matt 10:1); Ἀποθέμενοι: laying aside from yourselves (Heb 12:1). See Robertson, *Grammar*, 809, 810.

⁶⁷ Other examples listed: Matt 10:9, 16:22, 27:24; Mark 9:8, 14:47; Luke 8:27, 10:42, 16:19; John 21:7; Acts 5:2, 5:8, 9:39, 10:23, 13:46, 18:6, 19:24, 20:28, 25:11, 27:38; Rom 3:25, 11:1, 15:7; 2 Cor 3:18, 4:2; Gal 4:10; Phil 1:22; Col 4:5; 1 Tim 6:20; Heb 12:1, 12:25. Robertson, *Grammar*, 809–10.

⁶⁸ Robertson notes that this usage survives in Modern Greek. Other NT examples given: ἐμάχοντο (John 6:52) συνετέθειντο (John 9:22) ἐβουλεύσαντο (John 12:10) διαλεγόμενος (Acts 19:8) συναναμίγνυσθαι (1 Cor 5:9) κρινέσθαι (1 Cor 6:1). (*Grammar*, 810–11).

⁶⁹ Robertson, *Grammar*, 811. The point Robertson makes is that αὐτῶν is redundant, because the middle ἀπέθεντο suggests "laid aside from themselves" if read as an indirect middle. Similar examples occur in Titus 2:7; Acts 7:21, 20:24; 1 Tim 3:13.

⁷⁰ Robertson, *Grammar*, 811.

Robertson considers the term "deponent" to be "very unsatisfactory."[71] It was understood to mean the laying aside of active forms in middle verbs for which there was no corresponding active; yet in reality, most of these verbs had never had an active form.[72] He therefore employs the term "dynamic" to describe these middle verbs for which it is "hard to see the distinctive force of the voice." Nevertheless, he suggests that the Greeks themselves may have been more sensitive to this.[73] He concedes that an "intensive force" may partially be seen in many "deponents" of mental action, such as αἰσθάνομαι (Luke 9:45) ἀρνέομαι (Luke 12:9) εὔχομαι (Rom 9:3) λογίζομαι (Phil 4:8), and admits the reflexive idea in δέχομαι, but also draws attention to many middle verbs which are "very hard to explain" like γίνομαι (Matt 8:26), ἅλλομαι (John 4:14), ἀφικνέομαι (Rom 16:19), and ἐργάζομαι (Matt 25:16). Overall, Robertson does not presume to have an adequate explanation for this group of middle verbs. Nevertheless, he does not question that the form indicates that they are in fact expressing the middle voice.

2.1.6.3 Herbert Weir Smyth (1920)

Herbert Weir Smyth's Grammar of 1920 is a well-regarded authority on classical Greek.[74] He states that the middle voice indicates that "the action is performed with special reference to the subject[.]"[75] Further, in contrast to the active form, the middle lays stress on the "conscious activity, bodily or mental participation, of the agent." This is apparent in verbs which have both middle and active forms. Hence, for example, we find βουλεύσθαι meaning "deliberate" but βουλεύειν meaning "plan";

---

[71] Robertson, *Grammar*, 811.

[72] Robertson, *Grammar*, 811–12.

[73] Robertson, *Grammar*, 812.

[74] Herbert Weir Smyth, *A Greek Grammar for Colleges* (New York: American Book Company, 1920). Revised in 1956 by Gordon M. Messing and published by Harvard University Press with no change to the material on the middle voice, this work has remained in print for several decades.

[75] Smyth, *Greek Grammar*, §1713.

σταθμᾶσθαι meaning "calculate" but σταθμᾶν meaning "measure"—notwithstanding the fact that the "force of the middle often cannot be reproduced in translation[.]"[76]

Smyth endorses and brings further clarity to the basic types of middle voice noted above. He invokes the terms "Direct Reflexive Middle" to describe middle forms which represent the "subject acting directly on himself" such as λούομαι (I wash myself), while the "Indirect Reflexive Middle" refers to the subject "acting for himself, with reference to himself, or with something belonging to himself" for example πορίζεσθαι (provide for oneself); hence the self is often the implied indirect object.[77]

Smyth also comments on the "Causative Middle" in which case the subject has something done for himself, for example, ἐγὼ γάρ σε ταῦτα ἐδιδαξάμην (I had you taught this) and the "Reciprocal Middle" likely to occur with verbs of contending, conversing, greeting, and the like, such as ἀνὴρ ἀνδρὶ διέλεγοντο (they conversed man to man).[78] He affirms the same understanding of deponent verbs as Jannaris,[79] but notes that it is the aorist which determines the name of a deponent verb.

---

[76] Smyth, *Greek Grammar*, §1728.

[77] Smyth, *Greek Grammar*, §§1717–19. This nomenclature is logical: the indirect middle has an indirect object. William Douglas Chamberlain succinctly draws attention to this correlation with the indirect object and hence the dative case: "As the dative case is the case which expresses personal interest, so the middle voice is the voice of personal interest" (*An Exegetical Grammar of the New Testament* [New York: Macmillan, 1941], 81).

[78] Smyth, *Greek Grammar*, §§1725–1727. It is interesting to note that this example of the causative middle has an expressed accusative (direct) object, as opposed to the case of an active verb with a direct object in the accusative which expresses the direct reflexive relation. Hence this combination is distinctive and may be regarded as characteristic of the causative function. In such cases, the subject of the middle verb has the intention, while another subject (unspecified) carries out the action. Smyth notes that the active can also express mutuality when used with a reflexive pronoun e.g., φθονοῦσιν ἑαυτοῖς (they envied one another) or reciprocity with a reciprocal pronoun, e.g., ἀμφισβητοῦμεν ἀλλήλοις (we are at variance with one another).

[79] Smyth, *Greek Grammar*, §365c.

If the aorist has the middle form, it is called a middle deponent, for example, αἰτιάομαι (accuse), ᾐτιασάμην (aorist: accused); but if the aorist has the passive form, it is called a passive deponent, for instance, βούλομαι (wish), ἐβουλήθην (aorist: wished).[80] Middle deponents, he observes, often denote bodily or mental actions such as ἅλλεσθαι (jump); ἡγεῖσθαι (consider).[81]

2.1.6.4 H. E. Dana and Julius R. Mantey (1928)

Turning to another New Testament Grammar, H. E. Dana and Julius R. Mantey comment that the middle voice is "one of the most distinctive and peculiar phenomena of the Greek language."[82] It is one which has no "approximate parallel" in English and describes "the subject as participating in the results of the action." This is illustrated by the difference between βουλεύω (I counsel), and βουλεύομαι (I take counsel). Thus, we see "the subject acting with a view to participation in the outcome."[83] This is a helpful description, representing a subtle shift from other accounts that speak of the subject's involvement in the action itself. While they comment that no one definition can accommodate all the occurrences of the middle, they do identify some uses, noting nevertheless that demarcations are somewhat arbitrary.[84]

Like Smyth, they refer to the uncommon direct middle, indicating a direct action on the agent (being more often represented by the active with a reflexive pronoun), and the more common indirect middle. However, rather than defining this latter usage in terms of the subject as an indirect object (as Smyth) they refer mainly to the "intensive" sub-category of the indirect middle, discerning an emphasis the *writer* wishes to place on the subject producing the action. This, they explain, is rather

---

[80] Smyth, *Greek Grammar*, §§365c, 810, 811.

[81] Smyth, *Greek Grammar*, §1729.

[82] H. E. Dana and Julius R. Mantey, *A Manual Grammar of the Greek New Testament* (London: SPCK, 1928), §154.

[83] Dana and Mantey, *Grammar*, §155

[84] Dana and Mantey, *Grammar*, §§155–6

like an English writer using *italics* or an emphatic pronoun to stress the role of the subject. For example, they render αἰωνίαν λύτρωσιν εὑράμενος as "he himself secured eternal redemption" (Heb 9:12); similarly, ὃν καὶ σὺ φυλάσσου (2 Tim 4:15) is paraphrased as "*you* had better take heed for *yourself*.[85] A further use of the indirect middle they identify is to indicate personal engagement of the subject. Hence, we see στρατεύεσθαι (to be a soldier, as in 2 Tim 2:4) in contrast to στρατεύειν (to conduct a military campaign).[86]

Other categories identified by Dana and Mantey are the reciprocal and the permissive. The reciprocal sense requires a plural subject and "may represent an interchange of effort between the acting agents," for example, συνετέθειντο οἱ Ἰουδαῖοι: "the Jews had agreed with one another" (John 9:22).[87] The permissive middle represents the subject "voluntarily yielding himself to the results of the action," for example, διὰ τί οὐχὶ μᾶλλον ἀδικεῖσθε; "why not rather let yourselves be wronged?" (1 Cor 6:7).[88] They include in this category what Smyth nominates as the causative middle and describe it as "seeking to secure the results of the action in [one's] own interest."[89]

In discussion of "Irregularities in Voice" Dana and Mantey make a distinction between defective verbs (not used in every voice in every tense, for the root meaning lends itself to one voice rather than another) and deponent verbs, which not only lack the active form but use middle or passive forms in its place. Although a verb may be both defective and deponent, they emphasize that a deponent verb is distinctive in that "its voice form is different from its voice function" [90]

---

[85] Dana and Mantey, *Grammar*, §156.2.
[86] Dana and Mantey, *Grammar*, §156.2.iii. The examples given demonstrate the personal engagement of the subject in the activity specified.
[87] Dana and Mantey, *Grammar*, §156.4.
[88] Dana and Mantey, *Grammar*, §156.3.
[89] They do not give a New Testament example but do cite one from Homer: λυσόμενος θύγατρα: *to get his daughter set free* (*Grammar*, §156.3).
[90] Dana and Mantey, *Grammar*, §158.

2.1.6.5 F. Blass and A. Debrunner (1961)

The New Testament Grammar by F. Blass and B. Debrunner (1961) is a rigorous reference work rather than a teaching grammar. The authors do not describe the meaning of the middle voice but highlight instances of difference between the Greek of the New Testament and its classical ancestor. They note that "NT authors in general preserve well the distinction between middle and passive" but note that the *active* is sometimes used where a middle is expected from classical usage, for example, εἴ τις ὑμᾶς καταδουλοῖ (if someone enslaves you, 2 Cor 11:20).[91] They also observe the opposite, that is, a middle when the active is used in classical work, such as the middle ἐκδίδοσθαι for 'lease' in ἐξέδετο αὐτὸν γεωργοῖς (leased it to farmers, Matt 21:33).[92] In regard to αἰτεῖν and αἰτεῖσθαι, Blass and Debrunner note that αἰτεῖσθαι is generally used of requests in commerce, while the active is usually used for requests addressed to God.[93] Nevertheless, they consider the alternation of the middle and active in James 4:2, 3 to be arbitrary.[94]

The only specific uses of middle verbs identified (albeit briefly) are the reflexive, for example, ἀπήγξατο: he hung himself (used in Matt 27:5) and the causative/permissive, for example ὄφελον καὶ

---

[91] BDF, §316, §310.

[92] Other examples given of middle forms in the NT where classical Greek uses the active are καταλαμβάνεσθαι (Acts 4:13) for καταλαμβάνειν; ἀπειλεῖσθαι (Acts 4:17, 21) for ἀπειλεῖν (although acknowledging the active in 1 Pet 2:23) (BDF, §316.1).

[93] Matthew 27: 20, 58 are cited as middle voice requests in "commerce," although asking for Barabbas (27:20) or for Jesus' body (27:58) is not what one would normally consider commerce; perhaps there is a sense of transaction, however (BDF, §316.2).

[94] BDF, §316.2. Jas 4:2, 3 οὐκ ἔχετε διὰ τὸ μὴ αἰτεῖσθαι ὑμᾶς, αἰτεῖτε καὶ οὐ λαμβάνετε διότι κακῶς αἰτεῖσθε, ἵνα ἐν ταῖς ἡδοναῖς ὑμῶν δαπανήσητε. The use of both active and middle forms of αἰτέω in James 4:2, 3 invites a separate discussion, as given by Robertson, *Grammar*, 805 and Moulton, *Prolegomena*, 160. Briefly, the sense of asking from and for oneself where the middle is used is quite plausible; that is, you do not have because you do not ask (mid., from within/with intensity); you ask (act.) but do not receive because you ask (mid., for your own benefit), in order to spend on your pleasures.

ἀποκόψονται: would that they "get themselves emasculated" (Gal 5:12).⁹⁵ Like Moulton, they observe active verbs with future middle forms, noting that this was common in Attic but the trend in the Hellenistic era is towards active future forms instead.⁹⁶ Some active verbs, however, have retained the middle future, while ἀκούσω, ζήσω, κλαύσω, κράξω "vacillate between active and middle."⁹⁷

2.1.6.6 Maximillian Zerwick (1963)

For Maximillian Zerwick, the middle voice represents "the subject as acting (or causing another to act) with respect to himself (the subject)."⁹⁸ He offers a discerning assessment of the use of the middle in the New Testament, maintaining that, despite traces of obsolescence, "middle forms still retain a wide field of usage in the NT" for all the senses found in classical use.⁹⁹ He cites examples of the direct middle, the causative and permissive, and the indirect use, which he describes as the subject acting *of* itself, noting that this use in particular demonstrates an awareness of the "finer distinctions" between the active and middle voices.¹⁰⁰

Commenting on the active verbs with middle future forms, he notes that ἀκούσομαι and ἀκούσω are both found, as are ζήσομαι and ζήσω,

---

⁹⁵ BDF, §310.2, §317. This nuance in Gal 5:12 is missed in English translations. E.g., ESV, NAB, NIV, NJB, NKJV, NRSV translate this as reflexive, and KJV, passive. Other examples given for the causative middle: ἐβαπτισάμην (Acts 22:16) ἀπογράφεσθαι (Luke 2:1, 3).

⁹⁶ BDF, §77

⁹⁷ BDF, §77. Verbs retaining the middle future: -βήσομαι γνώσομαι ἀποθανοῦμαι λήμψομαι ὄψομαι πεσοῦμαι πίομαι τέξομαι φάγομαι φεύξομαι χαρήσομαι (Attic has χαιρήσω).

⁹⁸ Maximillian Zerwick, *Biblical Greek Illustrated by Examples*, 4th ed. trans., Joseph Smith (Rome: Pontificii Instituti Biblici, 1963), §225.

⁹⁹ Zerwick, *Biblical Greek*, §232

¹⁰⁰ Zerwick, *Biblical Greek*, §234. Direct middle: ἀπήγξατο (Matt 27:5), λουσαμένη (2 Pet 2:22), θερμαινόμενος (Mark 14:54). Causative or permissive: ἀπόλουσαι (Acts 22:16) ἀποκόψονται (Gal 5:12). Indirect: προεχόμεθα (Rom 3:9) ἐπιδεικνύμεναι (Acts 9:39), ἔθετο (Acts 12:4).

(as BDF above), but notes differences between authors.[101] His observations that the middle ἀκούσομαι is always used in Luke-Acts whereas ἀκούσω is found in the other gospels may suggest a greater awareness of the classical use by Luke.[102] Zerwick also notes the general retention of the classical idiom in which ποιεῖσθαι (middle voice) together with an accusative noun is used periphrastically as the equivalent of a singular verb. Hence, for example, δέησιν ποιεῖσθαι means 'to pray', as opposed to δέησιν ποιεῖν which would mean 'to compose a prayer', the object being independent of the verb. Although BDF maintains that this distinction is not strictly observed in the Koine, Zerwick disagrees, contending that "the active can generally be accounted for" especially in Luke.[103]

Nevertheless he also acknowledges instances which occur (not only in the New Testament but in Hellenistic Greek in general) of verbs being used in the middle voice which were previously active, for example περιβλέπεσθαι (looking around) in Mark 9:8 for the Attic περιβλέπειν; ἀπεκδύεσθαι used in Col 2:15 for stripping another (rather than stripping oneself as the middle would suggest) and φυλάττεσθαι (observed, kept) in Mark 10:20 for φυλάττειν.[104] Nevertheless, it is not difficult to see the self-interest in each of these examples; they cannot simply be said to be used "for" the active Attic form, as they are used in a different context. When middle and active forms

---

[101] Zerwick, *Biblical Greek*, §226. He notes that ἀκούσομαι is always used by Luke in Acts (3:22, 17:32, 21:22, 28:38) except for a citation from the LXX (28:26), whereas only ἀκούσω appears in the gospels (Matt 12:19; 13:14; John 5:25, 28; 10:16). ζήσομαι appears in Matt 9:18; Luke 10:28; John 11:25; and LXX quotations (Matt 4:4; Luke 4:4; Rom 1:17 = Gal 3:11 = Heb 10:38; Rom 10:5 = Gal 3:12) while ζήσω is used in John four times (not specified) and by Paul (Rom 6:2; 2 Cor 13:4; Heb 12:9). Significantly, however, there are variant readings which attest ἀκούσονται for ἀκούσουσιν in John 5:25, 28.

[102] This is consistent with the general view that Luke's Greek is more classical and less colloquial, as noted, e.g., in BDF, §3.

[103] Middle voice appropriately used: Luke 5:33; 13:22; Acts 1:1; 23:13; 27:18. Active appropriately used: Acts 15:3; 23:12; 24:12; 25:3 (Zerwick, *Biblical Greek*, §227; BDF, §310).

[104] Zerwick, *Biblical Greek*, §235.

of the same verb are used in the same context, however, Zerwick considers the distinction likely to be intentional.[105]

2.1.6.7 Stanley E. Porter (1992)

Drawing upon several earlier grammars, Stanley E. Porter's *Idioms of the Greek New Testament* is written at an intermediate level and treats the Greek of the NT as "an established corpus suitable for linguistic analysis," viewing it as a subset of the Hellenistic Greek texts of the first century.[106] He offers a considered discussion of the middle voice, and affirms that the reflexive middle, for example καωπλισμένος (having armed himself, Luke 11:21), is not the predominant use in this period.[107] In general, he asserts that the middle voice, which "carries the most semantic weight of the Greek voices," indicates "more direct participation, specific involvement or even some form of benefit of the subject doing the action."[108]

Whereas Robertson considers the use of the middle voice with a reflexive or intensive pronoun to be redundant, Porter suggests it may be used as an instrument for even greater emphasis, as, for example, διεμερίσαντο τὰ ἱμάτιά μου ἑαυτοῖς: "they divided up for themselves my garments" (John 19:24).[109] Such differences of opinion are indicative of attempts to adequately describe the use of the middle voice to the mind of an English speaker. Porter refers to the challenge of translating the Greek middle, noting that a reflexive or reciprocal pronoun or a prepositional phrase is generally needed.[110] Nevertheless, he

---

[105] Zerwick also discusses the distinction between αἰτω (simply "ask") and αἰτοῦμαι (avail oneself of one's right to ask) in Mark 6:23 and Jas 4:2. Zerwick, *Biblical Greek*, §76.

[106] Stanley E. Porter, *Idioms of the Greek New Testament*, 2nd ed. (Sheffield: Sheffield Academic, 1992) 13, 15.

[107] As do others. Porter cites, *inter alia*, Robertson, *Grammar*, 806; Moulton, *Prolegomena*, 155–56; Moule, *Idiom Book*, 24, Dana and Mantey, *Grammar*, §156.1.

[108] E.g., ἀπογράψασθαι: to participate in registering (Luke 2:5). Porter, *Idioms*, 67.

[109] Porter, *Idioms*, 68.

[110] Porter, *Idioms*, 68. Examples requiring reflexive pronoun: 2 Tim 4:15 σὺ

comments on the "importance of sorting out the Greek middle voice" and notes some exegetically significant examples.[111]

Porter claims that deponent verbs are considered to use the middle or passive form for active meaning *when an active form is not found*, citing ἔρχομαι as an example.[112] However, he displays some reservations about the notion, stating that there are a large number of ambiguous instances. Thus he cites examples given by Robertson of middle verbs which meet the formal criteria for deponency but which appear to retain their middle sense; e.g. αἰσθάνομαι (Luke 9:45), ἀρνέομαι (Luke 12:9), προαιτιάομαι (Rom 3:9), ἀσπάζομαι (Acts 25:13), διαβεβαιόομαι (Tit 3:8), ἐντέλλομαι (Heb 11:22), ἐπιλανθάνομαι (Matt 16:5), εὔχομαι (Rom 9:3), ἡγέομαι (Phil 3:8), λογίζομαι (Phil 4:8), μαίναμαι (Acts 26:25) μέμφομαι (Rom 9:19), φείδομαι (Rom 8:32).[113]

2.1.6.8 Francis Thomas Gignac (1981)

Francis Thomas Gignac comments on the trends in language observed in the Greek Papyri of the Roman and Byzantine period, many of which align with those observed for the Koine Greek under discussion. He observes the same trend with regard to the levelling of future middle forms of active verbs as in the New Testament; that is, some active verbs which had only a future middle form in Classical Greek have future

---

φυλάσσου (guard yourself); Mark 14:41 ἀναπαύεσθε; (are you resting yourself?); requiring reciprocal pronoun: Matt 26:4 συνεβουλεύσαντο (they counselled one another); John 9:22 συνετέθειντο οἱ Ἰουδαῖοι (the Jews had agreed with one another); requiring prepositional phrase: Luke 14:7 τὰς πρωτοκλισίας ἐξελέγοντο (they picked out for themselves the places of honor); Matt 16:22 προσλαβόμενος αὐτὸν ὁ Πέτρος (Peter, having taken him to himself).

[111] Porter, *Idioms*, 68–70. Exegetically significant passages discussed: 1 Cor 13:8, Col 2:15, Jas 4: 2–3. This matter is addressed in the investigation to follow.

[112] Porter, *Idioms*, 70.

[113] Porter, *Idioms*, 71; Robertson, *Grammar*, 812. Robertson comments that these are verbs of mental action.

active forms in the papyri, e.g., ἀκούσω in P.Oxy. 2.294 *l* 15, (22 CE).[114] He considers this to represent the "levelling of an irregular element in these mixed verbal systems" but comments that this phenomenon is less frequent in the papyri than in the New Testament and Koine literature.[115] Gignac observes however, that γενήσομαι, δυνήσομαι, and πορεύσομαι retained their future middle forms in the papyri as in the New Testament.[116] His observations overall confirm the attributes of middle verbs noted by the NT Grammars.

2.1.6.9 Daniel B. Wallace (1996)

Daniel B. Wallace notes the difficulty of defining the middle voice, because it encompasses "a wide and amorphous group of nuances" but in general, he claims that "the subject *performs* or *experiences* the action of the verb in such a way that *emphasizes the subject's participation.*"[117] His Grammar draws productively on the work of previous grammarians.[118] He clarifies their terminology for the different uses of the middle by grouping them where possible. Thus, for example, he notes that what he refers to as the indirect middle is also named the indirect reflexive, benefactive, intensive or dynamic by others when speaking of subjects acting for or by themselves.[119] While some separate the intensive middle (highlighting the subject as if an intensive pronoun were used) from the indirect middle (equivalent to the use of a reflexive pronoun in the dative), he considers them too similar to differentiate.[120] He accommodates those who hold that there is not a clear distinction between middle and active in the NT (e.g., Moule) and those who contend that the NT writers

---

[114] Gignac, *Greek Papyri*, 321. See §1.2n7, above.

[115] Gignac, *Greek Papyri*, 321–22.

[116] Gignac, *Greek Papyri*, 324.

[117] Wallace, *Exegetical Syntax*, 414; (italics original).

[118] Wallace refers to Moulton, Smyth, BDF, Moule, Robertson, Dana and Mantey, and Zerwick in his discussion on Voice (*Exegetical Syntax*, 408–30).

[119] Wallace, *Exegetical Syntax*, 419.

[120] Wallace, *Exegetical Syntax*, 420.

retain a sense of the classical distinction (e.g., Zerwick, above) by proposing that each instance of a middle verb should be examined carefully to determine "how much can be made of the voice."[121]

In regard to 'deponents', Wallace notes that the "criteria for determining deponency still await a definitive treatment."[122] He advises that before a middle verb is declared deponent (middle form functioning as active) it should be clear that no middle force is apparent *and* no active form exists, as determined by an investigation of its forms in wider Koine as well as in Classical Greek.[123] While he indicates that deponent verbs will generally have lexical entries in the middle/passive form, he notes that this can be deceptive. For instance, because ἐκλέγω has no active form in the NT, it appears in BAGD as ἐκλέγομαι; yet it does appear in the active in other Koine literature, therefore its middle forms in the NT are true middles and not deponent.[124] On the other hand, δέχομαι (receive, welcome) is not considered to be deponent because although it has no active form, the middle sense is clear, with the lexeme being "inherently reflexive."[125]

2.1.6.10 Guy L. Cooper III (1998)

The grammar by Guy L. Cooper III is a revision and translation of K. W. Krüger's *Attic Greek Prose Syntax* and has made this comprehensive work accessible to English readers.[126] In defining the character of the middle voice, Cooper states that it "denotes that the subject is in some especial manner involved or interested in the action of the verb"[127] and in distinction from the active, the "middle focuses on the subject of the

---

[121] Wallace, *Exegetical Syntax*, 420.

[122] Wallace, *Exegetical Syntax*, 430n65.

[123] Wallace, *Exegetical Syntax*, 429–30.

[124] Wallace points out that BAGD does indicate "the act. does not occur in our lit." (*Exegetical Syntax*, 428–29).

[125] Wallace, *Exegetical Syntax*, 429.

[126] Guy L. Cooper III, after K.W. Krüger, *Attic Greek Prose Syntax*, vol.1 (Ann Arbor: University of Michigan Press, 1998).

[127] Cooper, *Attic Greek*, 589.

verb and its personal capacities."[128] This is further articulated in his description of the "dynamic" middle (similar to Jannaris above) which warrants full citation here as it is adopted and referred to in the current study. Thus, Cooper states:

> The middle voice may be used to show that the faculties and resources of the subject, all thought of as pertaining naturally to it and lying within its natural sphere, are mobilized, energized, and applied. In these uses the subject is displayed as exerting itself, working and drawing adjacent conceptions into its own sphere of control and effectiveness. This range of the middle has been called, appropriately, the *dynamic middle*.[129]

In addition to the dynamic middle, (which he notes often applies to verbs having no active forms, the "so-called deponents")[130] he observes the tendency for the middle to express verbs of intelligence, volition, and emotion, which form the *source* of the "mobilization and expenditure of energy."[131] Cooper identifies the indirect middle or "middle of interest" as the most common, noting that the object of such a verb either pertains naturally to the subject or that the verbal action "draws the object into the sphere of the subject and establishes a relation of the object to the subject[.]" He also notes that the interest of the subject may be in the *removal* of an object.[132] Other middle types he identifies are the direct reflexive, reciprocal, and causal functions, as have others, above; however, Cooper aptly remarks that a verb may reflect two or more of these functions at once.[133]

---

[128] Cooper, *Attic Greek*, 590.

[129] Cooper, *Attic Greek* 589.

[130] Cooper, *Attic Greek* 592.

[131] Cooper, *Attic Greek*, 594. He does not label this group of verbs; the implication is that it may be a sub-set of the dynamic.

[132] Cooper, *Attic Greek*, 600, 601, 605. These descriptions suggest actions such as acquiring or rejecting.

[133] Cooper, *Attic Greek*, 595.

Concerning the use of the active and middle for a particular verb, Cooper notes that sometimes they are so sharply distinguished that they are "effectively separate elements of vocabulary," occurring particularly in situations of business and law, for example, ἀποδίδωμι: I pay what is due, restore, render, in contrast to ἀποδίδομαι: I sell.[134] In other instances, he asserts that the difference between active and middle "may be reduced to an untranslatable nuance" and the voice may be varied simply for stylistic purposes.[135] This work helpfully clarifies the variable senses of the middle voice in the Attic Greek which forms the basis of the Koine language under consideration.

2.1.7 Grammars of the Twenty-First Century

In recent years, a general shift may be observed in the discussion of middle voice and deponency, even in the elementary Grammars. The work by Conrad below, though not a grammar as such, may be seen to have been influential for subsequent works.

2.1.7.1 Carl W. Conrad (2002)

Carl W. Conrad's online article "New Observations on Voice in the Ancient Greek Verb" offers insight and clarity to the somewhat clouded understandings of the Greek middle voice in NT studies at the close of the 20th century.[136] Although unpublished, this work has been referred to by later writers, and has prompted a significant step forward in the endeavor to understand the morphology, in particular, of the middle voice in the New Testament.[137]

---

[134] Cooper, *Attic Greek*, 602.

[135] Cooper notes that the middle is frequently used in poetry, reflecting the tendency to focus on persons, whereas the active voice generates more objective literary expression, e.g., for narrative (*Attic Greek*, 603).

[136] Carl W. Conrad, "New Observations on Voice in the Ancient Greek Verb," 2002 available online at https://cpb-us-w2.wpmucdn.com/sites.wustl.edu/dist/8/2865/files/2020/10/newobsancgrkvc.pdf.

[137] Hence Conrad is given special acknowledgement by Rodney J. Decker, *Reading*

He remarks that the conventional terminology of transitivity and voice can be misleading when the basic polarity of the language is taken to be *active-passive* and an attempt is made to locate the middle voice somewhere between these two.[138] Accordingly, he contends that the middle voice must be understood in its own right, and this can only be done when the fundamental polarity of voice in ancient Greek is understood to be *active-middle*.[139] The distinctiveness of the middle verb, he asserts, is that the subject is "the focus of the verb's action or state[.]" Such verbs, whether transitive or intransitive, "indicate the deep involvement of the subject as the one experiencing, suffering, enduring, or undergoing an action or a change of state."[140]

In regard to morphology, Conrad contests the view that the -θη- endings in the aorist and future tenses are essentially passive voice markers. He prefers an opposition between middle/passive verbs on the one hand, marked morphologically for "subject-focus" and the unmarked active or "simple" verbs on the other.[141] Just as there is one set of endings ("morphoparadigm")[142] for middle-passive verbs in the present, imperfect and perfect tenses, he argues that the same occurs in aorist and future tenses; that is, the one form can indicate either middle or passive function.

In the aorist tense, there are two possible morphoparadigms for middle/passive function. Conrad designates the older sigmatic forms "MP1" and the theta forms "MP2" respectively.[143] To illustrate that theta

---

Koine Greek: An Introduction and Integrated Workbook (Grand Rapids: Baker Academic, 2014), xvi, and is recognized as a significant contributor in the field by Campbell, *Advances*, 94–95.

[138] Conrad, "New Observations," 3.
[139] As noted at the beginning of this survey.
[140] Conrad, "New Observations," 3
[141] Conrad, "New Observations," 7.
[142] Conrad employs the term "morphoparadigm" to indicate "a regular sequence of personal endings for singular and plural in each voice category, as they are employed in appropriate combinations for tense and mood with adjustments for loss of intervocalic sigma and contraction of vowels" ("New Observations," 2).
[143] Conrad, "New Observations," 11.

morphology does not necessarily indicate passive function (nor is it *essentially* passive) he cites a verb which exhibits all three voices: ἐγείρω, active (I arouse, awaken, cause to rise) and the middle/passive ἐγείρομαι: I rise, awake, (middle sense) or I am roused, awakened caused to rise (passive sense). In the aorist, there is no distinctly middle form (ἐγειράμην might be expected, he notes) but only ἠγέρθην which may be used in both the middle, intransitive sense (I woke up, got out of bed) and the passive (I was awakened).[144]

Conrad maintains that -θη- aorist forms arose to function for the middle/passive (subject-focused) voices in the aorist and future tenses and as they were adopted, the older middle forms (-μην, -σο, -το) of the same verb became obsolete.[145] In the particular state of flux of the language in the Koine Greek period therefore, at times both middle-passive forms existed side by side.[146]

This accounts for the use of so-called "passive" (theta) forms of verbs when the sense is clearly not passive; for instance, we find καὶ ἀποκριθεὶς αὐτῷ ὁ Ἰησοῦς εἶπεν: answering, Jesus said (Mark 10:51), using an MP2 form. However, MP1 forms are also found, for example, ὁ Πέτρος ἀπεκρίνατο πρὸς τὸν λαόν: Peter addressed the people (Acts 3:12).[147] Conversely, there are instances where MP1 forms are interpreted as passive, as in Mark 1:5, καὶ ἐβαπτίζοντο ὑπ' αὐτοῦ ἐν τῷ Ἰορδάνῃ ποταμῷ ἐξομολογούμενοι τὰς ἁμαρτίας αὐτῶν, Conrad notes that ἐβαπτίζοντο is almost always translated "were baptized" (passive) in English.[148] Similar phenomena occur with γίνομαι,

---

[144] Conrad, "New Observations," 3.

[145] Conrad, "New Observations," 6. Used with a verb stem, these endings generate the familiar λυσάμην, λύσω, λύσατο inflection pattern.

[146] Conrad lists 30 NT verbs for which this occurs ("New Observations," 15).

[147] Conrad locates 7 MP1 and 213 MP2 forms of ἀποκρίνομαι in the NT ("New Observations," 15).

[148] Hence, e.g., "and were baptized by him in the river Jordan, confessing their sins" (NRSV). Conrad notes, however, that the participial phrase ἐξομολογούμενοι τὰς ἁμαρτίας αὐτῶν (confessing their sins) indicates a voluntary action thus, even though the agent is expressed, the MP1 form may equally be read in a middle sense ("New

for which both MP1 (ἐγενόμην) and MP2 (ἐγενήθην) forms are evinced.[149] Thus Conrad advocates that when a middle-passive form is encountered, one should assume that it is middle unless the context clearly indicates it is passive.[150] These explanations offer helpful insights in regard to morphology.

2.1.7.2 David Alan Black (2009)

David Alan Black's publication of 2009 gives more credence to the force of the middle voice than earlier introductory texts. Like others, he comments that there is no single way of translating a middle verb into English since the specific way that the subject is being emphasized must be derived from the context.[151] He elucidates this comment by the example of λύομαι which (if middle rather than passive) could be translated: 'I am loosing myself', 'I myself am loosing', or 'I am loosing for myself'.[152] Such translations would correspond to the reflexive, the intensive/dynamic and the indirect middle respectively. Black notes that the active voice places emphasis on the action, but both middle and passive emphasize the subject. Further, he considers some deponents (having middle form but lacking the active) to be true middles in that the subject is being emphasized in some manner.[153] This questioning of the active

---

Observations," 13).

[149] Both forms are discussed in the investigations of middle verbs in 1 Thessalonians to follow. Conrad identifies forty-five MP2 aorists (ἐγενήθην morphoparadigm) of γίνομαι in the NT and judges that twenty-five appear passive in function, eleven middle, and nine ambiguous. He notes, nevertheless, that the MP1 forms (ἐγενόμην morphoparadigm) also exhibit passive function at times, concluding that both forms may indicate either middle or passive function ("New Observations," 18–21).

[150] Conrad asserts that the distinction between middle and passive function was not as significant to a Greek-speaker as it may be to an English speaker ("New Observations," 13).

[151] David Alan Black, *Learn to Read New Testament Greek,* 3rd ed. (Nashville: B&H Academic, 2009), 86.

[152] Black, *New Testament Greek,* 88.

[153] He asserts that deponents such as ἀσπάζομαι (I greet), ἀποκρίνομαι (I answer), and ψεύδομαι (I lie) express reciprocity. He considers ἐπενδύομαι (I put on) and

function of so-called deponents in introductory NT grammars was generally not apparent in the past.

2.1.7.3 Stanley E. Porter, Jeffrey T. Reed and Matthew Brook O'Donnell (2010)

The questioning of deponency is further posited by Stanley E. Porter, Jeffrey T. Reed and Matthew Brook O'Donnell, who state: "In our view, every verb expresses the meaning of its voice form, even when other forms—such as the active voice—may not exist."[154] This is a more radical stance than Porter's earlier work (*Idioms*, noted above). The authors maintain that although these verbs may be translated with an active English verb such as I became for ἐγενόμην, they retain the sense of the middle even though this may not be adequately captured in translation.[155]

The authors identify three uses of middle verbs. They note the reflexive and the reciprocal, as per custom but also the "proper middle" which is also known as the "intensive or dynamic middle" that "involves the subject doing an action to someone or something else in such a way as to affect itself also."[156] As an example, they suggest that the middle form αἱρήσομαι (I will choose) in Phil 1:22 expresses "focused

---

μιμέομαι (I imitate) to be reflexive, while ἔρχομαι (I go), διαλογίζομαι (I ponder), and βούλομαι (I wish) are true middles because they express processes that the subject alone can experience (*New Testament Greek*, 89).

[154] Porter, Stanley E., Jeffrey T. Reed and Matthew Brook O'Donnell, *Fundamentals of New Testament Greek* (Grand Rapids: Eerdmans, 2010), 125. Such a statement implies a one-to-one correlation between form and function. However, see Conrad in §2.1.7.1 above for a different view.

[155] Porter, Reed, O'Donnell, *Fundamentals*, 125. This position is not rigorously argued, and only this one example is given. However, the middle voice has been previously introduced, and such a comment directs the reader to look for the middle sense in so-called "deponent" verbs.

[156] Porter, Reed, O'Donnell, *Fundamentals*, 122. Notably this application of "dynamic" is different from both that of Robertson and Cooper noted above. Further, the description of the "proper middle" relates only to transitive verbs, yet many middles are intransitive.

involvement in the decision making process, which certainly had ramifications for his life."[157]

2.1.7.4 B. H. McLean (2011)

B. H. McLean's introduction to the Koine Greek language attributes little significance to the middle voice in the New Testament.[158] He notes its "special meanings" in the Attic period but claims that the "middle voice had more or less fallen into disuse" in the Hellenistic period.[159] He also maintains the traditional definition of deponent verbs as middle or passive in form but active in function.[160] This accords with the earlier Cambridge introductory texts by Duff and Wenham noted above, although McLean does give some indication that these features have been recently contested.[161] To conclude, he asserts that "in the majority of cases the middle voice of thematic verbs should be translated as an active voice" and that "one should never appeal to the force of a middle voice on the basis of morphology alone."[162] Such statements in a relatively recent work indicate that the traditional view is still being posited.

2.1.7.5 Rodney J. Decker (2014)

Rodney J. Decker's Grammar provides a succinct discussion and explanation of voice semantics and morphology in the Koine Greek language.[163] He indicates, along traditional lines, that in the active voice, although the subject is the agent (the entity performing the action) the focus

---

[157] Porter, Reed, O'Donnell, *Fundamentals*, 122.

[158] B. H. McLean, *New Testament Greek: An Introduction* (New York: Cambridge University Press, 2011).

[159] McLean, *NT Greek*, 99–100, citing Moule, *Idiom Book*, 24 (as noted above) in this regard.

[160] McLean, *NT Greek*, 100.

[161] McLean, *NT Greek*, 100n2.

[162] McLean, *NT Greek*, 100.

[163] Rodney J. Decker, Reading Koine Greek: An Introduction and Integrated Workbook (Grand Rapids: Baker Academic, 2014).

is not on the subject but on the action portrayed by the verb, for example, "I hit the ball." The middle also portrays the subject as agent but draws particular attention to the subject rather than the action, for example, "*I* hit the ball." On the other hand, the passive portrays the subject as the recipient of an action by some *other* agent, hence, "I was hit by the ball."[164] This is a lucid representation for the beginning student.

He further articulates that the active voice is "situation-focused," whereas passive and middle are both "subject-focused." This shifts attention from the situation to the role of the subject, the characteristic attribute being that the subject is affected "in or by the event denoted by the verb."[165] This observation places middle and passive verbs in the same category for this parameter, in line with Conrad's work, above. Decker's concept of voice function may be depicted thus in Figure 2.1.

Figure 2.1 Diagrammatic Representation of Voice Function

Active	Middle	Passive
Subject is agent		Subject is patient
Situation-focused	Subject-focused	

Although Decker affirms the existence of three voices, he acknowledges that these do not neatly align with three corresponding forms. He asserts that not only do the middle forms also represent the passive voice in present stem verbs as commonly acknowledged but the "passive" -ϑη- aorist forms may also represent the middle voice of intransitive

---

[164] Decker, *Reading Koine Greek*, 227–28.
[165] Decker, *Reading Koine Greek*, 227. Here Decker is citing Egbert J. Bakker, "Voice, Aspect and Aktionsart: Middle and Passive in Ancient Greek," in *Voice Form and Function*, ed. Barbara Fox and Paul J. Hopper, TSL 27 (Amsterdam: John Benjamins, 1994), 24. Bakker notes, however, that subject-affectedness is only an "abstract cover term" and must be considered in conjunction with the "lexical value" of the verb to generate the type of events represented by the middle voice.

verbs.[166] Hence, we find instances such as τῇ ὁδῷ τοῦ Κάϊν ἐπορεύθησαν: "they <u>have traveled</u> in the way of Cain" (Jude 1:11); Ἰωσὴφ δὲ ὁ ἀνὴρ αὐτῆς, δίκαιος ὢν καὶ μὴ θέλων αὐτὴν δειγματίσαι, <u>ἐβουλήθη</u> λάθρᾳ ἀπολῦσαι αὐτήν: "but Joseph her husband, being righteous and not wanting to disgrace her, <u>determined</u> to divorce her quietly" (Matt 1:19).[167] In these examples, the subject is clearly the volitional agent, so these theta forms do not signify the passive voice. These observations are depicted in Figure 2.2

Figure 2.2 Diagrammatic Representation of Voice Form

Tense Form	Active	Middle	Passive
Present	-ω	-ομαι	-ομαι
1st Aorist	-σα	-σάμην -θην	-θην

Decker also notes that in the present tense, the middle/passive form most commonly has middle function; but in the aorist, the dual-purpose theta form is mostly commonly passive in function, which suggests why this morphology has been traditionally considered passive in Koine Greek.[168] Decker asserts that the decision regarding voice must come from the context. If an agent other than the subject is evident, for instance, then passive function is indicated. On the other hand, if the verb has a direct object, middle function is implied.[169] Decker's clarification (again following Conrad) of the dual role of the theta aorist forms assists in a synchronic understanding of voice form and function in Koine Greek. Accordingly, theta aorist forms which have non-passive function need not be considered anomalies or described as "passive deponents" (having active function) but may be recognized as true middle verbs. In fact, Decker does not use the term deponent at all, but refers to middle-

---

[166] Decker, *Reading Koine Greek*, 283, 305.
[167] Decker, *Reading Koine Greek*, 283.
[168] Decker, *Reading Koine Greek*, 283.
[169] Decker, *Reading Koine Greek*, 248–49.

only verbs as those which have "an inherent middle meaning in the very lexis of the word itself."[170]

2.1.7.6 Recent Trends (2015–2020)

A trend exists in recent NT grammars to provide more extensive treatments of the middle voice and to endorse the move away from the category of "Deponent Verb," as noted by Fredrick J. Long who calls them "middle-formed verbs" in his *Koine Greek Grammar*.[171] The authors of *Going Deeper with New Testament Greek* affirm that most, if not all, (so called) deponent verbs are true middles; further, they note the "potential exegetical payoff for appreciating the significance of the middle voice."[172]

William D. Mounce (see §2.1.5 above) gives significantly more comment on middle verbs in the most recent edition of his grammar, also noting the advances in understanding that, although translated as active, "*the subject is affected by the action of the verb.*"[173] This is in line with Decker, above, and the specific middle voice studies of the section below. Benjamin L. Merkle and Robert L. Plummer give a succinct definition of the middle voice in their introductory grammar that is helpful for the beginning student, namely, "the subject both performs and is affected by the action."[174] They assert that "so-called deponent

---

[170] Decker, *Reading Koine Greek*, 252.

[171] Long notes that although middle-formed verbs are often translated actively, there is some stress on "*the subject's involvement in the action*" (*Koine Greek Grammar: A Beginning-Intermediate Exegetical and Pragmatic Handbook*, Accessible Greek Resources and Online Studies [Wilmore, KY: GlossaHouse, 2015], 57.

[172] Andreas J. Köstenberger, Benjamin L. Merkle, and Robert L. Plummer, *Going Deeper with New Testament Greek: An Intermediate Study of the Grammar and Syntax of the New Testament* (Nashville: B&H Academic, 2016), 197. Long also draws attention to the significance for interpretation (*Koine Greek Grammar*, 52).

[173] William D. Mounce, *Basics of Biblical Greek Grammar*, 4th ed. (Grand Rapids: Zondervan, 2019), 185–86 (italics original).

[174] Benjamin L. Merkle and Robert L. Plummer, *Beginning with New Testament Greek: An Introductory Study of the Grammar and Syntax of the New Testament* (Nashville: B&H Academic, 2020), 38.

verbs" are more aptly seen as middle-only verbs, not simply because of their form but because the action the verb describes is inherently "subject affected" (as Decker above). This places middle-only verbs firmly within the class of all middles.

While each of these grammars gives some examples of the use of middle verbs in various situations (reflexive, special interest, movement, etc.) the terminology still varies from one to another, as with the earlier grammars. Therefore, more specific studies on the middle voice will be examined in the next section to obtain a fuller sense of the ways in which the middle voice was used by the Greek speakers and writers themselves.

2.2 SPECIFIC MIDDLE VOICE STUDIES

2.2.1 Rutger J. Allan (2003)

Allan's comprehensive study of the middle voice is specific to Ancient Greek, from Homer to the Classical period.[175] In search of a model that adequately articulates the essence of the middle voice as well as its various applications, Allan draws on previous linguistic studies, notably those of John Lyons (general linguistics), Albert Rijksbaron (the verb in classical Greek), Suzanne Kemmer (a cross-linguistic middle voice study) and R. W. Langacker (cognitive grammar).[176] The verbs he classifies as 'middle' are those which have the middle inflection in the present indicative (such as λύομαι); consequently, passive verbs are within

---

[175] See §1.3, above.

[176] Albert Rijksbaron, *The Syntax and Semantics of the Verb in Classical Greek: An Introduction*, (Amsterdam: Gieben, 2002); John Lyons, *Introduction to Theoretical Linguistics* (Cambridge: Cambridge University Press, 1968); Suzanne Kemmer, *The Middle Voice*, TSL 23 (Amsterdam: John Benjamins, 1993); R. W. Langacker, *Foundations of Cognitive Grammar*, 2 vols. (Stanford, CA: Stanford University Press, 1987, 1991).

his purview.[177] Allan's work will be discussed in some detail as it forms a major interlocutor for the current investigation.

2.2.1.1 Linguistic Background

As the starting point from which to introduce and explain the necessary terminology for his investigation of the semantics of the middle voice, Allan employs the notion of the "prototypical transitive clause." In such a clause, an agent acts to effect a change of state on a patient, for example, "Mary cut the meat" or "John destroyed the house[.]"[178] The agent is the grammatical subject, and the patient is the direct object. This archetype serves as a reference point for other instances and may also be applied metaphorically to refer to mental events such as οἶδα τι (I know something); ὁράω τι (I see something).[179]

Because of the varying terminology among linguistic theories, Allan defines additional terms that he employs. Relevant to this discussion are the following: "*experiencer*: an animate entity engaged in a mental event"; "*beneficiary*: an animate entity receiving benefit as a result of the event"; and "*source*: the location from which an entity moves, or, metaphorically, the stimulus of a mental event."[180]

Another point of clarification relates to *markedness*, a term used in regard to two related words to positively indicate the presence of a particular attribute in one while the other is unmarked and consequently more general.[181] Allan argues that the active voice is unmarked (neutral) with respect to subject-affectedness, while the middle voice is marked (positive).[182] He emphasizes that this does not mean that the active

---

[177] Allan, *Polysemy*, 1n1.

[178] Allan, *Polysemy*, 6–8.

[179] Allan, *Polysemy*, 13–14. Throughout this section, English glosses are those given by Allan.

[180] Allan, *Polysemy*, 11–12 (italics original).

[181] Lyons provides an everyday example: The term *dog* is the unmarked, general term, while *bitch* is the marked term, applying only to female dogs (*Theoretical Linguistics*, 79).

[182] Allan, *Polysemy*, 19–29.

indicates the *absence* of subject-affectedness; it is simply unmarked. Indeed, the lexical meaning of some active verbs such as ἐσθίω (I eat) and πίνω (I drink) clearly indicate benefit for the subject and do not need to be marked or coded with the middle voice.[183] On the other hand, middle verbs *are* marked morphologically for subject-affectedness, hence "event types which do not involve subject-affectedness cannot be expressed by a middle verb."[184] This is tantamount to stating that middle morphology indicates subject affectedness.

Allan selected the criterion of subject-affectedness for the middle voice after considering other definitions. He notes that the idea of the subject being affected by the event is roughly equivalent to Kemmer's notion of the subject being conceptualized as both "Initiator" and "Endpoint."[185] However, he maintains this characterization is "not entirely adequate" for Ancient Greek, since it does not include the passive.[186] Therefore, he considers Lyons' definition of the middle voice to be the most apt, that is, "The implications of the middle, (when it is in opposition with the active) are that the 'action' or 'state' affects the subject of the verb or his interests."[187] As Allan remarks, this definition incorporates both the affected, patient-like sense of the middle and the indirect reflexive sense pertaining to the self-interest of the subject.[188] In keeping with Lyons' terminology, Allan employs the useful term "oppositional middles" for those middle verbs which have active counterparts; for the remainder, which do not appear in active form, he applies the term *media tantum* (middle only).[189]

---

[183] Allan, *Polysemy*, 26.

[184] Allan, *Polysemy*, 29.

[185] Allan, *Polysemy*, 46; Kemmer, *Middle Voice*, 73.

[186] Allan, *Polysemy*, 46. Nevertheless, Allan values Kemmer's typological study as fundamental to his work, noting her semantic map of middle-voice situation types (Allan, *Polysemy*, 42; Kemmer, *Middle Voice*, 202).

[187] Allan, *Polysemy*, 16–17; Lyons, *Theoretical Linguistics*, 373.

[188] Allan, *Polysemy*, 17.

[189] Allan, *Polysemy*, 2, 51.

2.2.1.2 Scope of the Middle Voice in Classical Greek

Adopting Langacker's theory of network categories, Allan seeks to demonstrate that the "grammatical category of middle voice can be insightfully analyzed as a complex network category."[190] That is, rather than simply listing an inventory of middle voice situations observed from usage, he represents them as part of a network, subsumed under the overarching characteristic of subject-affectedness but connected to other related situation types.[191]

2.2.1.3 Allan's categories of Middle Voice applications

Allan identifies eleven situation types which are marked by the middle voice. Each of these is briefly described below and compared, when relevant, with the classifications given in the grammars above. It should be borne in mind that Allan is not referring to the Greek of the Hellenistic era, but to earlier stages of the language. From Allan's examples and illustrations, those appearing in, or being pertinent to the language of the New Testament have been selected in the discussion to follow.

2.2.1.3.1 Passive Middle

In contrast to the grammars surveyed above, Allan includes the passive as a subcategory of the middle.[192] Indeed, this fits with his model in which subject affectedness is the essential criterion for the middle voice, for in the passive the patient (recipient of the action) has subject status. Although he emphasizes that the agent (the entity which performs the action) is "conceptually present" it may or may not be explicit, for example, ῥήγνυμαι (ὑπό): I am being broken (by). Allan also includes

---

[190] Allan, *Polysemy*, 39.
[191] See Allan, *Polysemy*, 119.
[192] Allan, *Polysemy*, 58–59.

πείθομαι: I am being persuaded (by) as an example, noting that passive middles may involve changes of state.[193]

2.2.1.3.2 Spontaneous Process Middle

The subject has the semantic role of patient, undergoing an "internal, physical change of state" which occurs without the direct initiation of an agent.[194] Allan notes that almost all these middles have an active causative counterpart; for instance, ἀπόλλυμαι (die, perish) has the active counterpart ἀπόλλυμι (destroy, kill). However, an unusual example, γίγνομαι (be born, come into being, become) has no corresponding active.[195] He notes that it is sometimes difficult to distinguish the spontaneous middle from the passive, as they are closely related. For example, καίομαι could be read in the sense of the intransitive spontaneous process middle (burn) or of the passive (be burnt).[196] In regard to morphology, Allan notes that this class of verbs never have a sigmatic middle form.[197]

2.2.1.3.3 Mental Process Middle

Allan applies this term to situations in which an animate subject experiences a mental effect, whether this be emotional (such as fear) or cognitive (such as knowing or remembering), noting that the present tense indicates that the subject is *in* a state, for example φοβέομαι (I am afraid), while the aorist signifies the *entering* of a state, thus ἐφοβήθην (I became afraid).[198] Although related to the passive in that a non-

---

[193] Allan, *Polysemy*, 59.

[194] Allan, *Polysemy*, 60.

[195] Allan, *Polysemy*, 60–61. Other examples given are: θέρομαι (become warm) cf. θέρω (make hot); φαίνομαι (become visible, appear) cf. φαίνω (cause to appear, show); τελεῖται (it is being fulfilled) cf. τελέω (accomplish).

[196] Allan, *Polysemy*, 63. Only context would distinguish.

[197] Allan, *Polysemy*, 60n72.

[198] Allan, *Polysemy*, 64–65.

volitional subject is affected, this category differs in that the effect does not come directly from an external agent, although it may be *caused* by an external stimulus. Hence, for instance, ὀργίζομαι + dat. (be angry with) suggests that the anger is experienced in response to a stimulus; the corresponding causative active being ὀργίζω (make angry).[199]. In such cases, a reading must depend on the context to determine whether it is the state of mind of the subject which is paramount; that is, whether the intention is to emphasize the mental experience of the subject, or whether an external agent is envisaged.

2.2.1.3.4 Body Motion Middle

Allan uses this term to describe situations in which an "animate entity volitionally brings about a change of state to himself."[200] This typically involves a change of location or body posture.[201] He notes that the corresponding active forms are causative. Hence, we find; στρέφομαι (turn around, intransitive) / στρέφω (turn, transitive); ἵσταμαι (stand still, stand up) / ἵστημι (set up, raise, make to stand); αἴρομαι (rise) / αἴρω (raise).[202] In these examples the middle form indicates action with reference to self, while the active refers to action on another, or outside oneself. Allan lists some *media tantum* verbs in this category, such as ἅλλομαι (jump); ἔρχομαι (go), which, according to his definition, are middle in meaning and not simply active, in contrast to many introductory grammars which classify them as deponent.[203]

---

[199] Allan, *Polysemy*, 65–67. Further examples: αἰσχύνομαι (be ashamed); λυπέομαι (be grieved about); μιμνήσκομαι (remember); ψεύδομαι + gen. (be mistaken); πείθομαι (believe, obey).

[200] Allan, *Polysemy*, 76.

[201] The subject is therefore both the initiator and the endpoint (affected entity) (*Polysemy*, 76).

[202] Allan, *Polysemy*, 77.

[203] Allan, *Polysemy*, 79. By contrast, see Duff, *Elements*, 93; Mounce, *Basics*, 150.

2.2.1.3.5 Collective Motion Middle

These are verbs of gathering and dispersing. Such actions are different from reciprocal middles in that the action does not occur *between* members of a group but involves a change of state brought about by a group as a whole. For example, (συλ)λέγομαι is a collective motion middle (gather, intransitive), whereas the active (συλ)λέγω expresses the transitive sense of gathering. Similarly, we find σκίδναμαι (disperse, intransitive) but σκίδνημι (disperse, transitive).[204] That is, the intransitive middle verb (συλ)λέγομαι indicates that individuals come together to form a group of which they are then part, whereas the active transitive counterpart indicates that an outside agent collects entities into a group, as in harvesting wheat.

2.2.1.3.6 Reciprocal Middle

As recognized by many of the grammars, verbs in this group denote events in which two (or more) participants act in the same manner on each other.[205] Therefore the subject is both initiator and endpoint of the same action type, as in fighting. Allan comments that reciprocal events often relate to contending, and defines all middle verbs in this category as *naturally reciprocal* events, noting that the majority are *media*

---

[204] Allan, *Polysemy*, 82–83. σκίδναμαι does not occur in the NT. συλλέγομαι occurs in the NT only as a passive (Matt 13:40); or active (Matt 7:16, 13:28-30, 40-41, 48; and Luke 6:44). In all cases it refers to gathering in the sense of harvesting, and clearly precludes a middle interpretation. BDAG s.v. "συλλέγω" refers only to the active meaning (gather by picking, as in harvest situations) whereas LSJ s.v. "συλλέγω" identifies active: bring together, collect; middle: collect for oneself; and passive: come together, assemble. Clearly it is a matter of interpretation whether the verb is middle or passive semantically. Allan does comment that the difference between the two lies in the extent to which the subjects are initiators. If gathered or dispersed by command, for instance, the verb would be passive. In the NT, συνέρχομαι is used to indicate the act of gathering to form a group (e.g., Luke 5:15; Acts 5:16; 1 Cor 11:17, 18) and may be interpreted in this middle sense because the action is voluntary.

[205] Allan, *Polysemy*, 84–85.

tantum, for example, ἀγωνίζομαι (contend, fight), διαλέγομαι + dat. (converse with) and μάχομαι + dat. (fight, quarrel with).[206] Whereas the grammars suggest that reciprocity may alternatively be expressed by an active verb and the reciprocal pronoun (ἀλλήλους), Allan specifies that such a construction is used for events not *normally* performed reciprocally.[207]

2.2.1.3.7 Direct Reflexive Middle

This use is invariably mentioned by the grammars. Allan applies the term "direct reflexive" to human agents volitionally performing an action on their person, the subject being both initiator and endpoint.[208] His prime examples are the familiar verbs of grooming such as κείρομαι (cut one's hair / have a hair-cut); λοῦομαι (bathe oneself); ἀλείφομαι (anoint oneself); ἕννυμαι (dress oneself); ζώννυμαι (gird oneself); κοσμοῦμαι (adorn oneself); νίζομαι (wash one's hands/feet).[209] Allan notes that these middles designate actions *normally* performed on oneself, whereas those not normally performed on self are expressed by an active verb with a reflexive pronoun, for example, ῥίπτει ἑαυτὸν εἰς τὴν θάλατταν: he throws himself into the sea.[210]

---

[206] Allan, *Polysemy*, 85. Accordingly, ἀγωνίζομαι (engage in contest, struggle, fight) occurs in the NT in Luke 13:24; John 18:36; 1 Cor 9:25; Col 1:29, 4:12; 1 Tim 4:10, 6:12; and 2 Tim 4:7. As noted in BDAG s.v. "ἀγωνίζομαι," this is often used figuratively, for instance in reference to striving on behalf of the gospel, or wrestling in prayer, e.g., εἰς τοῦτο γὰρ κοπιῶμεν καὶ ἀγωνιζόμεθα (for to this end we toil and struggle, 1 Tim 4:10, NRSV).

[207] Allan (*Polysemy*, 85), indicates that this is analogous to the use of the active with a reflexive pronoun to express reflexive events instead of using the middle (see below).

[208] Allan, *Polysemy*, 88.

[209] Allan, *Polysemy*, 89.

[210] Allan, *Polysemy*, 90.

2.2.1.3.8 Perception Middle

Allan applies this category of middle to situations in which an animate subject "perceives an object through one of the sensory organs."[211] The subject is mentally affected by the perception, hence becoming an *experiencer* in Allan's scheme. Such verbs tend to express volitional activity with the subject also acting as the agent, for example, γεύομαι (taste); σκέπτομαι (look at, consider), θεάομαι (look at, wondering).[212] Whereas active verbs may also express perception, they are unmarked, while the middle verbs of perception are marked to indicate subject-affectedness. This may be seen for instance in the contrast between σκέπτομαι, which indicates looking at something in order to gain information about it, and the active verb ὁράω (I see), that indicates nothing about an effect on the subject.[213] The middle verb signals that "the perception brings about a lasting effect on the cognitive state of mind of the perceiver."[214]

2.2.1.3.9 Mental Activity Middle

Allan describes mental activity situations as those in which an animate subject volitionally performs a mental activity whereby the subject is mentally affected, thus having the roles of both agent and experiencer, and sometimes beneficiary. As examples he notes βουλεύομαι (take counsel, plan, resolve); and λογίζομαι (calculate, reason, consider).[215]

---

[211] Allan, *Polysemy*, 95.

[212] Allan, *Polysemy*, 95.

[213] Allan, *Polysemy*, 99–100. Clearly these two verbs are not of the same root, but Allan is illustrating his point by noting that, when the effect on the subject is to be emphasised, a middle verb is appropriate. This, he notes, is consistent with Bechert's study of the use of ἰδεῖν and ἰδέσθαι in Homer, which concludes that the active is used when the action is emphasized, while the middle is used when the subject and its special participation in the act is emphasized. See J. Bechert, *Die Diathesen von ἰδεῖν und ὁρᾶν bei Homer* (München: Kitzinger, 1964), 424, 426.

[214] Allan, *Polysemy*, 100.

[215] Allan, *Polysemy*, 101.

He remarks that there is no "sharp boundary" between these verbs and the mental process type, however, the crucial difference is that mental activities are volitional (whereas mental processes react to stimuli).[216] In general, these verbs "designate that the subject conceives an idea by reasoning."[217] Further, he notes that some are related to indirect reflexives with concrete meaning by metaphorical extension to mental activity. Hence, for example, ὁρίζομαι (mark something out for oneself) becomes "determine for oneself, define[.]"[218]

2.2.1.3.10 Speech Act Middle

Allan asserts that speech acts expressed by the middle voice indicate that the subject is not only the agent but is also affected either as beneficiary or experiencer (for instance when a strong emotion is involved).[219] Examples given by Allan which also appear in the New Testament are: ἀπολογέομαι, (speak in defense), ψεύδομαι, (cheat by lies, speak falsely); ἀρνέομαι (refuse, deny); μέμφομαι (rebuke); ἐντέλλομαι (command); εὔχομαι (vow, pray, boast); δέομαι (beg, beseech). On the one hand, he explains the manner whereby the subject is affected in different instances, for example, lying is normally done for the benefit of the subject, On the other hand, a vow results in the speaker being bound by the promise and therefore mentally affected by the speech act. This contrasts with the more general verbs of speech, for example, λέγω (speak, say) and φημί (say), which Allan notes tend to be active.[220] This pattern is seen in the New Testament also.

---

[216] Allan, *Polysemy*, 102. Allan also notes that some verbs can express either a nonvolitional mental process or a volitional mental activity, e.g., φράζομαι: think, believe (mental process) or consider, contrive (mental activity).
[217] Allan, *Polysemy*, 102.
[218] Allan, *Polysemy*, 104.
[219] Allan, *Polysemy*, 105–7.
[220] Allan, *Polysemy*, 106.

2.2.1.3.11 Indirect Reflexive Middle

This class is commonly referred to by the grammars as something done in the interest of the subject (*to* or *for* the subject).[221] Allan indicates that in the typical case the volitional subject is affected by becoming a beneficiary or recipient, the latter occurring only with *media tantum* verbs.[222] Some of Allan's examples, such as δέχομαι (receive, accept); ἐργάζομαι (work at, make, perform); ἰάομαι (heal, treat, cure); κτάομαι (acquire); ῥύομαι (protect, rescue); ὠνέομαι (buy) also appear in the New Testament.[223] He asserts that the indirect reflexive middle is an *unemphatic* way of expressing that the subject is the beneficiary, whereas for greater emphasis, the reflexive pronoun in the dative may be used with either the middle or the active.[224] Allan considers the causative middle to be a sub-class of this category, as not only does the subject indirectly benefit, but it is the initiator of an event, (even though not a performer of it). For example, Θεμιστοκλῆς Κλεόφαντον τὸν υἱὸν ἱππέα μὲν ἐδιδάξατο ἀγαθόν (Thermistocles had his son Cleophantus taught to be a good horseman).[225] In such cases the subject is affected by the *results* of the action, not the action itself.

2.2.1.4 *Middle (sigmatic) and Passive (theta) Aorist Distinctions*

In addition to the *uses* of the middle voice, Allan examined the different *aorist forms* of the middle, that is, those having passive-like aorist endings employing theta, such as φοβέομαι (ἐφοβήθην) and those having sigmatic middle endings, for example, ποιέομαι (ἐποιησάμην). In accord with Conrad, above, he notes a "gradual expansion of the passive aorist form" mainly at the expense of the sigmatic middle aorist, noting

---

[221] As noted, for example, by Jannaris above.
[222] Allan, *Polysemy*, 112.
[223] Allan, *Polysemy*, 114.
[224] Allan, *Polysemy*, 114.
[225] Allan, *Polysemy*, 84.

that the latter has disappeared in Modern Greek completely.[226] The Koine language, in which both forms are present, thus represents a stage in this transition. Of particular interest to this study is his observation regarding the distribution of the two aorist forms among the different middle uses in his network schema.[227] For the classical era, this may be simplified on a linear scale as shown in Figure 2.3.

The consecutive order indicates a gradation from the strongest expression of subject affectedness (patient role) and minimal agent function to the reverse, that is, the strongest expression of agentive function and the least explicit expression of the subject as patient. Another feature analyzed by Allan is the volitional nature of the subject.

Figure 2.3 The Distribution of Aorist Forms among Allan's Middle Voice Categories

Passive	Spont. proc.	Men. process	Coll. motion	Body motion	Reciprocal	Dir. reflex.	Perception	Men. activity	Speech act	Ind. reflex.
Theta (passive) aorist forms					Sigmatic middle aorist forms					
Non-volitional			either	Volitional						

Allan finds that the subjects of sigmatic aorists are always volitional, as well as those of body motion middles, while the passive, spontaneous process and mental process are non-volitional. The collective motion middle may be either.[228]

---

[226] Allan, *Polysemy*, 148.
[227] Allan, *Polysemy*, 154–56.
[228] Allan, *Polysemy*, 175–76.

2.2.1.5 Concluding Observations

In summary, Allan presents a useful network model for the middle voice in Ancient Greek, articulating its polysemous nature while demonstrating the unifying attribute of subject-affectedness exhibited in various degrees and in various manners. An important distinctive feature of his work is that the passive is simply one use of the middle voice. While many of the categories align with those identified by others above, notably absent is the concept of a subject acting from within its own resources (Cooper's dynamic middle). Nevertheless, his classifications provide an apt vehicle of analysis for the investigations to follow.

Notably, Allan does not discuss deponent verbs as such. He does, however, mention that *media tantum* verbs are sometimes identified as *deponentia*, a term adopted from Latin grammar.[229] His analysis shows that many such verbs fall within the various middle voice categories he identifies. Thus, he does not class them as a separate group, consider them to lack middle voice meaning, or to be construed as active verbs disguised with middle morphology. They are simply verbs which are only used in the middle voice.

In New Testament Studies, however, verbs having middle, but not active forms (*media tantum*) have traditionally been labelled deponent. This designation brings with it the notion that although the form is middle, the function of the verb is active. Such an understanding arose from the misapplication of Latin grammar to Greek around the time of the Renaissance (see below) and has only recently been widely challenged.[230] Some of the significant contributions to this dispute are noted in the following sections.

2.2.2 Neva F. Miller (2005)

In an essay forming an appendix to the *Analytical Lexicon of the Greek New Testament* (of which she is co-editor), Neva F. Miller asserts the

---

[229] Allan, *Polysemy*, 2n4.
[230] See §2.2.3 and §2.2.4 below.

need for clarification regarding "deponent" verbs.²³¹ As she graciously affirms, her work is not a rigorous investigation, but driven by the need to classify forms for her lexicon, she draws attention to the problem and suggests some insights which may provide impetus for further investigation. Defining deponent verbs as those which have no active form, she comments that the traditional use of the term for verbs which are middle or passive in form but active in meaning implies two assumptions. It assumes that in the early stages of the language all verbs had an active form, and secondly that some verbs lost their active forms and became defective.²³² She questions these assumptions and in agreement with Robertson, considers that the middle form of a verb should be given due consideration. As an initial observation, she remarks that the subject "stays involved in the action" and articulates seven categories into which verbs "normally" classed as deponent may be placed.²³³ These are as follows:

1. Reciprocity, involving positive interaction, e.g., δέχομαι (welcome), δωρέομαι (bestow on), and χαρίζομαι (forgive); negative interaction, e.g., ἐπιλαμβάνομαι (grasp, seize hold of) and μάχομαι (fight); positive and negative communication, e.g., αἰτιάομαι (accuse) and ἐξηγέομαι (interpret, describe). Miller notes that "the removal of one party would render the verb meaningless and no action possible."²³⁴
2. Reflexivity, e.g., ἀπολογέομαι (make a defense, i.e., defend oneself) and ἐγκρατεύομαι (abstain, i.e., control oneself). Miller also includes verbs of motion in the sense of moving

---

[231] Neva F. Miller, "A Theory of Deponent Verbs," Appendix 2 of *Analytical Lexicon of the Greek New Testament*, ed. Timothy Friberg, Barbara Friberg, and Neva F. Miller (Victoria, BC: Trafford 2005), 423–30.

[232] Miller, "Deponent Verbs," 424.

[233] Miller, "Deponent Verbs," 426. The glosses given for the verbs in this section are those supplied by Miller.

[234] Miller, "Deponent Verbs," 427.

oneself, such as ἔρχομαι (come, go), πορεύομαι (journey), and ἐξάλλομαι (leap up).²³⁵
3. Self-Involvement, comprising verbs that "intimately involve the self in the processes going on within the action." These include intellectual activities, e.g., ἐπιλανθάνομαι (forget) and ἐπίσταμαι (understand); emotional states, e.g., ἐμβριμάομαι (be indignant); volitional activities, e.g., βούλομαι (wish, want).²³⁶
4. Self-interest, e.g., ἐργάζομαι (perform, accomplish) and κτάομαι (get, acquire).²³⁷
5. Receptivity (sensory perception), e.g., γεύομαι (taste), θεάομαι (see, behold).²³⁸
6. Passivity, which Miller sees as indicating that the subject is "unable to avoid the experience depicted in the verb." For example, γίνομαι (be born or come into being), κοιμάομαι (fall asleep, die), μαίνομαι (be mad, i.e., lunatic).²³⁹
7. State or Condition, in which the subject is the "center of gravity." For example, δύναμαι (be able), καθέζομαι (sit down), παράκειμαι (be at hand, be ready).²⁴⁰

Miller concludes that if the above types of verbs are true middles, and if the active form could not express the same meaning, there is no justification for considering them to be deponent.²⁴¹ It is evident that there is some correlation with the middle categories which have been identified by others (for instance her class designated 'Receptivity' may be

---

²³⁵ Miller, "Deponent Verbs," 427.
²³⁶ Miller, "Deponent Verbs," 428. The last example could perhaps be better described as 'acts of volition', rather than volitional activities, which suggests actions voluntarily undertaken as per Allan, above.
²³⁷ Miller, "Deponent Verbs," 429.
²³⁸ Miller, "Deponent Verbs," 429.
²³⁹ Miller, "Deponent Verbs," 429.
²⁴⁰ Miller, "Deponent Verbs," 429.
²⁴¹ Miller, "Deponent Verbs," 429.

equated to Allan's 'Perception Middle') yet there are also discrepancies; for example, Miller classifies καθέζομαι (sit down) as "State or Condition" whereas Allan classifies it as "Body Motion Middle."[242] Such differences affirm that the particular type of subject emphasis is to some extent a matter of personal discernment and difficult to perceive in isolation from context.

2.2.3 Bernard A. Taylor (2004, 2015)

Bernard A. Taylor offers a reappraisal of the notion of deponency in the context of his lexical work on the Septuagint, contending that "deponent" is a Latin term illegitimately applied to the Greek language, whereas 'middle voice' is an innately Greek concept.[243] It is not surprising, he claims, that verbs such as λογίζομαι (reckon, consider), αἰσθάνομαι (notice, perceive), and πυνθάνομαι (inquire) appear in the middle voice rather than the active because the subject is "directly and personally involved in the process—and hence the outcome[.]"[244] Therefore it is not necessary to assume that anything has been laid aside as is suggested when the term "deponent" is applied, for neither the active form nor a middle meaning has been abandoned; they are verbs whose lexical meaning is best expressed in the middle voice in Greek.[245]

In a more recent historical study, Taylor searches for the origins of this importation, noting, as observed above (§2.1.1, 2.), that the early grammars of Dionysius Thrax and Apollonius Dyscolus make no mention of the concept.[246] A Greek equivalent, ἀποθέτικος (related to

---

[242] Miller," Deponent Verbs", 429; Allan, *Polysemy*, 78.

[243] Bernard A. Taylor, "Deponency and Greek Lexicography," in *Biblical Greek Language and Lexicography: Essays in Honor of Frederick W. Danker*, ed. Bernard A. Taylor et al. (Grand Rapids: Eerdmans, 2004), 172. In Latin, deponent verbs are passive forms with active meaning, hence the assumed correspondence for Greek verbs with middle/passive forms but apparently active function.

[244] Taylor, "Deponency and Greek Lexicography," 174.

[245] Taylor notes that the English term "deponent" is derived from the Latin *depono*: "lay aside" ("Deponency and Greek Lexicography," 170).

[246] Bernard A. Taylor, "Greek Deponency: The Historical Perspective" 177–90 in

ἀποτίθημι, lay aside) does appear in the grammar of Constantinus Lascaris (1476), a teacher from Constantinople who had fled to the Latin west in the wake of its fall in 1453.[247] He identified five voices: active, passive, neutral (οὐδέτερον; i.e., intransitive), common or middle (used synonymously), and deponent (ἀποθέτικος).[248] Taylor states that during this Renaissance period Greek grammar was interpreted through the lens of Latin; that is, Latin paradigms were imposed on the Greek language and henceforth the notion of deponency has been applied to Greek.[249]

Taylor explains that this has resulted in an "eclipsing of the middle voice" by providing a way around it.[250] This custom has continued for centuries. However, the middle voice has come to the fore in recent times, following the work of Conrad (§2.1.7.1) and Allan (§2.2.1) in particular. Moreover, Neva Miller's call for further investigation of middle forms in relation to the New Testament (§2.2.2) has been embraced by other scholars as shown below.

2.2.4 Jonathan T. Pennington (2009)

In accord with Miller, Jonathan T. Pennington maintains that the traditional definition of deponent verbs as "middle-passive in form but active in meaning" has generated for New Testament studies a grammatical category that is erroneous.[251] He refers to the essay by Miller (above) as

---

Biblical Greek in Context: Essays in Honor of John A. L. Lee, ed. James K. Aitken and Trevor V. Evans, BTS 22 (Leuven: Peeters, 2015), 178–80.

[247] See also n19 above.

[248] Taylor, "Historical Perspective," 181–82. Taylor identifies only one earlier extant reference to ἀποθέτικος used in the sense of deponency, this being in the bilingual (Latin and Greek) *Ars Grammatica* by Dositheus (ca. fourth c. CE), written specifically for Greek speakers who wanted to learn Latin ("Historical Perspective," 189).

[249] Taylor, "Deponency and Greek Lexicography," 170–71.

[250] Taylor, "Historical Perspective," 189.

[251] Jonathan T. Pennington, "Setting Aside Deponency: Rediscovering the Greek Middle Voice in New Testament Studies" in *The Linguist as Pedagogue: Trends in the Teaching and Linguistic Analysis of the Greek New Testament*, ed. Stanley E. Porter and

well as the linguistic work of Klaiman, Bakker, and Kemmer, who have observed the particular situation types (Pennington refers to these as "lexical ideas") which are coded with the middle voice in several languages.[252] He commends the description given by Bakker, who states that the distinctive attribute of the middle voice is "the *affectedness* of the subject of the verb in, or by, the event denoted by the verb."[253] Bakker asserts that although this "affectedness" is the key factor, the exact sense of it depends on "interaction with the lexical value of each verb."[254] This clearly correlates with Allan's work discussed above.[255]

Pennington also considers the reasons why the subject-affectedness feature has not adequately been taken into account. Approaching the question from a pedagogical perspective, he suggests two factors. The first is the misapplication of a Latin grammatical category to the Greek language. He endorses the position of Taylor, above, noting that scholars "have adopted the category of deponency [from Latin] as if it were part of the Greek linguistic structure."[256] Second, he points to the lack of familiarity with the middle voice, noting that English (for example) "has no simple grammatical equivalent."[257]

Significantly, he comments that in learning another language we instinctively attempt to process it through our "own linguistic grid."[258]

Matthew Brook O'Donnell, NTM 11 (Sheffield: Sheffield Phoenix, 2009), 181–82.

[252] Pennington, "Setting Aside Deponency," 185. Kemmer's work has been referred to above; Klaiman's study is also cross-linguistic: M. H. Klaiman, *Grammatical Voice*, CSL 59 (Cambridge: Cambridge University Press, 1991); Bakker, "Voice, Aspect and Aktionsart" as noted above.

[253] Bakker, "Voice, Aspect and Aktionsart," 24, cited by Pennington, "Setting Aside Deponency," 185.

[254] Pennington, "Setting Aside Deponency," 185n4, referring to Bakker, "Voice, Aspect and Aktionsart," 24.

[255] Pennington does not mention Allan's study in this work.

[256] Pennington, "Setting Aside Deponency," 188.

[257] As noted above, translation of middle verbs into English requires additional terms such as reflexive pronouns or prepositional phrases if the force of the middle is to be accommodated ("Setting Aside Deponency," 182–83).

[258] Pennington, "Setting Aside Deponency," 186, 189.

Consequently, simply because a middle verb such as δέχομαι (receive, accept) appears active to the English mind, we construe an inconsistency between form and function in the Greek. Rather, he contends, it is our own lack of understanding of the meaning or function of the Greek middle voice which leads to this (mis)conception.

Pennington asserts that "most if not all verbs that are traditionally considered 'deponent' are truly middle in meaning."[259] Such a claim invites substantiation and underscores the rationale of this study. If correct, it has clear implications for the teaching of Greek and for New Testament Exegesis, as Pennington himself remarks. He recommends "middle only verbs" as a preferable classification, dispensing with the term and concept of deponency.[260]

As an illustration of the possible exegetical implications, he notes that ἐκλέγομαι (choose) is normally considered deponent, but could justifiably be read with the middle force of self-reference, such that ἐξελέξατο ἡμᾶς (Eph 1:4) would mean [God] chose us *for himself*.[261] In essence, he claims that any middle form should be carefully considered when reading and exegeting the New Testament, stating that "sensitivity to the middle voice may enable the interpreter to discern specific nuances" intended by the author.[262]

2.2.5 Stratton L. Ladewig (2010)

Stratton L. Ladewig does not primarily discuss the middle voice but rather sets out to establish a refined definition of deponency in Koine

---

[259] Pennington, "Setting Aside Deponency," 182.

[260] Pennington, "Setting Aside Deponency," 197.

[261] Pennington, "Setting Aside Deponency," 198. Possibly, Pennington states that ἐκλέγομαι would normally be considered deponent since it appears as the headword for this verb in BDAG. Nevertheless, LSJ lists the active, thus allowing for an enhanced meaning of the middle form. Wallace includes it among "verbs that look deponent but most likely are not" (*Exegetical Syntax*, 430).

[262] Pennington, "Setting Aside Deponency," 200.

Greek.²⁶³ Pointing to historical claims of a mis-match between form and function, he endorses the traditional view that middle or passive verb forms may have active function. He specifically rejects the arguments of Miller, Pennington, Taylor, and Allan, who, by contrast, all seek to grant the middle form its genuine middle voice.²⁶⁴

Ladewig affords only brief consideration to the meaning of the middle voice and essentially limits his considerations to direct and indirect reflexives.²⁶⁵ Accordingly, he concedes that verbs that only appear in the middle form and have a beneficiary/recipient subject (a term adopted from Allan) are truly middle in function.²⁶⁶ He considers all other *media tantum* verbs to have active function. Thus, he offers a revised definition of deponency:

> Deponency is a syntactical designation for the phenomenon in Koine Greek in which a lexically-specified set of verbs demonstrates incongruity between voice form and function by using middle and/or passive morphology to represent active voice function while simultaneously lacking active morphology for a particular principal part in Koine literature and lacking a beneficiary/recipient subject.²⁶⁷

Such a definition effectively retains the notion of deponency for some *media tantum* verbs but not others. By starting with the acceptance of deponency rather than an investigation of the middle voice, he arrives

---

²⁶³ Stratton L. Ladewig, "Defining Deponency: An Investigation into Greek Deponency of the Middle and Passive Voices in the Koine Period" (PhD diss., Dallas Theological Seminary, 2010).

²⁶⁴ Ladewig, "Defining Deponency," 167–93.

²⁶⁵ Ladewig, "Defining Deponency," 106.

²⁶⁶ Ladewig, "Defining Deponency," 130.

²⁶⁷ Ladewig, "Defining Deponency," 162.

at a position that is out of step with current understandings from linguistic studies and the more extensive grammars explored above.

2.2.6 Constantine R. Campbell (2015)

In a recent publication discussing developments in the study of Greek, Constantine R. Campbell devotes a chapter to "Deponency and the Middle Voice." This provides a succinct history of the development in thought on these matters from key contributors to the conversation.[268] Beginning with Moulton's critique of the term "deponent" in 1908 and culminating in its unanimous rejection by a panel at the 2010 SBL Conference,[269] his synopsis reveals the logical necessity for a clearer understanding of the middle voice should the notion of deponency be dismissed. Conversely, as Campbell expresses the logic of Miller and Allan, "a cohesive understanding of the middle voice will render deponency irrelevant."[270]

Campbell discerns that the task is more complex however, than simply discarding the nomenclature or the category of deponency. He calls for further investigations in this field, noting that what is required is "more complex than simply recognizing morphology" and draws attention to the remaining questions of "mixed deponents" such as active verbs having future middle forms, "passive deponents" and "lexical complexities" (the apparent interdependence of morphology, lexeme, and context). His concise survey of the state of scholarship on this matter is most accessible, providing an apt introduction to the field.

---

[268] Constantine R. Campbell, "Deponency and the Middle Voice," in *Advances in the Study of Greek: New Insights for Reading the New Testament* (Grand Rapids: Zondervan, 2015), 91–104. Moulton, Robertson, Miller, Taylor, Conrad, Allan, Pennington and Ladewig are mentioned, all of whom are discussed above.

[269] Campbell, Pennington, Porter, and Taylor formed the panel.

[270] Campbell, *Advances*, 96.

2.2.7 Rachel Aubrey (2016)

Writing from a linguistic perspective, Rachel Aubrey discusses the middle voice in NT Greek specifically in regard to the theta aorist morphology.[271] While broadly following Allan, she incorporates insights from cross-linguistic and diachronic studies, noting that the theta aorist was introduced into Greek for events which indicated a spontaneous change of state; it then spread to the passive, marking both these event-types in Homer.[272]

Through the Classical and into the Koine era the theta aorist spread further to displace the sigmatic middle aorist for other intransitive middle events.[273] She therefore affirms that in Koine Greek, as for the earlier stages of the language, the theta aorist is not specific to passive function.[274] An example she cites is τότε ἠγέρθησαν πᾶσαι αἱ παρθένοι ἐκεῖναι καὶ ἐκόσμησαν τὰς λαμπάδας ἑαυτῶν: "then all those bridesmaids <u>got up</u> and trimmed their lamps" (Matt 25:7).[275]

Aubrey also examines middle voice events with reference to energy transfer and focus of attention. For the prototypical transitive event such as *Matt hit the ball*, energy is transferred from agent (source) to patient (endpoint), inducing a change in the patient, with the focus of attention shifting accordingly, that is, from source to endpoint. However, for

---

[271] Rachel Aubrey, "Motivated Categories, Middle Voice, and Passive Morphology," in *The Greek Verb Revisited: A Fresh Approach for Biblical Exegesis*, ed. Steven E. Runge and Christopher J. Fresch. (Bellingham: Lexham, 2016), 563–625.

[272] Aubrey, "Motivated Categories," 571–72.

[273] Aubrey, "Motivated Categories," 572–73, 614. Aubrey adopts Allan's basic spectrum of events and draws her own semantic map, highlighting the trend from transitive active through the middle range (transitive and intransitive) to spontaneous and passive events ("Motivated Categories," 613).

[274] This is contrary to the traditional teaching of such in NT grammars. Such instruction leads to the treatment of non-passive "exceptions" of the theta aorist as passive-deponents. Aubrey states that cross-linguistically it is typical that passive markers are not exclusive to passive function ("Motivated Categories," 564).

[275] Aubrey, "Motivated Categories," 566. Other examples: ἐνθυμηθέντος (Matt 1:20); ἐμνήσθησαν (Luke 24:8); ἐκοιμήθη (Acts 7:60).

middle verbs, Aubrey notes that the focus of attention *remains* on the subject, which is both energy source and endpoint.[276] That is: "The one who began the event is also the one affected by it."[277] This position is, however, different from that of Allan as it does not include the passive as a type of middle.

By discussing voice in terms of number of participants and focus of attention, one matter which Aubrey's work reveals (though she does not emphasize this) is that when these parameters are considered, conceptually the passive is distinct from the middle. The passive is *like* the middle in that the spotlight is on the energy endpoint, which is another way of saying that the subject is affected. However, it is *unlike* the middle in that the energy comes from an external source. In this feature, it is a mirror image of the active, two participant transitive, for the passive expresses such events from the point of view of the affected entity rather than the source.[278] These wider insights will also help to inform the study of middle verbs to follow.

2.3 FURTHER LINGUISTIC AND PHILOSOPHICAL CONTRIBUTIONS

The survey thus far has been intentionally limited to studies of the middle voice in Greek; therefore cross-linguistic studies such as those of Kemmer have not been included in any detail. However, one little-known publication by linguist Emile Benveniste has been interpreted by Philippe Eberhard to generate an alternate perspective on Greek middle verbs that is pertinent to this study. It will become evident that this perspective on the middle voice is not entirely incongruent with those

---

[276] Aubrey, "Motivated Categories," 614.

[277] Aubrey, "Motivated Categories," 614.

[278] These matters become apparent in her final remarks (Aubrey, "Motivated Categories," 616–20). While a passive verb may not always have an active transitive counterpart in use, an active form is conceptually possible since passive verbs imply a transfer of energy from one entity to another.

above but is couched in different terminology and provides a useful criterion for this study.

2.3.1 Emile Benveniste (1966)

French linguist Emile Benveniste bases his brief study of the middle voice[279] on the fact that Proto-Indo-European, the common ancestor of Greek and many European languages, was "characterized by an opposition of only two diatheses": active and middle.[280] Consequently, all verbs are marked as one or the other; thus, *diathesis* (voice) is a fundamental attribute which is encoded in the verbal form (notably in the ending) along with person and number, the three factors pertaining to the subject.[281] He therefore seeks to identify the *basis* of this fundamental distinction, not merely instances or types of usage, and to articulate this difference between active and middle in linguistic terms.

Benveniste emphasizes that not all verbs can receive *both* active and middle endings; some are always expressed in the active (*activa tantum*) while some are always expressed in the middle (*media tantum*).[282] By comparing the types of verbs in each of these two classes, he aims to detect the distinguishing attribute which makes a particular verb suitable to one but not the other category.[283] He observes that verbs of action and

---

[279] Emile Benveniste, "Active and Middle Voice in the Verb," *Problems in General Linguistics*, trans. Mary Elizabeth Meek, MLS 8 (Coral Gables: University of Miami Press, 1971), 145–51; trans. of Emile Benveniste, *Problèmes de linguistique générale*, vol.1 (Paris: Gallimard, 1966).

[280] Benveniste, "Active and Middle," 145. Proto-Indo-European (PIE) is acknowledged by linguists as the common ancestor of many European and some Asian languages belonging to the Indo-European family, e.g., Greek, Latin, English, German, French, Sanskrit. See Lyons, *Theoretical Linguistics*, 21 and Horrocks, *Greek,* 9, 16. This is also assumed by Allan who refers to PIE in discussing cross-linguistic and diachronic middle voice studies. See, e.g., Allan, *Polysemy*, 4, 47, 48.

[281] Benveniste, "Active and Middle," 146, 150.

[282] This method contrasts with the more typical one of comparing active and middle forms of the same lemma.

[283] Benveniste selects verbs which are represented by the particular form in at least

condition are represented in both classes, but "[i]n the active the verbs denote a process which is accomplished outside the subject" whereas in the middle, the subject is inside the process.[284] Regarding the middle, he further states that the subject "achieves something which is achieved in him" such as being born or sleeping, and that "[h]e is inside the process of which he is the agent."[285]

This exterior and interior contrast is considered by Benveniste to be clearly applicable also to verbs of "double diathesis" (the oppositional middles noted by Allan). This is affirmed by examples such as πόλεμον ποιεῖ "he produces war (= provides the occasion for it or signals it)" and πόλεμον ποιεῖται "he makes war in which he takes part[.]"[286] Notably, his examples of oppositional middles are all transitive verbs such as λύει, λύεται; φέρει, φέρεται, which makes clear that his description of the middle voice as internal *diathesis* does not equate to intransitivity.[287] Nevertheless, many intransitive verbs *are* middle in form, and these, if expressed in active form, become causative (hence transitive), for example, κοιμᾶται 'he sleeps' produces κοῖμα 'he puts (someone) to sleep'.[288] Such a phenomenon endorses the opposition between active and middle he describes, that is, the subject is within the process in the case of middle forms, but external in the case of actives.

Benveniste further describes this opposition by noting that not only does the difference come down to the position of the subject with respect to the process, but also involves "qualifying it [the subject] as agent, depending on whether it effects, in the active, or effects while being

---

two IE languages.

[284] Benveniste, "Active and Middle," 148.

[285] Benveniste, "Active and Middle," 149.

[286] Benveniste, "Active and Middle," 149.

[287] It appears that Allan has interpreted Benveniste's "internal" to mean "intransitive"; this is briefly indicated as he discards this definition of the middle voice along with others that he considers insufficiently inclusive (*Polysemy*, 16–17).

[288] Benveniste, "Active and Middle," 149. Allan makes similar observations, e.g., φθείρομαι: perish, (intransitive) and φθείρω: destroy, ruin, (causative active) (*Polysemy*, 60).

affected, in the middle."[289] This requirement of an agentive subject distinguishes his definition from that of Allan by ruling out passive expressions, yet the notion of the subject being affected clearly aligns with Allan's fundamental criterion. Moreover, Benveniste emphasizes that active in contrast to passive has different meaning to the active in contrast to middle. He stresses that in contrast to the passive, the difference amounts to whether or not the subject is agent. In the opposition with the middle, the difference applies to whether the subject is external to the process (hence in control of it) or internal to the process and hence affected by it. These observations are similar to Decker's insight illustrated in Fig 2.1 above.

This effective definition of the middle voice has received little attention in the English-speaking world, yet it encapsulates the properties of middle verbs succinctly. Being a relatively small chapter, this work does not reflect the depth of investigation or breadth of explanation and illustration that is exhibited in Allan's rigorous monograph. Nevertheless, the notion appears justified and not at all inconsistent with previous studies; it simply describes the middle voice from another perspective. By placing the emphasis on the location of the subject within the verbal process, it allows for subject-affectedness and for both transitive and intransitive events. Nevertheless, it makes the distinction without depending on personal judgements such as the interest of the subject, or the particular type of affectedness. Furthermore, it distinguishes passive from middle by stipulating an agentive subject. This description of the middle voice is further developed in the work of Philippe Eberhard discussed below.

2.3.2 Philippe Eberhard (2004)

Philippe Eberhard perceives a resonance between the middle voice as internal *diathesis* and essential aspects of Gadamer's hermeneutics.[290]

---

[289] Benveniste, "Active and Middle," 149–50.

[290] Philippe Eberhard, The Middle Voice in Gadamer's Hermeneutics: A Basic Interpretation with Some Theological Implications, HUTh 45 (Tübingen: Mohr Siebeck, 2004), 15.

Although the full extent of his exploration is certainly beyond the scope of the present study, Eberhard's discussion and adaptation of Benveniste's concept provides fruitful insights for grasping the applicability and scope of internal *diathesis*. His own words may best explain his interpretation:[291]

> The middle voice ... points to a medium in the chemical sense: a medium in which and not only by which something takes place. It directs one's attention away from the subject/object distinction between "doer" and "done to" and shifts it toward the relation between the process of the verb and the subject ... the emphasis lies on the locality of the subject with respect to the verb.

One aspect of Gadamer's hermeneutics which Eberhard addresses is the notion of 'play';[292] Gadamer invokes the term "medial" in respect to play and this term is forthwith adopted by Eberhard in order to describe the middle voice.[293] That is, just as a person is involved interactively in a game such as a football match, so the middle voice indicates the *interactive* involvement of the subject in the verbal process or medium.[294] One cannot play a game from the outside; the player is within the game and *responds* to it, even in a one-person game; the subject not only plays the game, but the game *plays* the subject, causing it to adapt to the process. Correspondingly, the subject is internal to and active within the process denoted by the verb in the case of the middle voice.

---

[291] Eberhard, *Middle Voice*, 8.

[292] Eberhard, *Middle Voice*, 65–77. Gadamer refers to play in a very general sense, e.g., playing a game, the play of possibilities or a cat playing with a ball of wool; in all of these he sees an element of surprise as participants respond to the game itself. See Hans-Georg Gadamer, *Truth and Method,* rev. ed. (London: Continuum International, 2004), 102–9. The notion of a game of sport serves for illustration here.

[293] Eberhard, *Middle Voice*, 68; Gadamer, *Truth and Method*, 104.

[294] Thus, Eberhard comments: "Play is not something we master although we are still the players and make decisions within the game" (*Middle Voice*, 38).

Further resonance is seen in Gadamer's notion of the "fusion of horizons", a phrase applied to the process of interpretation.[295] Gadamer identifies "situation" as a "standpoint that limits the possibility of vision" and "horizon" as the "range of vison that includes everything that can be seen from a particular vantage point."[296] Applying this to the vision of the mind's eye, he asserts that there needs to be a fusion of horizons for understanding to occur. Hence, for example, in the interpretation of an historical text, to perceive only the historical horizon, or to maintain one's own horizon, does not enable true understanding; only when there is a fusion of horizons is there genuine understanding, only then "can we find in the past any truth that is valid and intelligible for ourselves."[297] This fusion is where understanding happens, yet the horizon expands only insofar as *the subject is active within it*. For Eberhard, this amounts to an "encompassing process that to a certain extent determines the subject who, far from being passive, can participate in the process that makes him or her what he or she is."[298] Therefore, he sees the interpretive process as a medial event, in which the horizon is "encompassing yet moveable from the inside!"[299]

This balance of "the hermeneutic event happening to the subject and the understanding subject's performance within it" is what Eberhard refers to as the "mediality of understanding."[300] He invokes as an example the middle-only verb διαλέγομαι (dialogue, discuss, dispute) to illustrate the generative sense of the middle voice in the process of understanding.[301] In a dialogue, the participants are not externally in control of the activity, but are medially involved in it. The dialogue itself is also

---

[295] See Eberhard, *Middle Voice*, 78; Gadamer, *Truth and Method*, 301–6.

[296] Gadamer, *Truth and Method*, 301. This is a technical use of the term, referring to space or scope as noted.

[297] Gadamer *Truth and Method*, 303.

[298] Eberhard, *Middle Voice*, 78.

[299] Eberhard, *Middle Voice*, 81.

[300] Eberhard, *Middle Voice*, 61. The subject actively seeks understanding; it is not passively imposed.

[301] Eberhard, *Middle Voice*, 17.

a subject, acting on the participants who are affected as they respond to its dynamics, just as horizons expand and fuse and in turn affect the subject in Gadamer's theory. Thus, as in any medial event, the subjects are inside the process that takes place, participants in the process that encompasses them.[302]

Eberhard further illustrates the medial notion by the use of the Greek verb γαμέω/γαμέομαι (marry).[303] In ancient Greek in general, he observes that when a man marries a woman, the verb is in the active voice, and the woman is the direct object; however, the woman 'gets married' to the man, with the verb in the middle voice.[304] This reflects the fact that in the active the subject is seen to be in control, directing the process from the outside, but in the middle, the subject gives herself to someone *within the process* of marriage which is happening to her. As this process takes place around her, she remains the subject because she is getting married, although she is not the exclusive subject. The medial notion therefore emphasizes the process encompassing the subject but does not "erase the subject's action within it."[305]

Eberhard does not use linguistic terms; hence, although he speaks of the subject being active, he does not specifically state that it is an agent in the conventional sense of an initiator in the prototypical transitive expression. In fact, in speaking of the middle voice he tries to avoid the notion of who does what to whom and emphasizes an interactive process which could have more than one active participant.

In the present study, this is taken to imply that the subject's action or behavior could be modified or adjusted during the process in response to the action of other participants or the process itself. Hence, depending on the twists and turns of a game or dialogue, the subject will act somewhat differently, although remaining subject of and internal to the same

---

[302] Eberhard, *Middle Voice*, 15, 16.

[303] Eberhard, *Middle Voice*, 16–17.

[304] Thus, Eberhard notes that the English use of "get" can reflect a middle sense, whereas "be" is used to indicate a passive (*Middle Voice*, 19). Hence the couple may 'be married' by a priest.

[305] Eberhard, *Middle Voice*, 82.

process.[306] This is an existential description of the middle voice, indicating the type of process portrayed by a middle verb. Although not inconsistent with the notion of subject-affectedness, it has a different emphasis and may provide a useful adjunct to the grammatical and linguistic descriptions.

2.4 SUMMARY COMMENTS

This survey has revealed that there are different ways of describing the middle voice from different perspectives. There is, nevertheless, a growing consensus among recent scholars that the notion of deponency as an explanation for middle-only verbs is no longer acceptable.[307] This intensifies the need for a genuine appreciation of the middle voice.[308] That is, if middle-only verbs are to be understood as true middles, we need a better understanding of this important feature of the Greek language in New Testament studies. To this end, the essence of the grammatical and linguistic perspectives discussed above are developed into more concise expressions below to provide succinct definitions against which we may examine middle verbs in various contexts.

The grammars tend to describe middle verbs from patterns of usage with respect to the subject; that is, the manner in which the subject acts in reference to itself. The terminology for particular manifestations of this syntax, however, varies considerably between authors. Hence, for example, Cooper employs the term "dynamic middle" to refer to a subject acting from its own inner resources, Porter applies the same term to his "intensive" or "proper" middle in which the subject is affected, while Robertson applies it to the so-called deponent verbs.[309]

Despite the variable terminology, the descriptions given by grammars may generally be summarized to say that the subject acts *on* itself

---

[306] This could also apply to intransitive events such as thought processes, in which the subject is essentially immersed in a dialogue with itself.

[307] See §2.1.7 above.

[308] As noted in §2.2.2 and §2.2.6 above.

[309] See §2.1.6.10; §2.1.7.3; §2.1.6.2 above.

(direct reflexive), *for* itself (indirect reflexive), or *by* itself (Cooper's dynamic middle). These all imply a volitional subject.

From linguistic studies, the emerging criterion of the middle voice is that of subject-affectedness. Taken as the sole criterion as in Allan's model, this is represented by many situation types and necessarily includes the "passive middle." However, in this study middle is distinguished from passive (wherein the subject only receives the action of another agent).

Finally, the middle voice may be described in terms of the location of the subject with respect to the verb, as in Benveniste's notion of internal *diathesis*. Eberhard interprets this to signify that the subject is acting within a process that encompasses it. Thus, Benveniste's terminology underscores position, while Eberhard's emphasizes participation in an interdependent process. These three perspectives may be summarised as follows:

1. The grammatical middle voice with the subject acting on, for or by itself.
2. Subject-affectedness as manifested in Allan's situation types (excluding passive).
3. The medial notion of a subject acting within the encompassing verbal process.

These three descriptors provide verifiable criteria which may now be applied to middle-form verbs to explore whether the middle form does indicate middle function. By examining the manner in which the verb functions in a particular context in the New Testament, it may be ascertained whether any of these descriptors apply. The descriptors are not mutually exclusive but are different ways in which the middle voice of either an oppositional middle or *media tantum* verb may be described and therefore discerned.

Chapter 3
The Middle Voice
in First Thessalonians

For reasons discussed below, Paul's first letter to the Thessalonians is selected as an initial source of middle verbs through which to explore the manifestations of the various understandings of the Greek middle voice discussed above. A good variety of verbs having middle voice morphology are used throughout the letter, with thirty-nine forms being identified across the five chapters.[1] Nevertheless, the frequency of middle verb forms (as a percentage of the total number of words) in this epistle is modest (2.63%) compared to that of some other books of the New Testament such as Luke (3.21%), Acts (3.71%), and James (4.08%). The relative frequencies of middle verbs in the books of the NA[28] text are displayed in Figure 3.1 below, demonstrating that 1 Thessalonians does not contain an unduly high or low proportion and may reasonably be regarded as an impartial sample.[2]

This sample enables one instance of the writing of a particular author to be studied, thus minimizing problems associated with the comparison of possible idiosyncratic uses of grammatical forms or vocabulary by different writers. The results of this investigation may then provide an impetus for the examination of Paul's usage of middle verbs elsewhere.

---

[1] Statistical data is obtained from *BibleWorks 10* NT morphological data base (BNM) for NA[28]. Dual purpose middle/passive forms are distinguished according to function, such that the total number of forms includes only those verbs which function as middles in context (39 in total). By contrast, the Accordance data base generates a figure of 3.3% because all middle/passive forms are included (49 verbs in total).

[2] This percentage in First Thessalonians aligns with the median frequency of 2.66% across the NT corpus.

Like all of Paul's epistles, 1 Thessalonians was composed in Greek, so it may be inferred that the precise choice of language is intentional and is employed in accordance with natural usage.[3] This will be illustrated by samples from the documentary papyri and other writings

Figure 3.1 Percentage of Middle Verbs per NT Book

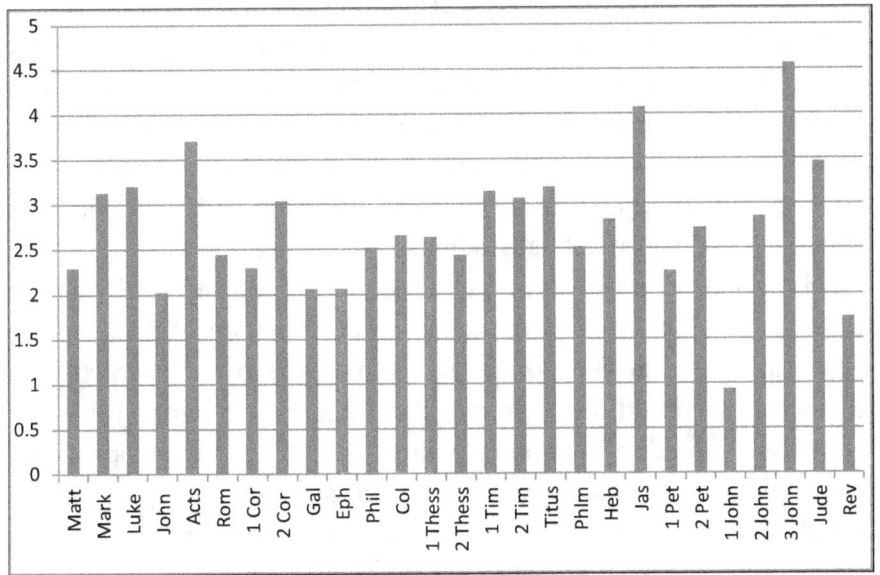

of the day. This methodology is consistent with the close correlation famously illustrated by Adolf Deissmann between the various registers of language in the New Testament and the colloquial modes of

---

[3] That is, Paul is using the language naturally, not as a translator and not depending on the conscious application of rules but nevertheless choosing the grammatical forms which would adequately express his thoughts. Accordingly, A. Andrew Das remarks that "Paul's vocabulary patterns are typical of an intelligent individual of the day" noting that he uses various literary devices which nevertheless do not necessitate formal training in rhetoric (A. Andrew Das, *Galatians*, Concordia Commentary: A Theological Exposition of Sacred Scripture [Saint Louis: Concordia, 2014], 61–62). In support of his assertion, he refers *inter alia* to Origen who admired the ability of Paul to communicate great truths in common language.

expression in the Hellenistic era.⁵ Where a middle form is observed in Paul's writing, it is therefore reasonable to assume that the choice is intended to adequately express his thoughts.

Rarely is any mention made of the function of middle verbs in commentaries, except perhaps regarding the ambivalence of a middle/passive form. This may reflect the lack of importance attributed to the middle voice in the New Testament in many grammars, as seen above. Given that a verb is the driving force of a sentence, however, and voice (*diathesis*) indicates the relationship between subject and verb, this omission calls for attention. This is particularly so if it can be demonstrated that middle form does signify middle function. Therefore, the following investigation examines each middle form verb within its context in the epistle to specifically address this inattention.

This survey does not purport to be an extensive exegetical study of each verse or segment cited but rather an examination of the syntactic function of the middle verbs *in situ* to determine the extent to which characteristics of the middle voice are evident. The lexical sense of the verb is initially explored in relation to biblical and contemporaneous usage. The verses in which each verb appears are then translated and briefly discussed in relation to the function of the middle verb within the immediate literary context.⁶ If any of the summary descriptors noted above are found to be applicable, this clearly speaks in support of the middle voice function of the verb. These descriptors are reiterated below.

---

⁵ Adolf Deissmann asserts that Paul chooses appropriate language for different purposes; yet whether forthright or reflective, "his Greek never becomes literary ... it remains non-literary"; he thus describes it as the "artless though not inartistic colloquial prose of a travelled city-resident of the Roman Empire" (*Light from the Ancient East: The New Testament Illustrated by Recently Discovered Texts of the Graeco-Roman World*, trans. Lionel R.M. Strachan, rev. ed. [London: Hodder & Stoughton, 1927], 70).

⁶ That is, the text surrounding the verb with due consideration given to the type of discourse in the section of the letter under consideration.

1. The grammatical notion of the subject acting on, for or with reference to itself.⁷
2. The linguistic notion of subject-affectedness as outlined by Rutger Allan.⁸
3. The medial notion of a subject acting within the encompassing verbal process.⁹

Since there could be some variation in middle function according to tense, this investigation will first explore the aorist middles in 1 Thessalonians in this chapter and then the present middle/passive forms in the next. The results of each investigation are summarized in tables at the conclusion of each chapter, listing the verbs according to the verses in which they appear. Where possible the verbs are classified according to Allan's categories, which are noted again below for reference.¹⁰

1. Passive middle, e.g., πείθομαι, be persuaded.¹¹
2. Spontaneous process middle, e.g., γίνομαι, come into being.
3. Mental process middle, e.g., φοβέομαι, fear.
4. Body motion middle, e.g., αἴρομαι, rise.
5. Collective motion middle, e.g., συλλέγομαι, gather.
6. Reciprocal middle, e.g., διαλέγομαι, converse with.
7. Direct reflexive middle, e.g., κοσμέομαι, adorn oneself.
8. Perception middle, e.g., θέαμομαι, look at, wondering.

---

⁷ As succinctly stated by Funk, *Grammar of Hellenistic Greek,* 157, representing the cumulative account of the grammars, and taken to include the "dynamic middle" as defined by Cooper, §2.1.6.10 above.

⁸ See §2.2.1 above.

⁹ This frequently but not necessarily correlates with Neva Miller's concept of reciprocity which she applies to activities wherein the subject is engaged with another participant. See §2.2.2 above.

¹⁰ As discussed in §2.2.1.3 above. The examples are those of Allan.

¹¹ The term "passive middle" refers to Allan's category of verbs denoting action effecting a change of state in the subject; an agent may conceptually be present but de-emphasized (Allan, *Polysemy,* 58). It is a reference to *function*. This term is distinct from 'middle/passive' which is used here to refer to the *form* of verbs having the ambiguous middle/passive morphology in tenses built on the present stem.

9. Mental activity middle, e.g., λογίζομαι, calculate, reason, consider.
10. Speech act middle, e.g., δέομαι, beg.
11. Indirect reflexive middle, e.g., δέχομαι, receive, accept.

One would not expect that every middle verb should neatly align with a particular classification however, for the categories are descriptive of samples of extant usage rather than prescriptive of all possible functions. Hence, whereas Allan assigns a middle verb to a category according to its most typical use,[12] the following investigations seek to identify the precise type of middle function exhibited by the inflected form in the specific context. In any given instance this may or may not align with the category to which the verb is assigned by Allan. Verbs are designated as *media tantum* (*m.t.*) for the purposes of this survey if they are listed in the middle but not the active form in BDAG. When an active form of a particular verb is also attested in Koine Greek, this is noted and the contrast between active and middle forms discussed. Lexical meanings are routinely drawn from LSJ, BDAG, and MM, with salient emphases noted.[13]

Before proceeding with the analysis, the following remarks may help to orientate the reader in respect to the literary context of the studies that follow. Written to the church Paul founded in Thessalonica, Macedonia, this epistle is widely regarded as the earliest extant letter of Paul.[14] The occasion of the letter is apparent from Paul's own remarks in 2:17–3:6. There he tells the young church that when he was unable to visit them himself, he had sent Timothy to strengthen and encourage them. He was particularly concerned about their faith in the face of hardship (3:2–3). Paul is most pleased with Timothy's report (3:6–8), although

---

[12] Allan, *Polysemy*, 60n73.

[13] Further lexical resources are consulted when necessary.

[14] As noted by Victor Paul Furnish, *1 Thessalonians, II Thessalonians*, ANTC (Nashville: Abingdon, 2007), 13. See also M. Eugene Boring, *I & II Thessalonians*, NTL (Louisville: Westminster John Knox, 2015), 3; Abraham J. Malherbe, *The Letters to the Thessalonians, A New Translation with Introduction and Commentary*, AB 32B (New York: Doubleday, 2000), 75.

he longs to see the congregation again himself. His concern for those he had brought to faith and nurtured is evident throughout the letter. Within this context of brotherly affection he writes to them, expressing thankfulness for their genuine response to the gospel and exhorting them to live upright lives as they support one another in love as they patiently await the return of the Lord.

3.1 Aorist Middle Verbs in 1 Thessalonians

Aorist middle verbs are often identified by their characteristic morphology, typically displaying the sigmatic aorist morpheme (e.g., ἐνδυσάμην) or a distinctive aorist stem in the case of second aorists (e.g., ἐγενόμην), along with the secondary middle personal endings. Nevertheless, as seen above, some aorist middle verbs exhibit the -(θ)η- morpheme and could be mistakenly assumed to be passive. In 1 Thessalonians, this matter is relevant to γίνομαι and κοιμάομαι as discussed below.[15] There are fifteen different middle aorist forms in 1 Thessalonians, representing nine different verbs, these being δέχομαι, γίνομαι, παρρησιάζομαι, εὐαγγελίζομαι, διαμαρτύρομαι, κοιμάομαι, ἐνδύομαι, τίθεμαι, and ἀσπάζομαι. Each verb form will now be examined within its context in the epistle to test for conformity to the descriptors of middle verbs noted above.[16]

3.1.1 Δέχομαι (media tantum)

Having the broad sense of receiving or accepting what is offered either concretely or mentally, δέχομαι frequently refers to welcoming or hospitable reception.[17] Accordingly, L&N state that while the

---

[15] All other theta aorist forms in 1 Thessalonians do exhibit passive function, viz., ὑβρισθέντες (2:2); πιστευθῆναι (2:4); σωθῶσιν (2:16); ἀπορφανισθέντες (2:17); καταλειφθῆναι (3:1); παρεκλήθημεν (3:7); τηρηθείη (5:23); ἀναγνωσθῆναι (5:27).
[16] Translations into English are original unless otherwise specified.
[17] BDAG, s.v. "δέχομαι."

initiative rests with the giver, the focus of attention is upon the receiver.[18] This sense of acceptance is evinced in a comment by Plutarch that is cited as an illustration of an apt reply given to a hostile audience: "τοὺς ταῦτα ποιήσαντας ἡμῶν ἐκβαλόντων ὑμεῖς ἐδέξασθε": "When we had driven out the doers of those deeds, you took them in[.]"[19] Similarly, the concluding lines of a notice of sale of land refers to the person who acts as surety, being Φαῆσις ὁ ἀποδόμενος ὃν ἐδέξατο Ὧ[ρο]ς ὁ πριάμενος: "Phaesis the vendor, whom Horus the purchaser has accepted."[20]

In the LXX, δέχομαι appears frequently in regard to the acceptance of gifts or offerings. For example, Moses accepted (ἐδέξατο) from the people the items to construct the golden calf (Exod 32:4) and it was said that God will not accept (δέξεται) any offering from the ungodly (Job 8:20). Similarly, δέχομαι is used in reference to words or advice. Accordingly, in speaking of Nineveh, Zephaniah states: "It listened to no voice. It accepted [ἐδέξατο] no correction" (Zeph. 3:2, NETS).[21]

This middle-only verb is also used throughout the New Testament, often in relation to receiving or accepting a person or their teaching. Hence, we find: καὶ ὃς ἂν μὴ δέξηται ὑμᾶς μηδὲ ἀκούσῃ τοὺς λόγους ὑμῶν: whoever would not receive you or listen to your words (Matt 10:14). Likewise, in James we read: ἐν πραΰτητι δέξασθε τὸν ἔμφυτον λόγον τὸν δυνάμενον σῶσαι τὰς ψυχὰς ὑμῶν: in humility accept the implanted word which is able to save your souls (Jas 1:21b). It is employed similarly by Paul in 1 Thess 1:6, in his complimentary introduction, as below:

---

[18] L&N, s.v. "δέχομαι." (57.125).

[19] Plutarch, *Prae.ger.rei.publ.* 810.F.8 (Fowler, LCL 321:222–223). Greek text of ancient authors is accessed via TLG, http://www.tlg.uci.edu; English translations are from LCL unless otherwise indicated.

[20] P.Ryl. 4.581 / 12 (121 BC). Unless otherwise stated, cited transcriptions and translations of papyri are accessed via DDbDP http://papyri.info/browse /ddbdp/.

[21] Similarly, Jer 5:3; 7:27; 9:19.

Καὶ ὑμεῖς μιμηταὶ ἡμῶν ἐγενήθητε καὶ τοῦ κυρίου, <u>δεξάμενοι</u> τὸν λόγον ἐν θλίψει πολλῇ μετὰ χαρᾶς πνεύματος ἁγίου[22]	And you became imitators of us and of the Lord, <u>accepting</u> the word amid much persecution with [the] joy of the Holy Spirit

Immediately prior (1:5) Paul indicates that the gospel came to them not only in word, but in power, in the Holy Spirit and with full conviction, thus emphasizing the effectiveness of the gospel message. In 1:6, he thus comments on their acceptance of the word and alludes to its effect, which is explicitly acknowledged in 2:13 discussed below. Thus, Karl Paul Donfried comments that the gospel message is a "performative word and it is actively at work (ἐνεργεῖται) in and among the believers (2:13) [.]"[23]

Accordingly, the NIV translates δεξάμενοι τὸν λόγον as "you welcomed the message"; NJB as "welcoming the word[.]" Such translations imply that the word was not simply imposed on hearers in an active-passive scenario, but was offered and welcomed, suggesting an interactive event in which the Thessalonians are volitional agents. Their receptivity occurs within the process of preaching and hearing, which is the medium, the milieu, in which they are acting by receiving the word. They could not welcome it if they did not first hear it, and their receptivity enables them to hear it in an eventful, life changing manner.[24] Therefore the medial notion applies.

That they are affected by their reception of the word is indicated within the text, for Paul notes that the Thessalonians experienced the joy of the Holy Spirit despite persecution. They became imitators of the Lord (1:6) and he commends them for the positive outcomes of their

---

[22] See §3.1.2.1 below for a discussion of ἐγενήθητε in this verse.

[23] Karl Paul Donfried, *Paul, Thessalonica, and Early Christianity* (Grand Rapids: Eerdmans, 2002), 148.

[24] This understanding intentionally draws on the context of the passage within the letter, according to the method adopted.

faith, hope and love (1:3). Therefore, Allan's notion of subject affectedness applies, Allan classifying δέχομαι as an indirect reflexive middle, in which the subject is the beneficiary.[25] In the grammatical sense, δεξάμενοι in 1:6 above could also be classed as an indirect reflexive, this being very much aligned with the lexical semantics of the verb, since one necessarily receives or welcomes *for* oneself. However, the nuance of Cooper's dynamic middle (§2.1.6.10 above) may also be seen, as the subjects' "faculties and resources ... are mobilized, energized and applied" in responding to the preaching of the gospel.[26]

This verb again appears in regard to reception of the word in 1 Thess 2:13.

| Καὶ διὰ τοῦτο καὶ ἡμεῖς εὐχαριστοῦμεν τῷ θεῷ ἀδιαλείπτως, ὅτι παραλαβόντες λόγον ἀκοῆς παρ' ἡμῶν τοῦ θεοῦ <u>ἐδέξασθε</u> οὐ λόγον ἀνθρώπων ἀλλὰ καθώς ἐστιν ἀληθῶς λόγον θεοῦ, ὃς καὶ ἐνεργεῖται ἐν ὑμῖν τοῖς πιστεύουσιν.[27] | And for this reason, we also thank God continually; that in receiving the word of God which you heard from us, you did not <u>accept</u> a human word, but—as it truly is—the word of God, which now operates with effect in you who believe. |

This verse contains two verbs commonly translated by 'receive' in English, viz., παραλαμβάνω and δέχομαι.[28] However, these do not have precisely the same meaning, for παραλαμβάνω typically refers to the reception of a tradition, while δέχομαι here, according to Abraham J. Malherbe, refers to more than "the outward acceptance of the

---

[25] Allan, *Polysemy*, 114.

[26] Cooper, *Attic Greek*, 589.

[27] See §4.9 below for a discussion on the present middle verb ἐνεργεῖται in this verse.

[28] Thus, for example, ESV, NAB, NKJV, and NRS all translate both δέχομαι in Matt 10:40 (ὁ δεχόμενος ὑμᾶς ἐμὲ δέχεται, καὶ ὁ ἐμὲ δεχόμενος δέχεται τὸν ἀποστείλαντά με) and λαμβάνω in the similar expression in John 13:20 (ὁ δὲ ἐμὲ λαμβάνων λαμβάνει τὸν πέμψαντά με) with 'receive'.

preaching" but rather "the acceptance of the practical consequences generated by the implanted word."²⁹ Likewise, James Everett Frame considers that there is a purposed distinction between the external reception (παραλαβόντες) and the welcome acceptance of the word (ἐδέξασθε).³⁰ Gordon Fee contends that παραλαβόντες had become a semi-technical term in the church for "teaching which had been handed down" (as in 1 Cor 11:23 and 15:3), whereas ἐδέξασθε indicates receiving by approval, accepting with commitment.³¹

Although commentaries such as those above often mention the similar yet nuanced lexical sense of these two verbs, conspicuous by its absence is any reference to the middle voice as a factor in this difference.³² Nevertheless, 1 Thess 2:13 provides an example of comparison of an external active (παραλαβόντες) with an internal middle *diathesis* (ἐδέξασθε). This juxtaposition is consistent with the thought that the Thessalonians not only heard the word that was preached but they accepted it by taking it to heart, thus allowing it to change them. This subject affectedness is expressed explicitly in the subsequent clause: *which now operates with effect in you who believe.*³³ The wider context of the letter further attests this effect, as Paul commends the Thessalonians for

---

²⁹ Malherbe, *Thessalonians*, 166–67.

³⁰ James Everett Frame, *A Critical and Exegetical Commentary on St. Paul's Epistle to the Thessalonians*, ICC (Edinburgh: T&T Clark, 1912), 107.

³¹ Gordon D. Fee, *The First and Second Letters to the Thessalonians*, NICNT (Grand Rapids: Eerdmans, 2009), 87n8, 88n10. This sense of commitment and acceptance is noted by BDAG, s.v. "δέχομαι." (5). This contrast is exemplified in the parable of the sower. Regarding reception of the word by those who are like the rocky soil, Mark has λαμβάνουσιν (4:16), but παραδέχονται (4:20) in reference to those who are like the good soil; that is, those who accept the word and produce its fruit.

³² Likewise, Jeffrey A. D. Weima, *1–2 Thessalonians*, BECNT (Grand Rapids: Baker Academic, 2014), 162, 163. Earl J. Richard, *First and Second Thessalonians*, SP 11 (Collegeville, MN: The Liturgical Press, 1995), 112; Charles A. Wanamaker, *The Epistles to the Thessalonians: A Commentary on the Greek Text*, NIGTC (Grand Rapids: Eerdmans; Carlisle, UK: Paternoster, 1990), 111.

³³ The middle verb ἐνεργεῖται (operates) is discussed with present middle verbs in the next chapter.

the positive outcomes of faith, hope and love which are active in their lives (1:3).

Regarding the middle voice descriptors, since 2:13 refers to acceptance of the word in a productive sense analogous to 1:6, the same considerations may be seen to apply; hence ἐδέξασθε in 2:13 likewise exhibits dynamic middle function, subject affectedness in the sense of indirect reflexivity, and the medial sense.

3.1.2 Γίνομαι (media tantum)

The verb γίνομαι (Attic form, γίγνομαι), appears frequently throughout the New Testament (669 times). It speaks of something coming into existence, coming to pass, or coming into a particular state such that it has "numerous nuances relating to being and manner of being."[34] While it generally has the sense of 'coming to be' rather than simply 'being,' γίνομαι sometimes provides the aorist for εἰμί. For example, οὐκ ἐγενόμην ἀπειθὴς τῇ οὐρανίῳ ὀπτασίᾳ (Acts 26:19) is rendered "I was not disobedient to the heavenly vision" (NAB, NIV, NKJV, NRSV). Similarly, Josephus employs the aorist in both senses in close textual proximity in *The Jewish War*. Hence, we read: ἐγενόμην δὲ σύμβουλος ἄριστος, ὡς οὐκέτι χρήσιμος ἤμην σύμμαχος: "When no longer useful as an ally, I became his best counsellor"[35] and προλαβὼν ἐξετασθήσεσθαι, ποταπὸς φίλος, οὐ τίνος, ἐγενόμην": "presuming that the subject of inquiry will be not whose friend, but how loyal a friend, I have been."[36]

As noted by Conrad above (§2.1.7.1), there are two inflectional patterns for the aorist of γίνομαι: that of ἐγενόμην (MP1) and that of ἐγενήθην (MP2 or -θη- form).[37] Both forms of the aorist appear in the

---

[34] BDAG, s.v. "γίνομαι"

[35] Josephus, *B.J.*, 1.389.1 (Thackeray, LCL 203:182–83).

[36] Josephus, *B.J.*, 1.390.5 (Thackeray, LCL 203:182–83).

[37] There are several uses of the -θη- form in the NT: ἐγενήθη appears in Matt 21:42; Mark 12:10; Luke 18:23, 20:17; Acts 4:4; Rom 16:2; 1 Cor 1:30, 15:10; 2 Cor 3:7, 7:14, 1 Thess 1:5, 1 Pet 2:7. It is commonly translated *has become*, e.g., "The stone the builders

text of 1 Thessalonians, the ἐγενόμην conjugation three times and the ἐγενήθην conjugation eight times.[38] While the database used to identify middle verbs for this study does not class the -θη- forms as middle (but rather as passive) it will be seen these -θη- aorist forms of γίνομαι do in fact function as middles in this epistle. This is consonant with Milligan's observation that both forms are used interchangeably in the New Testament and in late Greek generally.[39]

3.1.2.1 Γίνομαι in 1 Thess 1:5-7

⁵τὸ εὐαγγέλιον ἡμῶν οὐκ ἐγενήθη εἰς ὑμᾶς ἐν λόγῳ μόνον ἀλλὰ καὶ ἐν δυνάμει καὶ ἐν πνεύματι ἁγίῳ καὶ [ἐν] πληροφορίᾳ πολλῇ, καθὼς οἴδατε οἷοι ἐγενήθημεν [ἐν] ὑμῖν δι' ὑμᾶς. ⁶ Καὶ ὑμεῖς μιμηταὶ ἡμῶν ἐγενήθητε καὶ τοῦ κυρίου, δεξάμενοι τὸν λόγον ἐν θλίψει πολλῇ μετὰ χαρᾶς πνεύματος ἁγίου, ⁷ ὥστε γενέσθαι ὑμᾶς τύπον πᾶσιν τοῖς πιστεύουσιν ἐν τῇ Μακεδονίᾳ καὶ ἐν τῇ Ἀχαΐᾳ.

For our gospel <u>came</u> to you not only in word but also in power, in [the] Holy Spirit and with much conviction, as you know what kind of people <u>we were</u> among you for your sake. And you <u>became</u> imitators of us and of the Lord, accepting the word in [the midst of] much suffering with the joy of the Holy Spirit, so that you <u>have become</u> an example to all the believers in Macedonia and in Achaia.[40]

---

rejected *has become* the corner stone;" (Matt 21:42, NRSV), likewise 1 Pet 2:7. However, in 1 Thess 1:5 it is frequently translated *came*, e.g., our gospel *came* (ἐγενήθη) to you not in word only (NRSV, similarly ESV, NIV, NJB). See further discussion below on this verse.

[38] George Milligan notes that this "passive" form of γίνομαι is characteristic of this letter, reporting eight uses in 1 Thessalonians compared with thirteen in the remaining epistles in the WH text (*St. Paul's Epistles to the Thessalonians: The Greek Text with Introduction and Notes* [London: Macmillan, 1908], 9).

[39] Milligan, *Thessalonians*, 9.

[40] The different occurrences of γίνομαι in this passage may express different nuances of this verb, presenting a challenge for translation into English.

The verses above are in apposition to Paul's comments in 1:3–4 in which he testifies to the faith and service of the Thessalonians and his assurance that God had called them. In 1:5–7, above, he states that this is *because* the gospel came to them with (by/in) the power and conviction of the Holy Spirit (1:5). These verses speak of the eventfulness of the gospel, for there is a chain of events described in terms of the verb γίνομαι, speaking of phenomena coming into being. The gospel came (ἐγενήθη) to the Thessalonians with powerful inner conviction, such that they welcomed the word with joy in the Holy Spirit despite suffering opposition.[41] In this respect they became (ἐγενήθητε) imitators of the apostles and the Lord by replicating what the apostles were (ἐγενήθημεν) in regard to conduct. As a result, they themselves became (γενέσθαι) examples throughout the region (1:8–9) also. The gospel that was preached was accepted, actualized, and manifested in their changed behavior (1:7); it came into being as an event.[42]

In 1 Thess 1:5, ἐγενήθη is often translated by "come/came" (e.g., CEB, ESV, KJV, NAB, NIV, NKJV, NRSV), as also rendered above.[43] This representation focuses on the gospel becoming present to the Thessalonians and not on the one who brought it. By deemphasizing the role of the entity which caused the event, *our gospel came* is represented as a spontaneous process, thus "conceptualized as occurring without direct initiation by an agent" similar to statements such as "the tree fell over" or "the vase broke,"[44] This is consistent with Allan's listing of γίνομαι

---

[41] As noted by Richard, it is not immediately clear from the syntax whether the contrast between word, on the one hand, and power, Holy Spirit, and full conviction collectively on the other, refers to the preaching itself or to the effect on the hearers. (*Thessalonians*, 64–65). Translating ἐγενήθη as "came" could suggest the former but it is taken here to refer also to the reception by the Thessalonians, as affirmed likewise by Frame, *Thessalonians*, 73.

[42] See BDAG, s.v. "γίνομαι" (3).

[43] This sense of coming to is implied by the preposition εἰς. BDAG, s.v. "γίνομαι." (6). Paul uses γίνομαι with εἰς similarly in Galatians: ἵνα εἰς τὰ ἔθνη ἡ εὐλογία τοῦ Ἀβραὰμ γένηται ἐν Χριστῷ Ἰησοῦ: so that in Christ Jesus the blessing of Abraham might come to the Gentiles (Gal 3:14).

[44] See Allan, *Polysemy*, 60, 62, 63n82.

as an example of his spontaneous middle category, the subject being affected because it undergoes a change of state.⁴⁵ Hence, ἐγενήθη could be viewed as a spontaneous middle in Allan's scheme.

Considering the event signified by ἐγενήθη above, the context indicates that the gospel not only came or became present to them (εἰς ὑμᾶς) but that it also had an effect on the (receptive) hearers; hence the subject "effects while being affected[.]"⁴⁶ This corresponds to Eberhard's description of a medial event with the subject acting within a process that encompasses it; the coming is not distinguished from or opposed to the effect it has on the hearers. Hence, according to this view of the middle voice, the verb ἐγενήθη represents the dynamic engagement between the gospel, the hearers, and the Holy Spirit.⁴⁷

The grammatical description of the middle voice does not appear to apply here, since the notion of a subject acting to, for, or by itself most naturally applies to a volitional, hence animate subject. Nevertheless, the other two descriptors of the middle voice are applicable, as demonstrated above. These are two possible ways of perceiving the middle function of ἐγενήθη in this instance. In both, the subject is affected.

The second occurrence of γίνομαι appears as Paul notes (1:5 above) that the Thessalonians knew "what kind of people <u>we were</u> among you for your sake." Here he uses ἐγενήθημεν to express "we were" (as NAB, NJB, NKJV) or "we proved to be" (ESV, NRSV), and this is taken to refer to the way they conducted themselves. The context implies volitional behavior by the apostles among the Thessalonians: the apostles lived among the Thessalonians in a manner consistent with their preaching to provide an example for them.

From the grammatical perspective, such behavior implies that the apostles were acting volitionally, with heartfelt intent out of their own

---

[45] Allan, *Polysemy*, 60.

[46] Benveniste, "Active and Middle," 150. Similarly, Eberhard states: "In the middle voice ... the subject is within the action that happens to him or her and of which he or she is subject" (*Middle Voice*, 2).

[47] Accordingly, Bruce states regarding the gospel that "its author is God, whose Spirit is active both in those who declare it and in those who receive it" (*1 & 2 Thessalonians*, WBC 45 [Waco, TX: Word, 1982], 14).

resources. Hence, Cooper's dynamic middle, emphasizing the personal investment of the subject, may be discerned. They are not acting in their own interest but are acting from within themselves.

The medial notion of the middle voice may also be perceived, for the apostles were acting within a process which encompassed them, namely, their engagement with the Thessalonians. Their behavior was volitional, yet also determined by the specific circumstances to which they responded (as in Eberhard's illustration of participants playing a game and responding to its twists and turns).[48] They exhibited certain behavior and attitudes such as being fatherly and gentle in their interaction with the new Christians as well as being self-supporting (2:5–12). This behavior, this example of the gospel in action, is expressed as οἷοι ἐγενήθημεν [ἐν] ὑμῖν.

The use of ἐγενήθημεν rather than ἦμεν implies a change of state, thus corresponding to Allan's overarching criterion of subject-affectedness for the middle voice: they became a certain type of person, meaning they behaved in a certain manner among them. The qualification "for your sake" (δι' ὑμᾶς) suggests that their behavior was intentional. It is not represented as occurring spontaneously without any agent in view. It is more likely that ἐγενήθημεν corresponds to the mental process middle of Allan's scheme in this instance. This correlates to the sense of responding to a situation as suggested also by the medial notion.[49]

The second use of γίνομαι in 1:6, ἐγενήθητε, occurs in the expression ὑμεῖς μιμηταὶ ἡμῶν ἐγενήθητε καὶ τοῦ κυρίου: you became imitators of us and of the Lord. Paul refers to imitation in several of his letters, urging his converts to imitate him—a common custom among teachers of the period.[50] However, as Charles A. Wanamaker notes, Paul

---

[48] Eberhard, *The Middle Voice*, 68–69.

[49] The mental process middle involves "an animate subject that experiences mental affectedness." This may be due to an external stimulus (*Polysemy*, 64–65).

[50] For example, Phil 3:17, 1 Cor 4:16; and 11:1 (μιμηταί μου γίνεσθε καθὼς κἀγὼ Χριστοῦ), as noted by Wanamaker, *Thessalonians*, 80. Accordingly, Furnish comments that "Hellenistic teachers typically commended their own conduct as exemplary for their students" (*Thessalonians*, 45).

is not referring here to ethical conduct to be copied, but is emphasizing that the Thessalonians *have become* imitators of himself and of Christ as they experienced the joy of the Holy Spirit even amid their distress.[51] Thus he continues to commend them for the outworking of their faith.

Having become what they previously were not, namely, imitators of Paul and the Lord, a change in them is apparent, so the subjects are affected. Paul's use of μιμηταὶ ... ἐγενήθητε here indicates not that they actively imitated but *became* imitators. This expression therefore could be viewed as a spontaneous process in Allan's scheme, being "conceptualized as occurring without direct initiation by an agent."[52] Allan refers to the spontaneous classification as the default position in such situations, only being over-ruled by the passive when some "external initiator" is signaled by the context.[53]

Since their becoming imitators is not portrayed as intentional, the grammatical descriptors do not apply. Although there is a hint of direct reflexiveness in that they are acting on themselves in doing so, the verbal reference is to what they became in the sight of others, not what they themselves did. Their contribution is better accommodated by the medial position discussed below.

The wider context is instructive for analyzing this expression according to the medial notion, Since Paul commends the Thessalonians for the changes he sees in them, it implies that they do have some part to play in the process (of becoming imitators) themselves.[54] Hence they may be viewed as *participants* in an interactive situation, acting in a manner which replicates that of Paul and of Christ in the circumstances that surround them. The context indicates that this change occurs as a

---

[51] Wanamaker, *Thessalonians*, 81.

[52] Allan, *Polysemy*, 60.

[53] Allan, *Polysemy*, 64n84. This is in accord with Conrad's contention (§2.1.7.1 above) that for any middle-passive form the middle is to be preferred unless the context clearly indicates a passive sense.

[54] From the context, the Holy Spirit could also be seen to be a participant, as in Phil 2:12, 13, referring to the mutuality of the believers working out their salvation and God giving them the will to act according to his purposes.

result of their acceptance of the gospel, allowing it to bear fruit in their lives (1:3). Consequently, they are internal to the process of becoming imitators, active participants within a process that affects them—like a player becoming a winner through participating in a game.[55] The expression: "you became imitators" represents this whole process.

The final occurrence of γίνομαι in this passage is the middle aorist infinitive, γενέσθαι (1:7). English translations generally render γενέσθαι ὑμᾶς as "you became" (e.g., NIV, NRSV, NET, ESV, CEB, NAB, NKJV, NJB, CJB), with ὥστε plus the infinitive in this case referring to an actual result of their actions.[56] Paul is stating that not only have the Thessalonians become imitators of the apostle Paul and the Lord (1:6), but consequently they have become an example to the believers elsewhere (1:7).[57]

In a similar manner to the example above, γενέσθαι in 1:7 indicates subject affectedness because in becoming examples to others, the subjects became something which they previously were not. According to Allan's model, the event may be conceptualized as happening without direct agency; therefore, it conforms to his spontaneous middle process. From a medial perspective, however, as in the case above, this process of becoming examples happens to the subjects who are active participants within it, for it is only through their interaction with their situation that they become examples. Engaged in and inseparable from the process that is happening to them, they are internal to the event, so the medial

---

[55] This is consistent with Kemmer's assertion that middle situation types "involve a greater conceptual fusion between initiating and affected aspects of an entity than corresponding reflexive types. See Kemmer, *Middle Voice*, 94.

[56] Wallace notes that ὥστε + infinitive may refer to an actual or a natural (logical) result; see Wallace, *Exegetical Syntax*, 480n86. The context of Paul's commendation here indicates that their becoming an example is an actual result of their imitation of Paul and the Lord (v. 6).

[57] This is not necessarily to suggest that the imitation was deliberate; rather it came about as a result of their reception of the gospel. That is, they inadvertently duplicated the characteristic behavior of Christ and Paul; hence, Frame comments: "the taught have become the teachers" (*Thessalonians*, 83).

descriptor applies. However, as above, the grammatical descriptors of the subjects acting on, for or from within themselves do not readily apply to the process of becoming examples for it is not volitional of itself.

3.1.2.2 Γίνομαι in 1 Thess 2:5–8

In chapter 2 of his letter, Paul reminds the Thessalonians of his previous visit. He recalls their response to the gospel he brought (2:1, 5) and the caring, responsible conduct of the apostles toward the young church (2:7–12). This serves to affirm the benevolent relationship between Paul and the Thessalonians as a basis for his exhortation.[58]

| 1 Thess 2:5–8 Οὔτε γάρ ποτε ἐν λόγῳ κολακείας <u>ἐγενήθημεν</u>, καθὼς οἴδατε, οὔτε ἐν προφάσει πλεονεξίας, θεὸς μάρτυς ⁶οὔτε ζητοῦντες ἐξ ἀνθρώπων δόξαν οὔτε ἀφ' ὑμῶν οὔτε ἀπ' ἄλλων, ⁷δυνάμενοι ἐν βάρει εἶναι ὡς Χριστοῦ ἀπόστολοι. ἀλλὰ <u>ἐγενήθημεν</u> νήπιοι (ἤπιοι) ἐν μέσῳ ὑμῶν, ὡς ἐὰν τροφὸς θάλπῃ τὰ ἑαυτῆς τέκνα ⁸οὕτως ὁμειρόμενοι ὑμῶν εὐδοκοῦμεν μεταδοῦναι ὑμῖν οὐ μόνον τὸ εὐαγγέλιον τοῦ θεοῦ ἀλλὰ καὶ τὰς ἑαυτῶν ψυχάς, διότι ἀγαπητοὶ ἡμῖν <u>ἐγενήθητε</u>. | ⁵As you know and as God is our witness, we never <u>behaved</u> with flattering speech or a pretext for greed; ⁶ nor did we seek praise from mortals, whether from you or from others, ⁷ though we could have done as apostles of Christ. But we <u>behaved</u> gently in your midst, like a nurse tenderly caring for her own children. ⁸ Thus yearning for you, we consider it appropriate to share with you not only the gospel of God but also our own selves, because you <u>have become</u> very dear to us. |

---

[58] Abraham J. Malherbe draws attention to the paraenetic nature of this letter, and the way Paul adopts customary features of similar letters of the time, which exhibit a "philophronetic element" invoked to provide the framework for exhortation. Such letters "speak at length about the writer and firmly establish his relations with his readers" ("Exhortation in First Thessalonians," *NovT* 25 [1983]: 238–56 at 241).

There are various translations of the expression in which ἐγενήθημεν appears in 2:5 above. The NRSV and ESV read "we never came with" but others are more suggestive of the behavior or conduct of Paul and his companions, for instance, "nor did we ever appear with" (NAB), "we have never acted with the thought of" (NJB), or simply "we never used" (NIV, RSV).

While these different readings illustrate the challenge of translating the sense of this verb in its various applications,[59] it is clearly not perceived as passive. Rather, in this context the reference is to the *modus operandi* of the apostles, as in the case of ἐγενήθημεν in 1:5 above. Their behavior reflects their just motives (2:3) and implies an interactive, relational situation. Therefore, again, it is not spontaneous but volitional and may be described as medial (internal *diathesis*), and dynamic from the grammatical perspective (as in 1:5 above).

When the whole predicate (ἐν λόγῳ κολακείας ἐγενήθημεν) is taken into account, since the reference is to flattering speech, then in Allan's scheme this would be a speech act middle in which the subjects are affected psychologically and emotionally. This technically relates to the prepositional phrase rather than the verb, yet it illustrates the fact that γίνομαι is a difficult verb to analyze without further context. Another complicating factor is that the expression is negative; however, for the sake of analysis it must be taken as positive. The negation speaks for itself.

A further instance of ἐγενήθημεν appears in 2:7 where English translations commonly render ἐγενήθημεν νήπιοι as "we were gentle" (NAB, CEB, NRSV, NKJV, and RSV). Such translations apparently adopt the variant reading ἤπιοι (kind, gentle) in place of νήπιοι (children) in the NA²⁸ text.[60] Consistent with the NA²⁸ adoption of νήπιοι is

---

[59] The translation here adopts the phrase "behaved with flattering speech" as given by Ernest Best, *A Commentary on the First and Second Epistles to the Thessalonians*, BNTC (London: Black, 1979), 88.

[60] νήπιοι appears in the NA²⁸ text, following P⁶⁵ ℵ* B C* D* F G I Ψ* 104* *et al*, but ἤπιοι also appears in significant manuscripts, including ℵᶜ, 33, and the Majority Text. Milligan prefers the latter reading, commenting that νήπιοι possibly arose due to dittography of the final ν of ἐγενήθημεν (*Thessalonians*, 21).

that of the NET which reads "we became little children" while the NJB translation: "we lived unassumingly among you" possibly represents an abstraction of the childlike quality and could align with both variants. These latter translations admit a more interactive sense to the verb, suggesting a responsive, relational means of existence and behavior (again not a spontaneous process), thus conforming to the same criteria as ἐγενήθημεν in 1:5 and 2:5 above. That is, we see the criteria of medial process, dynamic middle, and subject affectedness (in the sense of becoming something different, but not doing so spontaneously). In this case Allan's mental process category could possibly apply.

The warm relationship between Paul and the Thessalonians is affirmed in 2:8 as Paul speaks of the affection with which the apostles regarded the Thessalonian believers who had <u>become</u> very dear to them (ἀγαπητοὶ ἡμῖν <u>ἐγενήθητε</u>). This refers to a change of state which is conceptualized as happening "without direct initiation by an agent" and is therefore spontaneous, like other examples given by Allan which refer to a process of changing into a particular state such as θέρομαι (become warm), φαίνομαι (become visible), or φύομαι (grow).[61]

The reference here is not to what the Thessalonians became themselves but what they had become in Paul's estimation. They are not represented as *deliberately* endearing themselves. The middle verb ἐγενήθητε here represents a spontaneous, passive-like process, in which the subjects are not volitionally involved. Therefore, in this instance the medial notion and the grammatical descriptors do not apply.

In this section of text (1 Thess 2:5–8), Paul denies any authoritarian or manipulative attitude on the part of the apostles and commends the caring and nurturing manner in which he and his companions ministered to the Thessalonians. This expression of behavior is middle voiced in the sense that they are not acting externally as would be the case if they were merely instructing the converts in a dictatorial manner. Instead, they are acting within the relationship of mutual affection by adopting a gentle, unassuming manner.

---

[61] Allan, *Polysemy*, 60, 61.

While the attribute of self-affectedness is apparent, the classification of γίνομαι as a spontaneous process middle is not appropriate for ἐγενήθημεν in 2:5 and 2:7 because the adoption of a particular attitude is volitional behavior. However, ἐγενήθητε in 2:8 could be so classified, as explained above. This observation implies that context should be a major factor when determining middle function.

3.1.2.3 Γίνομαι in 1 Thess 2:10

1 Thess 2:10 ὑμεῖς μάρτυρες καὶ ὁ θεός, ὡς ὁσίως καὶ δικαίως καὶ ἀμέμπτως ὑμῖν τοῖς πιστεύουσιν <u>ἐγενήθημεν</u>	you are witnesses, and so is God, how pure, upright, and blameless <u>we were</u> [in our behavior] toward you believers

Here again ἐγενήθημεν is used to refer to the way the apostles behaved within the encompassing relationship of interaction with the new believers.[62] Such *being* or *becoming* is not represented as passive or spontaneous, for the subjects are acting with volition.[63] Nevertheless, subject affectedness is apparent insofar as they become something in the particular circumstances. Thus, as in similar expressions above referring to the behavior of the apostles, ἐγενήθημεν could possibly be classed as a mental process middle in Allan's scheme. It can also be classed as a dynamic middle and a medial process, with the subjects acting from within their own resources in their engagement with the Thessalonians.

---

[62] Donfried (*Paul*, 187) comments that 2:9–12 describe the behavior of Paul as hardworking (2:9), moral (2:10), and fatherly (2:11-12).

[63] Weima comments on ἐγενήθημεν (we were), noting that since it is predicated by adverbs rather than adjectives, it emphasizes the conduct of Paul and the apostles (*Thessalonians*, 152). He does not, however, mention the middle voice.

3.1.2.4 Γίνομαι in 1 Thess 2:14

1 Thess 2:14 ὑμεῖς γὰρ μιμηταὶ ἐγενήθητε, ἀδελφοί, τῶν ἐκκλησιῶν τοῦ θεοῦ τῶν οὐσῶν ἐν τῇ Ἰουδαίᾳ ἐν Χριστῷ Ἰησοῦ, ὅτι τὰ αὐτὰ ἐπάθετε καὶ ὑμεῖς ὑπὸ τῶν ἰδίων συμφυλετῶν καθὼς καὶ αὐτοὶ ὑπὸ τῶν Ἰουδαίων[64]	for you, brothers, <u>turned out to be</u> imitators of the churches of God in Christ Jesus which are in Judea because you suffered the same things; you from your own compatriots just as they did from the Jews

As the Thessalonians had received the gospel as the word of God, it worked in them to produce a transformation (2:13). This resulted in persecution by their compatriots, just as those in Judea had been persecuted by the Jews.[65] As Malherbe comments: "The explicative *gar* ("for") connects the Thessalonians' reception of the word with their suffering for it."[66] Thus Paul affirms that the Thessalonians experienced not only the same faith produced by the word but also the same opposition as the apostles and the wider body of Christ.

When translated as "became" (e.g., ESV, NAS, NIV, NKJV, NRSV) ἐγενήθητε sounds passive, as though something befell them that they had no control over, as if they became victims. Nevertheless, the theme of mimesis is continued here, and draws attention to their suffering for the faith *in the process* of living the faith, just like their fellow Christians in Judea. Interestingly, the NJB translation renders this in a more active sense: "For you, my brothers, have modelled yourselves on the churches of God in Christ Jesus which are in Judaea[.]" Expressing it this way (as if active plus reflexive pronoun) brings out the volitional nature of the

---

[64] Paul turns from speaking of the way he and his companions conducted themselves to commending the Thessalonians for their faithfulness. In so doing, he revisits the notion of imitation discussed above (§3.1.2.1).

[65] Verse 13 is discussed in the following chapter dealing with present forms.

[66] Malherbe, *Thessalonians*, 167. Thus, Malherbe emphasizes that it was the working of the word in them (2:13) which resulted in their suffering.

process, suggesting that they chose to behave in a particular manner, that is, being steadfast in the face of suffering.

Rather than portraying the Thessalonians as victims (passive) or focusing on their response (active), the middle voice draws attention to the fact that this process *happened*. It happened as a consequence of their new life in Christ, and this was something Paul had taught them to expect. That is, they *turned out* to be imitators of their fellow believers in Judaea. [67]

Although the Thessalonians are active in the overall process, they are not controlling it from the outside but are active within the process which is happening to them.[68] Paul is speaking of what they became, thus the focus is on the subjects within the process, as represented by a third party. These considerations align with a medial interpretation of the middle voice of ἐγενήθητε in 1 Thess 2:14.[69]

In Allan's model, the Thessalonians are affected in becoming something that they previously were not. Since this change is represented as occurring without intervention from an external agent, the spontaneous classification of the prototypical use applies. This instance is therefore similar to expressions about becoming imitators (1:6) and examples (1:7) above.

The grammatical descriptors do not clearly apply in this instance, since the process is not volitional. As Bruce comments: "this was not a deliberate imitation ... rather, the experience of the Judean churches was reproduced in the Thessalonian church." Persecution, he asserts, is a "natural concomitant of the Christian faith[.]"[70]

---

[67] Paul reminds them of this in 3:3-4.

[68] Similarly, Eberhard refers to a medial process as encompassing but moveable from the inside (*Middle Voice*, 81).

[69] Similarly, becoming imitators and examples in 1:6 and 1:7 (§3.1.2.1 above).

[70] Bruce, *Thessalonians*, 45.

3.1.2.5 Γίνομαι in 1 Thess 3:4–5

The next occurrences of the aorist middle of γίνομαι appear in 1 Thess 3, where Paul explains his reason for writing and seeks to encourage the Thessalonians in the face of the opposition they are encountering.

1 Thess 3:4–5 καὶ γὰρ ὅτε πρὸς ὑμᾶς ἦμεν, προελέγομεν ὑμῖν ὅτι μέλλομεν θλίβεσθαι, καθὼς καὶ <u>ἐγένετο</u> καὶ οἴδατε.⁵ διὰ τοῦτο κἀγὼ μηκέτι στέγων ἔπεμψα εἰς τὸ γνῶναι τὴν πίστιν ὑμῶν, μή πως ἐπείρασεν ὑμᾶς ὁ πειράζων καὶ εἰς κενὸν <u>γένηται</u> ὁ κόπος ἡμῶν.	For even when we were among you, we used to tell you in advance that we would be afflicted, just as <u>has happened,</u> as you know. For this reason, when indeed I could bear it no longer, I sent to learn about your faith, in case the tempter had seduced you and our toil <u>had been</u> in vain

The predicted event, the affliction, happened or "came to pass" (KJV) (ἐγένετο, 3:4); it came into being where it previously was not. The conceptualized grammatical subject (the affliction) is therefore affected, being represented as a spontaneous process with no agent in view. Hence, Allan's spontaneous process middle applies. However, due to the inanimate nature of the subject, the grammatical descriptions are not readily applicable. The medial interpretation is also problematic in this case: although the focus is on the event, there is not a clearly identified subject that is acting within it. Therefore, it appears preferable in this instance to think in terms of a spontaneous process, with the agents being suppressed. Paul is not implicating anyone regarding the oppression but is simply stating that it happened as he warned them it would.[71]

---

[71] Allan comments that "the absence of an overt agent implies either that the agent is present somewhere in the background of the speaker's conception of the situation ... or that the agent is pragmatically irrelevant, or even that the event is conceptualized as lacking an agent altogether" (*Polysemy*, 63).

In verse 5 Paul expresses the expectation and hope of transformation, of spiritual fruit arising from the labor of himself and his colleagues among the Thessalonians. The overall sense is not that the grammatical subject, ὁ κόπος ἡμῶν, comes into being itself but that it should *prove to be, turn out to be* (γένηται) effective.[72] Although the expression above is negative by virtue of εἰς κενὸν (in vain, for nothing), the verb itself refers to a change in characteristic, so Allan's criterion of subject affectedness applies. Moreover, since the subject is inanimate, it must be classed as a spontaneous process. The grammatical criteria are not clearly applicable because it does not appear sensible to speak of an inanimate subject acting on, for or from within itself. This does not mean that γένηται does not have middle function, but simply that this way of describing it is not applicable.

An alternative way of thinking about the productiveness of the toil of the apostles is to think in terms of a medial event. The intimation in this section of the epistle is that there is a cosmic struggle in respect to the Thessalonians. Paul and Timothy, as God's co-workers in the (service of) the gospel (3:3), are working with God to bring about fruit in the lives of the Thessalonians and bring their faith to maturity; yet the tempter (ὁ πειράζων, 3:5) is striving to destroy it.[73] This speaks of an interactive, medial situation, where the work of preaching, teaching and encouraging is within the process of struggle for the growth in maturity of the converts. Paul is concerned that their work, though opposed, should be efficacious: it should amount to (γένηται) something, not nothing. Thus, the subject (the work of the apostles) is internal to the process expressed by the verb.

It is apparent that the verb γίνομαι, in testifying to the mutuality of the relationship between the apostles and the recipients of the letter, serves to link much of the thought expressed in chapters 1 and 2.[74] As

---

[72] See BDAG, s.v. "γίνομαι." (7) for this use: "to come into a certain state or possess certain characteristics, *to be, prove to be, turn out to be.*"

[73] For a discussion of the notion of the apostles being co-workers with God in the service of the Gospel, see Richard, *Thessalonians*, 149–52.

[74] Forms of γίνομαι appear ten times in ch. 1 and 2, yet only twelve times for the whole letter.

the apostles led by example, encouraging and nurturing the faith of their converts, the Thessalonians were transformed, leading them to exhibit the same attributes as the apostles by patiently enduring persecution and becoming witnesses of the gospel themselves. The aorist forms of γίνομαι discussed above as well as the present forms explored separately in the next chapter testify to the new phenomena coming into being in Thessalonica.

3.1.3 Παρρησιάζομαι *(media tantum)*

The middle-only verb παρρησιάζομαι refers to speaking freely or openly.[75] When used with an infinitive, it acquires the sense "have the courage, venture," according to BDAG.[76] The term παρρησία arose in the political sphere, referring to the freedom of speech that was characteristic of Athenian democracy and having the inherent nuances of: the right to speak, the sense of declaration of truth, and candour in the face of opposition.[77] It appears only five times in the LXX and nine times in the New Testament.[78] Not surprisingly, παρρησιάζομαι is used in the book of Acts to refer to the apostles speaking or preaching with boldness, for example, καὶ ἦν μετ' αὐτῶν εἰσπορευόμενος καὶ ἐκπορευόμενος εἰς Ἰερουσαλήμ, <u>παρρησιαζόμενος</u> ἐν τῷ ὀνόματι τοῦ κυρίου: "He moved about freely with them in Jerusalem and <u>spoke out boldly</u> in the name of the Lord" (Acts 9:28, NAB). Both the noun and the verb are attested by Plutarch, as below.[79]

> For as Lysander, we are told, said to the man from Megara, who in the council of the allies was <u>making bold</u> [παρρησια-

---

[75] LSJ, s.v. "παρρησιάζομαι."; BDAG, s.v. "παρρησιάζομαι."

[76] BDAG, s.v. "παρρησιάζομαι" (2).

[77] Heinrich Schlier, "παρρησια, παρρησιάζομαι," *TDNT* 5:871–873. Similarly, L&N comment on the sense of speaking openly, confidently, and fearlessly. L&N, s.v. "παρρησιάζομαι" (33.90), also of having the courage to do so (25.159).

[78] Acts 9:27, 28; 13:46; 14:3; 18:26, 19:8; 26:26. The only other occurrences are 1 Thess 2.2 and Eph 6:20.

[79] Plutarch, *Adul. amic.*, 71.E.6–7 (Babbitt, LCL 197:378–379).

ζόμενον] to speak for Greece, that "his words needed a country to back them"; so it may well be that every man's <u>frank speaking</u> [παρρησια] needs to be backed by character, but this is especially true in the case of those who admonish others and try to bring them to their sober senses.

This excerpt illustrates the philosophical tradition of the time. It was a common claim that the deeds of a teacher must match his words in order for him to have the right to boldness of speech in regard to moral instruction.[80] Malherbe points out that Paul does not draw attention to his own deeds but emphasizes that God is the source of his boldness and authority to exhort the new Christians,[81] as in 1 Thess 2:2 below:[82]

1 Thess 2:2 ἀλλὰ προπαθόντες καὶ ὑβρισθέντες, καθὼς οἴδατε, ἐν Φιλίπποις <u>ἐπαρρησιασάμεθα</u> ἐν τῷ θεῷ ἡμῶν λαλῆσαι πρὸς ὑμᾶς τὸ εὐαγγέλιον τοῦ θεοῦ ἐν πολλῷ ἀγῶνι.	But having suffered before and been mistreated at Philippi, as you know, <u>we had boldness</u> in our God to declare to you the gospel of God in the face of great opposition.

As Paul affirms that he and his companions had boldness to declare the gospel in the face of opposition, there is an emphasis on the mental state of the speaker. In Allan's scheme, the verb ἐπαρρησιασάμεθα could

---

[80] Malherbe comments: "That a philosopher's λόγος should match his ἔργον was a requirement not confined to Cynics, but in their case, it expressed their self-confidence … and justified their demands that they be emulated" ("Exhortation in First Thessalonians," 247).

[81] Malherbe, "Exhortation in 1 Thessalonians," 248–49. Similarly, in 2:4 Paul asserts: "but just as we have been approved by God to be entrusted with the message of the gospel, even so we speak, not to please mortals" (NRSV).

[82] This sense of ἐπαρρησιασάμεθα in 1 Thess 2:2 is translated variously, e.g., "we drew courage" (NAB), "we were bold" (KJV), "we had boldness" (ESV), "we had courage" (NRS), "we waxed bold" (ASV).

therefore be placed in the speech act category, consisting of verbs of speech which exhibit psychological or emotional involvement on the part of the speaker.[83] The subjects are active, but also affected because they *experience* boldness in the face of this opposition, which is contrary to the usual perception of this verb as a deponent.[84] However, the phrase (ἐν τῷ θεῷ) indicates that they were emboldened by God to preach the Gospel of God ἐν πολλῷ ἀγῶνι (with great struggle). They are internal to this process, active in boldly declaring the gospel but aware that this boldness comes from God working in and through them, despite the struggle. Therefore, there is simultaneity of reception and action in the speech-event: the subjects are acting within a process which encompasses them; they are internal to this medial event. According to grammatical descriptors, the dynamic middle sense is applicable since the subjects are acting from their own resources, drawing others into their sphere.

3.1.4 Εὐαγγελίζομαι (εὐαγγελίζω)

Having the generic sense of announcing good news, εὐαγγελίζομαι is widely used throughout the New Testament in a technical sense to refer to the preaching of the gospel. BDAG lists this verb in the active form, noting that this was common in later Greek, nevertheless indicating no difference in meaning from the classical middle form.[85] In the LXX the middle form predominates. For example, we find ἐπ' ὄρος ὑψηλὸν ἀνάβηθι <u>ὁ εὐαγγελιζόμενος</u> Σιων: "Go up on a high mountain, you

---

[83] Allan explains this in terms of the subject being a *"beneficiary* or an *"experiencer"* (*Polysemy*, 105). He does not include this verb in his examples but does list other *media tantum* verbs such as εὔχομαι (vow, pray, boast), κέλομαι (command), and ἀρνέομαι (refuse, deny). Each of these suggests commitment rather than indifference on the part of the speaker.

[84] BDAG, s.v. "παρρησιάζομαι."

[85] BDAG, s.v. "εὐαγγελίζω." as also noted in BDF §309. Nevertheless, it is the middle form which is most common in the New Testament.

who bring good tidings to Sion" in Isa 40:9 (NETS).⁸⁶ The middle is used similarly by Josephus in regard to Joab's messenger Achimas who "announced the welcome news of a decisive victory" (περὶ τῆς μάχης νίκην εὐαγγελίζεται καὶ κράτος) to King David.⁸⁷

In the New Testament, the middle form is almost exclusively used.⁸⁸ It is particularly frequent in Luke-Acts and common in the Pauline epistles in reference to preaching the gospel. Hence, we find: καὶ ταῖς ἑτέραις πόλεσιν εὐαγγελίσασθαί με δεῖ τὴν βασιλείαν τοῦ θεοῦ: "I must proclaim the good news of the kingdom of God to the other cities also (Luke 4:43, NRSV) and οὐ γὰρ ἀπέστειλέν με Χριστὸς βαπτίζειν ἀλλ' εὐαγγελίζεσθαι: "for Christ did not send me to baptize but to proclaim the gospel" (1 Cor 1:17, NRSV). It has been commented that 1 Thess 3:6 contains the only non-technical use in Paul, as

---

⁸⁶ An active form (εὐαγγελίζοντες) is used in reference to proclaiming the good news of Saul's death to the Philistines (1 Sam. 31:9), this being the earliest attestation of the active in TLG, having the same sense as the middle elsewhere, e.g., εὐαγγελιζόμενος (2 Sam. 4:10).

⁸⁷ Josephus, A.J., 7.250.2 (Marcus, LCL 281:136–137).

⁸⁸ The active only appears in Rev 10:7 (εὐηγγέλισεν) and Rev 14:6 (ἔχοντα εὐαγγέλιον αἰώνιον εὐαγγελίσαι). However, the former is widely interpreted as referring to the mystery of God which was *announced* to the prophets rather than to good news or gospel *per se*: accordingly, εὐηγγέλισεν is translated "announced" (ESV, NIV, NRSV), "declared" (KJV, NKJV), "proclaimed" (NET), "promised" (NAB), and "preached" (NAS, NAU). Likewise, in Rev 14:6; there is redundancy if εὐαγγελίσαι is understood to refer to good news, which is already specified in εὐαγγέλιον. It is more apt to translate ἔχοντα εὐαγγέλιον αἰώνιον εὐαγγελίσαι as 'having the eternal gospel to *announce*'. Although BDAG refers to an active form in a variant reading of Acts 16:17, (οἵτινες καταγγέλλουσιν ὑμῖν ὁδὸν σωτηρίας) according to NA²⁸ the only variant for καταγγέλουσιν (proclaim) is εὐαγγελιζονται (D 05) which is middle/passive in form, while the CNTTS critical apparatus (accessed via BibleWorks) lists εὐαγγελιζοντες (D 05*) and εὐαγγελιζοντε (D 05ᶜ). The latter may be dismissed on grounds of orthography, and the former, though grammatically possible, is unlikely since it would be more conventional to use the indicative (as in the NA²⁸ text) when there is a specified subject. Ultimately, since there is only one witness to this reading, which was later corrected, it cannot be said that there is significant attestation of the active form.

it does not explicitly refer to the preaching of the gospel.[89] However, there may well be a play on words intended, that is, just as Paul brought the good news of the gospel to them, now Timothy brings the good news of the fruit of the gospel *in* them to Paul.[90]

1 Thess 3:6 Ἄρτι δὲ ἐλθόντος Τιμοθέου πρὸς ἡμᾶς ἀφ' ὑμῶν καὶ <u>εὐαγγελισαμένου</u> ἡμῖν τὴν πίστιν καὶ τὴν ἀγάπην ὑμῶν καὶ ὅτι ἔχετε μνείαν ἡμῶν ἀγαθὴν πάντοτε, ἐπιποθοῦντες ἡμᾶς ἰδεῖν καθάπερ καὶ ἡμεῖς ὑμᾶς	But now Timothy has come to us from you and has <u>brought us good news</u> of your faith and love and [reported] that you always remember us well, longing to see us just as we also [long to see] you

While commentaries typically discuss the lexical meaning of εὐαγγελίζομαι, the technical and non-technical uses, the genitive absolute construction and general syntax of the verse, the distinctly middle form of the participle εὐαγγελισαμένου receives no mention.[91] English translations commonly render εὐαγγελισαμένου "has brought good news" (ESV, NAS, NIV, NKJV, NRSV, RSV), although the CEB and NJB translations read "has given us good news[.]" The latter reads much like an active transitive verb, whereas to *bring* news suggests that the subject who brings the news is an intermediary, relaying information from one situation to another. Thus, the subject (Timothy) is internal to the process, together with the recipients, bringing good news gained from personal experience. The subject is immersed in the event denoted by the verb; hence, the medial notion applies. In Allan's framework, εὐαγγελισαμένου could be classified as a speech act middle, the effect on the subject being regarded as the emotion associated with the

---

[89] As noted by Malherbe, *Thessalonians*, 200; Richard, *Thessalonians*, 154; Milligan, *Thessalonians*, 40; and Fee, *Thessalonians*, 122.

[90] As noted by Wanamaker, *Thessalonians*, 133; Boring, *Thessalonians*, 121.

[91] See, e.g., Weima, *Thessalonians*, 219; Fee, *Thessalonians*, 122; Malherbe, *Thessalonians*, 200.

bringing of the good news. In the grammatical sense, Timothy is acting from within himself (dynamic middle) in this situation, by expressing the good news of the faith of the Thessalonians, which he observed firsthand and now passes on.

3.1.5 Διαμαρτύρομαι (media tantum)

The verb διαμαρτύρομαι may refer to a solemn declaration like a sworn testimony in a legal scenario (thus emphasizing the truth of an assertion), or it may express serious concern in the form of exhortation, protest, or warning.[92] In the LXX both nuances are found, examples being: <u>διαμαρτύρομαι</u> ὑμῖν σήμερον τόν τε οὐρανὸν καὶ τὴν γῆν: "I call sky and earth <u>to witness</u> against you today" (Deut 4:26, NETS) and καὶ <u>διεμαρτυράμην</u> ἐν αὐτοῖς καὶ εἶπα πρὸς αὐτούς διὰ τί ὑμεῖς αὐλίζεσθε ἀπέναντι τοῦ τείχους: "And <u>I warned</u> them and said to them, "Why do you spend the night in front of the wall"?" (Neh 13:21, NETS). This sense of warning or entreating is also attested in a letter of Claudius (41 CE) to the people of Alexandria in regard to tensions between Greek citizens and Jews. He writes: : διόπερ ἔτι καὶ νῦν <u>διαμαρτύρομε</u> [διαμαρτύρομαι] εἶνα [ἵνα] Ἀλεξανδρεῖς μὲνπραέως καὶ φιλανθρόπως [φιλανθρώπως] προσφέροντε [προσφέρωνται] Ἰουδαίος [Ἰουδαίοις]: "Wherefore, still even now, <u>I entreat</u> you that, on the one hand, the Alexandrians behave gently and kindly towards the Jews[.]"[93]

In the New Testament, διαμαρτύρομαι is often used in Acts with reference to the apostles testifying to the gospel message. For example: καὶ παρήγγειλεν ἡμῖν κηρύξαι τῷ λαῷ καὶ <u>διαμαρτύρασθαι</u> ὅτι οὗτός ἐστιν ὁ ὡρισμένος ὑπὸ τοῦ θεοῦ κριτὴς ζώντων καὶ νεκρῶν: "and he commanded us to preach to the people and <u>to testify</u> that he is

---

[92] BDAG, s.v. "διαμαρτυρέω." LSJ, s.v. "διαμαρτυρέω."

[93] P.Lond. 6.1912 *l* 82–83, trans. John L. White, *Light from Ancient Letters* (Philadelphia: Fortress, 1986), 136. The orthographical errors (shown with corrections) in the transcript above may be explained by White's comment that the extant letter is a rather careless copy from Philadelphia in the Fayum, of what would have been an official document (*Light from Ancient Letters*, 131).

the one ordained by God as judge of the living and the dead" (Acts 10:42, NRSV). It is also used in the sense of warning, for instance: ἔχω γὰρ πέντε ἀδελφούς, ὅπως <u>διαμαρτύρηται</u> αὐτοῖς, ἵνα μὴ καὶ αὐτοὶ ἔλθωσιν εἰς τὸν τόπον τοῦτον τῆς βασάνου: "for I have five brothers—that <u>he may warn</u> them, so that they will not also come into this place of torment" (Luke 16:28, NRSV). This sense of warning, urging, or entreating is evident in the aorist indicative of διαμαρτύρομαι in 1 Thess 4:6, below:

| 1 Thess 4:6 τὸ μὴ ὑπερβαίνειν καὶ πλεονεκτεῖν ἐν τῷ πράγματι τὸν ἀδελφὸν αὐτοῦ, διότι ἔκδικος κύριος περὶ πάντων τούτων, καθὼς καὶ προείπαμεν ὑμῖν καὶ <u>διεμαρτυράμεθα.</u> | Not to transgress or take advantage of a brother in the matter, because the Lord is an avenger in all these things, as we told you before and <u>solemnly testified</u> |

As noted above, chapter 4 deals with ethical instruction and the context here is an admonition against unchastity and infidelity (4:3–7). Thus διεμαρτυράμεθα conforms to Allan's category of speech act middle verbs that reflect the heightened psychological involvement of the subject in the utterance.[94] Allan indicates that the subject is affected in such instances, for example in the utterance of a vow whereby the subject is bound, and this verb has a similar nuance.[95] There is the sense that Paul is utterly serious about his teaching and risks his life in order to proclaim it as can be seen from the broader context, despite any degree of "semantic generalization."[96] Such generalization may have weakened the

---

[94] Allan does not refer to διαμαρτύρομαι specifically but indicates that μαρτύρομαι is a speech act middle (*Polysemy*, 51).

[95] Allan, *Polysemy*, 107. Hence, e.g., "we solemnly forewarned you" (RSV), "as we told you before and solemnly affirmed" (NAB).

[96] Semantic generalization is discussed by Allan, *Polysemy*, 107. Nevertheless, this is a diachronic factor, whereas this study examines the meaning of verbs in context and is thus a synchronic approach.

original sense of declaration under oath, enabling the term to be more generally applied.[97]

Examining διεμαρτυράμεθα from the grammatical perspective, the verb may be seen to carry the middle nuance because of the investment and commitment of the subject in the event. With his earnestness being evident, Paul is not so much acting in his own interest as speaking from within his own convictions (speaking in the plural on behalf of his companions). Therefore, διεμαρτυράμεθα may be classed as a dynamic middle in the grammatical sense. From the medial perspective, the mental involvement and personal commitment to the truth of the statement means that the subjects are internal to the process. They are not represented as acting externally but are drawing on their convictions to warn the Thessalonians in a relational context. Solemnly testifying to a truth and affirming this to the Thessalonians, they are in an intermediary position; thus, the medial notion also applies.

3.1.6 Κοιμάομαι (κοιμάω)

In the New Testament and early Christian literature, according to BDAG, only the passive form with "active sense" is found,.[98] However, as discussed above, such verbs which have been traditionally designated "passive deponents" can simply be middle forms using the alternative -θη- morphology. This may be illustrated by examples from Homer who employed both the sigmatic and the -θη aorist middle forms of κοιμάω in his writing. As an example of the sigmatic aorist we have: ὡς ὁ μὲν ἔνθ' Ὀδυσεὺς κοιμήσατο, τοὶ δὲ παρ αὐτὸν ἄνδρες κοιμήσαντο νεηνίαι: "so there Odysseus slept and beside him slept the young men."[99] Illustrating the use of the -θη middle form we find: ἦμος δ' ἠέλιος κατέδυ καὶ ἐπὶ κνέφας ἦλθε, δὴ τότε κοιμήθημεν ἐπὶ

---

[97] Hence, e.g., διεμαρτύρατο is translated "protested" in Diodorus Siculus, *Bibl. Hist.*, 15.43.2.6 (Sherman, LCL 389:66–67).

[98] BDAG, s.v. "κοιμάω."

[99] Homer, *Odyssea*, 14.523 (Murray, Dimock, LCL 105:74–75). The context refers to natural sleep, not death.

ῥηγμῖνι θαλάσσης: "but when the sun set and darkness came on, then we lay down to rest on the shore of the sea."[100]

In the active form κοιμάω is transitive and refers to putting someone to sleep, while the middle/passive forms are used in reference to falling asleep or being asleep.[101] This common use is illustrated in the papyri. For example, in a villager's report of a household theft in 29 CE, the events are introduced as follows: κοιμωμένου μου ἐπὶ τῆς θύρας οὗ καταγείνομαι [καταγίνομαι] οἴκου: while I was sleeping at the door of the house which I inhabit (P.Ryl. 2. 127 *l* 8).

By figurative extension, the middle form is also used in reference to death or dying.[102] Hence, for example: καὶ ἐκοιμήθη Σαλωμων καὶ ἔθαψαν αὐτὸν ἐν πόλει Δαυιδ τοῦ πατρὸς αὐτοῦ: "And Solomon fell asleep, and they buried him in the city of David his father" (2 Chr 9:31, Brenton). Likewise: ἐξ ὧν οἱ πλείονες μένουσιν ἕως ἄρτι, τινὲς δὲ ἐκοιμήθησαν: "most of whom are still alive, though some have died" (1 Cor. 15:6, NRSV). Paul uses an aorist middle participle of κοιμάω in 1 Thess 4:14, 15 in a similar manner.[103] Although Paul is actually referring to death in these verses, he uses the verb for sleep. The metaphor is apt in this passage referring to resurrection.

1 Thess 4:14–15 εἰ γὰρ πιστεύομεν ὅτι Ἰησοῦς ἀπέθανεν καὶ ἀνέστη, οὕτως καὶ ὁ θεὸς τοὺς κοιμηθέντας διὰ τοῦ Ἰησοῦ ἄξει σὺν αὐτῷ. ¹⁵ Τοῦτο γὰρ ὑμῖν λέγομεν ἐν λόγῳ κυρίου, ὅτι ἡμεῖς οἱ	For if we believe that Jesus died and rose, in this way also God through Jesus will bring together with him those who have fallen asleep. For we tell you this by the word of the Lord, that we who are alive, who are left until the

---

[100] Homer, *Odyssea*, 9.169 (Murray, Dimock, LCL 104:356–357).

[101] LSJ, s.v. "κοιμάω."

[102] BDAG, s.v. "κοιμάω"; LSJ, s.v. "κοιμάω"; Frame, *Thessalonians*, 166. Milligan comments that it is commonly found in [burial] inscriptions (*Thessalonians*, 56).

[103] The form employed is typical of the passive, but as discussed above, the -θη- aorist forms were also used for some intransitive middles.

ζῶντες οἱ περιλειπόμενοι εἰς
τὴν παρουσίαν τοῦ κυρίου οὐ μὴ
φθάσωμεν τοὺς <u>κοιμηθέντας</u>·

coming of the Lord, will by no
means precede those <u>who have
died</u>.[104]

The participle κοιμηθέντας in both instances here refers to the sleep of death. Paul is reassuring the Thessalonians that those who have already died will in no way be disadvantaged in regard to the resurrection.[105] In the grammatical sense of the middle, it is difficult to discern any sense of the subjects acting on, for or by their own person. Such descriptions apply to volitional actions, rather than a more spontaneous process like falling asleep or dying. The subject is nevertheless affected in the process. Therefore, the verb fits Allan's overarching criterion and he refers to κοιμάομαι as a mental process middle, closely related to the spontaneous category.[106] Allan identifies such verbs as experiencers, noting that the aorist forms "generally designate that the subject *entered* a mental state (ingressive meaning of the aorist)."[107] This fits the present context well. Further, when one is sleeping, one is encompassed by the

---

[104] This translation of 4:14 takes διὰ τοῦ Ἰησοῦ with ἄξει in accord with NAB, NRSV, and Fee, *Thessalonians*, 172: "God through Jesus will bring with him those who are currently sleeping in death"; similarly, Malherbe, *Thessalonians*, 266. Alternatively, Frame argues that διὰ τοῦ Ἰησοῦ belongs with the participle; hence "those who fell asleep through Jesus" (*Thessalonians*, 169). Yet again, some translations render διὰ τοῦ Ἰησοῦ as "in Jesus" (e.g., NKJV, NJB). The two occurrences of the middle participle κοιμηθέντας are widely translated as "have fallen asleep" (e.g., NIV, NJB, RSV) though NRSV simply states "have died.", NKJ adopts "sleep" (4:14) or "are sleeping" (4:15). Milligan comments that κοιμηθέντας is used in a purely middle sense but does not discuss what that may mean (*Thessalonians*, 57). However, the comparison would necessarily be with the passive, in which case the subjects would be put to sleep (or death). No reference to voice was found in more recent commentaries.

[105] They may have misunderstood that as God's eschatological people they would not die before the Parousia (Boring, *Thessalonians*, 158).

[106] Allan, *Polysemy*, 150. Allan is referring here to the alternating sigmatic and theta aorist forms for certain verbs, including κοιμάομαι in Homer.

[107] Allan, *Polysemy*, 65.

event or process, so this intransitive verb also aligns with the notion of mediality; the subject is internal to the verbal process.[108]

3.1.7 Ἐνδύομαι (ἐνδύω)

The active verb ἐνδύω has the general sense of "go into," so with reference to clothing, this becomes "put on" or "clothe."[109] Hence, God ἐνέδυσεν (clothed) Adam and Eve with animal skins (Gen 3:21). In the New Testament, the active form appears only in Matthew 27:31 (and the parallel, Mark 15:20) referring to the soldiers putting Jesus' garments back on him, and in Luke 15:22 it refers to the father putting a robe on the prodigal son.

The middle form, ἐνδύομαι, predictably refers to putting something on oneself, or dressing. For example, priests are instructed to put on (ἐνδύσεται) a linen tunic (Lev 6:3) and metaphorically, to clothe themselves with righteousness: οἱ ἱερεῖς σου ἐνδύσονται δικαιοσύνην (Ps 131:9).[110] It is attested similarly in the contemporaneous literature. For example, Josephus writes that Mordecai rent his clothes and put on sackcloth: περιρρηξάμενος τὴν ἐσθῆτα καὶ σάκκον ἐνδυσάμενος.[111]

The middle form is found twenty-four times in the New Testament, fourteen of these occurrences being in the Pauline corpus. It is used literally, for instance: μὴ ἐνδύσησθε δύο χιτῶνας: you should not put on two tunics (Mark 6:9), and figuratively, particularly in Paul's writing. Hence, we see: ἐνδύσασθε τὸν κύριον Ἰησοῦν Χριστὸν: put on the Lord Jesus Christ (Rom 13:14) and Δεῖ γὰρ τὸ φθαρτὸν τοῦτο ἐνδύσασθαι ἀφθαρσίαν: for this perishable [nature] must put on the imperishable (1 Cor. 15:53).

In the last chapter of 1 Thessalonians wherein Paul discusses matters eschatological, he reassures the Thessalonians that they need not fear sudden judgement on the Day of the Lord like those who remain in

---

[108] Similarly, Eberhard states that "a dream is something that happens to me although I am the dreamer" (*Middle Voice*, 18).

[109] LSJ, s.v. "ἐνδύω."

[110] BDAG, s.v. "ἐνδύω."

[111] Josephus, *A.J.*, 11.221.2 (Marcus, LCL 326:420–421).

darkness: those who are, as it were, drunk and unaware (5:2–7). Accordingly, he writes in 1 Thess 5:8:

| 1 Thess 5:8 ἡμεῖς δὲ ἡμέρας ὄντες νήφωμεν <u>ἐνδυσάμενοι</u> θώρακα πίστεως καὶ ἀγάπης καὶ περικεφαλαίαν ἐλπίδα σωτηρίας | But we, who belong to the day, let us be sober, <u>putting on</u> a breastplate of faith and love, and for a helmet the hope of salvation |

Malherbe draws attention to the resonance with Isaiah 59:17 which states that the Lord put on (ἐνεδύσατο) righteousness as a breastplate in advance of coming in judgement on his enemies.[112] In 1 Thess 5:8, the participle ἐνδυσάμενοι is used figuratively in reference to putting a breastplate and helmet on oneself; hence, a clearly reflexive sense of the middle voice is apparent.[113] This naturally means that the subject is affected; therefore, in both the grammatical sense and Allan's model, the verb fits the direct reflexive category. However, there is also a sense that this is done in one's own interest (indirect reflexive). The notion of a medial event is likewise applicable, for in putting the breastplate on themselves, they are literally internal to the process of which they are agent. In putting on something, they get inside it, thus they are exhorted to put on, that is, *to get into*, the realm of faith and love, clearly identifying with the day (or light) to which they legitimately belong.

While some commentaries mention the aorist tense of the participle and hence translate ἐνδυσάμενοι as "having put on" or the like (as in ESV or NAS), they do not refer to its middle morphology.[114] This occurs even though the sigmatic form is unambiguously middle and as an oppositional middle, it stands in contrast to the active. If this were not

---

[112] Malherbe also notes Paul's frequent use of martial imagery (*Thessalonians*, 297).

[113] Allan does not list this verb but includes ἕννυμαι (dress oneself) and ζώννυμαι (gird oneself) as an example of direct reflexives used in ancient Greek (*Polysemy*, 89).

[114] Thus: Wanamaker, *Thessalonians*, 185; Boring, *Thessalonians*, 175–76, 183. Alternatively, Weima argues for contemporaneous action, hence "putting on," as translated above (*Thessalonians*, 362). The discussion centers on the significance of the aorist tense; no discussion is given of the middle form.

significant, there would be no reason to use a middle rather than an active verb. A middle form here suggests volitional action on the subject by the subject, which is consistent with the hortatory expression and general paraenetic tone of this section of the letter.

3.1.8 Τίθεμαι (τίθημι)

The very common verb τίθημι has many applications in the general sense of put, place, and set up, also institute, make, or ordain[115] The active and middle forms have similar applications, so the particular sense of the middle must be derived from the context.[116] In the LXX we find the middle used in regard to placing *things*, for example: καὶ ἔθετο Δαυιδ φρουρὰν ἐν Συρίᾳ: and David placed a garrison in Syria" (2 Sam. 8:6, Brenton).[117] It also refers to placing *people*, for example: καὶ νῦν ζῇ κύριος ὃς ἡτοίμασέν με καὶ ἔθετό με ἐπὶ τὸν θρόνον Δαυιδ τοῦ πατρός μου: "And now as the Lord lives who has established me, and set me on the throne of my father David" (1 Kgs 2:24, Brenton). Further, it is used in reference to setting *laws* in place, for example, καὶ ἀνέστησεν μαρτύριον ἐν Ιακωβ καὶ νόμον ἔθετο ἐν Ισραηλ: "and he raised up a testimony in Jacob and appointed a law in Israel" (Ps 77:5, Brenton). A similar use is found in Josephus regarding laws ordained by Osarsiph for his group of ill-treated insurgents: ὁ δὲ πρῶτον μὲν αὐτοῖς νόμον ἔθετο μήτε προσκυνεῖν θεοὺς: "By his first law he ordained that they should not worship the gods[.]"[118]

In the New Testament, the middle is found less frequently than the active (14 middle, 58 active).[119] The active is used typically for placing

---

[115] LSJ, s.v. "τίθημι." BDAG, s.v. "τίθημι." MM, s.v. "τίθημι."

[116] Hence, e.g., GE, s.v. "τίθημι," where active and middle uses are listed separately but are largely duplicated.

[117] Likewise, καὶ ἔθετο κύριος ὁ θεὸς σημεῖον τῷ Καιν: And the Lord God set a mark on Cain (Gen. 4:15).

[118] Josephus, *C. Ap.*, 1.239.2 (Thackeray, LCL, 186:260–261).

[119] In the LXX the number of middles and actives are more comparable (216:267). This is consistent with the diminishing use of middle verbs from Classical to Koine, as noted previously.

something somewhere, for example, a man building a house who <u>ἔθηκεν</u> θεμέλιον ἐπὶ τὴν πέτραν: laid the foundation upon rock (Luke 6:48, RSV). The middle occurs in more figurative senses such as: καὶ <u>ἔθεντο</u> πάντες οἱ ἀκούσαντες ἐν τῇ καρδίᾳ αὐτῶν: "and all who heard them <u>laid</u> them up in their hearts" (Luke 1:66, RSV). In Paul's letters, ἔθετο is similarly used in the sense *appointed,* for example, Καὶ οὓς μὲν <u>ἔθετο</u> ὁ θεὸς ἐν τῇ ἐκκλησίᾳ πρῶτον ἀποστόλους: "And God <u>has appointed</u> in the church first apostles" (1 Cor 12:28, RSV). A similar use is seen in 1 Thess 5:9 although it refers not to being appointed to a position or office of responsibility, but to a state of blessing, as below.[120]

1 Thess 5:9 ὅτι οὐκ <u>ἔθετο</u>	because God did not <u>ap-</u>
ἡμᾶς ὁ θεὸς εἰς ὀργὴν	<u>point</u> us for wrath but for
ἀλλὰ εἰς περιποίησιν	obtaining salvation
σωτηρίας διὰ τοῦ κυρίου	through our Lord Jesus
ἡμῶν Ἰησοῦ Χριστοῦ	Christ

This verse continues the thought of that discussed above (1 Thess 5:8); the Thessalonian Christians are exhorted to act in the prescribed manner *because* God has appointed (destined) them for salvation. Thus, Milligan comments that ἔθετο "clearly carries back the deliverance of the Thessalonians to the direct action and purpose of God," for God chose them (1:4) and called them into his own kingdom (2:12).[121] This accords with translations of ἔθετο as "intended" (CEB, CJB), or more commonly, "destined" (ESV, NAB, NET, NJB, NRSV, RSV).

It also reflects the similar use of ἔθετο expressing the wish of a testator through the will <u>he drew up</u> that his daughter should be his heir: δι' ἧς <u>ἔθετο</u> διαθήκης, ἠθέλησεν κληρονό[μο]ν ἑαυτοῦ γενέσθαι

---

[120] Weima notes the sense of "consign someone to something" for τίθημι (see BDAG, s.v. "τίθημι," 5) and thus translates ἔθετο as "destine," in this verse (*Thessalonians*, 365).

[121] Milligan, *Thessalonians*, 69.

τὴν θυγατέρα (SB 5.7558 *l* 4 [173 CE]).[122] These uses refer to ordaining something according to the will of the subject. Hence, in 1 Thess 5:9 above, Paul emphasizes that God wills for them a holy life consistent with their calling, leading to salvation and life with him (5:10) whether they be awake (living) or asleep (dead).

There is reference to the actions of both the believers and of God in the process of salvation in these two verses. The sense portrayed indicates an appointment or placing not simply into a particular category as an arbitrary, external act, but of an action that involves the subject (ὁ θεός) in an interactive, relational process. God ordains them to obtain salvation and therefore experience ongoing life with him (5:10).[123]

The medial notion is therefore applicable because the subject (ὁ θεός, God) is acting within the process designated by the verb, not externally to it. There is a sense of volition and purpose implied by the middle voice of τίθημι here. This action of appointing for salvation is initiated by God, involves God and is in God's interest, so the indirect reflexive is appropriate in the grammatical sense.[124] Allan does not list this verb in any of his categories but if God is acting according to his own desire as suggested, ἔθετο could be classed as an indirect reflexive on Allan's scale also. Such verbs refer to transitive events in which the subject derives benefit from the action.[125]

---

[122] A similar use of ἔθετο as an expression of purpose or will: "Daniel determined [ἔθετο] in his heart, that he would not defile himself with the King's table" (Dan 1:8, Brenton).

[123] For further examples of God choosing and saving people *for* himself see §4.2 ῥύομαι, below.

[124] This sense of being appointed resonates with the assurance of being loved and chosen expressed in Gal 1:4 (εἰδότες, ἀδελφοὶ ἠγαπημένοι ὑπὸ [τοῦ] θεοῦ, τὴν ἐκλογὴν ὑμῶν).

[125] Allan, *Polysemy*, 112.

3.1.9 ἀσπάζομαι (media tantum)

The verb ἀσπάζομαι is common throughout the New Testament (59 instances). It has a range of uses related to greeting, welcoming kindly or taking leave of another, BDAG noting that it may also refer to briefly visiting or looking in on someone.[126] Most notably, and relevant to the use in 1 Thessalonians, it is used to pass on greetings at the end of a letter.[127] An examination of papyrus letters shows that whereas χαίρειν is used at the beginning of a letter to greet the recipient, ἀσπάζομαι is typically used at the end to pass on greetings to the recipient, or in asking the recipient to salute others on behalf of the sender. Hence, for example, in a clearly written letter from the second century we find: Ἀπολλινᾶρις Ταησίῳ τῇ μητρὶ πολλὰ <u>χαίρειν</u>: "Apollinarios to his mother, Taesion, many <u>greetings</u>" at the beginning. while we read: <u>ἀσπάζομαι</u> πολλὰ τὰ ἀδέλφια: "<u>I greet</u> [salute] my brothers much" near the end.[128] Similarly, ἀσπάζομαι is used in the imperative form by Paul at the close of his letter to the Thessalonians, requesting the readers to greet each other, as in 5:26 below:

1 Thess 5:26 Ἀσπάσασθε τοὺς ἀδελφοὺς πάντας ἐν φιλήματι ἁγίῳ	<u>Greet</u> all the brothers and sisters with a holy kiss

Paul is asking the readers of the letter to greet everyone in the Church (τοὺς ἀδελφοὺς πάντας) with a holy kiss. Or perhaps, as Malherbe suggests, those who have the letter read to them are to greet any

---

[126] LSJ, s.v. "ἀσπάζομαι."; BDAG, s.v. "ἀσπάζομαι."

[127] The papyri conclusively affirm this custom according to MM, s.v. "ἀσπάζομαι." Likewise, Paul typically concludes his letters with some form of greeting, e.g., Ἀσπάσασθε πάντα ἅγιον ἐν Χριστῷ Ἰησοῦ: Greet every saint in Christ Jesus (Phil 4:21).

[128] P.Mich 8.490 ll 2, 16 (101–200 CE), translated by White, *Light from Ancient Letters*, 161–62.

other brothers and sisters in this manner.[129] Paul is not simply passing on *his* greetings to the Thessalonian church but is asking them to greet each other in this manner, thus exhorting them to show acceptance and brotherly love to one another.[130] Thus Paul is again asking them to imitate what he would do.

This type of expression is very much in accord with the middle voice. In warmly greeting another, the subject is acting within a process of exchange, neither acting outside of him/herself nor being a passive recipient. The subject and object are together within the process designated by the verb, corresponding to Eberhard's understanding of a medial event. As noted above, Miller applies the term 'reciprocal' to such expressions of mutuality or interaction, wherein the removal of one party would render the verb meaningless.[131] This is a subcategory of the indirect reflexive middle in the grammatical sense. Allan primarily refers to verbs of contending in the reciprocal category although does concede "that there is also a group of verbs with an accusative complement that may well be considered reciprocals" and cites ἀσπάζομαι as one example.[132] In this instance of ἀσπάζομαι, though not necessarily always, Allan's speech act category could also apply.

3.1.10 Summary and Analysis: Aorist Middle Verbs in First Thessalonians

Table 3.1 below summarizes how the middle verbs may be classified according to the contexts in which they appear in 1 Thessalonians. Grammatical middles are distinguished as direct reflexive (Dir.Ref.) indirect reflexive (Ind.Ref.) dynamic (Dyn.) or reciprocal (Recip.). If the subject is affected, the category to which Allan assigns the verb is given;

---

[129] Malherbe, *Thessalonians*, 341.

[130] As noted by Boring, *Thessalonians*, 205. Some see a more ecclesial purpose in the holy kiss, e.g., Richard comments that it was a command to express ecclesial unity on the occasion of the Lord's Supper when the letter would be read (*Thessalonians*, 287).

[131] See §2.2.2 above.

[132] Allan, *Polysemy*, 87 n141.

if the particular verb is not included among his examples, a category is proposed and marked with an asterisk.[133] Those verbs which fit the description of Eberhard/Benveniste are designated "Medial event." The "Deponent" (Dep.) classification is signified according to the entry in *ALGNT*, which identifies inflected forms as deponent if such is the common perception. This is not to endorse the category, which, some would maintain, has been clearly dismissed.[134] The point is to clarify whether verbs *previously* thought to be deponent may simply be those which are only used in the middle form. Verbs are classified here as *media tantum* (*m.t.*) if the middle but not the active form appears in BDAG.[135]

The following observations may be noted:

1. Perception of deponency does align with *media tantum* status.
2. Subject affectedness and the medial interpretation are widely applicable.
3. At least two of the three descriptors apply in most instances.
4. γίνομαι does not always conform to its prototypical spontaneous function.
5. The grammatical descriptors do not apply to events represented as spontaneous.
6. The -θη- forms of γίνομαι are functioning as middle verbs

The property of subject-affectedness is widely applicable, even though a particular category of Allan's may not always be clear, such as with the cases of ἐγενήθημεν in 1:5; 2:5, 2:7 and 2:10. These all refer to the behavior of the apostles and may be assigned the property of subject affectedness insofar as the verb is taken to indicate their *becoming* something in the relevant circumstances. The fact that γίνομαι rather than εἰμί is used supports this suggestion. Such instances may, however, be better represented by the medial notion because it focuses on

---

[133] Abbreviations for Allan's categories: Spont. = spontaneous, Sp. Act = speech act, M. Proc = mental process.

[134] As noted in §1.1 above.

[135] BDAG is not used as the arbiter of deponent perception as this property is not consistently noted.

the subject's location within a process without requiring the verb to be compressed into or confined within a category determined by the actual effect on the subject.

Table 3.1 Properties of Aorist Middle Verb Forms in 1 Thessalonians

Verb	Form	Ref.	m.t.	Dep.	Gramm. middle	Subj. Aff.	Allan category	Med.
δέχομαι	δεξάμενοι	1:6	✓	✓	Ind. Ref, Dyn.	✓	Ind. Ref.	✓
	ἐδέξασθε	2:13	✓	✓	Ind. Ref, Dyn.	✓	Ind. Ref.	✓
γίνομαι	ἐγενήθη	1:5	✓	✓	✗	✓	Spont.	✓
	ἐγενήθημεν	1:5	✓	✓	Dyn.	✓	M. Proc*	✓
	ἐγενήθητε	1:6	✓	✓	✗	✓	Spont.	✓
	γενέσθαι	1:7	✓	✓	✗	✓	Spont.	✓
	ἐγενήθημεν	2:5	✓	✓	Dyn.	✓	Sp. Act*	✓
	ἐγενήθημεν	2:7	✓	✓	Dyn.	✓	M. Proc*	✓
	ἐγενήθητε	2:8	✓	✓	✗	✓	Spont.	✗
	ἐγενήθημεν	2:10	✓	✓	Dyn.	✓	M. Proc*	✓
	ἐγενήθητε	2:14	✓	✓	✗	✓	Spont.	✓
	ἐγένετο	3:4	✓	✓	✗	✓	Spont.	✗
	γένηται	3:5	✓	✓	✗	✓	Spont.	✓
παρρησιάζομαι	ἐπαρρησιασάμεθα	2:2	✓	✓	Dyn.	✓	Sp. Act	✓
εὐαγγελίζω	εὐαγγελισαμένου	3:6	✗	✗	Dyn.	✓	Sp. Act	✓
διαμαρτύρομαι	διεμαρτυράμεθα	4:6	✓	✓	Dyn	✓	Sp. Act	✓
κοιμάω	κοιμηθέντας	4:14	✗	✗	✗.	✓	M. Proc.	✓
	κοιμηθέντας	4:15	✗	✗	✗	✓	M. Proc.	✓
ἐνδύω	ἐνδυσάμενοι	5:8	✗	✗	Dir. Ref.	✓	Dir. Ref.	✓
τίθημι	ἔθετο	5:9	✗	✗	Ind. Ref.	✓	Ind. Ref.*	✓
ἀσπάζομαι	ἀσπάσασθε	5:26	✓	✓	Recip.	✓	Recip.	✓

Furthermore, it is evident that the majority of verbs in the grammatical category are dynamic, in Cooper's sense of investing one's own particular resources into the action. This type of middle is less familiar than the direct or indirect reflexives, which may explain why such verbs have not always been recognized as having middle function. Taken as a whole, the evidence from this sample of verbs strongly suggests that middle form does indicate middle function, even for those verbs which are always used in middle form and were formerly considered to be deponent. There is therefore no need to regard such verbs as having active function or neglect to consider what their middle form may indicate.

CHAPTER 4
PRESENT MIDDLE VERBS IN FIRST THESSALONIANS

In the previous chapter, this study demonstrated that the aorist middle verb forms in 1 Thessalonians widely exhibit the properties of the middle voice. This current chapter continues this investigation in relation to the function of present middle/passive forms.

Since middle and passive verbs share the same morphology in the present tense, if there is ambiguity regarding the voice function of a verb in a given context, the matter is explored. While some commentaries address this question, once the passive is rejected in favor of the middle due to an agent subject, the middle voice function is generally not further explored. That is, although the distinction between passive and middle is established, the distinctive middle function compared to the active is not addressed.[1]

In the following investigations, therefore, the aim is to discern whether the present middle forms in 1 Thessalonians do in fact exhibit middle function in the context in which they are used.[2] The verbs examined are: ποιοῦμαι, ῥύομαι, ἔρχομαι, δύναμαι, ὀμείρομαι, ἐργάζομαι, παραμυθέομαι, μαρτύρομαι, ἐνεργέομαι, δέομαι, ἀπέχομαι, κτάομαι, φιλοτιμέομαι, κοιμάομαι, ἐφίσταμαι, προΐσταμαι, ἡγέομαι, ἀντέχομαι, and προσεύχομαι. The same descriptors of the middle voice are applied as for the aorist forms in the previous chapter:

---

[1] For example, see §4.9 below.

[2] The verbs examined are identified as middle by the *BibleWorks* 10 BNM database used throughout this investigation.

- The grammatical middle, with the subject acting on, for, or with reference to itself.[3]
- Allan's criterion of subject-affectedness within different types of events.
- The medial notion of the subject acting within the encompassing verbal process.

4.1 Ποιοῦμαι (ποιέω)

The common verb ποιέω essentially refers to doing or producing something, with various applications.[4] It is found in both active and middle forms in the New Testament, though the active is far more frequent (546 active, 21 middle). As examples of the active we may cite: ποιήσατε οὖν καρπὸν ἄξιον τῆς μετανοίας: produce fruit worthy of repentance (Matt 3:8), and τὰ ἔργα ἃ ἐγὼ ποιῶ: the works which I do (John 10:25). The middle is typically used in periphrastic constructions with a noun to indicate a single verbal idea,[5] for example, πάντοτε ἐν πάσῃ δεήσει μου ὑπὲρ πάντων ὑμῶν, μετὰ χαρᾶς τὴν δέησιν ποιούμενος: "In all my prayers for all of you, I always pray with joy" (Phil 1:4, NIV).[6]

Likewise, the idiom μνείαν ποιεῖσθαι (lit. to make remembrance) is employed for 'to mention', or 'to remember'. This expression is typically seen in the customary greeting at the beginning of ancient papyrus letters written in Greek.[7] An example appears in the well preserved letter

---

[3] As noted in ch. 3 this is taken to include Cooper's dynamic middle, with the subject acting from within its own resources.

[4] LSJ, s.v. "ποιέω"; BDAG, s.v. "ποιέω."

[5] LSJ, s.v. "ποιέω" II (5); BDAG, s.v. "ποιέω" 7a.

[6] Similarly, οἱ μαθηταὶ Ἰωάννου νηστεύουσιν πυκνὰ καὶ δεήσεις ποιοῦνται: the disciples of John frequently fast and pray (Luke 5:33).

[7] BDF refer to this as a "Hellenistic epistolary formula[.]" See BDF, §310.1. Malherbe comments similarly, although he emphasizes that whereas non-Christian prayers were generally petitions for health employed philophronetically, Paul takes the opportunity to give glory to God, acknowledging his initiative (*Thessalonians*, 107).

from Isais to her brother Hephaistion, found in the Sarapieion at Memphis: καὶ αὐτὴ δ' ὑγίαινον καὶ τὸ παιδίον καὶ ο ι ἐν οἴκωι πάντες σου διὰ παντὸς <u>μνείαν ποιούμενοι</u>: "and I myself am well, and the child, and all those in your household, <u>who</u> continually <u>remember</u> you."[8] In the New Testament, Paul also uses this expression in his letters, typically in connection with remembering or mentioning the recipients in prayer. For example, we find ἀδιαλείπτως μνείαν ὑμῶν ποιοῦμαι: I mention you constantly (Rom 1:9), Similar expressions occur in Eph 1:16, Phlm 4, and 1 Thess 1:2 as follows:

1 Thess 1:2–3 Εὐχαριστοῦμεν
τῷ θεῷ πάντοτε περὶ πάντων
ὑμῶν <u>μνείαν ποιούμενοι</u> ἐπὶ
τῶν προσευχῶν ἡμῶν,
ἀδιαλείπτως [3] μνημονεύοντες
ὑμῶν τοῦ ἔργου τῆς πίστεως ...

We always give thanks to God for you all, <u>making mention</u> of you in our prayers, constantly [3] remembering your work of faith ... [9]

Each of the selected descriptors point to middle function for ποιούμενοι here. Paul and his companions are mentally engaged with the persons for whom they are praying and with God; all are bound together in the process. Those praying are internal to the process as they make mention of those for whom they pray before God. Hence, the prayer is a medial process. They are also affected, since they are inspired to give thanks to God as they call to mind the good report of the fruitfulness of the gospel among the Thessalonians. [10] This volitional

---

[8] UPZ. 1.59 / 5a. (168 BC); translation from Roger S. Bagnall and Raffaella Cribiore, *Women's Letters from Ancient Egypt, 300 BC–AD 800* (Ann Arbor: University of Michigan, 2006), 111.

[9] This translation follows the punctuation of the NA[28] text. Alternatively, ἀδιαλείπτως (constantly) could be linked to μνείαν ποιούμενοι, as posited, e.g., by Wanamaker, *Thessalonians*, 74. Such a placement of the adverb would serve to highlight the mental involvement of the subject and hence the middle function of the verb, although Wanamaker does not mention the middle voice.

[10] As noted by Richard, *Thessalonians*, 59.

response could be classified under Allan's speech act or his mental activity category, but in either case, the element of subject-affectedness is apparent. Further, since the action arises within the heart and mind of the subjects, μνείαν ποιούμενοι conforms to the dynamic middle subset of the grammatical indirect reflexive middle category. Notably, since Allan's speech act middle requires an emotional or psychological investment on the part of the subject, this category often correlates with the dynamic middle.[11]

4.2 ῬΥΟΜΑΙ *(MEDIA TANTUM)*

The widely used verb ῥύομαι is listed in BDAG as a middle deponent, with the glosses "to rescue from danger, save, rescue, deliver, preserve."[12] An example from the papyri is seen in a well preserved letter from Dionysia to her husband Theon who is away on military service: ἐκ πολεμίων ἡμᾶς ἔρυσαι [εἴρυσαι] καὶ πάλι εἰς πολεμίους ἡμᾶς ἀφεὶς ἀπελήλυθας: "you both rescued us from enemies and again left us and went away against enemies."[13] Similarly, Josephus uses ῥύομαι in reference to priests supplicating God to rescue (ῥύσασθαι) them from their enemies;[14] and Philo speaks of Abraham pursuing the enemy to rescue (ῥύσασθαι) his nephew.[15]

In the LXX this basic sense of rescue from human enemies is again found, e.g., ὁ βασιλεὺς Δαυιδ ἐρρύσατο ἡμᾶς ἀπὸ πάντων τῶν ἐχθρῶν ἡμῶν: King David rescued us from all our enemies (2 Sam 19:10, NETS); καὶ ἐρρύσατο κύριος τὸν Ισραηλ ἐν τῇ ἡμέρᾳ ἐκείνῃ ἐκ χειρὸς τῶν Αἰγυπτίων: and the Lord delivered Israel in that day from the hand of the Egyptians (Exod 14:30, NETS). We also find ῥύομαι used in the sense of deliverance of the soul. For example, in Ps

---

[11] Data in tables 3.1 and 4.2 illustrate this correlation.
[12] BDAG, s.v. "ῥύομαι." LSJ and GE do not list ῥύομαι but indicate its relation to ἐρύω: to draw, pull or extract, LSJ, s.v. "ἐρύω." GE, s.v. "ἐρύω."
[13] P.Bad. 4.48 *l* 3 (127 BC), trans. Bagnall and Cribiore, *Women's Letters*, 107.
[14] Josephus, *A.J.*, 12.408.1, (Marcus, LCL 365: 212–213).
[15] Philo, *Abr.*, 231.1, (Colson, LCL 289: 112–113).

55:14 it is used in reference to God who "saved" (NETS) or "delivered" (Brenton) the soul of the Psalmist from death (ἐρρύσω τὴν ψυχήν μου ἐκ θανάτου).[16]

In the New Testament, ῥύομαι is always found in reference to God as deliver and to humans as the recipient of deliverance.[17] While this use of ῥύομαι is carried over from the LXX, Wilhelm Kasch notes that its meaning is further extended to include an "eschatological" sense.[18] Hence we see reference to deliverance from evil as a spiritual force or realm. For example, we find ῥῦσαι ἡμᾶς ἀπὸ τοῦ πονηροῦ: deliver us from evil / the evil one (Matt 6:13), and ὃς ἐρρύσατο ἡμᾶς ἐκ τῆς ἐξουσίας τοῦ σκότους: who delivers us from the dominion of darkness (Col 1:13). The passive form of ῥύομαι is also found, for example, ἵνα ῥυσθῶ ἀπὸ τῶν ἀπειθούντων ἐν τῇ Ἰουδαίᾳ: that I may be delivered from the unbelievers in Judea (Rom 15:31).[19] In 1 Thess 1:10, ῥύομαι appears in the form of a present middle participle, ῥυόμενον, as below:

| 1 Thess 1:10 καὶ ἀναμένειν τὸν υἱὸν αὐτοῦ ἐκ τῶν οὐρανῶν, ὃν ἤγειρεν ἐκ [τῶν] νεκρῶν, Ἰησοῦν <u>τὸν ῥυόμενον</u> ἡμᾶς ἐκ τῆς ὀργῆς τῆς ἐρχομένης.[20] | And to await his Son from heaven, whom he raised from [the] dead; Jesus, <u>the one who rescues</u> us from the coming wrath. |

On the basis of morphology alone, ῥυόμενον could be either middle or passive but the context indicates that it is middle, with Jesus as the agent

---

[16] See Wilhelm Kasch, "ῥύομαι" *TDNT* 6:1000–1002. Kasch asserts that in profane Greek, ῥύομαι may be used in reference to deliverance or salvation by the gods, observing a parallel use regarding the Lord as deliverer in the LXX (e.g., Isa 63:16). However, while both ῥύομαι and σῴζω may be used in the sense of save or rescue, he notes that σῴζω is the generic, more commonly used term, while ῥύομαι is more nuanced, noting in particular that only ῥύομαι is used in the sense of redemption.

[17] As noted in *ALGNT* s.v. "ῥύομαι." Similarly, Kasch, "ῥύομαι," *TDNT* 6:1002.

[18] Kasch, "ῥύομαι," *TDNT* 6:1003.

[19] See also Luke 1:74; 2 Thess 3:2; 2 Tim 4:17.

[20] ἐρχομένης (ἔρχομαι) is discussed separately below.

and ἡμᾶς, as the direct object.[21] This is consistent with the general use of the verb in the New Testament noted above, namely, that humans are the recipients of the deliverance.[22] The question that remains, then, is whether there is an observable middle nuance to this verb or whether it functions simply as an active. Traditionally, ῥύομαι has been considered "deponent" and treated as an active verb; accordingly, consideration of its middle function is typically absent in commentaries.[23] Being transitive, the function of rescuing someone appears typically active in English thought, but transitivity does not preclude middle function. Although many Greek middle verbs are intransitive, several are not.[24]

The subject affectedness of ῥυόμενον above may not immediately be apparent; however, Allan places it within his category of indirect reflexive middles, wherein the subject is considered to be a beneficiary or recipient.[25] The benefit to the subject (Jesus) in this case is more apparent if considered in the wider context of Christian Scripture, for it is consistent with the understanding that God desires a relationship with righteous people. Hence, there is a sense in which God (or Jesus) rescues them *for himself* as his own "treasured possession" (Deut 14:2, NIV).[26]

---

[21] This is affirmed by the fact that it is consistently translated in the active sense in English: "who delivers/rescues us" (ESV, NAB, NAS, NET, NIV, NKJV, NRSV).

[22] Thus, we find ἡμᾶς as object in Matt 6:13; 2 Cor 1:10; Col 1:13; and με as object in Rom 7:24; 2 Tim 3:11, 4:18. See also 2 Pet 2:7, 9.

[23] For example, Wanamaker comments on the lexical sense of ῥύομαι, noting that Paul more commonly uses "its synonym σῴζειν" (*Thessalonians* 88). Since σῴζειν is an active verb, this suggests (albeit perhaps unwittingly) a similar active function for ῥύομαι. Likewise, Fee, (*Thessalonians*, 50) comments on the subject of wrath and the designation of Jesus as God's son but includes no discussion on the function of ῥύομαι.

[24] As noted by Robertson, *Grammar*, 806. E.g., οὐ γὰρ νίπτονται τὰς χεῖρας (Matt 15:2). Here the action of washing is transferred to the hands even though the middle form indicates that self is the referent, so it speaks of washing their *own* hands (albeit in the negative). This verb is also used transitively in the active form, e.g., ἤρξατο νίπτειν τοὺς πόδας τῶν μαθητῶν (John 13:5). Therefore, both active and middle forms may be used transitively.

[25] Allan, *Polysemy*, 114.

[26] In similar vein: "Know that the LORD has set apart his faithful servant for himself; the LORD hears when I call to him" (Ps 4:3 NIV); "Return, faithless people," declares the

Likewise, Jesus prayed: "Father, I want those you have given me to be *with me* where I am and to see my glory" (John 17:24, NIV).

On the same basis as above, ῥύομαι would also be an indirect reflexive middle from the grammatical perspective, since the object of rescue is drawn *to* the subject, *for* the subject and *by* the subject (Jesus). Eberhard's medial concept is likewise apparent, as a dynamic, interactive situation is evoked: to rescue a person implies that s/he is being rescued *from* someone or something, in this case, ἐκ τῆς ὀργῆς τῆς ἐρχομένης.[27] The subject (as well as the object here) is situated within the process designated by the verb, participating in the rescue event. This is consistent with Neva Miller's observation (§2.2.2 above) that verbs of struggle and conflict (as implied by a rescue operation) are typically middle in form.[28] Hence ῥυόμενον displays all the characteristics of a middle voice verb in this particular context.

4.3 Ἔρχομαι (*Media Tantum* in Present Tense)

There are 632 instances of ἔρχομαι in the New Testament, where it commonly refers to coming or going in the sense of movement or travel.[29] For example, we see τῇ δὲ ἐπαύριον <u>ἐξελθόντες ἤλθομεν</u> εἰς Καισάρειαν: the next day we <u>departed</u> and <u>went</u> to Caesarea (Acts 21:8). However, BDAG also identifies uses in regard to making an

---

LORD, "for I am your husband. I will choose you ... and bring you to Zion" (Jer 3:14 NIV). This desire is also echoed in the NT, e.g., "but you are a chosen people, a royal priesthood, a holy nation, God's special possession" (1Pet 2:9, NIV). Similarly, "he has rescued (ἐρρύσατο) us from the dominion of darkness and brought us into the kingdom of the Son he loves (Col 1:13, NIV).

[27] This expression is consistent with the observation that Paul uses ἐκ of things and ἀπό of people in conjunction with ῥύεσθαι. See Frame, *Thessalonians*, 89.

[28] Eberhard comments that the middle voice does not do away with the subject and object, but merely with the opposition between them; they are both situated within the event designated by the verb. Email correspondence 4th February 2015.

[29] LSJ, s.v. "ἔρχομαι."

appearance, taking place, and the coming of events and circumstances, either natural or transcendent.[30] In such cases the subject is likely to be inanimate; hence, for example, καὶ κατέβη ἡ βροχὴ καὶ ἦλθον οἱ ποταμοί: the rain descended and the waters <u>came</u> (Matt 7:25).[31] Some uses of ἔρχομαι appear to be effectively passive, as when something is brought, for example, μήτι <u>ἔρχεται</u> ὁ λύχνος ἵνα ὑπὸ τὸν μόδιον τεῇ: is a lamp <u>brought</u> to be placed under a bushel? (Mark 4:21).[32]

Instances of ἔρχομαι in documentary papyri and ostraca attest its use with both animate and inanimate subjects. For instance, a first century ostracon letter (O.Berenike 2.198, *l* 9 [50–75 CE]) states that ὁ ἀδελφός σου <u>ἔρχεται</u> καὶ ἄμα σοῦ: "your brother <u>is coming</u> and together with you[.]" An inanimate subject is found in a personal letter in which Ptolemaios informs his sister that ὕπνος οὐ[κ]<u>ἔρχεταί</u> μοι διὰ νυκτός: "sleep does not <u>come</u> to me at night" (SB 1.4317, *l* 3–4 [ca. 200 CE]).

As seen in §4.2 above, ἔρχομαι appears in 1 Thess 1:10 as the present middle participle ἐρχομένης, referring to the '<u>coming</u> wrath' (τῆς ὀργῆς τῆς <u>ἐρχομένης</u>) from which the believers are being delivered. Allan classifies the prototypical usage of ἔρχομαι as 'body motion middle' in which an animate subject initiates a change in its own state.[33] However, he notes that some intransitive middle verbs such as κινέομαι (I move) can refer not only to animate subjects moving volitionally but also to inanimate subjects moving spontaneously.[34] Since Paul makes no

---

[30] BDAG, s.v. "ἔρχομαι." (4).

[31] Likewise: coming days (Luke 23:39); the harvest comes (John 4:25); rain coming (Heb 6:7).

[32] This impression may be due to the English translation however, and the original expression may be intended in a more metaphorical sense, i.e., does a light come (appear) to be placed under a bushel? This may well be the case in this instance which is preceded by the Parable of the Sower, speaking of the potential fruit or effectiveness of the word of God. Hence the emphasis may be intended to be on the process of light coming (hence middle function) in order to have an effect.

[33] Allan, *Polysemy*, 76.

[34] Allan comments that the body motion middle is closely related to the spontaneous middle in his network model, which accounts for the possibility of an inanimate subject

reference to an agent, he therefore represents the coming wrath in this instance as a spontaneous process. The grammatical description of the middle voice does not apply due to the impersonal nature of the subject; there is no indication that Paul is representing the wrath as acting on, for, or of itself.

The medial description of the middle voice may, however, be considered. It is apparent from the context in 1:10 and from the general use of ὀργή (wrath) in the New Testament that this phrase refers to the eschatological judgement on unbelievers.[35] Since the participle is functioning adjectivally, the "coming wrath" may be seen as an event, the cause of which is not explicitly mentioned. Eberhard's notion of mediality accommodates such a scenario, for the subject (wrath) and verb (coming) are inseparable in the event of the wrath coming upon someone. Active function (i.e., deponent use) is therefore excluded since the subject is not external to the process. This is consistent with the fact that ἔρχομαι is a *media tantum* verb in the present tense, supporting the notion that the verbal idea is inherently middle voiced.[36]

A similar instance of ἔρχομαι appears later in the epistle when Paul is writing at more length of eschatological matters:

---

with verbs that are also used as body motion middles with volitional (hence animate) subjects (*Polysemy*, 80).

[35] As noted, e.g., by Richard, *Thessalonians*, 52; Leon Morris, *The First and Second Epistles to the Thessalonians*, rev. ed. NICNT (Grand Rapids: Eerdmans, 1991), 50, 51; Wanamaker, *Thessalonians*, 88.

[36] Hence the two aorist uses of ἔρχομαι in this epistle, (2:18 and 3:6) focus on the movement of the subject from one place to another rather than an event generated by it. Διότι ἠθελήσαμεν ἐλθεῖν πρὸς ὑμᾶς: because we wanted to come to you (2:18) refers to travel, as does Ἄρτι δὲ ἐλθόντος Τιμοθέου πρὸς ἡμᾶς ἀφ' ὑμῶν: now that Timothy has come to us from you (3:6).

1 Thess 5:2 αὐτοὶ γὰρ ἀκριβῶς οἴδατε ὅτι ἡμέρα κυρίου ὡς κλέπτης ἐν νυκτὶ οὕτως ἔρχεται	For you yourselves well know that the day of the Lord <u>comes</u> as a thief in the night

In this verse the present form in Greek is commonly translated in the future sense in English (NAB, CEB, ESV, NET, NIV, NJB, NRSV, RSV).[37] Again there is an inanimate subject, "the day of the Lord."[38] Hence, the same considerations apply as to the discussion of "coming wrath" in 1:10 above.

When ἔρχομαι is used to refer to the coming of an event, there is a correlation with the sense of γίνομαι, insofar as it refers to something which comes into the existential realm of someone or something else.[39] The designated subject is not moving or travelling but being manifested and experienced. As in the previous instance in 1:10, the coming of the day of the Lord is seen as an event which comes upon people and can therefore be understood in the medial sense whereby subject and objects are both encompassed by the event. Without either party, there could be no event. In both these contexts, it is not appropriate to think of ἔρχομαι in the sense of a 'body motion' middle verb, although it could be seen as a spontaneous middle, as above. In both instances the grammatical concept of a subject acting on, for or by itself is difficult to apply because of the inanimate subject.[40]

---

[37] Likewise, for ἐφίσταται (come upon) in 1 Thess 5:3.

[38] For a succinct discussion of the phrase "[the] day of the Lord" in this context see Fee, *Thessalonians*, 187. Nevertheless, a particular interpretation of this expression is not essential for the present discussion.

[39] Likewise, γίνομαι is sometimes translated as come, as noted in §3.1.2.1 above.

[40] As for the aorist middle verbs in the previous chapter, spontaneous processes and conformity to grammatical descriptors are found to be incompatible.

4.4 ΔΥΝΑΜΑΙ (*MEDIA TANTUM*)

The middle-only verb δύναμαι refers to the capacity, power or ability to do something, with many nuanced applications.[41] It is very common throughout Christian Scripture. For example, God said to Abraham: ἀρίθμησον τοὺς ἀστέρας εἰ <u>δυνήσῃ</u> ἐξαριθμῆσαι αὐτούς: number the stars, if <u>you will be able</u> to count them (Gen 15:5, NETS). Similarly, a leper approaching Jesus said: ἐὰν θέλῃς <u>δύνασαί</u> με καθαρίσαι: if you will, <u>you can</u> make me clean (Mark 1:40). Interestingly, δύναμαι is frequently used in the negative with respect to humans but positively with respect to God (God is able, humans are unable).[42] It is widely used in other writings also. For example, Plutarch refers to οἱ δὲ μὴ <u>δυνάμενοι</u> ζῆν ἐν τῇ δημοκρατίᾳ: "those who are not <u>able</u> to live in a democracy[.]"[43] Likewise, in a private letter from 41 CE we see: ἀκολούθει δὲ Πτολλαρίωνι πᾶσαν ὥραν· τάχα <u>δύναταί</u> σε εὔλυτον ποι[ῆ]σαι: "Follow Ptollarion all the time; perhaps <u>he can</u> resolve your difficulty."[44] Throughout the New Testament epistles, δύναμαι also commonly appears as a present middle/passive participle in 1 Thess 2:6–7, as below.[45]

---

[41] BDAG, s.v. "δύναμαι." LSJ, s.v. "δύναμαι." BDAG identifies δύναμαι as deponent.

[42] Δύναμαι often relates to divine power, e.g., οὐδεὶς γὰρ δύναται ταῦτα τὰ σημεῖα ποιεῖν ἃ σὺ ποιεῖς, ἐὰν μὴ ᾖ ὁ θεὸς μετ' αὐτοῦ: no one can do these signs you do unless God is with him (John. 3:2) The examples are plentiful, inviting further exploration beyond the scope of this study.

[43] Plutarch, *Timoleon*, 5.2.1 (Perrin, LCL 98: 272–273).

[44] BGU 4.1079 *l* 10–14 (trans. White, *Light from Ancient Letters*, 130).

[45] The clause beginning with δυνάμενοι appears in v.7 of the NA[28] Greek text, but in v.6 of some English translations such as ESV, NAS, NIV, and RSV.

1 Thess 2:6–7 οὔτε ζητοῦντες ἐξ ἀνθρώπων δόξαν οὔτε ἀφ' ὑμῶν οὔτε ἀπ' ἄλλων, ⁷<u>δυνάμενοι</u> ἐν βάρει εἶναι ὡς Χριστοῦ ἀπόστολοι ἀλλὰ ἐγενήθημεν νήπιοι ἐν μέσῳ ὑμῶν

Nor did we seek human praise, neither from you nor from others. As apostles of Christ, <u>we could have</u> imposed our weight; but instead, we were gentle in your midst.

The sense expressed here is that the apostles could have claimed respect and honor from their hearers because of their position as apostles but instead they chose to be humble and gentle.[46] That is, they chose not to actualize the potential that was theirs. Paul had the *potential* to act with authority but did not act on this capacity. Accordingly, in relation to δύναμαι, Grundmann comments that the power or capacity is subservient to the *will* of the subject who possesses it.[47] Further, since their authority is given by the risen Christ,[48] one could discern a passive sense to δύναμαι in this instance, for they were *enabled* by dint of their position as apostles.

A second instance of δύναμαι appears in 1 Thess 3:9, where Paul asks a rhetorical question to indicate essentially that he is *not* able to render adequate thanks to God, again reflecting an internal state but not a change of state. Whereas above, they had the power but not the will to exercise it, in this instance they had the will but not the power to execute the action:

---

[46] In this, they were following the example and command of Christ himself (see Phil 2:3-8; Mark 9:35). Accordingly, Paul speaks of his converts becoming imitators of himself as one who imitates Christ (1 Thess 1:6; also 1 Cor 11:1).

[47] Walter Grundmann, "δύναμαι," *TDNT* 2:291.

[48] Grundmann, "δύναμαι," *TDNT* 2:310

1 Thess 3:9 τίνα γὰρ εὐχαριστίαν <u>δυνάμεθα</u> τῷ θεῷ ἀνταποδοῦναι περὶ ὑμῶν ἐπὶ πάσῃ τῇ χαρᾷ ᾗ χαίρομεν δι' ὑμᾶς ἔμπροσθεν τοῦ θεοῦ ἡμῶν	For what thanksgiving <u>are we able</u> to render to God for you, for all the joy we experience before our God because of you.

In both the above contexts, it is not reasonable to say that the subject is affected by the action of the verb, as the verb refers to an existing state, not a change of state. Allan himself declines to classify "the intriguing middle δύναμαι" stating: "It is not easy to understand what exactly is the contribution of the middle inflection[.]"[49] The grammatical descriptors likewise do not apply, as the subject is not actually performing a task; the reference is to potentiality, not actuality. Similarly, the medial notion applies to a subject acting within a process, but the verb itself in both these cases does not indicate action, but potential action. In this regard, it is perhaps similar to the future middles of otherwise active verbs which indicate a possibility in the mind of the speaker.

Scholars who comment on these verses typically do so in terms of the wider meaning in the context of thanksgiving or the relationship of Paul with the Thessalonians. The particulars of the verbal function of δύναμαι are not engaged, even by those commentators who normally discuss lexical and grammatical matters.[50] This verb invites and warrants further investigation in its own right.

4.5 ὉΜΕΙΡΟΜΑΙ (*MEDIA TANTUM*)

The present participle ὁμειρόμενοι in 1 Thess 2:8 is the only occurrence of ὁμείρομαι in the New Testament. This verb refers to desiring,

---

[49] Allan, *Polysemy*, 122n214. Allan discusses the possible semantic development of δύναμαι but ultimately treats it as an anomaly and declines to classify it.

[50] See, e.g., Frame, *Thessalonians*, 134. Frame discusses features of almost every other word in 3:9 but does not mention δύναμαι.

longing or yearning for someone or something.⁵¹ This is exemplified by its sole attestation in the LXX: οἳ ὁμείρονται τοῦ θανάτου καὶ οὐ τυγχάνουσιν: those who long for death and do not find it (Job 3:21, NETS).⁵² MM refers to it as a "rare verb"⁵³ while the ancient lexicon of Hesychius (fifth c. CE) notes its equivalence to the more common verb ἐπιθυμέω, which refers to desire or longing.⁵⁴ Hans Wolfgang Heidland also asserts that ὁμείρομαι is very rare but rather than equating it with ἐπιθυμεῖν, he states that "it is better taken med. as 'to feel oneself drawn to something', with strong intensification of the feeling."⁵⁵ Heidland therefore perceives the choice of this particular verb in 1 Thess 2:8 to be significant, stating that it "brings out the relation of the apostle to the community" which he describes as a "warm inward affection" that impels Paul to serve not only out of obedience to his commission, but also "in heartfelt love" for the believing community.⁵⁶

1 Thess 2:8 Οὕτως ὁμειρόμενοι ὑμῶν εὐδοκοῦμεν μεταδοῦναι ὑμῖν οὐ μόνον τὸ εὐαγγέλιον τοῦ θεοῦ ἀλλὰ καὶ τὰς ἑαυτῶν ψυχάς, διότι ἀγαπητοὶ ἡμῖν ἐγενήθητε.	Yearning for you in this manner, we were pleased to share with you not only the gospel of God, but even our very selves, because you had become so dear to us.

---

⁵¹ BDAG, s.v. "ὁμείρομαι." LSJ, s.v. "ὁμείρομαι."

⁵² Thayer notes that ὁμείρεσθαι is unknown among Greek authors and concludes that it is equivalent to ἱμείρεσθαι, GELNT, s.v. "ὁμείρομαι." This is confirmed by a TLG search which returns no attestations prior to the NT, except Job 3:21.

⁵³ MM, s.v. "ὁμείρομαι."

⁵⁴ Thus, Hesychius cites ἐπιθυμοῦσιν as an alternative for ὁμείρονται. K. Latte, *Hesychii Alexandrini lexicon*, vol. 1, Copenhagen: Munksgaard, 1953, s.v. "ομείρονται" (688).

⁵⁵ Hans Wolfgang Heidland, "ὁμείρομαι," *TDNT* 5:176. There is no indication of what is meant by "med." but middle or medial would certainly fit the comparison with the active ἐπιθυμεῖν and the meaning described.

⁵⁶ Heidland, "ὁμείρομαι," *TDNT* 5:176.

The participle here describes the feelings of the apostles towards the Thessalonians. Accordingly, this verb could be placed within Allan's mental process category, wherein the subject's response to a stimulus evokes an emotional or cognitive state, thus affecting the subject. This is similar to the medial notion in this instance, for ὁμειρόμενοι speaks of the apostles acting (mentally) within the process of yearning. They experience this feeling of longing as they think of the Thessalonians within the context of their relationship. They are active in the event of longing but are also affected by it, rather like Eberhard's illustration of understanding happening to the subject who is nevertheless actively engaged in the process.[57] They are not controlling the process from the outside (active), nor are they being controlled by another agent (passive) but are within the process (medial).

The context makes plain that ὁμειρόμενοι is not passive. While English translation requires an active verb, the middle nuance is in accord with, and enhances, the highly relational tone of this section of the epistle. Hence the yearning expressed is a response to (the recollection of) the heartfelt relationship which had been established between the apostles and the Thessalonian Christians. In a grammatical sense, since this longing arises from within the subjects it may be seen to conform to the dynamic middle subset of the indirect reflexive category. Therefore, ὁμειρόμενοι exhibits the three attributes of the middle voice under consideration.

4.6 ἘΡΓΑΖΟΜΑΙ (*MEDIA TANTUM*)

Having the various senses of labor, be active, expend effort, work for a livelihood, or accomplish something,[58] ἐργάζομαι occurs only in the middle form and takes a sigmatic aorist.[59] It first appears in the Bible in

---

[57] Eberhard, *Middle Voice*, 3, 108, 136.
[58] BDAG, s.v. "ἐργάζομαι"; LSJ, s.v. "ἐργάζομαι." LSJ provides an abundant list of various applications in ancient literature.
[59] Hence e.g., τὸ δὲ λοιπὸν εἰργάσαντο εἰς θεούς: but the rest they fashioned into

Genesis, in reference to working or cultivating the ground: ἄνθρωπος οὐκ ἦν ἐργάζεσθαι τὴν γῆν: there was not a human to till the earth (Gen 2:5, NETS) and appears throughout the LXX.⁶⁰. It is similarly used in a petition to Apollonios, Strategos of Arsinoite Nome, in which Petsiris reports an assault he suffered: ἐμοῦ ὄντος ἐργασζομένου ἐν ... ἀμπελωνος [ἀμπελωνι]: "while I was at work in the vineyard" (P.Mich. 5. 229, *l* 8–11, [48 CE]).⁶¹

In the New Testament ἐργάζομαι is used both transitively and intransitively. For example, καλὸν ἔργον ἠργάσατο ἐν ἐμοί: she did a good deed for me (Mark 14:6) and ἓξ ἡμέραι εἰσὶν ἐν αἷς δεῖ ἐργάζεσθαι: there are six days in which one must work (Luke 13:14), respectively. Forms of ἐργάζομαι appear in 1 Thess 2:9 and 4:11 as shown below. In both instances it is evident from the context that the verb refers to working in order to earn a living. Paul gave of himself in preaching the gospel (2:8) while working hard to support himself so as not to burden the flock (2:9).⁶² Having taught them also to be self-supporting, he reminds them of this principle in 4:11.

1 Thess 2:9 Μνημονεύετε γάρ, ἀδελφοί, τὸν κόπον ἡμῶν καὶ τὸν μόχθον· νυκτὸς καὶ ἡμέρας ἐργαζόμενοι πρὸς τὸ μὴ ἐπιβαρῆσαί τινα ὑμῶν ἐκηρύξαμεν εἰς ὑμᾶς τὸ εὐαγγέλιον τοῦ θεοῦ.	For you remember brothers, our toil and hardship; we preached the gospel of God to you while working night and day so as not to burden any of you.

---

gods (Isa 44:15, NETS).

⁶⁰ Hence, e.g., ἐμίσησας πάντας τοὺς ἐργαζομένους τὴν ἀνομίαν: you hate all those who work iniquity (Ps 5:6).

⁶¹ Corrected to ἐργαζομένου ἐν ... ἀμπελωνι. Similarly, ὕπαγε σήμερον ἐργάζου ἐν τῷ ἀμπελῶνι: Go work in my vineyard today (Matt. 21:28).

⁶² As noted by Boring, *Thessalonians*, 88.

1 Thess 4:11 καὶ φιλοτιμεῖσθαι ἡσυχάζειν καὶ πράσσειν τὰ ἴδια καὶ ἐργάζεσθαι ταῖς [ἰδίαις] χερσὶν ὑμῶν, καθὼς ὑμῖν παρηγγείλαμεν

and to aspire to live quietly and attend to your own affairs and to work with your [own] hands, just as we directed you.

While the notion of 'working' here is a generic reference to the activity of earning a living, the context indicates that Paul's attention is not on the work itself or the outcome of it but on the *efforts* of the workers, That is, the middle verb forms focus the reader's attention on the subjects being personally invested in the activity. Therefore, the criteria for the middle voice in grammatical terms are met, with the subjects acting *for* themselves (indirect reflexive) and since they are also acting *from within* their own resources, the dynamic middle function also applies.

Allan classifies ἐργάζομαι as an indirect reflexive middle, indicating that the subject is a recipient or beneficiary of the action, and such is the case in the verses above.[63] The use of ἐργάζομαι in these contexts is also consistent with the medial descriptor of the middle voice, for the subjects are functioning within a process of which they are part, both acting and being affected as they adapt to the process as required. Hence, the middle function may be discerned by examining all three descriptors, each one supplying a nuanced perspective.

4.7 ΠΑΡΑΜΥΘΕΟΜΑΙ (*MEDIA TANTUM*)

According to the lexica, this verb has a range of meanings in general usage, consonant with its compound structure: παρα-μυθέομαι (beside-speak). Thus, it can have the sense of exhort, encourage, console,

---

[63] Allan, *Polysemy*, 114. While the benefit may be seen in this context which refers to working for wages, the notion of beneficiary does not explain the use of this verb in regard to expending effort.

reassure, assuage, relieve, palliate, and explain.[64] The only occurrence in the LXX is in reference to Judas Maccabeus exhorting his people to trust in God, παραμυθούμενος αὐτοὺς ἐκ τοῦ νόμου καὶ τῶν προφητῶν: <u>encouraging</u> them from the law and the prophets (2 Macc 15:9). In his *Letter of Consolation to Apollonius*, Plutarch employs παραμυθέομαι in introducing words of poets and philosophers regarding suffering. For example, we see: ὁ δὲ <u>παραμυθούμενος</u> τὴν Δανάην δυσπαθοῦσαν Δίκτυς φησί: "And Dictys, who is <u>trying to console</u> Danaë in her excessive grief, says[.]"[65]

In the New Testament, παραμυθέομαι is used only four times: at John 11:19, 31 and 1 Thess 2:12; 5:14, with the focus being on the sense of drawing alongside to console or comfort by words. The attestations in John refer to those who came to visit Mary and Martha after the death of Lazarus, that <u>they might comfort</u> [<u>παραμυθήσωνται</u>] them concerning [their] brother (John 11:19). In 1 Thessalonians, Paul reminds the church of his behavior when he was with them (2:10). He was sincere and candid (2:4–6); not demanding, but gentle, (2:7); not a burden to them (2:9), and like a father to each one of them (2:11) as he urged and *encouraged* them to live according to their calling (2:12, below).[66] The verb is again attested in the latter paraenetic section of the letter, appealing to the community to minister to one another as they follow his teaching and example and *encourage* (or *comfort*) the faint hearted (5:14).

---

[64] LSJ, s.v. "παραμυθέομαι." BDAG, s.v. "παραμυθέομαι." GE, s.v. "παραμυθέομαι."

[65] Plutarch, *Cons. Apoll.*, 106.A.2 (Babbitt, LCL 222: 128–129). Malherbe notes that the consolation expressed philosophically and by the prototypical letter of consolation was not only an expression of grief but an appeal to reason, urging that suffering be placed in perspective (*Thessalonians*, 152, 153, 279).

[66] Boring comments that Paul's instruction of the converts reflects the fatherly responsibility for "socialization and moral instruction" (*Thessalonians*, 90). Thus, Paul is re-educating them for their new life in God's community.

1 Thess 2:12 παρακαλοῦντες ὑμᾶς καὶ <u>παραμυθούμενοι</u> καὶ μαρτυρόμενοι εἰς τὸ περιπατεῖν ὑμᾶς ἀξίως τοῦ θεοῦ τοῦ καλοῦντος ὑμᾶς εἰς τὴν ἑαυτοῦ βασιλείαν καὶ δόξαν.	Urging you and <u>encouraging</u> and charging you to live in a manner that is worthy of God who calls you into the kingdom and glory of himself.
1 Thess 5:14 παρακαλοῦμεν δὲ ὑμᾶς, ἀδελφοί, νουθετεῖτε τοὺς ἀτάκτους, <u>παραμυθεῖσθε</u> τοὺς ὀλιγοψύχους, ἀντέχεσθε τῶν ἀσθενῶν, μακροθυμεῖτε πρὸς πάντας.	We urge you, brothers, to admonish the idle, <u>encourage</u> the faint-hearted, support the weak and be patient towards everyone.

These two uses of παραμυθέομαι illustrate that the sense of this verb is not solely that of comforting but of speaking wisdom to encourage and help the hearers to deal appropriately with a particular situation. It requires a personal investment toward the other. In 2:12, by speaking words of encouragement, the apostles are not acting in their own interest, but are acting *from* within their own resources, from their heart, drawing others into their sphere of thought. Hence, the grammatical sense of Cooper's dynamic middle is apparent.[67] The verb παραμυθέομαι also fits Allan's speech act classification, wherein the subject is affected by the emotional or mental involvement associated with the type of speech.[68] The medial notion is evident in that the subjects (apostles) as well as the recipients of encouragement (the Thessalonians) are engaged relationally. The subjects need to adapt to the process by perceiving the specific need and providing the appropriate word

---

[67] Cooper, *Attic Greek Prose Syntax*, 589. See §2.1.6.10 above.
[68] Allan does not list the compound but does list μυθέομαι as an example of a speech act middle verb.

in response.[69] Hence the subjects are internal to the process. In 5:14, the same functions of the middle voice may be identified, as the Thessalonians are encouraged to minister to one another as they learn to live in Christian community.

4.8 Μαρτυρομαι (Μαρτυρεω)

The active and middle forms of μαρτυρέω are listed as separate entries in the lexica, suggesting that they have a different semantic sense, not only different voices.[70] The active is used in reference to bearing witness or giving evidence[71] as several examples from the papyri indicate. In the LXX the active μαρτυρέω appears thirteen times. For example, Laban and Jacob make a covenant with God as witness, then after setting up a monument, Laban states: ὁ βουνὸς οὗτος μαρτυρεῖ ἀνὰ μέσον ἐμοῦ καὶ σοῦ σήμερον: this mound bears witnesses between me and you today (Gen 31:46, NETS). Active forms appear seventy-seven times in the New Testament, notably in the Johannine corpus. For example, αὐτὰ τὰ ἔργα ἃ ποιῶ μαρτυρεῖ περὶ ἐμοῦ: these works which I do testify about me (John 5:36). Paul also employs the active. For instance, he testifies (μαρτυρῶ, 2 Cor 8:3) to the generosity of the Macedonian Christians when writing to the Corinthians about their contribution to the collection (2 Cor 8:1–15). In all these cases, witness is borne to someone or something other than the subjects themselves.

---

[69] The variation between παρακαλέω and the middle παραμυθέομαι is also discussed in §4.8 below. The notion of "action in response" often appears to correlate with the medial notion, this being suggested as an attribute of the middle voice by Dr. Stephen Curkpatrick of The University of Divinity, Melbourne, in personal communication.

[70] As seen in §2.1.6.2 above, this is not uncommon when the middle nuance is applied to the active verb.

[71] LSJ, s.v. "μαρτυρέω."; BDAG, s.v. "μαρτυρέω." MM notes that μαρτυρέω is used in reference to: witnesses to legal documents (P.Oxy. 1.105 / 13 [117–137 CE]); witnessing a crime (P.Amh. 2.66 / 35 [124 CE]); and testifying to character or behavior (P.Oxy. 6.930 / 16 [100–300 CE]). MM, s.v. "μαρτυρέω."

The middle form is far less frequent in Scripture, appearing only once in the LXX: "Against you we call to witness [μαρτυρόμεθα] heaven and earth and our God and the Lord of our fathers" (Jdt 7:28, NETS).[72] This sense of the middle form is also seen in a petition to a police magistrate (third c. CE). In this letter the complainant states that the offender "railed furiously at some of my daughter's sons, whom I called to witness" [ἐμαρτυράμην].[73] In addition to this use of calling upon someone or something to act as a witness, the lexica also note: "to affirm something with solemnity," or "to urge something as a matter of great importance[.]"[74] Thus Josephus writes of Sacchius (Zedekiah), that "the prophet Jeremiah came to him and solemnly protested [ἐμαρτύρατο], bidding him leave off his various impieties and lawless acts[.]"[75]

It is this sense of a solemn declaration or protest that is evident in the five NT uses of the middle form. Thus, in Paul's heartfelt farewell address to the elders of the church at Ephesus, he states: I declare to you [μαρτύρομαι ὑμῖν] that I am innocent of the blood of you all (Acts 20:26).[76] When brought before King Agrippa and being given permission to speak for himself Paul stands and testifies [μαρτυρόμενος] regarding his divine calling (Acts 26:22). In his concluding remarks to the Galatians, Paul writes: I testify [μαρτύρομαι] that any man submitting to circumcision is obligated to keep the whole Law (Gal 5:3).[77] Similarly, in Eph 4:17, μαρτύρομαι is used in reference to testifying in the

---

[72] Compounds of the middle appear more frequently, especially διαμαρτύρομαι, discussed in §3.1.5 above.

[73] SB 6.9421 / 23 (201–300 CE).

[74] BDAG, s.v. "μαρτύρομαι"; LSJ, s.v. "μαρτύρομαι." Milligan (Thessalonians, 25–26) notes that the original meaning of "summon to witness" was extended to "asseverate" or "solemnly charge."

[75] Josephus, A.J., 10.104 (Marcus, LCL 326: 214-215).

[76] "Declare" is given by NRSV, NIV. Some translations have "testify" instead (e.g., ESV, NKJ, RSV).

[77] The sense of μαρτύρομαι here is that of a solemn assurance or warning; hence "I warn you" (CJB); "I give my assurance" (NJB); "I declare" (NIV).

Lord that Christians must no longer live as the Gentiles do. In each case a sense of intensity and importance is portrayed. As opposed to the active, the subject is not testifying about another person or speaking as a witness to an event, but affirming something regarding himself or from within himself, hence the subject is the focus of the verb.

In 1 Thess 2:12 seen below, the participle μαρτυρόμενοι is coordinated with two other participles (παρακαλοῦντες, παραμυθούμενοι). These all describe the fatherly manner (2:11) in which Paul and his associates dealt with the Thessalonians. Although παρακαλέω and παραμυθέομαι have the similar sense of exhorting or encouraging, Boring contends that "the first term [παρακαλοῦντες] includes the others" in this verse.[78] This suggests that the active παρακαλοῦντες refers to the exhortation overall, while the two middle participles speak of the manner by which the subjects are personally invested in the action. Accordingly, the sense of 'charging' is posited for μαρτυρόμενοι below.[79]

1 Thess 2:12 παρακαλοῦντες ὑμᾶς καὶ παραμυθούμενοι καὶ μαρτυρόμενοι εἰς τὸ περιπατεῖν ὑμᾶς ἀξίως τοῦ θεοῦ τοῦ καλοῦντος ὑμᾶς εἰς τὴν ἑαυτοῦ βασιλείαν καὶ δόξαν.	Urging you and encouraging and charging you to live in a manner which is worthy of God who calls you into the kingdom and glory of himself.

The intensity and personal insistence evident in μαρτυρόμενοι, is sometimes translated "imploring" (NAS), "appealing" (NJB), or "pleading" (NRSV). These imply subject-affectedness in the sense of Allan's speech act middle category, implying an effect on the subject as

---

[78] Boring, *Thessalonians*, 90. Accordingly, Frame maintains that "παρακαλεῖν is general, παραμυθεῖσθαι and μαρτυρεῖσθαι specific," translating the expression as "we were urging both by encouragement and by solemn protest" (*Thessalonians*, 104). He does not, however, refer to middle voice.

[79] English translations of 1 Thess 2:12 render this verb variously, e.g., 'charged' (ESV, NKJV, RSV); 'pleading/pleaded' (CEB, NRSV); 'appealing' (NJB); 'urging' (NIV); 'insisting' (NET, NAB). All of these indicate an intensity of speech.

experiencer. Although Allan does not list this particular verb as an example, he refers to similar verbs of emotional speech or commanding, such as δέομαι (beg), ὑπισχνέομαι (promise), and ἐντέλλομαι (command)[80] These reflect nuances apparent in μαρτυρόμενοι in the above context.

From the grammatical perspective, the dynamic middle is evident, in that by emphatically making this charge, Paul is personally invested, acting *from* his own convictions. He is also to some extent acting *for* himself in the sense that he has a personal interest in their growth as Christians. It is somewhat difficult to discern if the medial sense is applicable here. Nevertheless, insofar as Paul is not simply reporting something he has seen (active sense) but is personally engaged in the process of imploring or charging them, he is internal to the process of the verb, as for παραμυθούμενοι discussed above. As he deals with each one of them like a father with his children (2:11), he is not simply admonishing or instructing them; he is not accomplishing something outside himself but is investing into his relationship with them. He is encouraging (παραμυθούμενοι) as needed and imploring (μαρτυρόμενοι) as needed. The medial sense is consistent with this understanding.

4.9 ἘΝΕΡΓΕΟΜΑΙ (ΕΝΕΡΓΕΩ)

The active form ἐνεργέω is used intransitively in reference to capabilities being put into operation; it may refer to being at work, being active, operating, or being effective.[81] In the LXX there are six active forms and one passive, referring to various subjects and types of working. It is used of the woman who toils (ἐνεργεῖ) for the benefit of her husband (Prov 31:12) and the Levites who enter the tabernacle to minister (ἐνεργεῖν) there (Num 8:24).[82] In a second century papyrus letter a woman writes

---

[80] Allan, *Polysemy*, 105–107.
[81] BDAG, s.v. "ἐνεργέω." LSJ, s.v. "ἐνεργέω."
[82] English terms are from NETS.

to her servant: καλῶς δὲ ποιήσεις καὶ περὶ τὰ λοιπὰ ἐνεργήσασα: "please <u>devote</u> your <u>energies</u> to the rest."[83] When Herod thought that Jesus must be John the Baptist returned from death, he stated: διὰ τοῦτο αἱ δυνάμεις ἐνεργοῦσιν ἐν αὐτῷ: this is why the miraculous powers <u>are at work</u> in him (Matt 14:2). Active forms are also used transitively in reference to producing something by working or bringing something to effect, for example, ἐνεργῶν δυνάμεις ἐν ὑμῖν: <u>working</u> miracles among you (Gal 3:5).[84]

No distinct sense is given for the middle of ἐνεργέω by the lexica. There are no instances of the middle form in the LXX but there are in literary sources. Hence, in discussing the value of skilled farmers compared to those who till the soil without knowledge, Philo states: τὰ δὲ τῶν γεωργῶν τὰ μετ' ἐπιστήμης ἐνεργούμενα πάντ' ἐστὶν ἐξ ἀνάγκης ὠφέλιμα: "but the scientific <u>labors</u> of the tillers of the soil are all of necessity beneficial."[85] The reference of the middle verb to the subject's personal involvement is illustrated by the use of ἐνεργέομαι by Marcus Aurelius in reference to "the blame of <u>inaction</u>" (ἡ αἰτία τοῦ μὴ ἐνεργεῖσθαι) [86] and to "<u>discharging</u> a function" (τι ... ἐνεργεῖσθαι).[87]

In the New Testament, there are nine middle and ten active forms of ἐνεργέω, BDAG noting that the middle is always used with an impersonal subject.[88] Hence, for example, Paul states ὥστε ὁ θάνατος ἐν ἡμῖν ἐνεργεῖται, ἡ δὲ ζωὴ ἐν ὑμῖν: so then, death <u>is at work</u> in us, but life in you (2 Cor. 4:12). Other instances appear in Rom 7:5 (sinful

---

[83] P.Giss. 78, *l* 3–4 (Bagnall and Cribiore, *Women's Letters*, 161).

[84] The implied subject here being God (the one who lavishly supplies the Spirit).

[85] Philo, *Det.* 104.6 (Colson and Whitaker, LCL 227:272–273).

[86] Marcus Aurelius, *Meditations*, 8.47.1.6. (Haines, LCL 58:220–221).

[87] Marcus Aurelius, *Meditations*, 3.7.1.11. (Haines, LCL 58:56–57).

[88] BDAG, s.v. "ἐνεργέω." Similarly, Wallace, (*Exegetical Syntax* 416n19) contends that the difference between the active and the middle is syntactical rather than lexical. While they both mean "I work" the active form is used with both personal and impersonal subjects, but the middle is used only with impersonal subjects in the NT. This is contested by Richard, however, who argues that the "alleged" impersonal subjects of finite verbs in the NT may be considered personified powers in the scheme of Hellenistic cosmology (*Thessalonians*, 114).

passions working), 2 Cor 1:6 (your comfort working), Gal 5:6 (faith working), Eph 3:20 (power working), Col. 1:29 (energy working), 2 Thess 2:7 (lawlessness at work), Jas 5:16 (prayer working), and 1 Thess 2:13, as follows:

1 Thess 2:13 Καὶ διὰ τοῦτο καὶ ἡμεῖς εὐχαριστοῦμεν τῷ θεῷ ἀδιαλείπτως, ὅτι παραλαβόντες λόγον ἀκοῆς παρ' ἡμῶν τοῦ θεοῦ ἐδέξασθε οὐ λόγον ἀνθρώπων ἀλλὰ καθώς ἐστιν ἀληθῶς λόγον θεοῦ, ὃς καὶ <u>ἐνεργεῖται</u> ἐν ὑμῖν τοῖς πιστεύουσιν.	For this reason we thank God without ceasing because, when you received the word of God which you heard from us, you accepted it not as a human word, but as it truly is, the word of God, which indeed <u>is operating</u> in you who believe.[89]

There are two sources of ambiguity in this verse. The verb ἐνεργεῖται, could be middle or passive based on morphology, and that to which the verb refers (ὅς), could be "God" or "the word of God." Thus, there are three possible readings, depicted in Table 4.1.[90]

Table 4.1 Possible Readings of 1 Thessalonians 2:13

Subject	Voice	Meaning
Word of God	middle	word of God is operating
Word of God	Passive	word of God is activated, made to operate
God	middle	God is working

The translation above reads ἐνεργεῖται as a middle verb and the word (of God) as its grammatical subject.[91] This appears to be the most

---

[89] See §3.1.1 above for comment on ἐδέξασθε in contrast to παραλαβόντες in this verse.

[90] God plus passive, (i.e., God is being activated or made to work) does not present as a viable option.

[91] Richard notes that most scholars consider 'word' rather than 'God' to be the antecedent because that is the dominant theme of the verse and it is consistent with the fact (noted above) that it is the active, rather than middle form that is used with a personal

natural reading of the Greek expression and accords with several major translations. Thus, ὃς καὶ ἐνεργεῖται is rendered: "which is at work" (ESV, NET, RSV, CJB); "which is indeed at work" (NIV); "which is also at work" (NRSV); "which is now at work" (NAB); "which effectively works" (NKJV); "which also performs its work" (NAS).[92] This reading conforms to the context, which clearly focuses on the word and its attributes, juxtaposing the "human word" which Paul mentions earlier in the verse with the "word of God" which is an *effective* word. Malherbe likewise reads ἐνεργεῖται as a middle verb, commenting that Paul is here stressing "the preached word as the means through which God acts."[93] Similarly, Best states that "the word possesses this power because it is the word coming from God who himself makes it effective."[94]

Interpreting the word to be a means in this manner readily illustrates the middle function, for it implies that the word of God is *working* (subject is agent) but that it is *made* to work by God (subject is affected). This conforms to internal *diathesis*, wherein the subject "effects while being affected[.]"[95] The focus is on the medial event with the subject within it. That is, the word of God *is* operating; it is being effective as Paul has previously remarked (1:3) and this is because it was taken to heart (ἐδέξασθε), not simply heard (παραλαβόντες λόγον ἀκοῆς). Therefore, the word, God and the believers are all involved in this process of bringing the word to effect. This has potential theological significance, for it speaks of the mutual interaction of God and believer in the process of salvation.[96]

---

subject (*Thessalonians*, 113–14). Weima likewise comments that Paul consistently uses the active form when God is the subject (1 Cor 12:6; Gal 2:8; 3:5; Phil 2:13) (*Thessalonians*, 164).

[92] In English, the active translations suggest a middle rather than passive reading.

[93] Malherbe, *Thessalonians*, 167.

[94] Best argues persuasively for this reading with ἐνεργεῖται as a middle verb, seeing in 2:13 an emphasis on the word at work and in 2:14 the evidence of its effect (*Thessalonians*, 112).

[95] Benveniste, "Active and Middle," 150.

[96] A corresponding notion in Phil 2:12, 13 is discussed by Philippe Eberhard, "The

In the grammatical scheme, the inanimate subject here makes it difficult to apply any sense of the subject acting *for* itself. However, a dynamic middle sense may be applied if it is accepted that the word possesses power, as, for example, "a power that is working among you believers" (NJB). To this extent it is acting from within its own resources. In Allan's scheme, the subject-affectedness could be accommodated as a spontaneous middle, since the focus of the concise expression is on what is happening to the subject, with no agent implied; it becomes effective, it comes into operation, like a flower blooming.[97]

Alternatively, ἐνεργεῖται could be read as a passive if God is the implied agent. Hence Milligan reads ὃς καὶ ἐνεργεῖται as "which also is set in operation," indicating that this brings out the Divine agency that is at work. He also states that God's word is an energizing power, but one which receives its power from God.[98] This then essentially corresponds to the first position above. Thus, Richard notes that some see little difference in viewing "word of God" as the subject of the middle verb, or God as the "virtual subject" of the passive (Milligan's position).[99]

Richard chooses to adopt a third position, namely, that God is the subject of a middle verb, which he understands to have a nuance of intensity or personal interest. He therefore translates the relative clause as: "who indeed is also at work in you who believe."[100] While this may sound appealing, it does not conform to the usual pattern of voice usage. Active forms of ἐνεργέω are used elsewhere when God is the subject, for example: ὁ Θεὸς ἐστιν ὁ ἐνεργῶν ἐν ὑμιν: for it is God who is

---

Mediality of our Condition: A Christian Interpretation," *JAAR* 67 (1999): 418–24. In similar vein, Malherbe remarks that "Paul thinks of the gospel as God's power, but only for those who believe (Rom 1:16; 1 Cor 1:18)" (*Thessalonians*, 167).

[97] Although there may be an ultimate cause, this is not expressed.

[98] Milligan correlates this reading with similar assertions relating to the power of God's word in Heb 4:12; Jas 1:21; 1 Pet 1:23 and Isa 55:11 (*Thessalonians*, 28).

[99] Richard, *Thessalonians*, 114–15.

[100] Richard, *Thessalonians*, 113. This would be an unusual combination, for when God is the subject, the verb is generally active, e.g., θεὸς ὁ ἐνεργῶν τὰ πάντα ἐν πᾶσιν: God working all things in all (1 Cor 12:6).

working in you (Phil 2:13). Therefore, for reasons also given above, the first reading is to be preferred. That is, word of God is the grammatical subject of ἐνεργεῖται, and this has middle function according to the dynamic (grammatical), spontaneous (Allan), and medial descriptors.

Although factors relating to passive or middle voice and choice of subject are discussed by commentaries, further consideration is lacking as to the specific attributes of the middle verb, or the way it differs in nuance from the active. In this regard, it is relevant to note that the active is used to speak of unilateral activity by a particular subject (including God) to produce a definite result.[101] For example, it is used of God working miracles (ἐνεργῶν δυνάμεις) among the Galatians (Gal 3:5), and the Spirit activating (ἐνεργεῖ) the spiritual gifts (1 Cor 12:11). In 1 Thess 2:13 above, we argue here that the middle voice represents a more generic, interactive process. It speaks of the word of God (the main topic of this verse) working within the believer.

4.10 ΔΕΟΜΑΙ (*MEDIA TANTUM*)

The middle-only verb δέομαι carries the sense of "asking for something pleadingly" whether of humans or of God.[102] Although the aorist has the -θη- form, the NT usage is consistent with that observed by MM in the papyri, that is, "there is no passive sense attached to any of the forms."[103] Δέομαι appears ninety-eight times in the LXX, for example, δέομαι κύριε προχείρισαι δυνάμενον ἄλλον ὃν ἀποστελεῖς: "<u>please</u> Lord, appoint another capable person whom you will send" (Exod 4:13, NETS). It is very common in Koine Greek, being frequently used in petitions to ruling sovereigns.[104] It appears thus in a letter to Zenon (assistant to Apollonius, the chief finance minister) from a widow

---

[101] Philippians 2:13 also conforms to this pattern as God works to produce an outcome in the believers.

[102] BDAG, s.v. "δέομαι," where it is identified as a "passive deponent." In LSJ, (s.v. "δέω"), δέομαι is also listed as a deponent, having the sense of being in need or lack or expressing such by pleading.

[103] MM, s.v. "δέομαι."

[104] MM, s.v. "δέομαι."

regarding the ill-treatment of her son in public service. Seeking an investigation into the matter, she writes: ἀξιῶ οὖν σε ἅμα δὲ καὶ <u>δέομαι</u>: "I request therefore, and I <u>beg</u> you" (P.Col. 3.6 *l* 12 [257 BC]).

In the New Testament δέομαι is used in similar manner, for example, πεσὼν ἐπὶ πρόσωπον <u>ἐδεήθη</u> αὐτοῦ λέγων· κύριε, ἐὰν θέλῃς δύνασαί με καθαρίσαι: Falling prostrate <u>he begged</u>: Lord, if you will, you can make me clean (Luke 5:12). Likewise, before King Agrippa Paul stated: διὸ <u>δέομαι</u> μακροθύμως ἀκοῦσαί μου: therefore, I <u>plead</u> that you listen to me patiently (Acts 26:3). It appears six times in Paul's letters (Rom 1:10, 2 Cor 5:20, 8:4, 10:2; Gal 4:12 and 1 Thess 3:10.) In 1 Thessalonians, Paul employs δέομαι in reference to his earnest prayer that he might see the church there again:

1 Thess 3:10 νυκτὸς καὶ ἡμέρας ὑπερεκπερισσοῦ <u>δεόμενοι</u> εἰς τὸ ἰδεῖν ὑμῶν τὸ πρόσωπον καὶ καταρτίσαι τὰ ὑστερήματα τῆς πίστεως ὑμῶν	Night and day <u>praying</u> most earnestly to see you face to face and to rectify what is lacking in your faith.

The participle δεόμενοι in this verse is clearly middle (not passive) in function. This is consistently reflected in English translations, for instance, "as we pray most earnestly" (ESV, NIV, NRSV) or "praying exceedingly" (NKJV). Nor would it be at all sensible to read it in the passive! Together with the double compound superlative ὑπερεκπερισσοῦ, the use of δέομαι rather than the more common term προσεύχομαι brings out the sense of pleading or begging.

The subjects are clearly acting out of personal interest by begging for something (albeit something honorable) *for* themselves. This fits the indirect reflexive middle of the grammatical descriptor. Allan recognizes the subject-affectedness in δέομαι but assigns it to his speech act category, in which the subject is both agent and experiencer.[105] On

---

[105] Allan notes that this verb differs from most speech act middle verbs which have a sigmatic aorist, since its aorist is only formed with -θη- (ἐδεήθην) (*Polysemy*, 105n179).

Eberhard's model, the subjects may be seen to be intermediaries, for as they think about the Thessalonian Christians with gratitude (3:9) they bring their petition to God for his attention. Accordingly, the subjects are *internal* to the process which, as Eberhard explains, means that "the subject though the seat or locus of the action—think of a dream—is inside the process going on."[106] Therefore, all three descriptors apply. It is clear from its lexical sense and its usage that δέομαι is intrinsically middle-voiced, thus accounting for its middle-only status in the New Testament.

4.11 ΑΠΕΧΟΜΑΙ (ΑΠΕΧΩ)

The active form, ἀπέχω may be used in the sense of being distant from, keeping away from, or receiving in full what is due.[107] In this latter sense it often occurs in receipts among the papyri, as G. Adolf Deissmann has demonstrated.[108] This sheds light accordingly on some uses in the New Testament. For example, in Matt 6:2 Jesus speaks of hypocrites who publicly announce their giving of alms and thus ἀπέχουσιν τὸν μισθὸν αὐτῶν (have their reward).[109] However, it is the sense of keeping away or being distant that is pertinent to the current investigation. This sense is attested in the LXX, for example, καθ' ὅσον ἀπέχουσιν ἀνατολαὶ ἀπὸ δυσμῶν ἐμάκρυνεν ἀφ' ἡμῶν τὰς ἀνομίας ἡμῶν: as far as east is from west, he has removed from us our acts of lawlessness. (Ps 102:12, NETS). The active is also used in reference to being distant in the NT, for instance, Ἔτι δὲ αὐτοῦ μακρὰν ἀπέχοντος εἶδεν αὐτὸν ὁ πατὴρ

---

[106] Eberhard, *Middle Voice*, 23.

[107] LSJ, s.v. "ἀπέχω." BDAG, s.v. "ἀπέχω."

[108] G. Adolf Deissmann, Bible Studies: Contributions Chiefly from Papyri and Inscriptions to the History of the Language, the Literature, and the Religion of Hellenistic Judaism and Primitive Christianity, trans. Alexander Grieve (Edinburgh: T&T Clark, 1901), 229. Hence, e.g., καὶ ἀπέχω τὴν συνκεχωρημένην τιμὴν πᾶσαν ἐκ πλήρους (I have received the whole agreed price in full), BGU 2.584 l 5–6 (44 BCE).

[109] Similarly, ἀπέχω δὲ πάντα καὶ περισσεύω· (I am paid in full and have more than enough, Phil 4:18).

αὐτοῦ: but while he was still far off his father saw him (Luke 15:20, NRSV).

The middle form, accordingly, refers to keeping *oneself* away, hence "avoid contact," "abstain," "refrain from," are listed as applications.[110] Thus, for example, Josephus refers to Daniel who "had resolved to live austerely and abstain [ἀπέχεσθαι] from the dishes that came from the king's table[.]"[111] Similarly, in the LXX Job is said to be righteous and devout, ἀπεχόμενος ἀπὸ παντὸς πονηροῦ πράγματος (staying away from every evil matter, Job 1:1). The middle form of ἀπέχω appears only six times in the New Testament[112] always in this sense of abstinence. Thus, in reference to the Gentiles who turn to God, James advises that the apostles should write to them to abstain [ἀπέχεσθαι] from the pollutions of idols (Acts 15:20 RSV).

In the paraenetic section of 1 Thessalonians, Paul exhorts the church to continue to make progress in living to please God (4:1–2) and to abstain from what is displeasing. Hence, he employs the present middle infinitive of ἀπέχομαι in 4:3 to address the matter of sexual morality (4:3–7), while in the final remarks of his letter, he employs the imperative in 5:22. Hence:

1 Thess 4:3 Τοῦτο γάρ ἐστιν θέλημα τοῦ θεοῦ, ὁ ἁγιασμὸς ὑμῶν, ἀπέχεσθαι ὑμᾶς ἀπὸ τῆς πορνείας,	For this is the will of God, your sanctification: that you keep yourself from sexual immorality;[113]
1 Thess 5:22 ἀπὸ παντὸς εἴδους πονηροῦ ἀπέχεσθε.	Abstain from every form of evil.[114]

---

[110] BDAG, s.v. "ἀπέχω."

[111] Josephus, *A.J.*, 10.190.2 (Marcus, LCL 326:262–263).

[112] Acts 15:20, 29; 1 Thess 4:3, 5:22; 1 Tim 4:3; 1 Pet 2:11.

[113] Wallace translates 1 Thess 4:3 as: "this is the will of God, your sanctification, namely, that you abstain from fornication" and identifies ἀπέχεσθαι as an infinitive in apposition ((*Exegetical Syntax*, 606). English translations of ἀπέχεσθαι include: "abstain" (ESV, NAS, NKJV, NRSV); "refrain" (NAB); "avoid" (NIV); "keep away" (NJB).

[114] For ἀπέχεσθε in 1 Thess 5:22, translations include "abstain" (ESV, NAS, NKJ,

In both these verses, this abstinence or keeping oneself away, is the required, volitional response in the face of temptation; it is the opposite of engaging in or embracing such activity. Since the subjects act on themselves (by restraint) it could therefore be classified as a direct reflexive in the grammatical sense. Allan recognizes the subject-affectedness implied by the middle form and classifies ἀπέχομαι: "keep oneself back from," as a body motion middle.[115] In both instances above, the middle forms of ἀπέχω may also be perceived in terms of mediality; the subjects are internal to the process of the verb as if in a dialogue with the forces of evil. As in a game of sport, there is potential unlawful interaction with another player, so Paul tells the Thessalonians that they are to avoid such engagement. Faced with a situation of temptation, they are to respond with restraint, keeping their distance from immoral actions and ungodly attitudes (e.g., 5:13, 14), thus becoming sanctified.

4.12 Κταομαι (*media tantum*)

A *media tantum* verb, κτάομαι has the general sense of acquiring, procuring for oneself (which immediately suggests middle function), possessing, or having in hand.[116] It is rare in Scripture, with only one instance in the LXX, viz., κτᾶσθαι ἐν ἀργυρίῳ πτωχούς: to acquire the poor with silver (Amos 8:6, NETS). Apart from its use in 1 Thessalonians, there is only one other occurrence in the NT: ὅτι τὴν δωρεὰν τοῦ θεοῦ ἐνόμισας διὰ χρημάτων κτᾶσθαι: because you thought you could obtain God's gift with money (Acts 8:20, NRSV). However, the use of this verb in relation to acquiring something is widely attested in other writings. A papyrus recording a decree dealing with protection of tax-paying cultivators of crown land states that officials are not on any

---

NRSV); "refrain" (NAB); "reject" (NIV): "shun" (NJB).

[115] Allan, *Polysemy*, 77. In the verses above, however, the reference is not simply to keeping away bodily.

[116] LSJ, s.v. "κτάομαι"; BDAG, s.v. "κτάομαι." The sense of procuring *for oneself* naturally indicates middle function.

pretext to acquire (κτᾶσθαι) implements required by the workers (P.Tebt. 1.5 / 242 [118 BC]). Josephus writes of one who seeks "to acquire [κτᾶσθαι] authority over others."[117] Diodorus Siculus likewise employs the middle infinitive in writing that the Greeks have learned "to gain [κτᾶσθαι] lands" by means of valor.[118]

While the above use in reference to acquiring something appears straightforward, in 1 Thessalonians the verb κτάομαι is used in conjunction with the noun σκεῦος. Generically, this may simply refer to an "object" or "thing." However, BDAG notes that it may also be employed to refer to persons functioning as vessels or instruments.[119] Accordingly, God says in regard to Paul: σκεῦος ἐκλογῆς ἐστίν μοι: he is my chosen instrument (Acts 9:15) and Paul refers to those destined for destruction as σκεύη ὀργῆς: vessels of wrath (Rom 9:22). Further, σκεῦος may also refer to a wife, L&N asserting that"[i]n ancient Jewish literature a wife was euphemistically called a 'vessel' in contexts relating to sexual relations."[120] This gives rise to the contextually appropriate interpretation of the use of κτάομαι in 1 Thess 4:4 below:

1 Thess 4:4 εἰδέναι ἕκαστον	Each of you knowing how
ὑμῶν τὸ ἑαυτοῦ σκεῦος	to possess your own wife
κτᾶσθαι ἐν ἁγιασμῷ καὶ τιμῇ	in holiness and honor

This verse follows Paul's admonition to avoid πορνεία in 4:3 (discussed above). Hence, his message is that honorable marriage, not lustful passion like the ungodly Gentiles (4:5), is the ethical standard the Thessalonians should observe. While this interpretation of σκεῦος as wife is adopted by NAB and RSV, some other English translations read κτᾶσθαι in the sense of control and σκεῦος as body, for example:

---

[117] Josephus, A.J., 17.32.4 (Marcus and Wikgren, LCL 410:180–181).
[118] Diodorus Siculus, Bibl. Hist., 11.5.5.7 (Oldfather, LCL 375:136–137).
[119] BDAG, s.v. "σκεῦος."
[120] L&N, s.v. "σκεῦος." (10.55).

"each one of you to know how to control his body" (NJB).[121] However, only in the perfect tenses does κτάομαι have this sense of control according to LSJ, and in 1 Thess 4:4 we have the present middle infinitive, not the perfect.[122] There is considerable discussion of these alternatives in commentary on this verse, with cogent arguments offered for both positions.[123]

In the former sense, κτᾶσθαι may be read in its usual meaning of acquiring or taking possession and the self-affectedness of this verb is clearly apparent.[124] This correlates with Allan's classification of κτάομαι as an indirect reflexive middle, the subject being the beneficiary of the action.[125] It could likewise be viewed as an indirect reflexive in the grammatical sense, as noted by Robertson, who assigns the sense of providing for yourself, or procure.[126] Thus "possess your own wife in holiness and honor" (as translated above) refers to the marriage relationship as a whole. Such an interpretation aligns with Eberhard's medial notion also, for then the subject is acting within a process that encompasses him.

The alternative reading also allows for a middle voice understanding of κτᾶσθαι. Since the subject acts on himself, this conforms to the

---

[121] Similarly, ESV, NIV, NRSV.

[122] LSJ, s.v. "κτάομαι." No examples from the Koine period are given for the sense of control.

[123] See Fee, *Thessalonians*, 145–50. Fee discusses various views and contends that no one interpretation is entirely satisfactory in this context. See also Ben Witherington III, *1 and 2 Thessalonians: A Socio-Rhetorical Commentary* (Grand Rapids: Eerdmans, 2006), 113–16. Witherington discusses both positions and lists proponents of each, concluding that Paul is advocating exclusive and respectful monogamy here, with κτᾶσθαι taken in the usual sense of *acquire* and σκεῦος as *wife*. Richard argues for the alternative, taking σκεῦος κτᾶσθαι to refer to mastery of one's body, in accord with "attested Greek idiom" (*Thessalonians*, 198–99).

[124] Paul expresses a similar thought, more explicitly, in 1 Cor 7:2, διὰ δὲ τὰς πορνείας ἕκαστος τὴν ἑαυτοῦ γυναῖκα ἐχέτω καὶ ἑκάστη τὸν ἴδιον ἄνδρα ἐχέτω: but because of sexual immorality, each man should have his own wife and each woman her own husband.

[125] Allan, *Polysemy*, 114.

[126] Robertson, *Grammar*, 810.

grammatical notion of the middle voice as a direct reflexive. Likewise, the subject is affected by the action, and the verb (read as "control oneself") fits Allan's direct reflexive category in the sense of acting (mentally) on oneself. It may also be perceived as a medial function for the subject is acting within the process described by the verb, an observation which is axiomatic for a direct reflexive function.

Although there is some uncertainty as to the intended meaning of σκεῦος κτᾶσθαι in this passage (perhaps even intended ambiguity by Paul), the verb clearly conforms to some middle function, whether the indirect middle in the first interpretation or the direct reflexive in the second. While attempts to translate the thought into English generate two rather different scenarios, the essential exhortation regarding appropriate sexual expression within marriage is clearly understood. Both interpretations generate an effect on the subject, and both can be read in a medial sense, although the latter perhaps more overtly so.

4.13 ΦΙΛΟΤΙΜΕΟΜΑΙ (*MEDIA TANTUM*)

In the broad sense, φιλοτιμέομαι refers to loving or seeking honor, hence to be ambitious or jealous, and in a less competitive sense, to endeavor earnestly or aspire.[127] These uses are widely attested in literary works of the first century; hence, Josephus writes: ἀλλήλοις ἁμιλλώμενοι καὶ ὑπερβάλλειν <u>φιλοτιμούμενοι</u> τὰς θυσίας, ἃς ἕκαστος ἐπιφέροι: "vying with and <u>striving</u> to surpass one another in their respective offerings[.]"[128] The non-competitive sense is also seen, for example, Νεάρχου τε τοῦ Κρητὸς καὶ Δημητρίου τοῦ υἱοῦ <u>φιλοτιμουμένων</u> τὸν Εὐμενῆ σῶσαι: "Demetrius his son and Nearchus the Cretan <u>being eager</u> to save the life of Eumenes[.]"[129]

In the LXX, φιλοτιμέομαι does not appear at all. In the New Testament it occurs only three times, all of these being in Paul's epistles. Thus, he states: "I make it my ambition [φιλοτιμούμενον] to proclaim

---

[127] LSJ, s.v. "φιλοτιμέομαι"; BDAG, s.v. "φιλοτιμέομαι".
[128] Josephus, *A.J.*, 3.207.2 (Thackeray. LCL 242: 414–415).
[129] Plutarch, *Eumenes*, 18.6.2 (Perrin, LCL 100:134–135).

the good news" (Rom 15:20, NRSV). Similarly, he asserts: "So whether we are at home or away <u>we make it our aim</u> [φιλοτιμούμεθα] to please him" (2 Cor 5:9, NRSV). In Paul's discussion of ethical conduct, his exhortation to continue to increase in brotherly love (4:9,10), is followed by another, using the middle infinitive φιλοτιμεῖσθαι as below:[130]

1 Thess 4:11 καὶ <u>φιλοτιμεῖσθαι</u>	and <u>to aspire</u> to live qui-
ἡσυχάζειν καὶ πράσσειν τὰ ἴδια	etly, attend to your own
καὶ ἐργάζεσθαι ταῖς [ἰδίαις]	affairs and to work with
χερσὶν ὑμῶν, καθὼς ὑμῖν	your [own] hands, just as
παρηγγείλαμεν	we directed you

A middle nuance may be detected in φιλοτιμεῖσθαι as it speaks of an attitude of mind. It therefore corresponds with Allan's mental activity middle category, along with verbs such as λογίζομαι (consider) or μέδομαι (plan, contrive). Allan maintains that such verbs function as both agents and experiencers because the activity affects their mental state.[131] In regard to mediality, the subject is internal to the process of the verb in the sense that their aspirations will interact with, determine, and be determined by their daily existence. It is not a mental function only but is outworked in various circumstances in appropriate ways. In such aspiration, the subjects need to draw on their own resources to bring other conceptions into their sphere (dynamic middle). Hence, φιλοτιμέομαι exhibits middle properties in the grammatical sense also.

---

[130] Fee notes that the infinitive φιλοτιμεῖσθαι functions as an imperative in 4:11, following from the exhortation (παρακαλοῦμεν) in 4:10 (*Thessalonians*, 161). Boring contends that "[t]he self-sufficiency for which Paul calls is ecclesial, not individual" (*Thessalonians*, 153). Thus, the exhortation is to the whole church, that they should mutually support one another. This correlates with the mention above of Paul educating them as to how to live in Christian community.

[131] Allan, *Polysemy*, 101.

4.14 ΚΟΙΜΑΟΜΑΙ (ΚΟΙΜΑΩ)

The aorist form of κοιμάομαι has been discussed in §3.1.8 above. Similar references to sleeping or lying down are attested for the present forms. For example, καὶ ἐν τοῖς μνήμασιν καὶ ἐν τοῖς σπηλαίοις κοιμῶνται: "they lie down to sleep in the tombs and in the caves" (Isa 65:4, Brenton); and τούτοις ὁ μὲν Πολύβιός φησιν ἔτι κοιμωμένοις ἐπιπεσεῖν τοὺς Ῥωμαίους: "These men, according to Polybius, were still asleep when the Romans fell upon them[.]"[132] Present forms of κοιμάομαι are likewise attested in the New Testament in the sense of natural sleep. Hence, we see: εἴπατε ὅτι οἱ μαθηταὶ αὐτοῦ νυκτὸς ἐλθόντες ἔκλεψαν αὐτὸν ἡμῶν κοιμωμένων: say that his disciples came during the night and stole him while we were sleeping (Matt 28:13). Paul uses the present tense in 1 Cor 11:30 euphemistically to refer to death: διὰ τοῦτο ἐν ὑμῖν πολλοὶ ἀσθενεῖς καὶ ἄρρωστοι καὶ κοιμῶνται ἱκανοί: because of this many of you are weak and sick and a good number are sleeping [have died]. The present middle participle is used in 1 Thessalonians similarly:

1 Thess 4:13 Οὐ θέλομεν δὲ ὑμᾶς ἀγνοεῖν, ἀδελφοί, περὶ τῶν κοιμωμένων, ἵνα μὴ λυπῆσθε καθὼς καὶ οἱ λοιποὶ οἱ μὴ ἔχοντες ἐλπίδα.	We do not want you to be ignorant, brothers, concerning those who are sleeping, so that you may not grieve like the remainder [of humankind] who have no hope.[133]

---

[132] Plutarch, *Aem.*, 16.2.1 (Perrin. LCL 98:394–395).

[133] The mid/pass subjunctive λυπῆσθε is parsed as passive by the database, yet English translations consistently render it in the active, indicating that it has been read as middle (agentive subject). Hence, we see: "do not grieve" (NIV, NJB); "may not grieve" (ESV, NAB, NAS, NRSV); "lest you sorrow" (NKJV); "you won't mourn" (CEB). However, it could sensibly be read as a passive also (be grieved).

In this section of the letter, Paul is addressing the matter of those who are sleeping (those who have died), assuring the Thessalonians that they can have hope because of the resurrection of Christ (4:14). Thus, Milligan comments that the present middle participle (κοιμωμένων) is suggestive of the temporary nature of the state of death for the Christian, with the thought of future awakening inferred.[134]

There are viable textual variants at 4:13, with the Western bilingual manuscripts (D, F, G) and the Majority Text having the perfect middle participle κεκοιμημένων in place of the present κοιμωμένων.[135] Nevertheless both forms refer to the current state of the dead, that is, they are "asleep"; this notion being rendered variously by English translations. Examples include "who have fallen asleep" (NAB, NJB, NKJV); "who are asleep" (NAS); and "who sleep in death" (NIV). The NRSV translation "who have died" does not reflect a temporary state of itself but since the context does speak of resurrection, this translation may have been adopted for clarity.

As discussed in relation to the aorist forms of κοιμάω (§3.1.6 above) the grammatical sense does not readily apply. However, the use of the present middle form here again refers to death as a temporary state, using the metaphor of sleep, so that a change of state occurs; hence subject-affectedness applies. As noted previously, Allan classifies κοιμάομαι as a mental process middle because of the (involuntary) change in mental state which occurs when one sleeps. Even though Paul is referring to the sleep of death here, the image is of one who is asleep. Further, when one is sleeping, a person is encompassed by the event, so the subject is internal to the process of the verb hence Eberhard's notion

---

[134] Milligan, *Thessalonians*, 55. This is affirmed in the next verse: εἰ γὰρ πιστεύομεν ὅτι Ἰησοῦς ἀπέθανεν καὶ ἀνέστη, οὕτως καὶ ὁ θεὸς τοὺς κοιμηθέντας διὰ τοῦ Ἰησοῦ ἄξει σὺν αὐτῷ (for if we believe that Jesus died and rose, in like manner God, through Jesus will bring together with him those who have fallen asleep). Death and sleep are also used synonymously in 1 Cor 15:20.

[135] As noted by Fee, *Thessalonians*, 164. The NA[28] text follows ℵ, A, B, 0278, 33 and others having the present participle.

of mediality also applies. The verb is therefore functioning in the middle voice, as the form suggests.

4.15 Ἐφίσταμαι (ΕΦΙΣΤΗΜΙ)

The basic sense of ἐφίστημι or ἐπίστημι (Ionic form) is setting or placing upon or over (ἐπι + ἰστημι) applied both literally and figuratively.[136] Thus, ἐφίστημι may refer to setting authorities in place over others. Hence, we read in reference to the Hebrews in Egypt: καὶ ἐπέστησεν αὐτοῖς ἐπιστάτας τῶν ἔργων: and he set task-masters over them (Exod 1:11).[137] When used intransitively, ἐφίστημι may refer to standing over in a more literal sense of orientation, for example, ἡ νεφέλη σου ἐφέστηκεν ἐπ' αὐτῶν: "your cloud has stood over them" (Num 14:14 NETS). In recounting the deliverance of the Hebrews from Egypt through Moses, Josephus writes that in response to the prayer of Amram, ὁ δὲ θεὸς ἐλεήσας αὐτὸν καὶ ... ἐφίσταται κατὰ τοὺς ὕπνους αὐτῷ: "God had mercy on him and ... appeared to him in his sleep."[138] Similarly, when telling of David's victory over Goliath, he states: δραμὼν δ' ἐφίσταται τῷ πολεμίῳ κειμένῳ: "Then, running forward, David stood over his prostrate foe[.]"[139]

---

[136] LSJ, s.v. "ἐφίστημι." In the NT, the Ionic ἐπίστημι predominates (17 times) cf. ἐφίστημι (4 times).

[137] Similarly, Num 1:50; Ruth 2:6. In papyri from the Ptolemaic period, the cognate noun ὁ ἐπιστάτης, is found in reference to the "Epistates," or "the head of a village or the village police" as defined by White, *Light from Ancient Letters*, 225. For example, in a petition (48 CE) to the Strategos of Arsinoite nome, Papontos speaks of investigating a robbery at his home in Talei, σὺν τῷ τῆς κώμης Ταλεὶ ἐπιστάτῃ: "together with the epistates of the village of Talei[.]" P.Mich 5.230 *ll* 11, 12.

[138] Josephus, *A.J.*, 2.212.2 (Thackeray, LCL 242:254–257).

[139] Josephus, *A.J.*, 6.190.1 (Thackeray and Marcus, LCL 490:420–421). The LXX reference to the same incident uses the active: καὶ ἔδραμεν Δαυιδ καὶ ἐπέστη ἐπ' αὐτόν (1 Sam. 17:51). This illustrates the fact that the choice of the middle is not always mandatory; it depends on the emphasis which the author wishes to convey. It is nevertheless evident that the subject is internal to the event.

BDAG notes that only intransitive uses such as these occur in the NT, so ἐφίστημι may refer to standing over, standing by, or coming upon. Moreover, these meanings are expressed by the 2nd aorist, perfect or pluperfect active, as well as the middle.[140] The active form is widely used in Luke-Acts, for example, καὶ <u>ἐπιστὰς</u> ἐπάνω αὐτῆς ἐπετίμησεν τῷ πυρετῷ καὶ ἀφῆκεν αὐτήν: and <u>standing over</u> her he rebuked the fever and it left her (Luke 4:39).[141] The sense is that someone or something comes into the presence or awareness of another. The only middle/passive form of ἐφίστημι in the New Testament appears in 1 Thess 5. Continuing the eschatological theme introduced in chapter 4, Paul speaks of the day of the Lord coming like a thief in the night (5:2), taking the unwary who live in darkness (5:4) by surprise.[142] Thus in 5:3 he states:

1 Thess 5:3 ὅταν λέγωσιν· εἰρήνη καὶ ἀσφάλεια, τότε αἰφνίδιος αὐτοῖς <u>ἐφίσταται</u> ὄλεθρος ὥσπερ ἡ ὠδὶν τῇ ἐν γαστρὶ ἐχούσῃ, καὶ οὐ μὴ ἐκφύγωσιν[143]	When they are saying "peace and security" then sudden destruction will <u>come upon</u> them, just like birth pangs on a pregnant woman, and they surely will not escape.

---

[140] BDAG, s.v. "ἐφίστημι."

[141] Apart from Luke-Acts, ἐφίστημι occurs in 1 Thess 5:3; 2 Tim 4:2 and 2 Tim 4:6 only.

[142] The sudden occurrence of the day of the Lord as judgment on God's opponents but deliverance for his people, may be traced back through apocalyptic tradition to the OT prophets, e.g., Isa 13:6–8, as noted by Wanamaker, *Thessalonians*, 179–80.

[143] Wanamaker suggests that this statement may be proverbial, stemming from an "apocalyptic milieu" noting that ἀσφάλεια, αἰφνίδιος and ἐφίσταται are all *hapax legomena* in Paul (*Thessalonians*, 180). Since ἐφίσταμαι is used in 2 Tim 4:2, 6, Wanamaker must be referring to the undisputed letters of Paul. Accordingly, Paul uses ἔρχομαι rather than ἐφίσταμαι in the similar expressions in 5:2 and 1:10 in reference to judgement coming upon people. Although both ἐφίσταται and ἔρχεται are middle verbs, Wanamaker does not address the matter of voice. Richard sees the echo of the cry of false prophets who proclaim peace and security in times of imminent judgement (*Thessalonians*, 251).

As a present verb, ἐφίσταται refers here to a surprise destruction which is yet to come and hence is commonly rendered in the future tense in English, as above.[144] According to form, ἐφίσταται could be passive, indicating that the destruction is placed or brought upon them, presumably by God. However, no agent is intimated, and English translations consistently render it in an active sense. This indicates that it is interpreted as a middle, not passive, verb. Hence, the destruction comes upon them; it comes into their experience.[145] As David stood over (ἐφίσταται) Goliath as the victor in the example above, so here also, the destruction stands over, or comes upon, the victim, this being expressed by a middle form.

We may now examine whether ἐφίσταται in the context of 1 Thess 5:3 aligns with the middle voice descriptors under consideration. The grammatical perspective is not readily applicable in this instance, since there is no volitional action on, for or from within the inanimate subject (ὄλεθρος: destruction). In Allan's scheme, if this subject is considered to experience a change in state by virtue of its coming upon people, then ἐφίσταται could be seen to fit his spontaneous process category.[146] It is difficult to decide if Eberhard's medial interpretation is applicable here. Although the inanimate subject is active in producing an effect and the emphasis is on the event, there is no indication of the subject being affected *within the process*. Therefore, it is better perceived as a sudden spontaneous process.

---

[144] Hence CEB, ESV, CJB, NIV, NRSV, although KJV, NAB, NET, NJB, retain the present. For a similar expression using the middle voice, see: "a sore trial shall come [ἐφίσταται] upon the mighty" (Wis 6:8, Brenton).

[145] Hence, e.g., "sudden destruction will come upon them" (NRSV); "sudden disaster comes upon them" (NAS).

[146] Only passive or spontaneous middle verbs may have an inanimate subject in Allan's scheme (*Polysemy*, 118).

4.16 ΠΡΟΪΣΤΑΜΑΙ (ΠΡΟΪΣΤΗΜΙ)

When used transitively, προΐστημι has the sense of "put before," or "set over," while it is used intransitively in the sense of "preside," "rule" or "govern" in the papyri records.[147] BDAG notes this sense of presiding over, but also lists: "to have an interest in, show concern for, care for, give aid."[148] The LXX employs προΐστημι in reference to those placed in charge, for example, καὶ ἐκάλεσεν τὸ παιδάριον αὐτοῦ τὸν προεστηκότα τοῦ οἴκου: "and he called the servant who had charge of the house" (2 Sam 13:17, Brenton).[149] Similar applications are found in the New Testament. For example, in Rom 12:8 Paul exhorts those who lead to do so with diligence (ὁ προϊστάμενος ἐν σπουδῇ). Similar uses are found in Epictetus, such as "as was fitting for Him who watches over and protects [προϊστάμενον] us like a father[.]"[150] Both middle and active forms are used in 1 Tim 3:4, 5, 12 in reference to the need for church leaders to be able to manage their own households well.[151]

As Paul draws towards the conclusion of this letter to the Thessalonians, he gives various exhortations. Urging them to respect their leaders in 5:12–13, he employs a present middle participle of προΐστημι appearing in 1 Thess 5:12 as below:

---

[147] MM, s.v. "προΐστημι," citing instances where it is applied to people (e.g., by use of the participle as a substantive) such as an estate agent (P.Ryl. 2.132 [32 CE]), a chief of a village (P.Ryl 2.122 [127 CE]) and a guardian (P.Tebt. 2.326 [ca. 266 CE]).

[148] BDAG, s.v. "προΐστημι."

[149] Similarly, 1 Macc 5:19; Amos 6:10.

[150] Epictetus, *Diatr.*, 3.24.4.1 (Oldfather, LCL 218: 184–185). Horrocks comments on the similarity of the language of Epictetus (ca. 60–140 CE) to that of the NT (*Greek*, 147).

[151] The only other occurrence in the NT is the middle infinitive προΐστασθαι (Tit 3:8, 14), commonly translated "to devote themselves" (ESV, NAB, NIV NRSV) i.e., to devote themselves to good works (καλῶν ἔργων προΐστασθαι). The sense of setting as a priority is apparent.

1 Thess 5:12 Ἐρωτῶμεν δὲ ὑμᾶς, ἀδελφοί, εἰδέναι τοὺς κοπιῶντας ἐν ὑμῖν καὶ <u>προϊσταμένους</u> ὑμῶν ἐν κυρίῳ καὶ νουθετοῦντας ὑμᾶς	Now we ask you, brothers and sisters, to acknowledge those who labor among you and who <u>have charge over</u> you in the Lord and admonish you

A passive reading of προϊσταμένους ὑμῶν in the sense of "who are placed over you" is not viable since no external agent is in view. Rather, the context of mutual respect and care suggests a middle reading, as given above.[152] This refers to the function of the leaders rather than their position. In support of this reading, Milligan notes that the general use of προϊστάμενος in the New Testament does not reflect the technical term found in the papyri where it refers to an official role such as superintendent.[153] Therefore, he considers that in the verse above it refers to the informal level of spiritual oversight given by elders.[154] This is consistent with the syntax, since it is placed between two other terms referring to functions, viz., κοπιῶντας (laboring) and νουθετοῦντας (admonishing). Consequently, as observed by Fee, it would appear to refer to a ministry of responsibility and guidance, not a position of status or directive leadership.[155] When read in the middle voice in this context,

---

[152] As noted by Conrad above (§2.1.7.1), a middle/passive form should be read as middle unless the context clearly indicates it is passive.

[153] Thus, e.g., superintendents of guilds are mentioned in BGU 4.1028 (100–200 CE); MM, s.v. "προϊστημι."

[154] Milligan, *Thessalonians*, 71–72. So also, BDAG, s.v. "προϊστημι" (2).

[155] For a discussion of translation possibilities, see Fee, *Thessalonians*, 204–6. Fee affirms function rather than status. He contends that the role of caring or being responsible for the converts is better sustained by the syntax since this participle is placed in sequence with two others that refer to the activities of the leaders. Accordingly, Boring contends that Paul is avoiding the impression of directive leadership, stating that there were no official roles in Thessalonica (no distinction between "clergy" and "laity") (*Thessalonians*, 191–92). He notes that Paul avoids foregrounding the "most official sounding word" (προϊσταμένους) and adds the qualification of being over them "in the Lord" (ἐν κυρίῳ), that is, as part of the Spirit-led community.

therefore, προϊσταμένους ὑμῶν ἐν κυρίῳ evokes the sense of protective oversight of the community.

The middle nuance may therefore be seen in terms of Eberhard's notion of mediality, when "having charge over" is understood in this sense of caring for and guiding. These processes imply an engagement between those who preside and their charges, encompassing the subject in an interactive manner with other participants.[156] From the grammatical perspective, an understanding of προϊσταμένους in terms of caring, responsible leadership would indicate that the leaders would be mobilizing and applying their personal resources. Allan does not list this verb, but the closest category with an agentive subject would appear to be his indirect reflexive middle, being an *"unemphatic* way of expressing that the subject is the beneficiary."[157] The benefit to the subject in such an instance could be the quality of fellowship achieved.

4.17 Ἡγέομαι (*media tantum*)

The middle-only verb ἡγέομαι is used in two senses. It can refer to leading or guiding, for example, ἐκ σοῦ γὰρ ἐξελεύσεται ἡγούμενος: for from you [Bethlehem] shall come a leader, (Matt 2:6). Alternatively, it can have the sense of "think," "regard," "consider."[158] This latter sense occurs in the NT, for example, Πᾶσαν χαρὰν ἡγήσασθε ἀδελφοί μου, ὅταν πειρασμοῖς περιπέσητε ποικίλοις: consider it all joy, my brothers, when you encounter various trials (Jas 1:2). It is used similarly in the LXX, for example, ἥγηται δὲ τὴν θάλασσαν ὥσπερ ἐξάλειπτρον: "and he regards the sea as a pot of ointment" (Job 41:23, Brenton). Philo also uses this sense of ἡγέομαι in reference to God,

---

[156] This verb could likewise fit Miller's notion of reciprocity which she applies to activities that are dependent on more than one participant. This does not imply symmetrical action between subject and object, but, like a medial process, an involvement of the subject in an interactive situation. See §2.2.2 above.

[157] Allan, *Polysemy*, 114.

[158] BDAG, s.v. "ἡγέομαι." LSJ adds the senses of *believe, hold* and *deem*. LSJ, s.v. "ἡγέομαι."

thus: δεῖ γὰρ ἡγεῖσθαι καὶ ἄποιον αὐτόν: "but we must <u>deem</u> that he belongs to no type...."[159]

It is always in this latter sense that ἡγέομαι occurs in the epistles of Paul, for example, ἀλλὰ τῇ ταπεινοφροσύνῃ ἀλλήλους <u>ἡγούμενοι</u> ὑπερέχοντας ἑαυτῶν: but in humility <u>consider</u> others as surpassing yourself (Phil. 2:3).[160] In 1 Thess 5:12 discussed in the previous section, the Thessalonians were asked to "acknowledge" (NIV) or "respect" (NAB) those presiding over them. In the subsequent verse (1 Thess 5:13) Paul continues his exhortation regarding the attitude the believers ought to have toward their leaders, again expressing a concern for proper order, mutuality, and peace:

| 1 Thess 5:13 καὶ <u>ἡγεῖσθαι</u> αὐτοὺς ὑπερεκπερισσοῦ ἐν ἀγάπῃ διὰ τὸ ἔργον αὐτῶν. εἰρηνεύετε ἐν ἑαυτοῖς. | And <u>to regard</u> them most highly in love because of their work. Be at peace among yourselves. |

The middle infinitive ἡγεῖσθαι aligns with Allan's mental activity category. This comprises actions in which subjects act voluntarily but are also affected by their (mental) actions, somewhat like the process of perception.[161] Although Allan does not list ἡγέομαι among his examples, he does include similar verbs, viz., λογίζομαι ("calculate, reason, consider") and σταθμάομαι ("measure, estimate, conjecture") in this category.[162] The use of ἡγεῖσθαι with imperative force here balances the notion of προϊσταμένους (presiding over) discussed above. Hence, the leaders are to care for the people who in turn are to esteem and respect their leaders. This (asymmetrical) reciprocity reflects a medial situation, where subject and object are both within the event of pastoral

---

[159] Philo, *Leg.* 1.51.8 (Colson, Whitaker, LCL 226:178–179). Similarly, in Josephus: "we ought to acknowledge (ἡγεῖσθαι) the greatness of the Deity" (*A.J.*, 8.418.2 [Marcus, LCL 281:440–441]).

[160] See also, 2 Cor 9:5; Phil 2:6, 25; 3:7, 8; 1 Thess 5:13; 2 Thess 3:15; 1 Tim 1:12; 6:1.

[161] Allan, *Polysemy*, 101–4.

[162] Allan, *Polysemy*, 103.

supervision. There is a relational aspect to the sense of ἡγεῖσθαι in this context, for leaders can only supervise those who submit to their authority; moreover, by such submission, the people are in fact esteeming their leaders in love. The situation is medial in that it is not a matter of who does what to whom, but of mutual interaction. Finally, according to grammatical descriptions, this action of "regard" (NIV) or "esteem" (NKJ) may best be considered to arise from the application of the subjects' own resources and thus be seen as a dynamic middle.

4.18 Ἀντέχομαι (ΑΝΤΕΧΩ)

The active form ἀντέχω literally means hold against (ἀντι-έχω), while the middle ἀντέχομαι may take on the sense of hold against oneself, so cling to, hold fast, or demonstrate a strong interest or loyalty. BDAG notes that only the middle is found in early Christian literature.[163] Josephus employs ἀντέχομαι in this sense of holding fast: ὁ δὲ παλαίων τοσούτοις πάθεσιν ὅμως τοῦ ζῆν ἀντείχετο: "Yet, struggling as he was with such numerous sufferings, he clung to life[.]."[164] Similar uses are seen in the LXX, for example, ἀντεχομένους τῆς διαθήκης μου: "and hold fast my covenant" (Isa 56:6, NETS). In Job, the middle is used of attachment in the sense of support or showing mercy: ἀνθέξεται τοῦ μὴ πεσεῖν αὐτὸν εἰς θάνατον: "he will provide support so that he does not fall into death" (Job 33:24, NETS).

Ἀντέχομαι appears only four times in the New Testament. It is used in parallel passages in the gospels in reference to being *devoted* or loyal to one master and despising another (Matt 6:24, Luke 16:13). In Titus it appears in the advice that elders should *hold fast* to the faith they were taught (Tit 1:9). Continuing Paul's exhortations to the Thessalonians (ἀδελφοί) concerning mutual care, Paul employs ἀντέχεσθε in reference to loyal support in 5:14 as below:

---

[163] LSJ, s.v. "ἀντέχω"; BDAG, s.v. "ἀντέχω."
[164] Josephus, *B.J.*, 1.657.1. (LCL 203: 312–313).

1 Thess 5:14 παρακαλοῦμεν δὲ ὑμᾶ ἀδελφοί, νουθετεῖτε τοὺς ἀτάκτοι παραμυθεῖσθε τοὺς ὀλιγοψύχους, ἀντέχεσθε τῶν ἀσθενῶν, μακροθυμεῖτε πρὸς πάντας.	We urge you, brothers and sisters, to admonish the idle, comfort the faint-hearted, <u>support</u> the weak and be patient towards everyone

Interestingly, of the four behaviors that Paul invokes here, three are designated by active verbs and two are middle voiced. The two middle verbs παραμυθεῖσθε (discussed in §4.7 above) and ἀντέχεσθε (under discussion) each evoke interaction and relationship: a personal involvement. To comfort or console (παραμυθεῖσθε) requires a sense of empathy and compassion on the part of the subject toward the other. Likewise, to support, help or be devoted to (ἀντέχεσθε) the weak requires a personal engagement, a response to their needs.[165] Such response would necessarily be adjusted to the need of the moment.

On the other hand, the active forms of the verbs 'urge' (παρακαλοῦμεν) admonish (νουθετεῖτε) and 'be patient' (μακροθυμεῖτε) reflect the fact that these concepts do not inherently require a relational context.[166] In urging or admonishing someone to do something, the subject is acting outside itself, seeking to influence the one addressed to comply with the will of the subject. Being patient reflects a state but not a change in state, hence the active is appropriate. In 1 Thess 5:14 above, it is the phrase πρὸς πάντας which directs this towards others; this sense is not inherent in the verb.

---

[165] τῶν ἀσθενῶν could refer to those who are spiritually weak, physically weak, or needy; thus, Wanamaker is of the opinion that "Paul left these exhortations intentionally vague" so that the readers could interpret manifest needs and respond accordingly (*Thessalonians*, 198). It seems likely that the pastoral care is directed generally, rather than at specific groups as suggested by Boring, *Thessalonians*, 193.

[166] For example, a merchant could urge a customer to buy an expensive item; a traffic officer could admonish a person who was about to walk against a red light; one could be patient on encountering transport delays. Although there must be some interface when addressing another, no innate sense of mutuality is implied.

In the middle form ἀντέχεσθε, the sense of interactive behavior associated with supporting others is indicative of medial function. The subjects are acting but they are involved in a process which encompasses them, and are consequently internal to the event. Allan does not include this verb in his main examples. However, he does refer to "emotionally motivated actions" in which the subject functions as a beneficiary (as in the case of indirect reflexive middles) since it is "either ill-disposed or well-disposed towards the object."[167] From the grammatical perspective, the middle sense of supporting one another suggests an internal motivation, such that the subjects' own resources are mobilized and applied, as for Cooper's dynamic middle.

4.19 ΠΡΟΣΕΥΧΟΜΑΙ (*MEDIA TANTUM*)

The frequently used middle verb προσεύχομαι refers to the offering of prayers or vows, or petitioning a deity by prayer in Jewish, Christian, and pagan contexts.[168] In non-biblical Greek the simple form εὔχομαι is far more common.[169] However, προσεύχομαι is also found, for example, ἀνατέλλοντι τῷ ἡλίῳ προσευξάμενος: "addressing his prayers to the rising sun[.]"[170] This preference is further illustrated by the prolific attestation of εὔχομαι in non-literary papyri in opening and closing expressions of prayer for good health in personal letters. For example, a soldier writes to his mother as follows: πρὸ μὲν πάντων εὔχομαί σε ὑγειαίνειν [ὑγιαίνειν] καὶ εὐτυχεῖν: before all things I pray for your health and prosperity (P.Mich. 3.203 [114–116 CE]).

By contrast, although both verbs are attested in the LXX and NT, the compound form is more common, especially in the NT where it is

---

[167] Allan, *Polysemy*, 113n199.
[168] LSJ, s.v. "προσεύχομαι." BDAG, s.v. "προσεύχομαι."
[169] As noted by Heinrich Greeven, "εὔχομαι," *TDNT* 2:775. Accordingly, TLG searches reveal that the ratio of uses of εὔχομαι to προσεύχομαι in Plutarch is 129:28, Josephus 76:2, and Philo 117:4.
[170] Plutarch, *Dion*, 27.4.2 [Perrin, LCL 98: 58–59].

the dominant verb for prayer.[171] Accordingly, προσεύχομαι is widely found throughout the LXX (110 times), for example, <u>προσηύξατο</u> δὲ Αβρααμ πρὸς τὸν θεόν καὶ ἰάσατο ὁ θεὸς τὸν Αβιμελεχ: so Abraham <u>prayed</u> to God and God healed Abimelech (Gen 20:17). In the NT it is used eighty-five times, for example, γρηγορεῖτε καὶ <u>προσεύχεσθε</u>: stay alert and <u>pray</u> (Matt 26:41). Paul uses προσεύχομαι twice as an imperative in his concluding remarks in 1 Thessalonians, as below:

1 Thess 5:17 ἀδιαλείπτως <u>προσεύχεσθε</u>	Pray without ceasing
1 Thess 5:25 Ἀδελφοί, <u>προσεύχεσθε</u> [καὶ] περὶ ἡμῶν	Brothers and sisters, pray [also] concerning us

Both these occurrences may be discussed together. Although Allan does not list προσεύχομαι among any of his middle verb examples, he does list εὔχομαι ("pray, vow, boast") in his speech act category, in which the subject is affected by heart-felt types of speech.[172] Grammatically, it may be classified as a dynamic middle, the prayer emerging from within the subject's own resources. At times it could also be an indirect reflexive, when performed in the subject's interest. Accordingly, while BDAG identifies προσεύχομαι as middle deponent, Wallace considers that "it takes little imagination to see a true (indirect) middle force to this verb, however."[173] It can also be understood as a medial activity, for both the person praying and the deity are mutually involved in the event, as in a dialogue.[174] Even though one may be praying for another person, it is one's own thoughts, whether of thanksgiving or supplication, which are being expressed in response to thoughts of the other. This scenario

---

[171] The ratio of the verbs εὔχομαι to προσεύχομαι is 86:110 in the LXX and 7:85 in the NT.

[172] Allan, *Polysemy*, 105. This is not surprising given Allan's sources (Homer and Classical literature). Many NT verbs do not appear among his samples.

[173] BDAG s.v. "προσεύχομαι"; Wallace, *Exegetical Syntax*, 430n66.

[174] This assumes that God hears the prayers of believers, as affirmed throughout the New Testament, e.g., Matt 6:6; Luke 18:1; Rom 8:26.

aligns with Eberhard's notion of mediality, for the person praying, those prayed for, and God, are all held together conceptually within the process of prayer. The subject is the locale of the action but is also internal to it.

4.20 SUMMARY AND ANALYSIS

The results of the investigations into the function of verbs with present middle form in 1 Thessalonians are summarized in the table below. This indicates where there is conformity in function to the descriptors of the middle voice employed in this study, as for the aorist forms in the previous chapter.[175]

Table 4.2 Properties of Present Middle Verb Forms in 1 Thessalonians

---

[175] Abbreviations as previously, also M. Act = mental activity; Bod. M. = body motion.

Middle Voice Verbs in the New Testament

Verb	Form	Ref.	MT	Dep.	Gramm. middle	Subj. Aff.	Allan category	Med. event
ποιέω	μνείαν ποιούμενοι	1:2	✗	✗	Dyn.	✓	Sp. Act, M. Act.	✓
ῥύομαι	ῥυόμενον	1:10	✓	✓	Ind. Ref.	✓	Ind. Ref.	✓
ἔρχομαι	ἐρχομένης	1:10	✓	✓	✗	✓	Spont.	✓
	ἔρχεται	5:2	✓	✓	✗	✓	Spont.	✓
δυναμόω	δυνάμενοι	2:7	✗	✓	✗	✗	✗	✗
	δυνάμεθα	3:9	✗	✓	✗	✗	✗	✗
ὁμείρομαι	ὁμειρόμενοι	2:8	✓	✓	Dyn.	✓	M. Proc.	✓
ἐργάζομαι	ἐργαζόμενοι	2:9	✓	✓	Dyn.	✓	Ind. Ref.	✓
	ἐργάζεσθαι	4:11	✓	✓	Dyn.	✓	Ind. Ref.	✓
παραμυθέομαι	παραμυθούμενοι	2:12	✓	✓	Dyn.	✓	Sp. Act	✓
	παραμυθεῖσθε	5:14	✓	✓	Dyn.	✓	Sp. Act	✓
μαρτυρέω	μαρτυρόμενοι	2:12	✗	✓	Dyn.	✓	Sp. Act	✓
ἐνεργέω	ἐνεργεῖται	2:13	✗	✗	Dyn.	✓	Spont.	✓
δέομαι	δεόμενοι	3:10	✓	✓	Ind. Ref., Dyn.	✓	Sp. Act	✓
ἀπέχω	ἀπέχεσθαι	4:3	✗	✗	Dir. Ref.	✓	Bod. M.	✓
	ἀπέχεσθε	5:22	✗	✗	Dir. Ref.	✓	Bod. M	✓
κτάομαι	κτᾶσθαι¹	4:4	✓	✓	Ind./ Dir. Ref.	✓	Ind./ Dir. Ref.	✓
φιλοτιμέομαι	φιλοτιμεῖσθαι	4:11	✓	✓	Dyn.	✓	M. Act.	✓
κοιμάω	κοιμωμένων	4:13	✗	✓	✗	✓	M. Proc.	✓
ἐφίστημι	ἐφίσταται	5:3	✗	✗	✗	✓	Spont.	✗
Προΐστημι	προϊσταμένους²	5:12	✗	✗	Dyn.	✓	Ind. Ref.	✓
ἡγέομαι	ἡγεῖσθαι	5:13	✓	✓	Dyn.	✓	M. Act.	✓
ἀντέχω	ἀντέχεσθε	5:14	✗	✗	Dyn.	✓	Ind. Ref.	✓
προσεύχομαι	προσεύχεσθε	5:17	✓	✓	Dyn.	✓	Sp. Act	✓
	προσεύχεσθε	5:25	✓	✓	Dyn.	✓	Sp. Act	✓

The following observations may be noted:

- Subject affectedness is applicable to every instance except δύναμαι.[176]
- There are many instances of dynamic middle function.
- Grammatical descriptors do not apply to events represented as spontaneous.[177]

---

[176] Allan treats δύναμαι as an anomaly, and declines to classify it (*Polysemy*, 122n214).

[177] Hence, e.g., ἔρχομαι, for which the subject is the wrath of God.

- In most instances, three, or at least two of the descriptors apply.
- The present forms exhibit middle function to a similar degree as the aorists.

The notions of subject affectedness and mediality are widely applicable, while the most frequent type of grammatical middle is the dynamic function. This reflects that the action often comes from within as an emotional, compassionate, or respectful attitude, consistent with the tone of the letter. Far less frequent is the more commonly acknowledged indirect reflexive, indicating action in one's own interest.

It may be seen that although *media tantum* verbs generally correlate with deponent classification, δύναμαι, μαρτύρομαι and κοιμάομαι have active forms even though their middle form is regarded as deponent by *ALGNT*. Therefore, so-called deponent verbs cannot be said always to lack active forms. Likewise, these results do not support the notion that "deponent" verbs have active function, since those examined here (except for δύναμαι) display middle function according to the descriptors applied. If these descriptors are accepted as properties of the middle voice, the idea that deponency indicates active function is refuted for these instances, confirming the assertions to this effect in the introduction. That is, middle form widely indicates middle function.

Combining the results for the aorist and present verbs in 1 Thessalonians, it is found that for the forty-six middle forms investigated, thirty-one (67%) exhibit grammatical middle functions, forty-four (97%) exhibit subject affectedness and forty-one (89%) exhibit medial function. Further, it may be seen that two or more descriptors apply in forty-one (89%) of cases, the two forms of δύναμαι and certain spontaneous processes being the exceptions. These results for both aorist and present tenses indicate that middle verbs in 1 Thessalonians widely exhibit middle function. Consequently, a similar investigation of another sample of middle forms is deemed worthwhile in this investigation of the function and significance of middle verbs in the Greek New Testament.

CHAPTER 5
MIDDLE VERBS IN SECOND CORINTHIANS

In the previous chapter it was seen that all middle form verbs (except δύναμαι) in 1 Thessalonians exhibited middle function according to the descriptors applied. Specifically, the grammatical descriptors applied frequently, subject-affectedness and medial function applied widely. For a further source of middle verb forms to investigate from Paul's writings, Second Corinthians has been selected. This epistle contains the highest proportion of middle verbs among Paul's letters to church communities, as may readily be seen in Fig 2.1 above. Verbs with middle voice morphology constitute 3.04 percent of all words in Second Corinthians compared to 2.63 percent in 1 Thessalonians. Since middle function was observed consistently for both the aorist and present middle forms in 1 Thessalonians, this distinction will not be maintained in the present chapter. Accordingly, the analysis will be undertaken by lexeme, not tense form.

In 2 Corinthians, 136 middle forms appear, representing 51 different verbs as listed in the Appendix. Twelve of these have already been studied in 1 Thessalonians, viz., δύναμαι, ἐνεργέομαι, γίνομαι, ῥύομαι, φιλοτιμέομαι, τίθημι, δέομαι, δέχομαι, ἡγέομαι, ἔρχομαι, εὐαγγελίζομαι, ἀσπάζομαι. The remaining middle-inflected verbs in 2 Corinthians provide a further sample for study along the same lines as those in previous chapters. That is, their lexical sense is clarified with reference to usage and their function in the immediate context in the epistle is examined to ascertain whether the three descriptors of middle voice apply. The following middle verbs are examined below in the sequence in which they appear in 2 Corinthians: βούλομαι, βουλεύομαι, χράομαι, σφραγίζομαι, ἐπικαλοῦμαι, φείδομαι, χαρίζομαι, ἀποτάσσομαι, ἄρχομαι, λογίζομαι.

While an understanding of the Corinthian correspondence is complex and will not be attempted here, a brief comment on the second canonical epistle may provide some context for the excerpts examined below. Clearly, in addition to 1 Corinthians, Paul had written another letter, sometimes referred to as the harsh or severe letter, which called on the church to address a matter of misconduct (2 Cor 2:3–10). This caused Paul some anxiety concerning the manner in which it would be received (2 Cor 7:8–12). Further, Paul addresses certain adversaries, variously called false apostles (11:13) or super-apostles (12:11) who had rivalled and therefore challenged Paul's authority in the eyes of some of the Corinthians. Therefore, throughout the letter we find that Paul is affirming his divine calling and spiritual authority with respect to the congregation he founded.

5.1 ΒΟΥΛΟΜΑΙ (*MEDIA TANTUM*)

Two senses of βούλομαι are documented by BDAG.[1] The first refers to a "desire to have or experience something, with the implication of planning accordingly" hence, "*wish, want, desire*." For example, ὃς ἐὰν οὖν βουληθῇ φίλος εἶναι τοῦ κόσμου, ἐχθρὸς τοῦ θεοῦ καθίσταται: therefore, whoever wants (purposes) to be a friend of the world is essentially an enemy of God (Jas 4:4). The second sense of *actually* planning a course of action may be rendered by "intend," "plan," or "will[.]"[2] This sense of planning to achieve what is willed is also noted by MM, who indicate that the sense of "purpose, intention, not mere will, but will with premeditation" frequently underlies the use of this verb.[3] Such usage is clearly apparent in P.Oxy. 10.1263 (128–29 CE) which

---

[1] BDAG, s.v. "βούλομαι."

[2] Josephus, *A.J.*, 14.233.2 is cited as an example: βούλομαι ὑμᾶς εἰδέναι ὅτι πρέσβεις Ἰουδαίων μοι προσῆλθον: I want you to know that envoys have come to me from the Jews. The desire for the recipients to know of the envoys is actualized in the writing which informs them of such. There is an indication of acting on the wish. A similar use appears in Phil 1:12; Γινώσκειν δὲ ὑμᾶς βούλομαι, ἀδελφοί, ὅτι τὰ κατ' ἐμὲ μᾶλλον εἰς προκοπὴν τοῦ εὐαγγελίου ἐλήλυθεν: "I want you to know, brothers, that my situation has turned out rather to advance the gospel" (NAB).

[3] MM, s.v. "βούλομαι." This definition is attributed to Hort in commenting on βούλομαι in Jas 4:4. See F. J. A. Hort, *The Epistle of St. James: The Greek Text* (London: Macmillan, 1909), 93.

documents an application addressed to the city-scribe of Oxyrhynchus concerning the author's intention to practice a trade: βούλομαι πρώτως ἀπὸ τοῦ ἐνεστῶτος τρισκαιδεκάτου [τρεισκαιδεκάτου] ἔτου[ς] Ἀδριανοῦ Καίσαρος τοῦ κυρίου χρήσασθαι τῇ τῶν ἐργ[ατῶν] ποταμοῦ τέχ[νῃ]: "I wish to begin from the present thirteenth year of Hadrianus Caesar the lord to practise the trade of a river-worker[.]"

The verb βούλομαι is used thirty-seven times across the New Testament, most often in Acts (14 occurrences). For example, in Acts 18:15 we read that Gallio is unwilling to rule on the charges that the Jews in Achaia bring against Paul, stating: κριτὴς ἐγὼ τούτων οὐ βούλομαι εἶναι: *I do not wish* to be a judge of these things. The more popular word for wish or want in Hellenistic Greek, however, is θέλω, which appears 208 times in the New Testament.[4] Both verbs appear in Matt 1:19, θέλω being used to express a desire and βούλομαι referring to the intended course of action to fulfil the desire. Thus, we see: Ἰωσὴφ δὲ ὁ ἀνὴρ αὐτῆς, δίκαιος ὢν καὶ μὴ θέλων αὐτὴν δειγματίσαι, ἐβουλήθη λάθρᾳ ἀπολῦσαι αὐτήν: Joseph her husband, being a righteous man and not wanting to disgrace her, determined to dismiss her secretly.[5]

In explaining his change of travel plans to the Corinthians, Paul poses rhetorical questions in defense of his integrity, the use of μήτι indicating that the answer expected would be *no*. That is, he was not being frivolous but had good reasons for the change. Thus, βούλομαι is

---

[4] The increasing use of θέλω in preference to βούλομαι in the Hellenistic era is noted in BDF §101, and by Gottlob Schrenk, *TDNT* 1:630. A comparison of the number of occurrences of θέλω and βούλομαι in the LXX and NT supports this observation. In the LXX, θέλω: βούλομαι = 118:76 (approx. 3:2), whereas in the NT θέλω: βούλομαι = 208:37 (approx. 11:2).

[5] Since the aorist of βούλομαι exhibits the -θη- morpheme it is typically classified as a passive deponent, as, e.g., Robertson, *Grammar*, 817. Such terminology was shown above to be unnecessary. The -θη- aorist also appears in James 1:18, 4:4; and 2 John 1:12, without passive sense. This is made clear by the translations e.g., βουληθεὶς (Jas 1:18) is rendered "He willed" (NAB) and "He chose" (NIV), i.e., it functions as a middle verb.

used to express Paul's intentions, his will with purpose, in 2 Cor 1:15, 17 as follows:

2 Cor 1:15–17 Καὶ ταύτῃ τῇ πεποιθήσει ἐβουλόμην πρότερον πρὸς ὑμᾶς ἐλθεῖν, ἵνα δευτέραν χάριν σχῆτε, ¹⁶ καὶ δι' ὑμῶν διελθεῖν εἰς Μακεδονίαν καὶ πάλιν ἀπὸ Μακεδονίας ἐλθεῖν πρὸς ὑμᾶς καὶ ὑφ' ὑμῶν προπεμφθῆναι εἰς τὴν Ἰουδαίαν. ¹⁷ τοῦτο οὖν βουλόμενος μήτι ἄρα τῇ ἐλαφρίᾳ ἐχρησάμην; ἢ ἃ βουλεύομαι κατὰ σάρκα βουλεύομαι, ἵνα ᾖ παρ' ἐμοὶ τὸ ναὶ ναὶ καὶ τὸ οὒ οὔ; ⁶	So with this confidence, I was intending to come to you first so that you might have a double benefit; that is, to go via you into Macedonia and to come back to you from Macedonia and to be sent on to Judea by you. Intending this, therefore, did I consequently act with levity? Or when I resolve [something], do I resolve [it] according to merely human inclinations, so that it is 'yes, yes' and 'no, no' with me?

The sense of ἐβουλόμην, and βουλόμενος translated 'intended' and 'intending' respectively in the verses above, is consistent with both subject affectedness and the medial notion of middle verbs described previously. The lexical sense indicates not only wishing but planning a particular course of action, which presupposes a dialogical process with oneself, as described by Allan in reference to his mental activity category of middle verbs.[7] Similarly, the subject is interior to the activity

---

[6] Verse 17 has variant readings. Βουλόμενος is attested by, e.g., P⁴⁶, ℵ, A, B, C, F, *et al*; βουλεύμενος by the Majority Text. Hence, "I intended" (NIV) cf. "I was planning" (NKJV). For comment, see Margaret E. Thrall, *The Second Epistle to the Corinthians*, vol. 1, ICC (Edinburgh: T&T Clark, 1994), 140n85. Thrall draws attention to this variant and considers the Majority text reading to be explained by assimilation to the verbs which follow.

[7] Allan, *Polysemy*, 101. Allan lists βουλεύομαι among his examples of mental

denoted by the verb (it is encompassed by it) so the medial notion described by Eberhard also applies. In the grammatical understanding of the middle voice, it is evident that the subject (Paul) is acting with reference to himself, that is, from within his own resources.

Despite the fact that there are five middle verb forms in 1 Cor 1: 15–19, viz., ἐβουλόμην βουλόμενος, ἐχρησάμην, βουλεύομαι (x 2), the matter of voice typically receives no mention in commentaries.[8] The middle voice, however, is appropriate in this context for Paul is speaking of his personal investment in regard to his desires, his intentions, and his resolution of the matter of travel plans; he is also personally concerned about the opinion of the Thessalonians in regard to his integrity. The other two middle verbs in this section of text are discussed below.

5.2 ΒΟΥΛΕΥΟΜΑΙ (ΒΟΥΛΕΥΩ)

For this oppositional middle, the general sense is thinking about or deciding upon a course of action. Hence, "deliberate" or "resolve" capture the essential meaning, with the middle voice indicating reference to oneself.[9] Both voices are used in Plutarch, such that we find βουλεύσας translated "making a plan"[10] and βουλευόμενοι as "held deliberations" in the same work.[11] In the LXX there is only one instance of the active: τίς ταῦτα ἐβούλευσεν ἐπὶ Τύρον: "Who has devised this counsel against Tyre?" (Isa 23:8, Brenton), yet in the following verse, the middle is used in a similar sense: "The Lord of hosts has purposed

---

activity middle verbs, but not βούλομαι. However, there appears to be an overlap in the semantic range of these two verbs since both require thinking or planning.

[8] No instances were found. Harris, for example, comments on various grammatical and lexical matters in the Greek text but makes no mention of the middle voice. See Murray J. Harris, *The Second Epistle to the Corinthians,* NIGTC (Grand Rapids: Eerdmans, 2005), 192–198.

[9] BDAG, s.v. "βουλεύω." LSJ, s.v. "βουλεύω."

[10] Plutarch, *Romulus*, 8.8.4, (Perrin, LCL 46:112–113).

[11] Plutarch, *Romulus*, 16.2.3, (Perrin, LCL 46:134–135).

[ἐβουλεύσατο] to bring down all the pride of the glorious ones" (Isa 23:9, Brenton). If there is any distinction, it appears that the middle refers to the mental planning and the active to implementing the plans.[12] Hence, for example, Plutarch says that Lysander "took measures (ἐβούλευσεν) at once to change their form of government."[13]

It is noted by BDAG that only middle forms of βουλεύω occur in the New Testament or early Christian literature.[14] Luke 14:31 is cited as an example of the first use. Jesus asks: "what king, going out to wage war against another king, will not sit down first and consider (βουλεύσεται) whether he is able with ten thousand to oppose the one who comes against him with twenty thousand?" (NRSV). The second sense of reaching a decision is seen in John 11:53, "so from that day they planned (ἐβουλεύσαντο) that they would kill him" (NRSV).[15] This usage is similarly found in a papyrus letter from a tax farmer regarding official business in respect to an upcoming meeting. Βεβουλεύμεθα ἐκσπάσαι τὸ ἐπιδεδομένον ὑπόμνη(μα) μή ποτε ἐπὶ τοῦ διαλόγου χειμασθῶμεν "We have <u>determined</u> to abstract the memorandum in order that we may not come to grief at the audit."[16] This second sense appears to align with Paul's expression in 2 Cor 1:17, already discussed above in regard to βούλομαι.

---

[12] However, NETS renders both ἐβούλευσεν and ἐβουλεύσατο with "planned."

[13] Plutarch, *Lysander*, 15.1.5 (Perrin, LCL 80:272–273).

[14] BDAG, s.v. "βουλεύω." The middle form, βουλεύομαι, occurs 56 times in the LXX, e.g., ὑμεῖς ἐβουλεύσασθε κατ' ἐμοῦ εἰς πονηρά ὁ δὲ θεὸς ἐβουλεύσατο περὶ ἐμοῦ εἰς ἀγαθά: you purposed evil against me, but God purposed for good concerning me (Gen 50:20). It only occurs 6 times in the NT: in Luke 14:31, John 11:53, 12:10; Acts 27:39, 1 Cor 1:17 (x2).

[15] NIV and NKJV have "plotted" which suggests following through on a decision. The middle form is used similarly by Josephus, e.g., ἐκ γὰρ τοῦ φανεροῦ διακινδυνεύοντες οὐκ ἐνόμιζον εἶναι τοῖς Ἰωνάθου ἀξιόμαχοι. φυγὴν οὖν <u>ἐβουλεύσαντο</u>: "for they did not consider themselves a match for Jonathan's men, if they were to fight in the open. They therefore <u>resolved</u> on flight[.]" Josephus, *A.J.*, 13.177–178 (Marcus, LCL 365:314–315).

[16] P.Tebt. 1.58 *l* 28 (111 BC).

2 Cor 1:17 τοῦτο οὖν
βουλόμενος μήτι ἄρα τῇ
ἐλαφρίᾳ ἐχρησάμην; ἢ ἃ
βουλεύομαι κατὰ σάρκα
βουλεύομαι, ἵνα ᾖ παρ' ἐμοὶ
τὸ ναὶ ναὶ καὶ τὸ οὒ οὔ;

Intending this, then, did I consequently act with levity? Or when I <u>resolve</u> [something], do I <u>resolve</u> [it] according to merely human inclinations, so that it is 'yes, yes' and 'no, no' with me?

In the rhetorical question in the verse above, Paul is asking: do I resolve (βουλεύομαι) the matters I resolve (βουλεύομαι) according to human inclinations?[17] Paul indicates that he is not simply acting on impulse (κατὰ σάρκα), rather that there are other factors affecting his considered decision; he is thus internal to and encompassed by the process (medial event). As he comes to a firm decision, he is also affected by the process. Accordingly, Allan includes βουλεύομαι among his examples of mental activity middle verbs. This is an oppositional middle and while there appears to be no sharp distinction between the lexical sense of the active and that of the middle, in this context the middle verb refers to deliberation within or by oneself. Hence, Paul is acting from within his own resources (dynamic middle) and has a genuine interest in the outcome of the decision (indirect reflexive). Therefore, all three descriptors apply.

5.3 ΧΡΑΟΜΑΙ (*MEDIA TANTUM*)

Only middle forms of χράομαι appear in the New Testament. Accordingly, BDAG identifies χράομαι as a "middle deponent" and lists no active form.[18] In this study, on the other hand, middle verbs listed in BDAG without an active form are identified as *media tantum*. Active forms do appear in earlier literature, having various applications such as

---

[17] The NRSV translates βουλεύομαι as "I make my plans" and βουλόμενος as "when I wanted" thus retaining a distinction between intention (βούλομαι) and actually constructing a plan (βουλεύομαι).

[18] BDAG, s.v. "χράομαι."

"proclaim", "furnish with", "attack."[19] There are both active and middle forms in the LXX. For example, when the Hebrews left Egypt, it is said that the Lord gave his people favor in the sight of the Egyptians, who actually ἔχρησαν αὐτοῖς: "supplied them" (Exod 12:36, NETS). The middle form is used more frequently, often in reference to the way people are treated. Hence, in making a covenant with Isaac, Abimelech asserts ἐχρησάμεθά σοι καλῶς: "we have treated you well" (Gen 26:29, NETS).

BDAG identifies three related uses of χράομαι in the NT, as below.

1. Using or employing something, with the item being used stated in the dative, e.g., Μηκέτι ὑδροπότει, ἀλλὰ οἴνῳ ὀλίγῳ χρῶ: no longer drink water but use a little wine (1 Tim 5:23).
2. Treating a person in a particular manner, e.g., φιλανθρώπως τε ὁ Ἰούλιος τῷ Παύλῳ χρησάμενος: Julius treated Paul in a friendly manner (Acts 27:3).
3. Acting or proceeding in a certain manner, with either an adverb or the dative of the characteristic shown, e.g., 2 Cor 1:17, cited above and discussed further below.[20]

Forms of χράομαι occur eleven times in the NT (Acts 27:3,17; 1 Cor 7:21, 31, 9:12, 15; 2 Cor 1:17, 3:12, 13:10; 1 Tim 1:8, 5:23). Notably, seven of these appear in the Corinthian correspondence. The three instances of χράομαι in 2 Corinthians are discussed below.

---

[19] LSJ, s.v. "χράω." GE, s.v. "χράω."

[20] A similar use by Josephus: κατέσχε δὲ οὗτος καὶ τὰ Ἱεροσόλυμα δόλῳ καὶ ἀπάτῃ χρησάμενος: and this king seized Jerusalem by resorting to cunning and deceit[.]" Josephus, *A.J.*, 12.4.2 (Marcus, LCL 365: 2–3). That is, he *acted with* or *used*, cunning and deceit.

2 Cor 1:17 τοῦτο οὖν βουλόμενος μήτι ἄρα τῇ ἐλαφρίᾳ <u>ἐχρησάμην</u>;	Intending this, then, did I consequently <u>act</u> with levity?
2 Cor 3:12 Ἔχοντες οὖν τοιαύτην ἐλπίδα πολλῇ παρρησίᾳ <u>χρώμεθα</u>	Therefore, having this hope, we <u>act</u> with great boldness[21]
2 Cor 13:10 Διὰ τοῦτο ταῦτα ἀπὼν γράφω, ἵνα παρὼν μὴ ἀποτόμως <u>χρήσωμαι</u> κατὰ τὴν ἐξουσίαν ἣν ὁ κύριος ἔδωκέν μοι εἰς οἰκοδομὴν καὶ οὐκ εἰς καθαίρεσιν	For this reason, I write these things while absent, so that when present I may not <u>act</u> harshly, in accordance with the authority which the Lord gave me for the purpose of edification and not for pulling down

We see that χράομαι is used in 2 Corinthians in reference to Paul acting in a particular manner in each instance: acting with levity (1:17), with boldness (3:12), or harshly (13:10). The medial nature of such behavior is apparent, since (as for the characteristics of encouragement and support in 1 Thessalonians) these attributes inherently require a relational encounter. Paul is speaking of acting in a certain manner or employing a particular attitude towards the Corinthians, being conceptually within a situation which encompasses him. This is consistent with the relational, interactive characteristic of many middle verbs observed in the previous chapter.

In Allan's scheme, though it may not be readily apparent that the subject is affected, Paul is acting in his own interest indirectly, that is, for the effectiveness of his ministry. Hence, this verb conforms to Allan's indirect reflexive category, in which a subject becomes a beneficiary or recipient and is therefore affected by the process. According to the grammatical criteria, Paul is acting *from* within his own resources

---

[21] Similarly, "we *use* great boldness" (NAS, NKJV); "we *act* very boldly" (NAB); we *act* with great boldness (NRSV).

or powers (dynamic middle) as he adopts the appropriate behavior in each instance; nevertheless, the indirect reflexive (*for* himself) could also apply as above.

5.4 ΣΦΡΑΓΙΖΟΜΑΙ (ΣΦΡΑΓΙΖΩ)

BDAG lists the active form σφραγίζω and records the sense of sealing something either for security, to keep it secret, or for identification. In the latter case the mark denoting ownership also carries the protection of the owner.[23] This is illustrated in the record of Pilate sealing (σφραγίσαντες) Jesus' tomb and posting guards (Matt 27:66). However, no specific use or examples are given for the middle form σφραγίζομαι.[24] This suggests that the middle voice may be used at the writer's discretion to highlight the specific relation of the subject to the verb. Accordingly, LSJ notes that the middle sense of σφραγίζομαι is to seal an article to show that it is pledged.[25] This implies that there is a personal commitment on the part of the subject, as illustrated by several instances in the LXX. For example, it is used of writing and sealing a marriage contract (Tob 7:14), to refer to sealing a deed for the purchase of a field (Jer 39:10), and to King Darius sealing the stone of the lions' den, hence irrevocably committing Daniel to the beasts. (Dan 6:18).

In the ancient world, sealing was a common practice. It was used in practical matters such as sealing goods for delivery to protect and guarantee the integrity of the contents, as well as in the authentication and protection of documents.[26] Hence, a contract could be made legally valid by the inclusion of seals pertaining to the relevant parties and witnesses on the document itself. Then, after rolling, it could be protected from tampering by tying with string and sealing with stamped clay bullae.[27]

---

[23] BDAG, s.v. "σφραγίζω."

[24] Examples of use for σφραγίζω given by BDAG include all voice forms.

[25] LSJ, s.v. "σφραγίζω."

[26] "Seals, Mesopotamian," Bonnie S. Magness-Gardiner, *ABD*, 5:1062–1063; Gottfried Fitzer, "σφραγίς, σφραγίζω," *TDNT* 7:944–6.

[27] Katelijn Vanthorpe, "Seals in and on the Papyri of Graeco-Roman and Byzantine

Illustrations of the use of sealing are found in papyri such as P.Oslo 2 53 *ll* 2–4 (101 CE): ἐκομισάμην παρὰ Πετεχῶντος κίστην ἐσσφραγισμένην[ἐσφραγισμένον] μεστὴν σταφυλῆς χλω[ρ]ᾶς: "From Petechon I received a <u>sealed</u> chest full of fresh grapes." In P.Tebt. 2 413 *l* 6 (101–300 CE) Aphrodite assures her mistress that a letter has been safely delivered: καὶ τὸ χαρταριν [χαρτάριον] ἔλαβεν Σερηνίων ἐσσφραγισμένον [ἐσφραγισμένον]: "and Serenion took the papyrus <u>sealed</u>."

This awareness of the use and purpose of seals in the ancient world is helpful in interpreting Paul's metaphorical use of σφραγισάμενος in 2 Corinthians. In his efforts to justify his change of plans (1:15, 16), Paul claims that he is not fickle but faithful, as surely as God is faithful (1:18). Accordingly, he duly calls on God as witness to his declaration that his motive was to spare the Corinthians, not lord it over them (1:23, 24). In characteristic Pauline fashion, embedded in discourse about ostensibly mundane matters, he pauses to affirm that both he and the Corinthians all belong securely to God; hence we find the theologically charged statements of 2 Cor 1:21–22 below:

| 2 Cor 1:21, 22 ὁ δὲ βεβαιῶν ἡμᾶς σὺν ὑμῖν εἰς Χριστὸν καὶ χρίσας ἡμᾶς θεός, ²²ὁ καὶ <u>σφραγισάμενος</u> ἡμᾶς καὶ δοὺς τὸν ἀρραβῶνα τοῦ πνεύματος ἐν ταῖς καρδίαις ἡμῶν. | Now God is the one who, having anointed us, establishes us together with you in Christ; the one who indeed <u>sealed</u> us by giving the down-payment of the Spirit in our hearts.[28] |

Egypt" in *Archives et sceaux du monde hellénistique*, ed. M. F. Boussac and A. Invernizzi (Athens: École française d'Athènes, 1996), 231–91.

[28] The present participle (βεβαιῶν) followed by three aorist ones (χρίσας, σφραγισάμενος, δούς) with the metaphorical use of commercial language suggests that the two instances of καί in v. 22 are epexegetical. The whole focus is on the faithfulness of God who anointed both Paul and the believers into Christ by the Holy Spirit, by whom they are also "sealed", as noted by Gordon D. Fee, *God's Empowering Presence: The Holy Spirit in the Letters of Paul* (Peabody, MA: Hendrickson, 1994), 287–95. Frank J.

The use of σφραγισάμενος in 2 Cor 1:22 is one of only two middle forms of σφραγίζω in the NT. The other occurs in Rom 15:28 where Paul refers to sealing the collection for the poor in Jerusalem, which he was eager to deliver safely.[29] Since most uses are active or passive, the middle may be considered to be used purposefully[30] (as in the examples from the LXX above where the subject is pledging authentication). Hence, the subject is personally invested in the process. While recent commentaries consulted did not remark on the middle form of σφραγισάμενος, Alfred Plummer (1915) comments that: "The meaning here may be that, in confirmation of a covenant, God sealed us as His own (mid.) and attested our value[.]"[31]

English translations sometimes render σφραγισάμενος ἡμᾶς in 2 Cor 1:22 in a manner that implies sealing as a form of identification, for instance, "marked us with his seal" (NJB), "set his seal of ownership on us" (NIV), "put his seal (up)on us" (ESV, RSV). In the commercial and legal imagery here, although the sense of ownership may be primary, the action of sealing also provides authentication and security.[32] In the context of 2 Cor 1:22, we have persons, not physical objects, who are the recipients of the seal.[33] This is interpreted to indicate that God seals

---

Matera also posits that the last two particles (σφραγισάμενος, δούς) refer back to the anointing (χρίσας) (*II Corinthians: A Commentary*, NTL [Louisville: Westminster John Knox, 2003], 55–56).

[29] Referring to the collection as fruit, it appears that Paul draws on the commercial imagery of sealing to indicate that everything is in order and ready for delivery, as noted by James D. G. Dunn, *Romans 9–16*, WBC 38b (Dallas: Word, 1988), 877.

[30] Active forms: Matt 27:66; John 3:33, 6:27; Rev 7:3, 10:4, 20:3, 22:10; passives: Eph 1:13, 4:30; Rev 7: 4, 5, 8. The references in Revelation are evocative of the protective sign or mark mentioned in Ezek 9:4–6 which was to protect the righteous from destruction; thus, the seal is a form of identification which serves as protection.

[31] Alfred Plummer, *A Critical and Exegetical Commentary on the Second Epistle of St. Paul to the Corinthians*, ICC (Edinburgh: T&T Clark, 1915; repr., 1966), 41.

[32] As noted by Harris, *Second Corinthians*, 207; this is consistent with the comment by BDAG noted above.

[33] There are no instances in the LXX of God acting as the subject of this verb, nor

or marks the believer for himself, with his authority, by the giving of the Spirit as a guarantee or down-payment.³⁴

In this process of sealing the believer, it may be construed that God is acting in his own interest to the extent that the seal indicates a claim of ownership or identification. Therefore, in Allan's terminology, σφραγισάμενος could be classified as an indirect reflexive middle verb in which the volitional subject is also a beneficiary of the action. Likewise, the grammatical indirect reflexive would apply, as God seals the believers *for* himself. In the Trinitarian context of the verse, God gives the Holy Spirit in sealing the believer, therefore there is also a sense that this is accomplished *by* himself which aligns with the dynamic middle.³⁵ The medial notion, however, does not seem readily applicable in this instance, for God is not represented as being encompassed by the process. The explanations of middle function in terms of the affectedness or involvement of the subject are more appropriate in this instance.

5.5 ἘΠΙΚΑΛΟΥΜΑΙ (ΕΠΙΚΑΛΕΩ)

The verb ἐπικαλέω has the general sense of "call upon," "summon," or "call out" in the active. Accordingly, the middle form, ἐπικαλοῦμαι, frequently refers to calling upon or invoking the name of a deity or

---

of people as its object.

³⁴ Although English translations commonly read the καί before δούς as a conjunction (sealed *and* gave the Holy Spirit) Harris argues that καὶ δοὺς τὸν ἀρραβῶνα τοῦ πνεύματος ἐν ταῖς καρδίαις ἡμῶν is explicative of σφραγισάμενος, such that it indicates the means by which the persons are sealed (*Second Corinthians*, 209). This is consistent with Fee's reading noted above, and appears reasonable, especially in light of the passive use of σφραγίζομαι in Eph 1:13 (ἐν ᾧ καὶ πιστεύσαντες ἐσφραγίσθητε τῷ πνεύματι τῆς ἐπαγγελίας τῷ ἁγίῳ, (in whom [Christ] you were sealed by the promised Holy Spirit). That is, the giving of the Holy Spirit constitutes the sealing of the believer.

³⁵ Hence, Fee comments that vv. 21, 22 strongly invoke the notion of the Trinity, being one of a "series of semi-creedal soteriological texts that are full of Trinitarian implications" (*Empowering Presence*, 293).

person in authority for some form of assistance for oneself.³⁶ Thus, Jeremiah says of the Lord: εἰς τὴν βοήθειάν μου ἤγγισας ἐν ᾗ σε ἡμέρᾳ ἐπεκαλεσάμην: "you came near to help me in the day when I called on you" (Lam 3:57, NETS). Similarly, when Paul faces accusation from the Jewish authorities, he denies any wrong-doing and appeals to Caesar: Καίσαρα ἐπικαλοῦμαι (Acts 25:11).

The active occurs only once in the NT (Matt 10:25), the passive ten times, generally in reference to someone's name, such as Σίμων ὁ ἐπικαλούμενος Πέτρος: Simon, who is called Peter (Acts 10:18). The middle form appears seventeen times, most commonly in Acts, but also in Paul's writings, in which it always refers to calling upon the Lord.³⁷ A familiar example is πᾶς γὰρ ὃς ἂν ἐπικαλέσηται τὸ ὄνομα κυρίου σωθήσεται: for all who call upon the name of the Lord will be saved (Rom 10:13).³⁸

In 2 Corinthians, Paul does not call upon God for salvation or assistance, but as a witness. Plummer states that calling upon "Heaven" to witness is common in Greek literature, citing examples from Homer, Plato and Xenophon in which the middle form indicates "that Heaven is invoked as a witness on one's own side."³⁹ Josephus uses this verb similarly in describing Abraham's sending of his servant to Rebekah to secure her hand in marriage for Isaac. "These pledges are given on this wise: each party places his hands under the other's thigh, and they then invoke (ἐπικαλοῦνται) God as witness of their future actions."⁴⁰ In like manner, in 2 Cor 1:23 Paul calls upon God as his witness as he attests

---

³⁶ BDAG, s.v. "ἐπικαλέω"; LSJ s.v. "ἐπικαλέω." Accordingly, Harris (*Second Corinthians*, 212) comments: "In the middle voice ἐπικαλέομαί τινα means "I appeal to someone in my favor."

³⁷ Rom 10:12, 13, 14; 1 Cor 1:2; 2 Cor 1:23.

³⁸ The same expression appears in Acts 2:21.

³⁹ Plummer, *Second Corinthians*, 43.

⁴⁰ Josephus, *A.J.*, 1.243.3 (Thackeray, LCL 242: 120–121).

his unselfish intentions in changing his travel plans. This is effectively an oath before God,[41]

2 Cor 1:23 Ἐγὼ δὲ μάρτυρα τὸν θεὸν <u>ἐπικαλοῦμαι</u> ἐπὶ τὴν ἐμὴν ψυχήν, ὅτι φειδόμενος ὑμῶν οὐκέτι ἦλθον εἰς Κόρινθον	I <u>call upon</u> God as witness upon my life, that it was to spare you that I did not subsequently come to Corinth[42]

The middle form ἐπικαλοῦμαι here serves to indicate that the action of calling upon God is done with reference to Paul himself—in his own interest, in the sense of adding weight to his claim. This correlates with the indirect reflexive middle as described by Allan, in which the subject "derives benefit from the action performed[.]"[43] It could similarly be placed in his speech act category.[44] Grammatically, ἐπικαλοῦμαι could also be indirect reflexive (acting *for* oneself), yet the intensity of his oath suggests that his words are heartfelt, from deep within (dynamic middle). The emphatic ἐγώ further emphasizes the subject, while the expression ἐπὶ τὴν ἐμὴν ψυχήν indicates that Paul stakes his life upon his integrity in this matter.[45] From the perspective of mediality, it is apparent that Paul is placing himself and his integrity under scrutiny. He is internal to the process of calling upon God as

---

[41] See Ralph P. Martin, *2 Corinthians*, 2nd ed. WBC 40 (Waco, TX: Word, 2014), 171. Martin considers Ἐγὼ δὲ μάρτυρα τὸν θεὸν ἐπικαλοῦμαι to be "a mild example of oath taking" noting OT precedents. Harris considers it a formal oath and formal curse, indicating the "seriousness of the charges levelled against him" and a deep sense of accountability to God (*Second Corinthians*, 212–13).

[42] Φείδομαι is discussed separately below.

[43] Allan, *Polysemy*, 112.

[44] Allan asserts that: "in many cases the subject intends to gain benefit from the speech act ... These middle verbs are similar to indirect reflexive middles in that the subject can be assigned the semantic role *beneficiary*" (*Polysemy*, 107).

[45] Harris notes that ἐπὶ τὴν ἐμὴν ψυχήν is a Hebraism, literally meaning "against my soul," i.e., "on my own life" (*Second Corinthians*, 212).

witness, a process which conceptually draws together and involves God, Paul and the Corinthians. Thus, ἐπικαλοῦμαι in this context aligns with the medial notion also.

5.6 ΦΕΙΔΟΜΑΙ (*MEDIA TANTUM*)

Listed in BDAG as a middle deponent, φείδομαι has the general sense of sparing someone or something (from harm or loss), drawing back, or refraining from something.[46] For example, ὅς γε τοῦ ἰδίου υἱοῦ οὐκ ἐφείσατο ἀλλὰ ὑπὲρ ἡμῶν πάντων παρέδωκεν αὐτόν: indeed, he who did not spare his own son but delivered him up for us all (Rom 8:32). This verb appears frequently in the LXX. For example, οὐ φείσομαι ἐπ' αὐτοῖς καὶ οὐ μὴ οἰκτιρήσω αὐτούς: I will not spare them, and I will not have compassion upon them (Jer 21:7, Brenton). Similarly, it is used by Josephus in telling of Simeon and Levi who killed all the males of the city to avenge their sister Dinah, sparing (φείδονται) only the women.[47] Φείδομαι occurs only ten times in the New Testament; it does not appear at all in the gospels but is mainly used by Paul.[48] It occurs three times in 2 Corinthians: in 1:23 (above), and in 12:6 and 13:2 as below:

2 Cor 12:6 Ἐὰν γὰρ θελήσω καυχήσασθαι, οὐκ ἔσομαι ἄφρων, ἀλήθειαν γὰρ ἐρῶ· φείδομαι δέ, μή τις εἰς ἐμὲ λογίσηται ὑπὲρ ὃ βλέπει με ἢ ἀκούει [τι] ἐξ ἐμοῦ	Though if I wish to boast, I shall not be a fool, for I would be speaking the truth; but I refrain, lest anyone may think more of me than he sees in me or hears from me.

---

[46] BDAG, s.v. "φείδομαι." LSJ, s.v. "φείδομαι."
[47] Josephus, *A.J.*, 1.340.4 (Thackeray, LCL 242: 162–163)
[48] NT occurrences are Acts 20:29; Rom 8:32, 11:21; 1 Cor 7:28; 2 Cor 1:23, 12:6, 13:2; 2 Pet 2:4, 5.

2 Cor 13:2 προείρηκα καὶ προλέγω, ὡς παρὼν τὸ δεύτερον καὶ ἀπὼν νῦν, τοῖς προημαρτηκόσιν καὶ τοῖς λοιποῖς πᾶσιν, ὅτι ἐὰν ἔλθω εἰς τὸ πάλιν <u>οὐ φείσομαι</u>	I said before when present on my second visit and I say in advance being absent now, to those who sinned before and all the rest, that if I come again, I <u>will not hold back</u>.[49]

In 2 Cor 1:23 (discussed above) Paul explains that it was in order to <u>spare</u> (ὅτι <u>φειδόμενος</u> ὑμῶν) the Corinthians that he did not come to Corinth as previously planned. In 12:6 he states that he *refrains* from boasting for the purpose of integrity. In 13:2, he asserts that he will not *spare* (ESV, NAS, NIV, NKJV, RSV) or *be lenient* (NAB, NRSV) toward those who have not repented (12:20, 21). In each case, Paul is motivated by his desire to maintain an appropriate relationship with the Corinthians, maintaining trust, integrity, and authority. He does so for the purpose of building up the Corinthians in the faith, always aware of his accountability before God (12:19). Hence the notion of sparing (or not) refers to his considered intention, something he does within the context of his relationship with the church at Corinth.

In order to spare the Corinthians by acting towards them in an attitude of mercy, Paul must restrain his own impulses or actions Therefore, he is also acting on himself, holding himself back. Hence, οὐ φείσομαι in 13:2 has the sense: "I will not hold (myself) back," so it is essentially a direct reflexive in the grammatical sense (considering the positive sense for the purpose of analysis). Yet also, the dynamic middle could apply, for Paul is acting from within his own heartfelt intentions, making a considered decision.[50]

---

[49] This firm language appears in the context of Paul signaling his third visit (13:1) to Corinth, in anticipation that they will examine themselves and repent so that he may not need to be harsh with them when he comes (12:20–13:5).

[50] This evokes the definition of the middle by Nigel Turner, *Syntax*, vol. 3 of *A Grammar of New Testament Greek* (Edinburgh: T&T Clark, 1963), 54. He comments that "the middle involves the whole subject in the verb's action and expresses the subject in some special relationship to himself."

From the medial perspective, we can see that the subject (Paul) is positioned within the process of the verb since the action, although carried out with respect to the Corinthians, also affects him. Therefore, the subject is medially located within the process, responding to the situation by holding himself back.

Allan discusses φείδομαι in connection with indirect reflexives, referring to it as one of a "group of verbs that designate emotionally motivated actions that seem to be related to the indirect reflexive middle."[51] The subject, being well-disposed toward the object, may be considered to benefit from the action. Nevertheless, if the sense of the verb is understood as 'holding oneself back', the direct reflexive could also apply in Allan's scheme.

The other two instances may also be seen to have middle function. In 2 Cor 1:23, it was in order to spare the Corinthians that Paul decided not to visit at that stage. That is, he held himself back, so that although he was acting towards the Corinthians in the sense of extending mercy (sparing them) he was also acting upon himself in restraint and the same descriptors apply as above.

In 2 Cor 12:6, φείδομαι is used intransitively, indicating even more explicitly that Paul is 'holding himself back' (refraining) from boasting, acting upon himself in a volitional response to the possibility. Hence the direct reflexive sense is apparent, yet because of the emotional motivation, so too is the sense of acting within a process, a mental process of deciding to act in a particular manner, a process which encompasses the subject. Likewise, the sense of benefit (indirect reflexive) noted by Allan above is again apparent in Paul's motivation to demonstrate his integrity. In each case there is the sense of acting according to the relationship Paul has with the Corinthians.

Here is an example of a verb commonly construed as deponent that has been shown to be truly middle. If 'deponent' is simply taken to mean

---

[51] Allan, *Polysemy*, 113n199. This type of emotional motivation resonates with the dynamic middle, as noted above. Such an explanation of the middle voice of φείδομαι could also apply in 2 Cor 1:23; 12:6, and 13:2 if the benefit Paul derives is the establishment of the type of relationship that he desires with the Corinthians.

that the verb has no active form, there is no conflict. However, if deponent is taken to mean "middle in form but active in function" as is commonly held, the classification is to be disputed. Rather than applying to the meaning of the Greek verb in context, the active designation actually applies to a translation such as the English "spare" (ESV, KJV, NAB, NIV, NRSV). On the contrary, φείδομαι exhibits middle function wherever it appears in 2 Corinthians.

5.7 ΧΑΡΙΖΟΜΑΙ (*MEDIA TANTUM*)

While LSJ lists the active form χαρίζω, noting that it was usually used in the middle voice, BDAG lists χαρίζομαι as a middle deponent, thus suggesting that the active was not used in NT times.[52] The middle is used in the New Testament to refer to giving graciously or generously (Rom 8:32), cancelling a debt (Luke 7:42), or forgiving a wrongdoing (Eph 4:32), as noted by BDAG.[53] Hans Conzelmann asserts that the primary sense of the word χαρίζομαι is giving, the specific nuance being derived from its context, so that when used in the sense of forgiveness it relates to a "special form of giving, namely, pardoning[.]"[54]

In the LXX, χαρίζομαι appears always in the sense of giving, granting, bestowing, or releasing but not, however, in regard to forgiveness. For example, εἰ πάντα τὰ ὑπάρχοντα Αμαν ἔδωκα καὶ <u>ἐχαρισάμην</u> σοι: "if everything belonging to Haman I gave and <u>turned over</u> to you" (Esth 8:7, NETS).[55] The lemma appears twenty-three times in the NT, occurring in Luke-Acts in the sense of bestowing (Luke 7:21, Acts

---

[52] LSJ, s.v. "χαρίζω." BDAG, s.v. "χαρίζομαι."

[53] One nuance of the sense of giving is that of handing over or releasing someone on request, e.g., Pilate being asked to release a murderer (Acts 3:14), Paul (not) being handed over to the Jews (Acts 25:11, 16), and Paul being restored to Philemon (Phlm 1:22). The sense appears to be to grant the wishes of those who ask for the surrender.

[54] Hans Conzelmann, "χάρις, χαρίζομαι, χαριτόω, ἀχάριστος," *TDNT* 9:372–402; here, 396–7.

[55] χαρίζομαι is used similarly in 2, 3 and 4 Maccabees and in Sirach. There are no active forms.

27:24), cancelling a debt (Luke 7:42, 43) and handing over upon request (Acts 3:14, 25:11, 16).

In the Pauline corpus it is used in the sense of bestowing graciously (Rom 8:32, 1 Cor 2:12; Gal 3:18; Phil 1:29, 2:9; Phlm 1:22) and in relation to forgiveness of wrongdoing (2 Cor 2:7, 10 (x3), 12:13; Eph 4:32 (x2); Col 2:13, 3:13 (x2). These facts suggest that "forgiving" is a characteristically Pauline usage of χαρίζομαι; this does not necessarily indicate that he is using it in an unconventional manner, however. Rather, this usage may be explained by the subject matter of his letters, for what is graciously conferred is the remission of sins, consistent with Conzelmann's comments above.[56]

While there are no active forms of χαρίζομαι in the NT, there are both MP1 and MP2 aorist forms as encountered previously in the case of γίνομαι.[57] However, in contrast to the equivalence observed in uses of ἐγενόμην and ἐγενήθην (both being used in the middle voice), in the case of χαρίζομαι the MP2 forms *do have* passive sense,[58] for example, ἵνα εἰδῶμεν τὰ ὑπὸ τοῦ θεοῦ <u>χαρισθέντα</u> ἡμῖν: so that we may perceive the things freely <u>given</u> to us by God (1 Cor 2:12).[59] This correlates with the fact that χαρίζομαι is used transitively. Middle forms of χαρίζομαι appear three times in 2 Corinthians as below:

| 2 Cor 2:7 ὥστε τοὐναντίον μᾶλλον ὑμᾶς <u>χαρίσασθαι</u> καὶ παρακαλέσαι, μή πως τῇ | On the contrary rather, you should <u>forgive</u> and console [him], otherwise he may be |

---

[56] This is likewise noted by Harris, *2 Corinthians*, 233.

[57] See §3.1.2 γίνομαι, above.

[58] As noted by both BDAG and LSJ, the latter indicating that the passive has the sense of being favoured. This correlates with χαρίζομαι being a transitive verb.

[59] Other NT attestations of the passive are χαρισθῆναι (Acts 3:14), and ἐχαρίσθη (Phil 1:29). These also refer to the sense of being granted, rather than being forgiven. Middle aorists of χαρίζομαι: ἐχαρίσατο (Luke 7:21, 42, 43; Eph 4:32; Phil 2:9), χαρίσασθαι (Acts 25:11; 2 Cor 2:7), χαρίσασθε (2Cor 12:13), and χαρισάμενος (Col 2:13).

περισσοτέρᾳ λύπῃ καταποθῇ ὁ τοιοῦτος	overwhelmed by excessive sorrow [60]
2 Cor 2:10 ᾧ δέ τι <u>χαρίζεσθε</u>, κἀγώ· καὶ γὰρ ἐγὼ ὃ <u>κεχάρισμαι</u>, εἴ τι <u>κεχάρισμαι</u>, δι' ὑμᾶς ἐν προσώπῳ Χριστοῦ,	And to whom you <u>forgive</u> anything, I do also; for what I <u>have forgiven</u>, if I <u>have forgiven</u> something, is for your sake in the sight of Christ
2 Cor 12:13 τί γάρ ἐστιν ὃ ἡσσώθητε ὑπὲρ τὰς λοιπὰς ἐκκλησίας, εἰ μὴ ὅτι αὐτὸς ἐγὼ οὐ κατενάρκησα ὑμῶν; <u>χαρίσασθέ</u> μοι τὴν ἀδικίαν ταύτην	For in what way were you made inferior to the rest of the churches, except that I myself did not burden you? <u>Forgive</u> me this wrong!

Although in the last example Paul is clearly being facetious, the verb χαρίζομαι is used in the sense of forgiving in each of the verses above, rather than in the sense of bestowing a gift. Nevertheless, it could be said that what is bestowed is grace itself. The medial function of such an action is clear, for in responding to an offence with grace, the subjects in each case are involved in a process which encompasses them (Eberhard). The subject is not acting merely externally in a manner which leaves itself unaffected, but is interior to, the action designated by the middle verb.

Whereas Allan does not definitively classify this verb among the examples for any of his categories, he includes χαρίζομαι among a number of verbs which designate "emotionally motivated actions"[61] perceiving these to be related to the indirect reflexive middle, the subject benefiting from the action in some manner.[62] For the purpose of

---

[60] English translations such as CJB, ESV, KJV, NAB, NIV, NJB, and NRSV, typically render this verb by the appropriate form of 'forgive' in each of these verses.

[61] As for φείδομαι above.

[62] In this comment Allan also includes: αἰκίζομαι (maltreat), δηλέομαι (hurt,

affirming the middle function of χαρίζομαι in the verses above, it is sufficient to recognize that the subjects are affected by the act of forgiving due to the associated change in their emotional state and/or social relations. This is highlighted in the parable Jesus told of the unforgiving servant (Matt 18:23–35) in which the state of a person who does not forgive is likened to that of being in jail. Forgiveness brings release from anger and negative emotions arising from an offence, as well as improved relationships, so in this sense, there is a benefit to the subject. It is volitional, arising from within a person (dynamic middle) directed to another and occurring in the context of relationship. Such attributes are typically reflected in the middle verbs considered throughout this investigation.

5.8 ἈΠΟΤΑΣΣΟΜΑΙ (ἈΠΟΤΑΣΣΩ)

The active form, ἀποτάσσω and the middle form ἀποτάσσομαι have somewhat different applications; the former, which is not found in the New Testament, refers to appointing, positioning or setting apart, removing.[63] The middle form ἀποτάσσομαι is classed as a verb of communication by L&N, meaning "to employ formalized expressions appropriate to leaving or saying farewell to someone, possibly involving the communication of final arrangements for leaving—'to say goodbye'."[64] Hence, for example, a private papyrus letter from Ptolemaios to his mother and sister (SB 18.13867 *l* 95 [125–175 CE]) includes the remark: ὀργίζομε [ὀργίζομαι] δὲ ὅτι οὐκ ἀπετάξατό μοι: "but I am angry because she did not <u>bid me good-bye</u>." The semantic link between

---

damage), φείδομαι (spare), φιλοφρονέομαι (treat kindly). The benefit may be power, when the subject is ill-disposed, or pleasure when well-disposed, toward the object (*Polysemy*, 113n199).

[63] LSJ, s.v. "ἀποτάσσω." Example of active use: καὶ <u>ἀπέταξεν</u> ἐκεῖ δύναμιν τηρεῖν αὐτὸ καὶ ὠχύρωσεν αὐτὸ τηρεῖν τὴν Βαιθσουραν: and he <u>stationed</u> a force there to defend it, and he fortified it to defend Baithsoura (1 Macc 4:61, NETS).

[64] L&N, s.v. "ἀποτάσσομαι" (33.23). This verb is not very common in Scripture, occurring only 7 times in the LXX and 6 times in the NT.

the active and middle forms may be construed as being that the middle involves positioning or setting *oneself* apart, hence, taking leave, as illustrated also by the NT examples below.⁶⁵ That is, while the sense of the verb may have become associated with the speech act of 'saying good-bye', in essence it refers to the *intention of parting*.

This sense is clearly apparent in Acts 18:21 in reference to Paul bidding farewell to the Ephesians: ἀλλὰ <u>ἀποταξάμενος</u> καὶ εἰπών· πάλιν ἀνακάμψω πρὸς ὑμᾶς τοῦ θεοῦ θέλοντος: but on <u>taking leave</u> of them he said: "I will return to you if God wills[.]" Ἀποτάσσομαι is similarly used when Jesus took leave of his disciples to go up to the mountain to pray (ἀποταξάμενος αὐτοῖς, Mark 6:46). In Luke 14:33 the verb is used metaphorically in the stronger sense of renouncing or forsaking: πᾶς ἐξ ὑμῶν ὃς οὐκ <u>ἀποτάσσεται</u> πᾶσιν τοῖς ἑαυτοῦ ὑπάρχουσιν οὐ δύναται εἶναί μου μαθητής: anyone of you who does not <u>renounce</u> all that he has cannot be my disciple.⁶⁶

The only other occurrence of ἀποτάσσομαι in the NT is in 2 Cor 2:13, as Paul refers to leaving Troas, where a door had opened for him to preach the gospel (2:12). Although this was an opportunity Paul would normally have heartily engaged, he was anxious because he did not meet Titus. This meant that he had no news as to how the Corinthians had received his harsh letter (previously delivered to them by Titus).⁶⁷ Therefore, he went on to Macedonia hoping to meet him there.

---

⁶⁵ The sense of parting is also noted by LSJ for the middle form.

⁶⁶ ἀποτάσσεται is typically translated "renounce" (CJB, DRA, ESV, NAB, RSV), "forsake" (KJV, NKJV, GNV), or "give up" (CEB, NAS, NIV, NRSV) in this verse. *ALGNT* identifies this as a metaphorical use. In taking leave of all that they have, they are effectively renouncing or forsaking it.

⁶⁷ In 2 Cor 7:6–14, Paul continues his reference to Titus and the severe letter which the Corinthians duly accepted.

2 Cor 2:13 οὐκ ἔσχηκα ἄνεσιν τῷ πνεύματί μου τῷ μὴ εὑρεῖν με Τίτον τὸν ἀδελφόν μου, ἀλλὰ <u>ἀποταξάμενος</u> αὐτοῖς ἐξῆλθον εἰς Μακεδονίαν	I had no rest in my spirit because I did not find my brother Titus, so I <u>took leave</u> of them and went on to Macedonia

As in the examples above, the middle form here refers to saying farewell. There could be an element of the stronger sense also, because he is choosing to forsake the opportunity to preach the gospel in Troas (2 Cor 2:12) in favor of going to Macedonia. The middle function is seen in the activity of parting *himself* from the people at Troas. Thus, in a grammatical sense ἀποτάσσομαι could be considered a direct reflexive, although this does not reflect any emotional or relational component normally associated with farewells. The notion of mediality is apparent in that the process encompasses the subject acting within it; the subject is not the sole participant. The action is volitional but results in a change of state for Paul as he removed himself from their company. The subject is clearly affected by the process.

Although Allan does not list ἀποτάσσομαι among his examples, it could be classified as a speech act middle. For this category, Allan asserts that the "subject is involved in the speech act in a special way" and that such verbs are "rather specific with respect to their lexical meaning."[68] That is, "neutral" verbs of speech such as λέγω tend to be active, whereas those in which the subject is emotionally or mentally involved, such as μέμφομαι (rebuke) are inclined to have middle form.[69] On this basis, ἀποτάσσομαι also fits the speech act category, for the severing of a relationship produces an effect on the subject.[70] However, since he chose to leave so that he might meet up with Titus in Macedonia, he is

---

[68] Allan, *Polysemy*, 105–6.

[69] Allan, *Polysemy*, 106–7.

[70] Although we are not told about Paul's feelings toward the people of Troas, his departure meant tearing himself away from an opportunity to preach the gospel. He was also anxious about Titus; therefore, there was some emotional component to his departure.

also acting in his own interest, seeking a benefit from the departure. Hence, Allan's indirect reflexive category is also appropriate. Whether or not ἀποτάσσομαι fits neatly into one of Allan's categories does not refute the fact that the subject is clearly affected in this process.

5.9 Ἄρχομαι (Ἄρχω)

Although ἄρχομαι has an active form, the semantic relationship between the two forms is not immediately apparent. Whereas ἄρχω indicates the function of ruling or governing, the middle form ἄρχομαι refers to beginning an action.[71] There is however, a semantic link of primacy common to both forms; that is, primacy of time (ἄρχομαι) or primacy of power status (ἄρχω).[72] The middle form is pervasively used in the New Testament, the active form occurring only twice (Mark 10:42, Rom 15:12), both being in reference to ruling the nations. Therefore, having a distinct lexical sense, ἄρχομαι is effectively a *media tantum* verb in the New Testament, which probably explains why it is sometimes referred to as a middle deponent verb.[73]

It is commonly used as an auxiliary with an infinitive to indicate commencement of an activity. Hence, we see ἤρξατο ὁ Ἰησοῦς κηρύσσειν: Jesus <u>began</u> to preach (Matt 4:17) and similarly, γράφειν ἤρξατο τὴν ἐπιστολήν: he <u>began</u> to write the letter.[74] Occurring frequently in narrative texts, it appears eighty-four times in the NT altogether but most prolifically in the gospel of Luke, for example, καὶ ἀνεκάθισεν ὁ νεκρὸς καὶ ἤρξατο λαλεῖν: the dead man sat up and

---

[71] BDAG, s.v. "ἄρχω." Accordingly, L&N lists the two verbs in different semantic domains: L&N s.v. "ἄρχω" (37.54) to rule or govern; L&N s.v. "ἄρχομαι" (68.1), to initiate an action, process, or state of being. Wallace comments that this is an example of verbs which have followed separate paths for active and middle, having virtually no overlap in the field of meaning (*Exegetical Syntax*, 415n17).

[72] As noted by Gerhard Delling, "ἄρχω," *TDNT* 1:478.

[73] See Duff, *Elements*, 97; Jay, *NT Greek*, 86.

[74] Plutarch, *Vitae decem oratum*, 847.B.1 (Fowler, LCL 321: 428–429).

began to speak (Luke 7:15). It is used only once in the writings of Paul, this being in 2 Corinthians 3:1, as below.

2 Cor 3:1 Ἀρχόμεθα πάλιν ἑαυτοὺς συνιστάνειν; ἢ μὴ χρῄζομεν ὥς τινες συστατικῶν ἐπιστολῶν πρὸς ὑμᾶς ἢ ἐξ ὑμῶν;	Are we <u>beginning</u> to commend ourselves again? Or do we, like some, need letters of commendation to you or from you?

The middle voice function of this verb can be recognized in that it is distinctly volitional yet because the subject is beginning to engage in an activity, it is also affected. When people begin something, they act with reference to themselves, moving from a state of inertia to one of activity, or from one activity to another. Therefore, there is a change of state. While Allan does not include ἄρχομαι in any of his categories, it could be regarded as an indirect reflexive in his scheme because the subject would become an 'experiencer' or 'beneficiary' with respect to the action.[75] Likewise, grammatically, there could be the sense here of acting *for* himself (if he *were* beginning to commend himself), yet also *by* himself, mobilizing his capacities, so ἀρχόμεθα in 2 Cor 3:1 could be classed as both an indirect reflexive and a dynamic middle.

The situation is also medial, for the subject would be acting within the process of beginning to commend himself—a process "in and of which the subject partakes."[76] This descriptor highlights the process (beginning) but does not suppress the subject, who can determine the extent to which he engages in the new activity, the degree to which the process happens.[77] These middle voice attributes are also linked to the lexical semantics of the verb. That is, beginning something necessarily means that the subject is affected and participates in the results of the action;

---

[75] Allan, *Polysemy*, 112.
[76] Eberhard, *Middle Voice*, 77.
[77] See Eberhard, *Middle Voice*, 75.

such participation being another indicator of the middle voice and one which is readily apparent in this instance.[78]

5.10 ΛΟΓΙΖΟΜΑΙ (*MEDIA TANTUM*)

The verb λογίζομαι is found throughout a wide range of Greek writing.[79] The primary sense, according to H. W. Heidland, refers to "an act of thought according to strict logical rules."[80] He notes that it is used commercially in regard to counting or reckoning, referring, for example, to charging a debt or evaluating something in a legal context.[81] In classical literature, it means "deliberate, to conclude." commonly referring to the non-emotional thinking of the philosopher, especially in Plato.[82] Further, he notes that in rendering Hebraic thought in the LXX there appears a more subjective, emotional nuance such that it refers to reckoning or regarding people as something, as well as planning or devising.[83] For example. καὶ ἐν τοῖς ἀνόμοις ἐλογίσθη: "and he was reckoned among the lawless" (Isa 53:12, NETS), that is, he was regarded or considered as such.[84]

---

[78] See Dana and Mantey, *Manual Grammar*, 157.

[79] LSJ provides many examples from classical literature. Among the Hellenistic writings, the lemma appears frequently in Plutarch (89 times), Josephus (70 times), and the LXX (120 times), according to TLG and BibleWorks searches respectively.

[80] H. W. Heidland, "λογίζομαι, λογισμός," *TDNT* 4:284–92.

[81] Heidland, *TDNT* 4:284.

[82] Heidland refers to "the non-emotional thinking of the philosopher seeking suprapersonal knowledge ... the receptive apprehension of something objectively present" (*TDNT* 4:284). The notion of receptive apprehension resonates with concepts of the middle voice such as the perception middle. Thus, Allan notes that in the case of the verb σκέπτομαι, the subject gains information from (carefully) observing an object, such that the perception brings about a lasting effect on the cognitive state of mind of the perceiver (*Polysemy*, 99–100).

[83] Heidland, *TDNT* 4:284–85.

[84] The sense of planning or purpose is also seen, e.g., καὶ μετανοήσω περὶ τῶν κακῶν ὧν ἐλογισάμην τοῦ ποιῆσαι αὐτοῖς: "then will I repent of the evils which I purposed to do to them" (Jer 18:8, Brenton).

Of interest regarding this more subjective nuance is the example provided by a papyrus letter from *Arsinoite nome* in Egypt, written to account for five particular camels, one of which had since been sold and one hired out. In reference to simply counting the remaining three camels, the verb used is ἐξαριθμέω (count or enumerate), whereas when the writer refers to the one calf who is now "reckoned" among the fully grown camels, the verb used is λογίζομαι. This reflects the subjective sense of considered evaluation or estimation rather than simple enumeration. Hence, we see: κάμηλ(οι) ἐξαριθ(μηθέντες) γ: "3 camels counted," but καμήλων δ καὶ πώλου α, <u>λογιζομένου</u> νυνεὶ [νυνὶ] ἐν τελείοις: "four camels and one calf, now <u>reckoned</u> among the full-grown ones" (BGU 3.762 *ll* 1, 7–9, [163 CE]).

All of the above uses are found in the New Testament, as noted by BDAG.[85] The primary sense of simple reckoning or calculating is used by Paul in Romans, for example, μακάριος ἀνὴρ οὗ οὐ μὴ <u>λογίσηται</u> κύριος ἁμαρτίαν: blessed is the man against whom the Lord <u>does not reckon sin</u> (Rom 4:8).[86] In the wider sense of consider, regard or estimate, we see, for example, <u>ἐλογίσθημεν</u> ὡς πρόβατα σφαγῆς: <u>we are regarded</u> as sheep for slaughter (Rom 8:36, citing Ps 43:23). The use of λογίζομαι to refer to mental activity, that is, thinking upon a matter, is seen in Paul's exhortation to the Philippians to think about matters of virtue: ταῦτα <u>λογίζεσθε</u>: <u>think on</u> these things (Phil 4:8). Illustrating the sense of holding an opinion, Silvanus is said to be a faithful brother ὡς λογίζομαι (in my estimation) in 1 Pet 5:12.

The verb λογίζομαι appears forty times in the New Testament, primarily in the writings of Paul. This includes eight occurrences in 2 Corinthians (3:5, 5:19, 10:2 x2, 10:7, 10:11, 11:5, 12:6) which are all in the middle form. Although there are no active forms, there are several

---

[85] BDAG, s.v. "λογίζομαι."

[86] English translations commonly render this in the sense of a credit and debit account, e.g., "will not reckon to his account" (CJB), "whose sin the Lord does not record" (NAB), "to whom the Lord imputes no guilt" (NJB).

Middle Voice Verbs in the New Testament 199

occurrences of the MP2 aorist form in the New Testament.[87] For this particular verb, the MP2 forms appear to be true passives, while the sigmatic (MP1) aorist represents the middle voice.[88] Accordingly, Paul uses the passive ἐλογίσθη to speak of Abraham's faith being reckoned to him as righteousness in Romans, e.g., ἐλογίσθη τῷ Ἀβραὰμ ἡ πίστις εἰς δικαιοσύνην (Rom 4:9).[89] Middle forms of λογίζομαι appear throughout 2 Corinthians, as itemized below. The voice function for each instance is discussed in §5.10.8.

5.10.1 Λογίζομαι in 2 Cor 3:5

2 Cor 3:5 οὐχ ὅτι ἀφ' ἑαυτῶν ἱκανοί ἐσμεν λογίσασθαί τι ὡς ἐξ ἑαυτῶν, ἀλλ' ἡ ἱκανότης ἡμῶν ἐκ τοῦ θεοῦ	Not that we are qualified of ourselves <u>to regard</u> anything as [coming] from ourselves; rather, our sufficiency is from God

Paul here is speaking of the church at Corinth being the evidence of his ministry. In this verse λογίσασθαι is rendered variously by English translations, for example: "to think" (GNV, KJV, NKJV), "to consider" (NAS, NET) "to claim" (CEB, ESV, NIV, NJB, NRSV), "to take credit" (NAB), and "to count" or "to account" (ASV, CJB, ERV). Having denied that he is commending himself (3:1), he argues that the Corinthians themselves are his letter of commendation (3:2) and that God is the one who qualifies the apostles for their ministry (3:6). The sense is that Paul denies any credit for the successful ministry which God has achieved

---

[87] LSJ does not list an active form, only the middle and passive.

[88] Occurrences of aorist passives in Paul: Rom 2:26; 4:3, 9, 10, 11, 22, 23; 8:36; Gal 3:6 (also 2 Tim 4:16). Sigmatic middle aorists appear only in this epistle: 2 Cor 3:5; 12:6.

[89] Although the passive is often an inversion of an active form, the middle λογίζομαι is one of many middle verbs that can be transitive and hence may be inverted into a passive expression. Hence, e.g., God reckoned Abraham's faith becomes Abraham's faith was reckoned.

through him among the Corinthians.⁹⁰ Therefore, λογίσασθαι is used in the usual sense of considering or reckoning as Paul speaks of his self-evaluation in this verse.

5.10.2 Λογίζομαι in 2 Cor 5:19

| 2 Cor 5:19 ὡς ὅτι θεὸς ἦν ἐν Χριστῷ κόσμον καταλλάσσων ἑαυτῷ, μὴ <u>λογιζόμενος</u> αὐτοῖς τὰ παραπτώματα αὐτῶν καὶ θέμενος ἐν ἡμῖν τὸν λόγον τῆς καταλλαγῆς | that is to say, God was in Christ reconciling the world to himself, not <u>reckoning</u> their trespasses [against] them, and assigning to us the message of reconciliation |

This can be understood in the context of the pericope 5:14–21 which speaks of the substitutionary death of Christ. Christ died for all (5:14) and God made Christ, the one who knew no sin, to be sin, so that in him we might become the righteousness of God (5:21). This speaks metaphorically in terms of an account or ledger. Christ is placed on the side of sin and death while people are deemed to be righteous. Their trespasses are not recorded against them (5:19) but are effectively removed from their account, remitting their debt.⁹¹ Here λογιζόμενος is used transitively in terms of counting or reckoning the trespasses (τὰ παραπτώματα) of the offenders (αὐτοῖς).

---

⁹⁰ Harris understands that Paul is referring to the thoughts expressed in 1 Cor 15:9–10, in which he speaks of his unworthiness to be an apostle and of God's grace working through him (*2 Corinthians*, 268).

⁹¹ Similarly, Col 2:13–14. He forgave us all our sins, having cancelled the charge of our legal indebtedness, which stood against us and condemned us; he has taken it away, nailing it to the cross (NIV).

5:10.3 Λογίζομαι in 2 Cor 10:2

2 Cor 10:2 δέομαι δὲ τὸ μὴ παρὼν θαρρῆσαι τῇ πεποιθήσει ᾗ λογίζομαι τολμῆσαι ἐπί τινας τοὺς λογιζομένους ἡμᾶς ὡς κατὰ σάρκα περιπατοῦντας.	Now I beg [you] that when present I may not [need to] be bold with the firmness that I expect to challenge some who consider us to be living in a worldly manner.

Paul has begun a new section of the letter in 10:1, referring to himself emphatically: Αὐτὸς δὲ ἐγὼ Παῦλος παρακαλῶ ὑμᾶς: I, Paul myself, urge you. Thus, he pleads according to the gentleness of Christ (10:12), for the Corinthians to respond to his concerns, before proceeding (10:3–4) to defend his apostolic authority.[92] Unless they do so, he imagines or expects (λογίζομαι) that he will need to be harsh with them later in person. This is an intransitive use of the term, akin to the thought process of Greek philosophy, rather than from commercial transactions. The second use of this verb in 10;2, λογιζομένους, has a slightly different sense, namely that of considering or having an opinion.[93] However, both uses are intransitive and refer to consideration of evidence.

---

[92] There is a disjunction between 2 Cor 9 and 10, as will be discussed briefly in the next chapter of this work. Nevertheless, Paul is appealing for their obedience (10:1–6) and proceeds to support that appeal by reference to the apostolic authority he has exercised in the church at Corinth (10:7–18), as noted by Victor Paul Furnish, *II Corinthians*, AB 32A (Garden City, NY: Doubleday, 1984), 475.

[93] As noted by Harris, *2 Corinthians*, 673–74.

5.10.4 Λογίζομαι in 2 Cor 10:7

2 Cor 10:7 Τὰ κατὰ πρόσωπον βλέπετε. εἴ τις πέποιθεν ἑαυτῷ Χριστοῦ εἶναι, τοῦτο <u>λογιζέσθω</u> πάλιν ἐφ' ἑαυτοῦ, ὅτι καθὼς αὐτὸς Χριστοῦ, οὕτως καὶ ἡμεῖς	Look at the facts before you. If anyone is confident in himself that he is of Christ, he should further <u>consider</u> this for himself: that just as he is of Christ, so also are we[94]

Paul addresses the matter of his authority as Christ's representative in this section of the chapter. The imperative λογιζέσθω is juxtaposed with πέποιθεν, the perfect active form of πείθω (persuade). Paul is contending that any persons (most likely the rival apostles) claiming to be of Christ should think about the matter and be as sure of Paul's standing in Christ as they are of their own. Therefore, again the notion of reasoning and evaluating, even judgement, is evident in the use of λογίζομαι, for Paul is challenging such persons to weigh up the evidence κατὰ πρόσωπον (in front of them) and draw a conclusion.

5.10.5 Λογίζομαι in 2 Cor 10:11

2 Cor 10:11 τοῦτο <u>λογιζέσθω</u> ὁ τοιοῦτος, ὅτι οἷοί ἐσμεν τῷ λόγῳ δι' ἐπιστολῶν ἀπόντες, τοιοῦτοι καὶ παρόντες τῷ ἔργῳ	Let such people <u>take account of</u> this – that as we are in word through letters when absent, so also [we will be] in deed when present

---

[94] The translation above does not expand on the expression Χριστου εἶναι, (to be of Christ). However, in the context of the defense Paul is making against those who contest his apostleship, it appears that he is referring to the function of an apostle, i.e., an authorized representative of Christ, rather than simply one who belongs to Christ as a believer. Thus, he is likely referring to the rival apostles. See discussion in Thrall, *II Corinthians*, vol.2, 619–22; Martin, *2 Corinthians*, 490–91; Harris, *2 Corinthians*, 688–90.

Here Paul is referring to those who assert that he is bold in his letters but weak in personal presence (10:10), and warns them to take account of the fact that he will be just as firm in person (10:11). The imperative λογιζέσθω is translated variously, for instance, "consider" (NAS, NET, NKJV), "understand" (ESV, NAB, NRSV), "realize" (CJB, NIV, NLT), and "reckon" (ASV, ERV). The translation by Harris— "Such a person should reckon with this"—brings out the imperative tone.[95] They should therefore consider Paul's exhortation carefully and not disregard his written warnings that challenge them to amend their behavior. Therefore, λογιζέσθω is a call to logical reasoning in this verse.

5.10.6 Λογίζομαι in 2 Cor 11:5

2 Cor 11:5 <u>λογίζομαι</u> γὰρ μηδὲν ὑστερηκέναι τῶν ὑπερλίαν ἀποστόλων	For <u>I consider</u> that I am not at all inferior to the 'super-apostles'

Continuing his defense of his apostolic authority, Paul expresses divine jealously toward the Corinthians, anxious that his opponents should not lead them astray from their sincere devotion to Christ (11:2, 3). Accordingly, he announces that he does not consider himself in anyway inferior to them. Although it would be difficult to accommodate fluently in English translation, the sense of calculating or estimating is apparent in λογίζομαι here, for Paul is evaluating his own credentials in light of the claims of the super-apostles.

5.10.7 Λογίζομαι in 2 Cor 12:6

2 Cor 12:6 Ἐὰν γὰρ θελήσω καυχήσασθαι, οὐκ ἔσομαι ἄφρων, ἀλήθειαν γὰρ ἐρῶ· φείδομαι δέ, μή τις εἰς ἐμὲ <u>λογίσηται</u> ὑπὲρ ὃ βλέπει με ἢ ἀκούει [τι] ἐξ ἐμοῦ	Though if I wish to boast, I shall not be a fool, for I would be speaking the truth; but I refrain, lest anyone <u>may think</u> more of me than he sees in me or hears from me

---

[95] Harris, *2 Corinthians*, 700.

In 2 Cor 12:6 (also discussed above with reference to φείδομαι), Paul again compares two options. He refers, on the one hand, to the impression he may give by boasting of his credentials, and that which the Corinthians may discern from his speech and actions on the other. He declines to boast, so that they must evaluate his integrity by drawing their own conclusions based on the evidence of his words and actions.

5.10.8 Middle function oF λογίζομαι

In consideration of the middle function of λογίζομαι, the comment by Heidland pertaining to the philosophical use of this term is helpful (see above). To speak of the "receptive apprehension of something objectively present" is effectively to say that the subject is in a middle disposition to the verb. In acting to process information, whether in the more concrete manner of accounting or reckoning or in the more abstract sense of logical reasoning and evaluation, the subject is within the process described by the verb (medial function).

Accordingly, Allan places λογίζομαι in his mental activity category, consisting of middle verbs in which the subject has the semantic role of both 'agent' and 'experiencer', (or 'initiator' and 'endpoint' in Kemmer's terminology).[96] That is, the subject engages volitionally in some mental activity and is affected by the process. The effect or change of state involved may be construed as the acquisition of new knowledge. In the grammatical sense, the subject may be seen to be acting from within, mobilizing his or her intrinsic resources (dynamic middle).

In the verses discussed above, this sense of thoughtful reasoning is apparent as Paul speaks of his *considered opinion* about his ministry (3:5, 11:5) and his *expectation* that he will need to be bold towards some who *consider* his behaviour to be at fault (10:2). He posits a challenge to his opponents to *think* again (10:7) or to *be mindful* of his admonition (10:11) and expresses his concern that their *evaluation* of him is based

---

[96] Allan, *Polysemy*, 101, 103.

on just evidence (12:6). In 5:19, Paul states that God is reconciling people to himself, not *deeming* their sins to their account.⁹⁷ Although the reference here is to *not* deeming or attributing sin to people, the verb itself, in the positive sense, involves an act of consideration, just as in the example from the papyri in which the calf was considered or deemed to be full-grown and hence counted as such. A calculated decision needed to be made as to which side of the ledger the transgressions should be placed. Hence, in all the instances of λογίζομαι in 2 Corinthians, all three descriptors of the middle voice are affirmed.

5.11 SUMMARY AND ANALYSIS

Table 5.1 below summarizes the function of each middle verb analyzed in this chapter. In some instances, it was seen that more than one of Allan's categories or more than one type of grammatical middle function could apply. Hence, for example, φείδομαι could be classed as a direct reflexive or a dynamic middle; these functions are not mutually exclusive. However, only one function is displayed in the table for clarity. Similarly, some of the dynamic middles could also be classed as indirect reflexives, for example, ἐπικαλοῦμαι, which appears as such in Allan's classification.

---

⁹⁷ Harris provides an interesting discussion on the use of καταλλάσσω (reconcile) (*2 Corinthians*, 435–36). He observes that the verb is unique in the NT to Paul, who gives it a distinct reference to reconciliation of estranged humanity with God through Christ. In 2 Cor 5:18 & 19 he notes that God is both the initiator and goal of reconciliation, citing Porter: "Paul uses καταλλάσσω in the active voice with the offended and hence angered party in a relationship (i.e., God) as (grammatical) subject taking the initiative in effecting reconciliation between himself and the offending party" (from S. E. Porter, *Καταλλάσσω in Ancient Greek Literature, with Reference to the Pauline Writings*, EFN 5 [Córdoba, Spain: El Almendro, 1994], 16). While the mention of initiator and goal is suggestive of middle voice, instead the active is used with the dative reflexive pronoun ἑαυτῷ to indicate that God acts to draw people *to himself*. The use of the active with the reflexive pronoun here instead of the middle (an equivalence noted in ch. 2 above), could possibly make the reflexivity more explicit than the middle voice would necessarily convey.

Table 5.1 Properties of Middle Verb Forms in 2 Corinthians

Verb	Form	Ref.	MT	Dep.	Gramm. middle	Subj. Aff.	Allan category	Med. event
βούλομαι	ἐβουλόμην	1:15	✓	✓	Dyn.	✓	M. Act	✓
	βουλόμενος	1:17	✓	✓	Dyn.	✓	M. Act	✓
βουλεύω	βουλεύομαι	1:17	✗	✗	Dyn.	✓	M. Act	✓
χράομαι	ἐχρησάμην	1:17	✓	✓	Dyn.	✓	Ind. Ref.	✓
	χρώμεθα	3:12	✓	✓	Dyn.	✓	Ind.Ref.	✓
	χρήσωμαι	13:10	✓	✓	Dyn.	✓	Ind.Ref.	✓
σφραγίζω	σφραγισάμενος	1:22	✗	✗	Ind. Ref.	✓	Ind. Ref.	✗
ἐπικαλέω	ἐπικαλοῦμαι	1:23	✗	✗	Ind. Ref.	✓	Ind. Ref.	✓
φείδομαι	φειδόμενος	1:23	✓	✓	Dir. Ref.	✓	Ind. Ref.	✓
	φείδομαι	12:6	✓	✓	Dir. Ref.	✓	Ind. Ref.	✓
	φείσομαι	13:2	✓	✓	Dir. Ref.	✓	Ind. Ref.	✓
χαρίζομαι	χαρίσασθαι	2:7	✓	✓	Dyn.	✓	Ind. Ref.	✓
	χαρίσεσθε	2:10	✓	✓	Dyn.	✓	Ind. Ref.	✓
	κεχάρισμαι	2:10	✓	✓	Dyn.	✓	Ind. Ref.	✓
	χαρίσασθε	12:13	✓	✓	Dyn.	✓	Ind. Ref.	✓
ἀποτάσσω	ἀποταξάμενος	2:13	✗	✗	Dir. Ref.	✓	Sp. Act.	✓
ἄρχομαι	ἀρχόμεθα	3:1	✗	✗	Ind. Ref.	✓	Ind. Ref.	✓
λογίζομαι	λογίσασθαί	3:5	✓	✓	Dyn.	✓	M. Act.	✓
	λογιζόμενος	5:19	✓	✓	Dyn.	✓	M. Act.	✓
	λογίζομαι	10:2	✓	✓	Dyn.	✓	M. Act.	✓
	λογιζομένους	10:2	✓	✓	Dyn.	✓	M. Act.	✓
	λογιζέσθω	10:7	✓	✓	Dyn.	✓	M. Act.	✓
	λογιζέσθω	10:11	✓	✓	Dyn.	✓	M. Act.	✓
	λογίζομαι	11:5	✓	✓	Dyn.	✓	M. Act.	✓
	λογίσηται	12:6	✓	✓	Dyn.	✓	M. Act.	✓

All twenty-five middle verbs in this investigation clearly display middle function. This includes many *media tantum* verbs that have been perceived as deponent in the past. Notably, subject-affectedness is applicable in every case, as is some type of grammatical function. The subcategories are included in these classifications to assist the identification of each verb with an already recognized class rather than to delimit the possible ways in which a verb may function in the middle voice. Clearly there are various ways of describing the function of a middle verb, as may be seen by the correlation of Allan's mental activity with the dynamic middle. Both involve the engagement of the subject's particular mental capacities but describe this engagement differently. The medial notion also applies widely but draws attention to the subject's participation within a process rather than what is happening to the subject itself. This sample of verbs amply demonstrates middle function for the different descriptors employed in this investigation.

CHAPTER 6
SELECTED MIDDLE VERB STUDIES IN SECOND CORINTHIANS

In the previous chapter, a sample of twenty-four middle forms representing ten different verbs in 2 Corinthians was investigated. These were selected on the criterion that they were not included in the 1 Thessalonians investigation, then examined in the order they appear in 2 Corinthians. It was found that these verbs clearly demonstrated middle function in their context according to the three descriptors employed throughout this study. Such results encourage continued investigation along the same lines.

While there are many more middle verbs in 2 Corinthians, (in fact, too many to investigate individually) a closer exegetical examination of a portion of text may serve to summarize and illustrate some of the issues associated with understanding and translating the middle voice. Further, since the high proportion of middle verbs in 2 Corinthians may be attributed to the particularly frequent use of καυχάομαι a study of middle verbs in 2 Corinthians would be found wanting if the function of this significant verb were not addressed.[1] The selection of these two investigations is informed by the distribution of middle verbs throughout this epistle as displayed in the graph of Figure 6.1 below.

As is widely recognized, the tone of 2 Corinthians changes markedly at the beginning of ch. 10. Indeed, so distinctly polemical does Paul's writing appear in the final chapters (chs. 10–13) that some scholars consider them to be part of a different letter altogether, possibly part of the harsh letter to which Paul refers in 2 Cor 2:4, 7:6, and 7:12.[2]

---

[1] Καυχάομαι is used twenty times in this epistle.

[2] Among those who consider chs. 10–13 to belong to a different letter, R. H. Strahan

Figure 6.1 Frequency of Middle Verbs per Chapter in 2 Corinthians

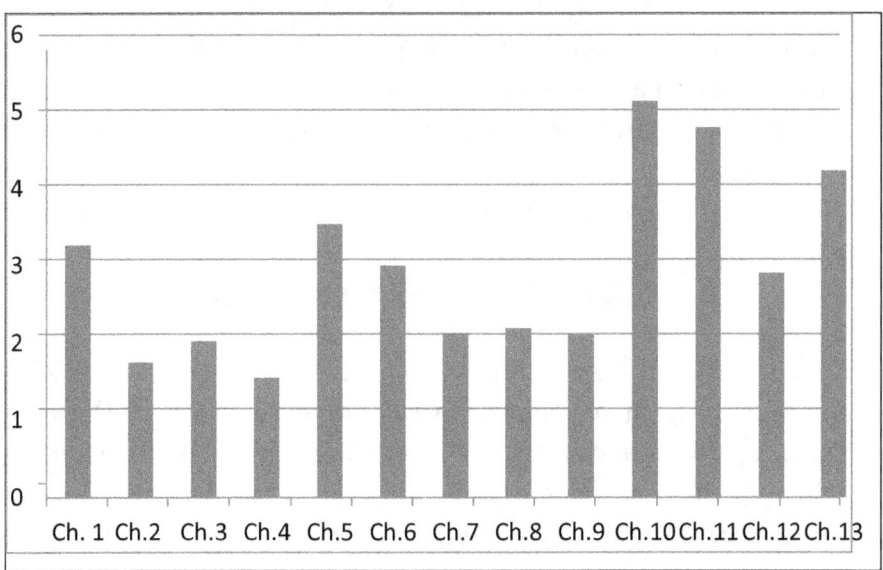

Others maintain that these chapters are a valid and integral part of the one letter, the distinctive tone being attributable to the nature of the issues addressed.³ That is, Paul assumes the need to defend and assert his

---

contends that they belong to the previous harsh letter (*The Second Epistle to the Corinthians*, MNTC (London: Hodder & Stoughton Ltd, 1935, repr., 1954), xvi-xx); while Furnish argues that chapters 10–13 belong to a later letter (*II Corinthians*, 30–41). Thrall presents a comprehensive account of arguments for and against this matter. ultimately favoring the separate position (*II Corinthians*, vol. 1, 5–20).

³ Arguments directly in favor of these chapters being original and integral to this epistle are given by Philip Edgcumbe Hughes, *Paul's Second Epistle to the Corinthians*, NICNT (Grand Rapids: Eerdmans, 1979), xxi–xxxv. Similarly, see Jan Lambrecht, *Second Corinthians*, SP 8 (Collegeville: Liturgical Press, 1999), 7–9. The "theological content remains remarkably constant" throughout all chapters, according to Mark A. Seifrid, The *Second Letter to the Corinthians* (Grand Rapids: Eerdmans, 2014), 368. He maintains that in all probability chapters 10–13 do not represent a separate fragment. Likewise, Harris considers that the position with fewer difficulties is that which posits the integrity of the letter in its canonical form (*Second Corinthians*, 29–51).

authority and integrity as an apostle of Christ due to the teaching of the rival apostles. Similarly, the higher proportion of middle verbs in chs.10–13 can be accounted for by the subject matter, for in this section Paul particularly speaks of boasting (καυχάομαι), seventeen times and reasoning (λογίζομαι), six times.[4] Since this study deals with the letter in its canonical form, this debate need not be discussed further here, so chs. 10–13 will be considered part of 2 Corinthians as it appears in NA[28].

6.1 CASE STUDY—2 COR 10:3–5

Paul is addressing the perception by some that the apostles are walking according to the flesh, of behaving in a worldly fashion (10:2). He therefore takes up this notion and uses it to speak of spiritual battle, asserting that although they are living in the world (Ἐν σαρκὶ περιπατοῦντες), they do not contend on worldly terms (κατὰ σάρκα: according to flesh):

2 Cor 10:3–5. Ἐν σαρκὶ γὰρ περιπατοῦντες οὐ κατὰ σάρκα <u>στρατευόμεθα</u>, τὰ γὰρ ὅπλα τῆς στρατείας ἡμῶν οὐ σαρκικὰ ἀλλὰ δυνατὰ τῷ θεῷ πρὸς καθαίρεσιν ὀχυρωμάτων, λογισμοὺς καθαιροῦντες καὶ πᾶν ὕψωμα <u>ἐπαιρόμενον</u> κατὰ τῆς γνώσεως τοῦ θεοῦ, καὶ αἰχμαλωτίζοντες πᾶν νόημα εἰς τὴν ὑπακοὴν τοῦ Χριστοῦ,	For although we live in the flesh, we do not <u>engage in battle</u> according to the flesh, for the weapons of our warfare are not merely human but are mighty in God for the tearing down of fortresses, demolishing arguments and every exalted thing <u>rising</u> against the knowledge of God, taking every thought captive to obey Christ.

---

[4] By contrast, καυχάομαι occurs three times and λογίζομαι two times in the remainder of the letter.

Paul speaks figuratively of engaging in a battle—not one which is fought on mere human terms or with human weapons (οὐ σαρκικά)—rather, it is by God's power that resistance to the knowledge of God through the gospel is overcome.[5] This resistance is expressed in terms of military metaphor (ὀχύρωμα, fortress, stronghold, or prison), and in terms of verbal defense (λογίσμός, reasoning or argument). Then, alluding to warfare imagery once more, he refers to *any* high thing (πᾶν ὕψωμα), of whatever kind, rising (ἐπαιρόμενον) in opposition to God being made known through Paul's preaching.

6.1.1 Στρατεύομαι (στρατεύω) in 2 Cor 10:3

The metaphor of warfare, with reference to weapons and fortresses, is introduced by the present middle indicative στρατευόμεθα.[6] Although BDAG refers to στρατεύομαι as a middle-deponent in the New Testament,[7] this verb has both active and middle forms in the wider literature (see below). Thus, LSJ distinguishes between the active form στρατεύω which is used to indicate the strategic waging of war or the advancing of an army, and the middle which refers to being enlisted or physically serving as a soldier.[8] The latter is, accordingly, the apt choice for expressing the engagement of a person or persons in battle. The middle form therefore indicates that Paul is speaking in 2 Cor 10:3 above of personal involvement (στρατευόμεθα) in the spiritual warfare campaign (στρατεία).

These respective uses of active and middle forms of στρατεύω are attested in the corpus of Josephus. Thus, λέγεται δ' ὡς οὗτος ὁ Ἑώφρην <u>στρατεύσας</u> ἐπὶ τὴν Λιβύην: "it is said moreover that this

---

[5] The adjectives σαρκικά and δυνατά here are opposites, contrasting human limitation with Godly power, as noted by Furnish, *II Corinthians*, 457. Similarly, Paul contrasts σαρκικά (material things) with πνευματικά (spiritual things) in 1 Cor 9:11.

[6] Accordingly, Furnish states that in using this verb "Paul begins a portrayal of his apostolic service as a military campaign" (*II Corinthians*, 457).

[7] BDAG, s.v. "στρατεύω."

[8] LSJ, s.v. "στρατεύω."

Eôphrên <u>led an expedition</u> against Libya" illustrates the active use.⁹ As an example of the middle form, we see: ἀλλὰ πάντες ἐν ὅπλοις ἐφ' ἁρμάτων καὶ ἵππων <u>στρατευόμενοι</u> μᾶλλον ἢ δουλεύοντες διῆγον: "but they all bore arms and <u>served in the field</u> on chariots and horses rather than lead the lives of slaves."¹⁰ The middle use is similarly attested in a papyrus petition to a centurion regarding the retrieval of valuable goods a veteran had deposited with a fellow soldier while in military service. The letter thus begins: ἡνίκα <u>ἐστρατευόμην</u>, κύριε ἐν Πηλουσίῳ: "when <u>I was serving in the army</u>, lord, in Pelusium" (BGU 1.4 [177 CE]).

Only the middle form, στρατεύομαι, is found in the New Testament. It is used either literally to refer to individuals serving as soldiers (Luke 3:14, 1 Cor 9:7, 2 Tim 2:4) or metaphorically to speak of agents involved in spiritual or psychological battles (2 Cor 10:3, 1 Tim 1:18, Jas 4:1, 1 Pet 2:11).¹¹ In 2 Cor 10:3, above, Paul employs the middle indicative στρατευόμεθα which, by virtue of its lexical semantics and its middle voice form indicates the engagement of the subjects in the action, their vested interest in the outcome of it and the reciprocal nature of the activity.¹²

Applying the descriptors of the middle voice, we see that it may therefore be classed as an indirect reflexive in the grammatical sense. It also corresponds with Eberhard's notion of mediality, for the subjects are clearly acting within a process (the battle, or even being enlisted in the military) which encompasses them. They are not acting outside or alongside the process but are immersed in it. Likewise, the criterion of subject-affectedness is also apparent, for it is axiomatic that the subjects

---

⁹ Josephus, *A.J.*, 1.239.4 (Thackeray, LCL 242:118–119)

¹⁰ Josephus, *A.J.*, 8.161.4 (Marcus, LCL 281:302–303).

¹¹ Hence, e.g., Τίς στρατεύεται ἰδίοις ὀψωνίοις ποτέ; who serves as a soldier at his own expense? (1 Cor 9:7) and Πόθεν πόλεμοι καὶ πόθεν μάχαι ἐν ὑμῖν; οὐκ ἐντεῦθεν, ἐκ τῶν ἡδονῶν ὑμῶν τῶν στρατευομένων ἐν τοῖς μέλεσιν ὑμῶν; what is causing the quarrels and fights among you? Isn't it your desires at war among your members? (Jas 4:1).

¹² The reciprocal function is often noted by grammarians (e.g., §2.1.6.2 above).

engaged in a battle are affected by such involvement. Although Allan comments that στρατεύομαι could be seen as a body motion middle,[13] this does not appear to be the most appropriate sense here. Rather, the indirect reflexive in which the subject is both agent and experiencer, or the reciprocal (agent and patient) are more suitable.

6.1.2 Ἐπαίρομαι (ἐπαίρω) in 2 Cor 10:5

The second middle verb in this text, ἐπαιρόμενον, a present middle/passive participle of ἐπαίρω, may now be considered. According to BDAG the lexical sense of the active is "to cause to move upward, lift up, hold up"; with metaphorical extensions having the sense of "offer resistance to, be in opposition to, rise up," or "suggest that one is better than one really is, be presumptuous, put on airs[.]"[14] In the New Testament, the active form appears sixteen times, typically in reference to lifting up one's eyes (Matt 17:8; Luke 6:20, 16:23, 18:13; John 4:35, 6:5, 17:1), or voice (Luke 11:27; Acts 2:14, 14:11, 22:22). These active forms are always transitive.[15] The passive aorist (-θη- form) appears only once, in reference to Jesus being lifted (ἐπήρθη) into the clouds (Acts 1:9).[16] The middle/passive form occurs only in 2 Corinthians: at 10:5 as above, and at 11:20.

In 2 Cor 11:20 Paul writes: ἀνέχεσθε γὰρ εἴ τις ὑμᾶς καταδουλοῖ, εἴ τις κατεσθίει, εἴ τις λαμβάνει, εἴ τις <u>ἐπαίρεται</u>, εἴ τις εἰς πρόσωπον ὑμᾶς δέρει: for you are forbearing if someone enslaves you, or devours you or exploits you or, <u>raises himself</u> [against] you; if he hits you in the face.[17] The verb <u>ἐπαίρεται</u> can be understood

---

[13] Allan, *Polysemy*, 229.

[14] BDAG, s.v. "ἐπαίρω." As noted by Harris, BDAG does not distinguish a specific middle sense in the NT (*Second Corinthians*, 682n87).

[15] Similarly, lifting up hands, Luke 24:50; 1 Tim 2:8.

[16] This is generally translated as passive, e.g., he was lifted up (ESV, NAB, NJB), taken up (CJB, KJV, NIV).

[17] The middle, rather than passive function of ἐπαίρεται is implied here by the tone of the verse which comprises a list of aggressive behaviors, the other verbs being active

from the context to have middle (not passive) function, for volitional activity is implied. This use of the middle of ἐπαίρω to refer to rising up against another person, particularly an authority, is also evident in the LXX. For example, we see: καὶ Αδωνίας υἱὸς Αγγιθ ἐπήρετο, λέγων, ἐγὼ βασιλεύσω: "And Adonias the son of Aggith exalted himself, saying, I will be king" (1 Kgs 1:5, Brenton).[18]

With respect to Paul's use of ἐπαιρόμενον with military imagery in 2 Cor 10:5, the voice function is not immediately obvious. Both middle (e.g., NAB, NIV, NKJV) and passive (e.g., NJB, NRSV) readings are represented among the English translations. The RSV actually circumvents the decision regarding voice by omitting the verb altogether, translating πᾶν ὕψωμα ἐπαιρόμενον κατὰ τῆς γνώσεως τοῦ θεοῦ as "every proud *obstacle* to the knowledge of God[.]" Despite differences in translation, the image generated is that of any high or exalted thing (ὕψωμα) standing in opposition to the knowledge of God, like a military fortress stands in opposition to an attacking force.[19] Such opposition, Paul states, is demolished by weapons which are δυνατὰ τῷ θεῷ (powerful in God).[20] It will be seen that the choice between middle and passive function is related to the wider context in which the verb appears and specifically to the manner in which πᾶν ὕψωμα is interpreted. An outline of salient factors is given below.

Translations that interpret ἐπαιρόμενον as middle do so by representing it as a direct reflexive. For example, we read "every arrogance which raises itself up" (CJB), "every pretension raising itself" (NAB), "every high thing that exalts itself" (NKJV), and "every pretension that sets itself up" (NIV). Such readings raise a question as to the nature of

---

in function, with implied transitivity. The middle form could be translated as a reflexive, e.g., "exalts himself" (NAS) or simply intransitive, e.g., "behaves arrogantly" (NET).

[18] A similar sense of rising up in rebellion is found in Ezra 4:19; 1 Macc 8:5; 10:70; 2 Macc 7:34; and 3 Macc 2:21.

[19] Thus Seifrid states, "The "knowledge of God" is on the offensive, pressing its attack against everything raised up in rebellion against it" (*Second Corinthians*, 383).

[20] Translations of this phrase include: "powered by God" (CEB), "have divine power" (ESV), "mighty through God" (KJV), "divinely powerful" (NAS).

the subject, for the reflexive function normally refers to an animate agent, to something that is capable of volitional action.[21] Since πᾶν ὕψωμα is neutral, such a reading lends itself to the notion that Paul is speaking of spiritual powers or beings which are capable of such action, for arguments or attitudes are not capable of raising themselves.

Against reading ἐπαιρόμενον as a direct reflexive middle, however, is that it sounds rather active and could equally be expressed by the active form with a reflexive pronoun, which is the more common mode of expressing action on oneself in the New Testament.[22] Further, as discussed above, the direct reflexive function is the least frequent use of the middle form, rarely occurring in the New Testament.[23]

On the other hand, some translations reflect the passive sense which suitably accommodates an inanimate neuter subject (ὕψωμα) by allowing for an implied agent. The sense would be that the high thing is raised by those who resist the knowledge of God. For example, we see "every proud obstacle raised up" (NRSV), "every defence that is raised up" (CEB), "every lofty opinion raised" (ESV), and "every presumptuous notion that is set up" (NJB). In whatever manner the military metaphor is interpreted, the sense is that the opposition is raised *by* someone. Such a reading tends to suggest that the battle is an intellectual one, as if a philosophical position is argued or an arrogant attitude adopted in opposition to the gospel. Hence, Furnish comments that Paul "writes of reasonings as strongholds" that are "raised up in opposition to the knowledge of God," noting a similar use of the "stronghold" metaphor by Philo when referring to strategic and defensive arguments.[24]

---

[21] Allan considers the direct reflexive category to be limited to a "human agent that volitionally performs an action on him or herself" (*Polysemy*, 88).

[22] As noted in §2.1.6.4 above.

[23] See §2.1.6.7 above. An alternative middle reading is discussed below.

[24] Furnish, *II Corinthians*, 454, 462. Thus, Philo writes, "For the stronghold which was built through persuasiveness of argument was built solely for the purpose of diverting and deflecting the mind from honoring God" (*Conf.*, 129.3 [Colson, Whitaker, LCL 261:80–81]). See also, R. H. Strachan, *The Second Epistle of Paul to the Corinthians*, MNTC (London: Hodder & Stoughton, 1954), 11. Strachan comments that Paul's

Both middle and passive options discussed above appear plausible;[25] however, they do not exhaust all possibilities. Paul has already referred to tearing down strongholds, (ὀχυρωμάτων, maintaining the warfare metaphor) and arguments, (λογισμοὺς, interpreting the metaphor) yet adds πᾶν ὕψωμα ἐπαιρόμενον. Both subject and participle are open to interpretation, yet the emphasis is clear: *whatever* arises in opposition will be torn down, not by human arguments, but by the power of God.[26]

Given the above considerations, further types of middle function (other than the direct reflexive noted above) may be considered. From the grammatical perspective, the indirect reflexive function is also possible, for rising up in battle suggests that the subject has a vested interest, a self-interest in so doing. Further, the action would require the mobilization of intrinsic powers, as in the case of the dynamic middle. Like the direct reflexive considered above, these possibilities invoke the question as to the nature of the agent (subject). Nevertheless, each of the grammatical descriptors refers to the subject acting volitionally and thus suggest an animate subject.

Another possible type of middle function for ἐπαιρόμενον is Allan's spontaneous process. Such verbs indicate a change of state, but the focus is on what is happening rather than on the agent of change, as when one might say "the wax is melting."[27] In this case Paul would be speaking of *anything* that rises up (πᾶν ὕψωμα ἐπαιρόμενον) in opposition, not just arguments raised by human agents. This would allow for

---

opponents are offering moral resistance rather than serious attempts at disproof.

[25] Thus, e.g., Plummer (*Second Corinthians*, 277) asserts that ἐπαιρόμενον is probably middle on the basis of the middle form in 11:20, yet he also states that it could be passive. Thrall translates this expression as "every arrogant attitude raised in opposition" which suggests, as her comments also imply, a passive reading, although she does not state this explicitly. Thrall, *II Corinthians*, 2: 613.

[26] Thrall (*II Corinthians*, 2: 611–2) asserts that Paul maintains the warfare metaphor in καθαίρεσιν ὀχυρωμάτων (lit. the demolition of fortresses) but interprets it in λογισμοὺς καθαιροῦντες (lit. demolishing arguments/reasonings) and continues to interpret it by reference to ὕψωμα (lit. height, high place, spiritual realm).

[27] Allan, *Polysemy*, 60, 61. A similar expression could be: "the glass broke." The focus is on what happened, not on the agent.

spiritual opponents as well (as Eph 6:12).[28] Similarly, the imperfective aspect of the present participle together with the middle voice resonates with the medial notion that emphasizes the subject as a participant in an encompassing process rather than a specific cause and effect. According to this conception, the ὑψώματα would be actively opposed to the knowledge of God, engaged in, and encompassed by the spiritual battle, without requiring further specification as to identity. Both these options allow for the flexibility of interpretation which the context invites.

Nevertheless, since those speaking the ancient Greek language did not always distinguish the middle and passive voices morphologically, straining to choose between them may not be the correct or necessary approach. It should be recalled that the fundamental distinction in ancient Greek was not active/passive as in English, but active/middle. Hence, we may unwittingly think essentially in terms of the wrong polarity, trying to understand the Greek in terms of an English mindset or frame of reference.[29] Allan, for instance, as seen in ch. 2, subsumes the passive under the umbrella of the middle. Accordingly, he places the spontaneous-middle adjacent to the passive-middle in his network scheme, noting that they are very similar except that in the passive there is an implied, if not explicit, agent.[30]

Therefore, it may be construed that the ambiguity generated by the middle/passive form of ἐπαιρόμενον contributes to the exegetical richness of Paul's expression here. Rather than trying to specify whether πᾶν ὕψωμα is subject or object, hence, whether the verb is middle or passive, we may read this passage in reference to the superiority of

---

[28] "For our struggle is not against enemies of blood and flesh, but against the rulers, against the authorities, against the cosmic powers of this present darkness, against the spiritual forces of evil in the heavenly places." (Eph 6:12, NRSV)

[29] For comment on the original distinction of active/middle see §2.1.7.1 above; also, Robertson, *Grammar*, 332, 803; Lyons, *Theoretical Linguistics*, 373–4.

[30] Allan, (*Polysemy*, 118) indicates that spontaneous middle verbs legitimately have animate or inanimate subjects. Nevertheless, he does not list ἐπαίρομαι in any of his categories.

God's power over *any* form of opposition.[31] Nevertheless, thinking in terms of a spontaneous or medial middle function appears to accommodate the maximum exegetical flexibility. Therefore, as the first middle verb (στρατευόμεθα) speaks of engaging in battle, a process involving exertion from within the subject, and the second (ἐπαιρόμενον) speaks of opposition, the middle voice thread contributes to the notion of engagement and interaction on a spiritual plane throughout this pericope.

6.2 ΚΑΥΧΑΟΜΑΙ (*MEDIA TANTUM*)

The middle-only verb καυχάομαι invites special consideration. It represents a major motif in chapters 10, 11, and 12 of 2 Corinthians, where its numerous occurrences may well account for this epistle having the highest frequency of middle verbs of all the New Testament books.

Figure 6.2 Number of Occurrences of Καυχάομαι in the NT

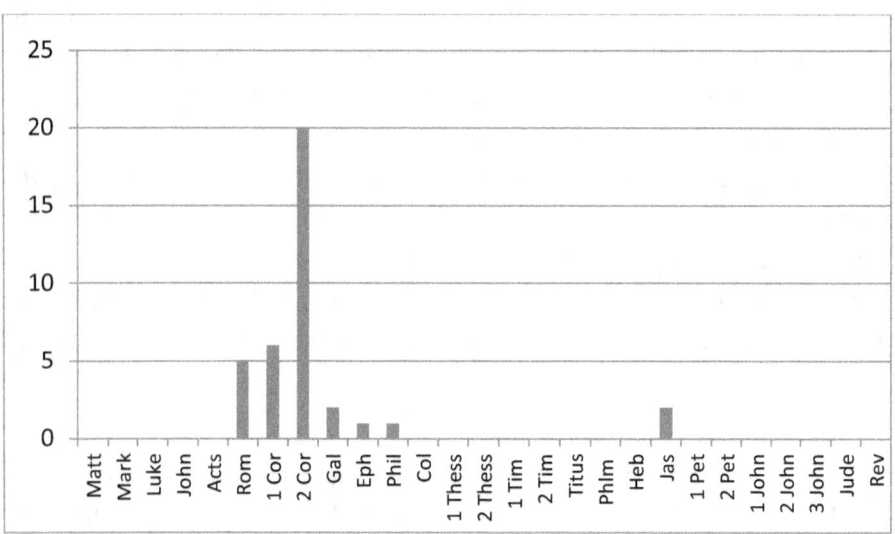

---

[31] Since English cannot adequately portray the full amplitude of the middle voice, the RSV translation noted above, which omits the verb, may well be a preferable option.

While there are thirty-seven forms of καυχάομαι altogether in NA[28], all but two of these (Jas 1:9 and 4:16) occur in Pauline epistles, while the majority (20 in total) are found in Second Corinthians (5:12; 7:14; 9: 2; 10:8, 13, 15, 16, 17x2; 11:12, 16, 18x2, 30x2; 12:1, 5x2, 6, 9).[32] As a requisite prelude to the investigation of its middle function, the semantic range and general usage of καυχάομαι will be explored. Since Paul employs this verb to generate a significant thread in his argument, all tense forms of καυχάομαι that occur in this epistle will be examined.[33]

Aligned with the theme of self-commendation in 2 Corinthians, καυχάομαι is commonly translated as 'boast', 'take pride', 'glory', or 'rejoice'.[34] BDAG identifies it as a middle deponent and articulates two related, but nuanced applications of the verb: 1. "[T]o take pride in something" 2. "[T]o make a boast about something...."[35] These uses point to both an attitude of mind and a proclamation in speech about such an attitude. Accordingly, LSJ includes the senses of "speak loudly" and "vaunt oneself" as well as boasting about or in something.[36]

6.2.1 General Use of καυχάομαι

Before turning to examine each specific occurrence of καυχάομαι in context, it is instructive to consider the connotations of existing usage. In discussing the broad use of this verb, Bultmann asserts that the sense of καυχᾶσθαι is to boast in the sense of vaunting oneself or glorying in oneself, noting that such a character trait was reprehensible to the Greek philosophers.[37] Hence, for example, Plutarch addresses the matter

---

[32] Καυχάομαι also occurs throughout the LXX (41 times).

[33] For example, the future is followed by the present and aorist in one train of thought in 10:13–16. Hence the tense forms examined are not limited to the present and aorist as in previous cases.

[34] Accordingly, the sense of καυχωμένους in 2 Cor 5:12 is rendered by "glory" (ASV, ERV, KJV), "pride" (NAU, NET, NIV, NJB, RSV), "boast" (CJB, ESV, NAB, NKJV, NRSV), "brag" (NLT), and "rejoice" (GNV, TNT).

[35] BDAG s.v. "καυχάομαι."

[36] LSJ, s.v. "καυχάομαι."

[37] Rudolf Bultmann, "καυχάομαι, καύχημα, καύχησις," TDNT 3:646. Thus, for

of self-praise from an ethical point of view in his essay *De laude ipsius* (*On Self-praise*). While he asserts that speaking of one's own importance or prowess is generally offensive to the hearer, he proposes certain circumstances in which it may be appropriate and need not provoke a negative reaction.[38] Thus Plutarch states:[39]

> Yet in spite of all this there are times when the statesman might venture on self-glorification [περιαυτολογία] as it is called not for any personal glory or pleasure, but when the occasion and the matter in hand demand that the truth be told about himself, as it might about another—especially when by permitting himself to mention his good accomplishments and character he is enabled to achieve some similar good.

Aune maintains that words based on the καυχ- stem have stronger negative connotations than those which refer more generally to speaking of oneself, such as περιαυτολογία above.[40] Hence the verb καυχάομαι is widely represented in literary narratives, typically in relation to boasting of a victory in battle as well as in relation to the folly of inappropriate boasting.[41] For example, Diodorus Siculus (first c. BCE)

---

example, Plutarch comments: "In theory, my dear Herculanus, it is agreed that to speak to others of one's own importance or power is offensive, but in practice not many even of those who condemn such conduct avoid the odium of it." Thus, he comments that although Pindar states: καὶ τὸ καυχᾶσθαι παρὰ καιρὸν μανίαις ὑποκρέκειν: "untimely vaunting plays the tune for madness," he does not follow his own admonition, but "never wearies of extolling his own powers" (*De laude*, 539 A.1– C.4, [De Lacy and Einarson, LCL 405: 114–117]).

[38] As discussed by David E. Aune, "Boasting," *The Westminster Dictionary of New Testament and Early Christian Literature and Rhetoric* (Louisville: Westminster John Knox, 2003), 81–84. Aune itemizes Plutarch's conditions for acceptable self-praise and relates these to Paul's boasting in 2 Corinthians.

[39] Plutarch, *De laude*, 539.E.1-7 (De Lacy and Einarson, LCL 405:116–119).

[40] Aune, "Boasting," 83.

[41] The lemma appears 2,902 times in the TLG corpus.

tells of a distinguished Macedonian warrior and companion of King Alexander who challenged a Greek athlete, Dioxippus, to individual combat. The Greek won, but since this was not the desired outcome, the king instigated a deadly plot against Dioxippus and consequently, his victory was short-lived. Diodorus states: οὐ μὴν ἡ τύχη γε εἴασεν ἐπὶ πολὺν χρόνον <u>καυχήσασθαι</u> τὸν ἄνδρα τῇ νίκῃ: "Fortune, however, did not allow him to <u>boast</u> of his victory for long."[42] In this account, boasting appears to be used in a general sense of taking pride in the victory, not necessarily boastful speech (which would hardly be perspicacious in the circumstances).

The non-literary papyri of the Hellenistic period provide limited but significant attestation to καυχάομαι.[43] This is not unexpected, considering the genre and subject matter of the specimens, namely, personal and family letters, business letters, petitions and the like.[44] There is, however, a clear example in a papyrus letter found at Oxyrhynchus. The extract below illustrates the use of καυχάομαι in reference to Trophimus' insistence that he did in fact send money to his father.[45] Ἔγραψάς μοι διὰ τῶν σῶν γραμμάτων ὅτι <u>καυχώμενος</u> ἐχόνομα Διοδώρου ὅτι ἔπεμψά σοι ἀργύρια ἐγὼ γὰρ <u>οὐ καυχῶμαι</u> ἐμαυτὸν <ἃ> ἔπεμψά σοι διὰ Φιλοξένου: "You wrote me in your letter that I <u>am</u>

---

[42] Diodorus Siculus, *Bibl. Hist.* 17.101.2.5. (Welles, LCL 422:408–409). Similarly, referring to Aristotle, we find: "To one who boasts [καυχώμενον] that he belonged to a great city his reply was, 'That is not the point to consider, but who it is that is worthy of a great country'" (Diogenes Laertius, *Vitae philosophorum* 5.19.11 [Hicks, LCL 184:462–463]). Likewise, we find the caution: "But Achab replied that the time to boast [καυχᾶσθαι] was not when arming oneself but after coming off victorious in battle" (Josephus, *A.J.*, 8.372.1 [Marcus, LCL 281:414–415]).

[43] A search of DDbDP identified only one papyrus attesting καυχάομαι viz., P.Oxy. 8.1160 (201–400 CE) discussed below.

[44] Such categories are discussed and exemplified by Stanley K. Stowers, *Letter Writing in Greco-Roman Antiquity*, LEC 5 (Philadelphia: Westminster, 1989), 109. Stowers comments on similarities between the letters of the NT and conventional letters of the period. In relation to 2 Corinthians, he observes that it contains a mixture of elements from common types of letters: exhortation, advice, rebuke, invective, and apology.

[45] P.Oxy. 8.1160, *l* 7–11.

boasting in the presence of Diodorus because I sent you money; but I do not boast idly; I did send [it] by Philoxenus."[46] The letter proceeds to mention that the son is willing to send further provisions if his father has need, but also explains that he has been idle (presumably unemployed) for two months, otherwise he would have sent more. Thus, καυχῶμαι in this letter appears to denote a genuine claim, despite the doubt expressed by the father. Notwithstanding that a sender and recipient of a letter best understand its meaning, if this interpretation is correct, the two senses of the verb as used in this letter, namely, a truthful claim as opposed to an idle boast, reflect the general observations already noted above.

As elsewhere in writings of the Hellenistic period, the LXX expresses disapproval of self-praise.[47] For example, ἐγκωμιαζέτω σε ὁ πέλας καὶ μὴ τὸ σὸν στόμα: Let your neighbor and not your own mouth, praise you (Prov 27:2). Similar disdain applies to the self-confident attitude of one who boasts about the future: μὴ καυχῶ τὰ εἰς αὔριον οὐ γὰρ γινώσκεις τί τέξεται ἡ ἐπιοῦσα: "Do not boast about tomorrow for you do not know what the next day will bear" (Prov 27:1, NETS).[48]

---

[46] Translation by John Garrett Winter, *Life and Letters in the Papyri: The Jerome Lectures* (Ann Arbor: University of Michigan Press, 1933), 61. Winter cites and rejects Hunt's translation: "You wrote to me in your letter that my boastfulness earns me the name of 'Gift of Zeus' because I sent you money; but I do not boast about what I sent you by Philoxenus." The main point of contention is the interpretation of ἐχόμενα at the end of line 8, which Hunt reads as ἔχω ὄνομα. In either case, the claim regarding the money is clear; the matter in dispute is whether he is unduly asserting an attitude of pride or protesting his honesty.

[47] Aune comments: "Self-praise or boasting about one's person or achievements was a social taboo throughout the ancient world" ("Boasting," 81). In Israelite and Jewish culture, he notes that it "implicitly diminished the majesty and power of God (Ps 75:4–7)."

[48] Similarly, Jas 4:13–16 reproves anyone who counts on tomorrow, noting that all such boasting is evil (πᾶσα καύχησις τοιαύτη πονηρά ἐστιν).

On the other hand, boasting or glorying *in the Lord* is encouraged.[49] In Psalm 31, for instance, we see: εὐφράνθητε ἐπὶ κύριον καὶ ἀγαλλιᾶσθε δίκαιοι καὶ <u>καυχᾶσθε</u> πάντες οἱ εὐθεῖς τῇ καρδίᾳ: "be glad in the Lord and rejoice, O righteous, and <u>boast</u>, all you upright in heart" (Ps 31:11, NETS).[50] Here καυχάομαι is used in conjunction with verbs of praise and rejoicing with respect to the Lord. Hence, the LXX draws a distinction based on the source of one's boast, placing the self-sufficient attitude of the one who boasts in his own prowess in contrast to an attitude of humility before God, as below:

| Jer 9:22–23 τάδε λέγει κύριος μὴ <u>καυχάσθω</u> ὁ σοφὸς ἐν τῇ σοφίᾳ αὐτοῦ καὶ μὴ <u>καυχάσθω</u> ὁ ἰσχυρὸς ἐν τῇ ἰσχύι αὐτοῦ καὶ μὴ <u>καυχάσ</u>ί ὁ πλούσιος ἐν τῷ πλούτῳ αὐτοῦ ἀλλ᾽ ἢ ἐν τούτῳ <u>καυχάσθω</u> ὁ <u>καυχώμενος</u> συνίειν καὶ γινώσκει ὅτι ἐγώ εἰμι κύριος ποιῶν ἔλεος καὶ κρίμα καὶ δικαιοσύνην ἐπὶ τῆ γῆς ὅτι ἐν τούτοις τὸ θέλημά μου λέγει κύριος | Thus says the Lord: Let not the wise man <u>boast</u> in his wisdom, and the strong man <u>boast</u> in his strength, and let not the rich man <u>boast</u> in his wealth; but rather, let him that <u>boasts</u>, <u>boast</u> in this: to understand and know that I am the Lord who exercises mercy and judgment and righteousness upon the earth; for in these things is my desire, says the Lord.[51] |

The positive or negative connotation of καυχάομαι depends on whether a person is praising himself or another (namely, God, in the case above), that is, to the actual basis of trust, confidence, or rejoicing.[52]

---

[49] Hence, e.g., Perschbacher designates one sense of καυχάομαι as "to undertake laudatory testimony to," *NAGL*, s.v. "καυκάομαι."

[50] Ps 5:12 likewise employs καυχάομαι in reference to praise: "and all that love thy name shall rejoice [καυχήσονται] in you" (Brenton).

[51] Verse 22 and part of 23 appear also in 1 Sam 2:10.

[52] True boasting in the sense of humbling oneself before the Lord not only implies trust but can also have the sense of rejoicing or exulting according to Bultmann, *TDNT* 3:646. Hence, e.g., where the LXX uses καύχημα in 1 Chr 16:27 and 1 Chr 29:11, the NRSV has 'joy' and 'glory' respectively.

Those who boast in the sense of praising themselves demonstrate confidence or pleasure in their own achievements, whereas those who praise or rejoice in God indicate a confidence or boast in God. In 2 Corinthians, Paul expresses this same distinction: Ὁ δὲ <u>καυχώμενος</u> ἐν κυρίῳ <u>καυχάσθω</u>: Let the one who <u>boasts,</u> boast in the Lord (2 Cor 10:17).[53] Accordingly, Paul states that the very existence of the church in Corinth amounts to a letter of commendation for him (2 Cor 3: 2, 3).[54] Thus Paul places his confidence in the Lord and in the work the Lord has done through him (2 Cor 3: 4, 5).[55]

In light of these attitudes to boasting, as well as the negative connotations of boasting in the English language today, the sense and rhetorical use of καυχάομαι in this epistle invites careful consideration. An awareness of prevailing cultural attitudes regarding boasting and the custom of self-commendation are both important in understanding the verbal contest between Paul and his opponents.[56] George Guthrie, for example, affirms that self-commendation by way of presentation of credentials was conventional practice in first century Greco-Roman culture, being somewhat like a letter of recommendation but without the third party involvement.[57] This implies that καυχάομαι may not

---

[53] Paul writes the same expression in 1 Cor 1:31.

[54] Hence, "the Christian's καύχησις [boasting] includes glorying in the acts of God that are brought about in the course of apostolic ministry" (Moisés Silva, "καυχάομαι," *NIDNTTE*, 2:654).

[55] As emphasized by Scott Hafemann, "'Self-Commendation' and Apostolic Legitimacy in 2 Corinthians: A Pauline Dialectic?" *NTS* 36 (1990): 66-88.

[56] Hafemann asserts that "it is the theme of 'self-commendation' which ought to be considered the key to understanding the focus of Paul's apologetic in 2 Corinthians" ("Self-Commendation," 69, 70). Nevertheless, this is not undertaken as an intellectual confrontation. Rather, it is the substance of Paul's boasting viz., his self-humbling to boast in weakness, that generates the distinction between Paul and his opponents.

[57] He argues that Paul may have recommended himself to the Corinthians on first acquaintance but in this letter, he is reminding them of the genuine reasons why they can be confident in him (see discussion on 5:12 below). George H. Guthrie considers boasting and self-commendation to be used nearly synonymously by Paul in this letter (*2 Corinthians*, BECNT [Grand Rapids: Baker Academic, 2015], 182–87). Aune, however, is

necessarily be viewed in a pejorative sense, depending on the manner and context in which it is used. As each instance is explored below, various considerations therefore arise in relation to the substance of the boast, the motivation of the speaker and the rhetorical function of the language employed.[58]

6.2.2 Καυχάομαι in Context in 2 Corinthians

In turning to examine specific instances of the voice function of καυχάομαι in this epistle, the understanding discussed above is borne in mind. That is, while boasting may be seen as trusting or expressing confidence in something, it is the object of one's trust which can determine whether the boast has moral legitimacy, as well as the motive and circumstances. In this regard, L&N comment: "In a number of languages ... quite different terms are employed, depending upon the differing degrees of justification for such boasting."[59] Hence, the application of the English gloss 'boast' with its attendant negative connotation, is unlikely to be the most appropriate interpretation in every instance.

6.2.2.1 Καυχωμένους in 2 Cor 5:12

Having affirmed his calling and strong sense of accountability before God (2 Cor 5:5–10), Paul appeals to the Corinthians to be assured of his good conscience (5:11). Then, in 2 Cor 5:12, which attests the first use of καυχάομαι in this epistle, Paul alludes to the distinction noted above between legitimate and inappropriate boasting. He indicates that the

---

careful to draw a distinction between negative boasting and genuine self-commendation, which he asserts, is a social institution ("Boasting," 83).

[58] See, e.g., Christopher D. Land, *The Integrity of 2 Corinthians and Paul's Aggravating Absence* (Sheffield: Sheffield Phoenix, 2015), 218. Land comments on the rhetorical aspect of Paul's boasting of his weaknesses, for his ironical speech generates a parody of his opponents' boasting of worldly attributes.

[59] L&N, s.v. "καυκάομαι" (33.368).

Corinthians may well be proud of him on the basis of his God-given ministry in contrast to the face-value boasting of others.[60]

2 Cor 5:12 οὐ πάλιν ἑαυτοὺς συνιστάνομεν ὑμῖν ἀλλὰ ἀφορμὴν διδόντες ὑμῖν καυχήματος ὑπὲρ ἡμῶν, ἵνα ἔχητε πρὸς τοὺς ἐν προσώπῳ <u>καυχωμένους</u> καὶ μὴ ἐν καρδίᾳ.	We are not commending ourselves to you again but rather giving you an opportunity to have a ground for boasting on our behalf toward those who <u>boast</u> in outward appearance and not in reference to the heart.

This verse also contains the cognate noun καυχήμα, signifying a boast or ground for boasting. The participle καυχωμένους designates a sense of confidence here, for Paul asserts that his opponents (the false apostles) trust in their outward credentials (ἐν προσώπῳ) whereas Paul implies that one's confidence should be a matter of inward integrity.[61] It is not so much the act of boastful speech that is at issue here for Paul, but the locus of one's trust.[62] This indeed is indicated by the inclusion of prepositional phrases introduced by ἐν in this verse (**ἐν** προσώπῳ καυχωμένους καὶ μὴ **ἐν** καρδίᾳ).[63]

---

[60] Those who boast in outward appearance are generally considered to be Paul's adversaries. See, e.g., Harris, *Second Corinthians,* 414 and Furnish, *II Corinthians,* 324. Likewise, Plummer suggests that Paul refers to the Judaizers who "glory in external privileges not in internal worth" (*Second Corinthians,* 171).

[61] See Paul's earlier comment: "So whether we are at home or away, we make it our aim to please him" (2 Cor 5:9, NRSV)

[62] Paul makes a similar remark in Philippians: ἡμεῖς γάρ ἐσμεν ἡ περιτομή, οἱ πνεύματι θεοῦ λατρεύοντες καὶ καυχώμενοι ἐν Χριστῷ Ἰησοῦ καὶ οὐκ ἐν σαρκὶ πεποιθότες: for it is we who are the circumcision, who worship in the Spirit of God and boast in Christ Jesus, not having confidence in the flesh (Phil 3:3).

[63] Attention is drawn to the different prepositions used in association with καυχᾶσθαι by Adolf Deissmann, *Die Neutestamentliche Formel "In Christo Jesu"* (Marburg: N.G. Elwert'sche, 1892), 64. As Plummer notes: "In N.T., as in LXX, ἐν after καυχᾶσθαι introduces that in which people glory" (*Second Corinthians,* 171).

Nevertheless, insofar as this boasting was known, it must also have been spoken, so the criteria for Allan's speech act middle may be expected to apply. This refers to verbs of speech for which the subject is both agent and beneficiary (or experiencer) that express a strong emotional or mental investment in the speech. While Allan does not list καυχάομαι in any of his categories, he does list εὔχομαι. This verb may be used in the senses of "pray," "vow or promise," or "profess loudly, boast, vaunt" as a speech act middle.[64] While εὔχομαι is not used to refer to boasting in the LXX or NT, it is widely attested in this sense in earlier Greek writing, which is the object of Allan's study.[65] Accordingly, the expression εὔχομαι εἶναι was used in making a profession or claim regarding valor or parentage. For instance, in Plato's *Gorgias*, Socrates induces Gorgias to admit that he claims (εὔχομαι) to be a rhetorician. Ἀγαθόν γε, ὦ Σώκρατες, εἰ δὴ ὅ γε εὔχομαι εἶναι, ὥς ἔφη Ὅμηρος, βούλει με καλεῖν: "Yes, Socrates, and a good one too, if you would call me what—to use Homer's phrase—'I vaunt myself to be'[.]"[66] When used in this manner, εὔχομαι is a near synonym for καυκάομαι which could therefore also viably be placed in Allan's speech act category.[67]

---

[64] Allan, *Polysemy*, 105, 107. LSJ, s.v. "εὔχομαι."

[65] The LXX attests the first two uses, e.g., εὔξομαι πρὸς τὸν θεόν: I will pray to God (Exod 8:25), and ὃς ἂν εὔξηται κυρίῳ δῶρον αὐτοῦ: whoever would vow his gift to the Lord (Num 6:21) but does not appear to use εὔχομαι in the sense of boast. In the New Testament εὔχομαι is consistently used for "pray", e.g., εὐχόμεθα δὲ πρὸς τὸν θεὸν μὴ ποιῆσαι ὑμᾶς κακὸν μηδέν: we pray to God that you would not do anything wrong (2 Cor 13:7). For the sense of boasting, see below.

[66] Plato, *Gorgias*, 449.a.7 (Lamb, LCL 166:264–265). Lamb notes that εὔχομαι εἶναι was "the regular phrase of a Homeric hero in boasting of his valor, parentage etc." (Lamb, LCL 166 265n1). For example, "From broad Crete I claim [εὔχομαι] my lineage, the son of a wealthy man" (Homer, *Odyssea* 14.199 [Murray and Dimock, LCL 105:50–51]).

[67] Further evidence of their synonymous nature may be seen in S. C. Woodhouse, *English-Greek Dictionary: A Vocabulary of the Attic Language* (London: Routledge, 1910), s.v. "boast," where both εὔχομαι and καυχάομαι are found. Accordingly, Bultmann notes that Homer used εὔχομαι but not καυχάομαι (*TDNT* 3:646).

Regardless of the mechanics of assigning καυχάομαι to a particular category, Allan's overarching attribute of subject-affectedness is clearly apparent in the use of the middle form καυχωμένους in 2 Cor 5:12. The subjects (those that express confidence in outward appearance) are seemingly empowered or seek to be empowered by the action. Since this boast is undertaken in their own interest and for their benefit, the grammatical concept of an indirect reflexive middle (which is also one of Allan's categories) applies. The medial notion is likewise apparent as the sense of boasting or trusting *in* something indicates that the subjects are conceptually within the process expressed by the verb. It is not accomplished outside the subject; rather, they are within the process as they express their confidence (either by word or deed) in their presumed credentials and act toward the Corinthians accordingly.

6.2.2.2 Κεκαύχημαι in 2 Cor 7:14

2 Cor 7:14 ὅτι εἴ τι αὐτῷ ὑπὲρ ὑμῶν <u>κεκαύχημαι</u>, οὐ κατῃσχύνθην, ἀλλ' ὡς πάντα ἐν ἀληθείᾳ ἐλαλήσαμεν ὑμῖν, οὕτως καὶ ἡ καύχησις ἡμῶν ἡ ἐπὶ Τίτου ἀλήθεια ἐγενήθη.	For if I <u>have boasted</u> about you to him, I have not been disgraced; but just as everything we said to you was true, so also our boasting towards Titus [about you] has turned out to be true.

The context of this verse (2 Cor 7:6–14) is charged with emotion on the part of Paul. Having learnt from Titus that the Corinthians responded to his letter of correction with godly grief and repentance, Paul is encouraged regarding their standing as new people in Christ. The perfect form of κεκαύχημαι (7:14) indicates that Paul is in a state of having boasted about them, that is, his status has become "Paul who boasts about the Corinthians" so he is anxious that they live up to his commendation. Therefore, he expresses his relief and joy, remarking that his boasting to Titus about them was not invalidated (7:14). Consequently, he is able to say, "I rejoice, because I have complete confidence in you" (7:16).

Whereas in 5:12 the reference was to boasting (trusting) *in* something, here it is to boasting *about* (ὑπέρ) something to someone. This indicates a transitive use of the verb, corresponding to a speech act which emanates from one and is received by another.[68] Paul is not boasting about himself, but expressing his confidence in the Corinthian church. Again, a cognate noun, καύχησις (act of boasting) appears in close proximity to the verb, καυχάομαι, enhancing the theme of boasting, which is the actual term widely used in English translations in this instance.[69]

The function of κεκαύχημαι here is clearly not directly reflexive, since Paul is speaking of others, not himself; nor is he acting in his own interest. However, the personal investment in the act of boasting here as a form of testimony, rather like the action of solemnly testifying (§3.1.5 διαμαρτύρομαι), indicates that Paul was acting from within, as per Cooper's dynamic middle. Similarly, Allan's speech act middle may be applied, due to the psychological effect of placing his integrity at stake, placing himself in a position of vulnerability (hence self-affectedness).[70] In commending the Corinthians to Titus, Paul is active in boasting but also affected by the process of boasting, for his testimony is open to confirmation. Therefore, he is acting medially, within the process of the verb, a process which conceptually involves all three parties: Paul, the Corinthians and Titus.

6.2.2.3 Καυχῶμαι in 2 Cor 9:2

In chapter nine of 2 Corinthians, Paul is speaking of the offering he is collecting from his various congregations to deliver to those in need in Jerusalem (Rom 15:25–27). He refers to this in 2 Cor 9:1 as "the ministry to the saints." Here, Paul also refers to boasting about something, as he recalls the pleasure and pride he felt when speaking to the Macedonians of the eagerness demonstrated by the Corinthians, as below:

---

[68] Harris notes that the characteristic construction of 'boasting about something to someone' appears whenever καυχάομαι is used transitively in the NT (*Second Corinthians*, 619).

[69] Hence: CJB, CSB, ESV, KJV, NAB, NASB, NET, NIV, NJB, NKJV, NRSV.

[70] The dynamic middle and Allan's speech act are often found to correlate, for the latter implies the former.

2 Cor 9:2 οἶδα γὰρ τὴν
προθυμίαν ὑμῶν ἣν ὑπὲρ ὑμῶν
<u>καυχῶμαι</u> Μακεδόσιν, ὅτι
Ἀχαΐα παρεσκεύασται ἀπὸ
πέρυσι, καὶ τὸ ὑμῶν ζῆλος
ἠρέθισεν τοὺς πλείονας.

for I know your eagerness,
which I <u>boast</u> about to the
people of Macedonia, [saying]
that Achaia has been ready
since last year; and your zeal
has stirred up the majority.

The function of the present middle indicative καυχῶμαι is intimated by the verse itself, for it is apparent that Paul's boasting had the effect of stirring up the Macedonians. That is, he was boasting of the Corinthians' eagerness with the intention of persuading the Macedonians to respond in similar fashion.[71] Therefore, it is apparent that Paul was personally concerned with the outcome of his action, indicating an indirect reflexive middle function from the grammatical view. Further, his speech is purposeful; he is not simply speaking into the air as if rehearsing a speech. Rather, he is boasting to a particular audience in order to persuade or influence them, so the function here implies subject affectedness in the manner of Allan's speech act middle.[72] Being syntactically equivalent to the case above, the medial function is again apparent. Paul is speaking of an event in which he is internal to the process of boasting about one person or thing to another.

---

[71] Nevertheless, Paul is challenging the Corinthians to be ready to act on their commitment, notifying them that he is sending brothers to collect their contribution (9:3–5).

[72] As noted above, Allan observes that verbs of straightforward speech tend to be active (e.g., λέγω, φημί) whereas those which are emotionally invested tend to be middle in form (*Polysemy*, 106). Further, as noted by Harris, when Paul was writing this epistle, the Macedonian collection was well under way (8:2–5) (*Second Corinthians*, 622). There was therefore a certain reciprocity in effect; Paul applauded the generosity of the Macedonians in face of their hardship in order to spur on the Corinthians to complete their offering (8:1–6), while he also boasted of the eagerness of the Corinthians (Achaians) to encourage the Macedonians as above.

6.2.2.4. Καυχήσωμαι in 2 Cor 10:8

As noted above, chapter ten begins a distinct section of 2 Corinthians, wherein Paul embarks on boasting in regard to himself in defense of his authority in the face of opposition from the rival apostles.

2 Cor 10:8 ἐάν [τε] γὰρ περισσότερόν τι <u>καυχήσωμαι</u> περὶ τῆς ἐξουσίας ἡμῶν ἧς ἔδωκεν ὁ κύριος εἰς οἰκοδομὴν καὶ οὐκ εἰς καθαίρεσιν ὑμῶν, οὐκ αἰσχυνθήσομαι	Now, even if <u>I boast</u> a little too much about our authority, which the Lord gave for building you up and not for tearing you down, I will not be put to shame[73]

Paul boasts of authority which the Lord gave him; therefore, he is ultimately not pointing to his own abilities but to his apostolic calling. It could be that the reference to "boasting a little too much" of his authority alludes to demands he made in his severe letter.[74] That is, he may be saying in effect that although he continues to speak of, or claim authority from the Lord, this is not an empty boast; he will not be put to shame and his presence will in fact match his words (10:10, 11). He assures them that the Lord gave him authority to build them up, thus intimating that any chastisement on his part towards them was also directed to this goal as a facet of his pastoral ministry. The authority he claims in the Lord is central to his argument against the rival apostles.

The boasting (or claim) is intended to influence them; he is not exalting himself *per se* but is drawing their attention to his apostolic authority in order to secure (or re-secure) their allegiance and trust. Therefore, Paul is claiming God-given authority *for* himself, authority to enable him to achieve his goal and minister to them more effectively (hence indirect reflexive function). In Allan's scheme, the subject-affectedness could be seen in either the indirect reflexive (as above) or the speech act middle, for there is again a sense of personal investment, an emphatic

---

[73] In this verse περί is generally translated "about" (CJB, NAS, NET, NIV, NKJV) or "of" (KJV, NAB, NRSV, RSV).

[74] As suggested by Colin Kruse, *The Second Epistle of Paul to the Corinthians*, TNTC (Leicester: Inter-Varsity Press, 1987), 176.

assertion in his claim. The medial function may be seen with the whole process in view, for Paul is encompassed by the process of affirming the authority given to him by the Lord. In making this claim, he is pointing to something beyond himself yet not acting externally to himself; he is the locale of the action and is himself affirmed in the process.

6.2.2.5 Καυχάομαι Forms in 2 Cor 10:13–17

| 2 Cor 10: 13–17 ἡμεῖς δὲ οὐκ εἰς τὰ ἄμετρα <u>καυχησόμεθα</u> ἀλλὰ κατὰ τὸ μέτρον τοῦ κανόνος οὗ ἐμέρισεν ἡμῖν ὁ θεὸς μέτρου, ἐφικέσθαι ἄχρι καὶ ὑμῶν. ¹⁴ οὐ γὰρ ὡς μὴ ἐφικνούμενοι εἰς ὑμᾶς ὑπερεκτείνομεν ἑαυτούς, ἄχρι γὰρ καὶ ὑμῶν ἐφθάσαμεν ἐν τῷ εὐαγγελίῳ τοῦ Χριστοῦ, ¹⁵ οὐκ εἰς τὰ ἄμετρα <u>καυχώμενοι</u> ἐν ἀλλοτρίοις κόποις, ἐλπίδα δὲ ἔχοντες αὐξανομένης τῆς πίστεως ὑμῶν ἐν ὑμῖν μεγαλυνθῆναι κατὰ τὸν κανόνα ἡμῶν εἰς περισσείαν ¹⁶ εἰς τὰ ὑπερέκεινα ὑμῶν εὐαγγελίσασθαι, οὐκ ἐν ἀλλοτρίῳ κανόνι εἰς τὰ ἕτοιμα <u>καυχήσασθαι</u>. ¹⁷ Ὁ δὲ <u>καυχώμενος</u> ἐν κυρίῳ <u>καυχάσθω</u>· | Now *we* will not <u>claim credit</u> beyond the appropriate limit, but [only] according to the domain which God apportioned to us—a domain which indeed reaches as far as you. We are not overextending ourselves as if we did not reach you, for we were the first to come to you with the gospel of Christ, not <u>boasting</u> unjustifiably in the work of others, nevertheless we have the hope that, as your faith increases, our sphere of activity among you may be enlarged to overflowing, so as to proclaim the gospel beyond you, not to <u>glory</u> in that already done in the realm of another.[75] So, whoever <u>boasts</u>, should <u>boast</u> in the Lord. |

---

[75] Harris discusses at some length the possible interpretations for κανών in these verses (*Second Corinthians*, 712). While the general use of the term ranges from the yardstick or measuring line of a craftsman to a territory in the sense of a geographical or administrative region, he asserts that it is the territorial sense which Paul employs here. Accordingly, Plummer notes that while κανών generally refers to a length, the essence

In these verses Paul asserts that he is the true apostle to the Corinthians: the one who brought the gospel to them. Consequently, he claims (boasts of) legitimate authority over them.[76] He argues that he does not extend his boast or testimony beyond proper limits (10:13, 15) nor does he extend it to the realm of another (10:16). Thus, he sets the stage and establishes his right to testify (or boast) of his work among them. He affirms that he restricts his claims to those of his God-given assignment, in contrast to those who offered themselves as ministers at Corinth, a ministry they had neither started nor nurtured.[77]

The use of καυχάομαι in 10:13–16 may be interpreted in two ways. It may be read in relation to Paul if the negative assertions are transformed into positives for the sake of the exercise. Hence, by saying that he does not boast beyond acceptable limits Paul is essentially saying that he is boasting appropriately, that is, making legitimate claims about himself. He is therefore acting for himself and with reference to himself, so the indirect reflexive grammatical function is apparent. He is not controlling an action outside himself, but is within the process, affirming himself and being affirmed, so the medial notion also applies. Allan's speech act classification could also apply since Paul is emphasizing the validity of his authority. As for the near synonym εὔχομαι discussed above, the subject in this case also is affected psychologically by the intensity of the assertion.[78]

Alternatively, if καυχάομαι is interpreted in reference to the inappropriate boasting of the false apostles, the matter is straightforward. Acting for themselves, in their own interest, the grammatical indirect reflexive applies. Allan's speech act classification again applies, and the

---

is that Paul "does not exceed the limits set for him" (*Second Corinthians*, 287). See also BDAG s.v. "κανών." (2) "set of directions or formulation for an activity[.]" This interpretation certainly appears justified by the context. Hence, e.g., "we will keep to the field God has assigned to us" (10:13, NRSV).

[76] Although he uses the epistolary first-person plural (hence καυχησόμεθα in v. 13) the context indicates that Paul is essentially speaking of his own authority aligned with his calling to be an apostle of Christ Jesus.

[77] As noted by Guthrie, *2 Corinthians*, 490.

[78] For similar reasons, the dynamic middle could also apply.

subjects are within the process of the verb, in a medial situation. For either interpretation, the middle sense of the verb forms is apparent.

Concluding his discussion on the topic of assertions about oneself, in 2 Cor 10:17 Paul integrates his rhetoric with his theology, making the emphatic assertion that those who boast should do so in the Lord. This remark directs the readers' attention again to the legitimate source of confidence for a Christian, with the participle καυχώμενος referring to boasting in a generic sense and the imperative, καυχάσθω, being specific in referring to boasting, glorying, asserting confidence *in* the Lord (ἐν κυρίῳ καυχάσθω).[79] Paul clearly applies this ethic to his boasting about his authority, claiming that he is in fact glorying (boasting) in the Lord who called him and works through him, not going beyond appropriate boundaries (whether geographical or ethical).[80]

The participle καυχώμενος in 10:17 is used in an absolute sense; nevertheless, the context suggests that Paul is referring to boasting of credentials as a source of authority. Therefore, it may be viewed in the same manner as above, with the indirect reflexive, speech act and medial functions of the middle voice being evident. The imperative καυχάσθω is an instruction for them to boast in, or with reference to, the Lord; that is, to affirm the Lord as the source of their confidence.

Since the implication is one of trusting rather than boasting to another for self-edification or personal benefit, in the grammatical sense, καυχάσθω aligns more with the dynamic middle than the indirect reflexive of self-interest. Similarly, in Allan's scheme, the reference is not to a speech act but rather to mental activity. The subject (the one who trusts) is internal to the process, actively trusting but also affected by the encompassing process, finding confidence in the Lord.

---

[79] In 1 Cor 1:31 Paul makes the same assertion prefaced by "as it is written"; hence it is likely to be a paraphrased reference to Jer 9:22–23, cited above. This allusion is recognized in commentaries, e.g., Guthrie, *2 Corinthians*, 497; Harris, *Second Corinthians*, 724; Seifrid, *Second Corinthians*, 398.

[80] This could be interpreted to mean that he is not boasting beyond what is legitimate just as, and because of, the fact that he refers to the geographical parameters of his calling.

Middle Voice Verbs in the New Testament

These two instances resonate with the two uses noted by BDAG at the outset; one is an attitude of confidence in something while the other refers to speaking of such. Therefore, in understanding Paul's use of καυχάομαι in this epistle, it would appear to refer to *(pro)-claiming as a source of joy, pride, or confidence*.[81] These nuances cannot be adequately captured by the active sounding translation of "boast." Moreover, the discussion above illustrates that the specific middle function is related to the semantic nuance of the verb in a particular context.

6.2.2.6 Καυκάομαι Forms in 2 Cor 11

In chapter 11 Paul embarks on a different kind of boasting. He is not simply stating his legitimate trust in his calling, but is boasting in an ostensibly competitive manner, speaking of his credentials (which, he nevertheless admits, is foolishness). Paul seeks to point out that the false apostles (11:13) surpass him in nothing, except perhaps their unjustified excessive boasting according to their own standards (10:12). He therefore matches their claims and demonstrates that he is equal to or greater than them on whatever ground of boasting they may have as ministers of the gospel (11:22–27). Yet even beforehand, he prefaces his argument by stating that he will continue to support himself and not rely on the Corinthians financially (11:7–10). This is a claim the false apostles cannot match. Therefore, he states:

| 2 Cor 11:12 Ὃ δὲ ποιῶ, καὶ ποιήσω, ἵνα ἐκκόψω τὴν ἀφορμὴν τῶν θελόντων ἀφορμήν, ἵνα ἐν ᾧ καυχῶνται εὑρεθῶσιν καθὼς καὶ ἡμεῖς. | So what I am doing I will continue to do, in order to prohibit an occasion, for those wanting an occasion, to be found equal to us in the things they <u>boast</u> about, |

---

[81] Such an expression makes sense of assertions akin to 'boast in the Lord' (as a source of joy) as well as claims to specific credentials. It may be seen that Silva uses boast and claim in parallel in his comments cited in n54 above.

The things in which they may boast (ἐν ᾧ καυχῶνται) can be inferred from Paul's rejoinders (e.g., they are Israelites, 11:22); they refer to human attributes. Hence the verb καυκάομαι here refers to boasting in the typical sense of claiming a qualification or testifying to a source of pride. Again, this could be considered a speech act middle in Allan's scheme, with the subject becoming a beneficiary, yet also could be classed as an indirect reflexive for the same reason.[82] Both are volitional actions with agentive subjects.[83] Similarly, in the grammatical scheme, the subjects are acting in their own interest (*for* themselves), again evincing the indirect reflexive property. Insofar as they boast to others about their own attributes, they are internal to the process of the verb "in and of which the subject partakes."[84] Hence, the medial notion also applies.

Paul subsequently denounces the rival ministers as false apostles and deceitful workers (11:13) who disguise themselves as ministers of righteousness (11:15). He further indicates that although he considers their boasting of certain credentials to be foolish, he will also boast like a fool, apparently to discredit any claims to superiority they may have on human grounds. Thus, he states:

2 Cor 11:16 ἵνα κἀγὼ μικρόν τι <u>καυχήσωμαι</u>	that I too <u>may boast</u> a little
2 Cor 11:18 ἐπεὶ πολλοὶ <u>καυχῶνται</u> κατὰ σάρκα, κἀγὼ <u>καυχήσομαι</u>	since many <u>boast</u> on human grounds, I will also <u>boast</u>

---

[82] The inference from Paul's reference to his desire to continue to be self-supporting is that the false apostles were not. Accordingly, he makes reference to those who prey on the Corinthians (11:20).

[83] Allan notes the similarity between speech acts that affect the subject as beneficiary and the indirect middle (*Polysemy*, 107).

[84] Eberhard, *Middle Voice*, 77.

The substance of this boasting is given in 11:22–23, as Paul speaks of his credentials, matching his opponents' claims to be Hebrews, Israelites, descendants of Abraham and ministers of Christ point by point (although he does claim superiority in respect to the latter [ὑπὲρ ἐγώ]). Martin notes the "rhetorical asyndeton" employed here by Paul as he rapidly dismisses any advantage suggested by the opponents.[85] Consequently, even in written form, a strongly emotional tone is apparent, so the boasting conforms to Allan's speech act category in which the subject is experiencer. In these verses, as before, the verb may be classed as an indirect reflexive middle in grammatical terms, relating to an action undertaken for the benefit of the subject. It also reflects the internal *diathesis* of Eberhard's medial concept as the subject is immersed in the process, as above.

Paul quickly changes, however, from matching his opponents' boasts above to declare that he will boast of his weakness. Thus in vv. 23–29 he documents a catalogue of his trials and sufferings, both physical and mental, that he has endured as an apostle, concluding with the comment in 11:30 as follows:

2 Cor 11:30 εἰ καυχᾶσθαι δεῖ, τὰ τῆς ἀσθενείας μου καυχήσομαι	if it is necessary to praise oneself, I will boast of the matters of my weakness

Harris, among others, asserts that boasting was important to the Corinthians, suggesting that εἰ here could be interpreted as "since,", and that καυχᾶσθαι δεῖ (boasting is a necessity) may have been "one of their watchwords."[86] The generic sense implied by καυχᾶσθαι is taken

---

[85] Martin, *2 Corinthians*, 561.

[86] Harris is referring to C. K. Barrett, *The Second Epistle to the Corinthians*, BNTC (London: Black, 1973), 306 (*Second Corinthians*, 817). Similarly, Timothy B. Savage speaks of the value afforded to an individual's status in Graeco Roman society in the first century, noting that "the quest for personal glory, δόξα, became an ideal" (*Power through weakness: Paul's understanding of the Christian ministry in 2 Corinthians*, SNTSMS 86 [Cambridge: Cambridge University Press, 1996], 23, 54). Furthermore,

to be praising or affirming oneself by boasting here. The infinitive would therefore be a direct reflexive, yet the sense of self-interest would fit the indirect reflexive as well; these two categories being common to the grammatical descriptors and to Allan's scheme. Although this verse does not explicitly refer to speech, Allan's speech act category could apply as it is implied in the semantics of praise. The medial notion also applies since in the act of boasting, the subject is affirmed, so is therefore encompassed and affected by the process in which it participates.

In turning to speak of his weaknesses, Paul generates a shift in his argument. Although he felt compelled to boast in competition with his opponents, he does so "in the only fully legitimate way open to a Christian—that is in weakness that discloses the Lord's power[.]"[87] In articulating and enumerating the sufferings he endured, Paul is mindful of the grace of God upon him, thus claiming (or attesting) his weakness and vulnerability with God's saving grace in view.[88] This aligns with his comment in 1 Cor 1:27–29. There he states that God chooses people who are weak or unwise in the worlds' eyes to shame those who are strong and wise, such that no human person may boast (καυχήσηται) in the presence of God (1 Cor 1:29). It is God who is the source of their life in Christ, thus the one who boasts or makes any claim, must do so

---

"When people turned to evaluate their contemporaries, they looked for the same evidence of personal worth and glory that they prized for themselves: impressive displays of status worthy of public applause and esteem." He remarks, "There can be little doubt that boasting was a matter of great importance in the Corinthian church."

[87] Barrett, *Second Corinthians*, 306.

[88] Second Corinthians 12:9 records the Lord's words to Paul: "My grace is sufficient for you, for power is brought to perfection in weakness." That is, the experience of God's power follows the acknowledgement of weakness.

with deference to God.⁸⁹ In boasting of his weakness, therefore, Paul is ultimately boasting of God.⁹⁰

In 2 Cor 11:30, the middle function of boasting by way of speech act may be recognized as in the previous examples; what has changed, however, is the focus of the boast. Rather than speaking of his credentials, Paul now directs his boast towards his weaknesses and hence to God's grace, using the theme of boasting as a thread in his theological argument. Feeling obligated (perhaps by way of rhetorical convention) to boast in the face of his opponents' claims, he continues to act for himself (indirect reflexive function) that is, to defend his claim of apostolic authority. The emotional involvement in his declaration (Allan's speech act category) is clearly apparent. Again, he is internal to the process designated by the verb (medial function), for his weakness is affirmed as he testifies to it; the subject is active in the process that is happening to him.

6.2.2.7 Καυχάομαι Forms in 2 Cor 12

The expression καυχᾶσθαι δεῖ appears again at the beginning of chapter 12, where Paul speaks of boasting in an absolute sense, that is, in the general sense of praising oneself. Hence, the same descriptors apply as for καυχᾶσθαι in 11:30 above, that is, direct or indirect reflexive, speech act middle and the medial sense.

---

⁸⁹ The sense here is that humans owe everything to God, hence have no reason to claim any credit for anything. Paul speaks of spiritual wisdom imparted by the Holy Spirit in contrast to human wisdom in 1 Cor 2. In proclaiming his weakness, Paul is therefore indirectly praising or boasting in God, who has delivered him and worked through him in ministry to the Gentiles.

⁹⁰ In relation to boasting of his weaknesses, see Christopher D. Land, *The Integrity of 2 Corinthians and Paul's Aggravating Absence*, NTM 36 (Sheffield: Sheffield Phoenix, 2015), 218. Land comments that Paul "subverts his critics' manner of boasting, setting aside things that might earn him worldly respect and taking pride instead in his manifest weakness and his total dependence on Christ." This, he asserts, results in a parody of the behaviour of his opponents, so that "Paul's foolish imitation takes on the form of a scathing ridicule."

> 2 Cor 12:1 Καυχᾶσθαι δεῖ, | It is necessary to praise one-
> οὐ συμφέρον μέν, ἐλεύσομαι | self; not that it is profitable,
> δὲ εἰς ὀπτασίας καὶ | but I will go on to visions
> ἀποκαλύψεις κυρίου. | and revelations of the Lord.

Paul acquiesces to convention but does so on his own terms. He speaks of visions and revelations given to a person he knows who was caught up into paradise fourteen years ago and heard matters of which it is not permissible to speak (12:2–4). This is an indirect reference to himself, as is apparent in 12:6–8, yet Paul deftly avoids focusing on himself and as always, turns the discourse into a testimony to the grace of God (12:8–9).[91] Thus in 12:5–6 he asserts the veracity of the visions without claiming any credit for himself.

> 2 Cor 12: 5, 6 ὑπὲρ τοῦ | I will boast about such a per-
> τοιούτου καυχήσομαι, ὑπὲρ δὲ | son, but about myself I will
> ἐμαυτοῦ οὐ καυχήσομαι εἰ μὴ | not boast, except in regard to
> ἐν ταῖς ἀσθενείαις. Ἐὰν γὰρ | weaknesses; [nevertheless]
> θελήσω καυχήσασθαι, οὐκ | if I should wish to boast, I
> ἔσομαι ἄφρων, ἀλήθειαν γὰρ | would not be foolish, for I
> ἐρῶ· | would be speaking the truth.

The uses of καυχάομαι are somewhat more difficult to analyze here, because of the use of the third person to represent Paul, the future verbs, and the sense of *I will not but if I did*. However, καυχήσομαι is first used in the sense of praising or testifying to the credentials of (technically) a person other than himself (ὑπὲρ τοῦ τοιούτου) as in 7:14, above. In this regard, Allan's speech act middle applies (as for εὔχομαι, discussed above), yet there is no sense of Paul seeking benefit from this

---

[91] Various explanations have been suggested for Paul's use of the third person here, including similarity with rabbinic or philosophical practices, e.g., Martin, *2 Corinthians*, 590–91; Furnish, *II Corinthians*, 543–44. Nevertheless, the specific motivation does not affect the analysis of the text itself.

testimony. Rather, there is the personal investment characteristic of the dynamic middle. A medial sense is not readily apparent in this instance, however, for the process does not appear to encompass the subject.[92]

In the second use of καυχήσομαι, Paul states that he will not boast, except of his weakness, so this is equivalent to 11:30 above. The indirect reflexive, speech act and medial functions apply as he refers to himself, building his overall argument regarding his divine appointment. Paul concludes here (12:6) by asserting that if he were to boast (καυχήσασθαι) about the revelation, then it would simply amount to telling the truth, to making a genuine claim regarding himself.[93] In this case, Allan's indirect reflexive would be appropriate due to the associated benefit, rather than any sense of emotional investment in a speech act. In the grammatical sense, he would be claiming something *for* himself (indirect reflexive), and in the medial sense he would be partaking of the process of which he is subject.

The final occurrence of καυχάομαι in this epistle occurs in 12:9, when Paul's play on the word rounds off his argument. Having taken up the challenge to boast of his credentials and then extending this to boasting in his weaknesses and therefore in God's grace, he has come full circle. Here the sense returns to one of rejoicing, for he affirms that he will boast but not in a worldly manner about himself. Rather, he will rejoice (καυχήσομαι) in his sufferings and weaknesses because they ultimately cause him to trust and rejoice in God who delivers him and works through him in ministry to the Gentiles. After referring to his thorn in the flesh, and his prayer for its removal which was not granted, Paul recounts the Lord's reply to him, and makes his own final affirmation on the matter of boasting:

---

[92] Curiously, in boasting of such a person, i.e., speaking of what he may claim as credentials in a spiritual sense, no human credit is involved, for the experience of revelation was initiated by God.

[93] As in the Homeric phrase, εὔχομαι εἶναι, and Plutarch's notion of acceptable self-talk discussed above.

2 Cor 12:9 καὶ εἴρηκέν μοι· ἀρκεῖ σοι ἡ χάρις μου, ἡ γὰρ δύναμις ἐν ἀσθενείᾳ τελεῖται. ἥδιστα οὖν μᾶλλον <u>καυχήσομαι</u> ἐν ταῖς ἀσθενείαις μου, ἵνα ἐπισκηνώσῃ ἐπ᾽ ἐμὲ ἡ δύναμις τοῦ Χριστοῦ	yet he said to me: My grace is sufficient for you for my strength is brought to fullness in weakness. Gladly therefore I will <u>boast</u> even more in my weaknesses, in order that the power of God may dwell in me

The middle function is evident insofar as Paul speaks of his weaknesses as a vehicle through which he experiences God's power as a source of joy and delight. This is the pinnacle of his argument, evincing speech invested with determination and passion (Allan's speech act category) from which it could be said that he derives, or seeks to derive, the benefit of the rhetorical victory (indirect reflexive). Existentially, he derives the benefit of the experience of the power of God; therefore, he is decidedly internal to the process, whether by the assertion of his intention to boast or glory in his weakness or by the action itself.

6.2.3 Summary Comments

The middle-only verb καυχάομαι is used in various ways throughout Second Corinthians to refer to "boasting about" or "boasting in" or simply to the act of boasting. In the latter case, it is used in an absolute sense (10:13; 11:16, 18, 12:6) and the verb functions intransitively. Elsewhere it is associated with (usually followed by) a prepositional phrase that indicates the object of the boast. Such phrases are introduced by ὑπέρ when referring to boasting about or on behalf of others (7:14; 9:2; 12:5); more commonly however, a phrase beginning with ἐν indicates the source of one's boast or confidence (5:12; 10:15, 16, 17; 11:12, 12:5, 9).

According to context, καυχάομαι may imply a sense of pride or may forthrightly refer to a truthful claim. These various uses, despite and because of their different nuances, are seen to form an essential thread in Paul's argument regarding his authority and his essential theological assertion regarding God's strength operating through weakness. In every contextual instance, the middle function of καυχάομαι has been recognized. It consistently exhibits the indirect reflexive attribute of self-interest and frequently the mental or emotional investment of both the dynamic middle and Allan's speech act category, to which may be assigned the prototypical use of the verb. Likewise, a medial sense is widely recognized and sometimes a direct reflexive function also. Notably, different types of middle function are evident for different contexts, and at times more than one grammatical or subject-affected classification may apply; this reflects the fact that these are descriptors of middle function and not sole determinants.

This consistent evidence of middle function for καυχάομαι is in conflict with the middle-deponent designation of the lexical form by BDAG and of the deponent status assigned to every inflected form of καυχάομαι in *ALGNT*. Thus, καυχάομαι is not simply active (or deponent) in its many applications in this epistle. It functions in the middle voice, as do the oppositional middles στρατευόμεθα and ἐπαιρόμενον appearing in 10:3–5, as discussed above. The functions of these verbs in context are summarized in Table 6.1 below.[94]

---

[94] The same parameters apply as in previous chapters.

Table 6.1 Properties of Selected Middle Verbs in 2 Corinthians

Verb	Form	Ref.	MT	Dep.	Gramm. middle	Subj. Aff.	Allan category	Med. event
στρατεύω	στρατευόμεθα	10:3	✘	✘	Ind. Ref.	✓	Ind. Ref.	✓
ἐπαίρω	ἐπαιρόμενον	10:5	✘	✘	Dir. Ref. Ind. Ref.	✓	Spont.	✓
καυχάομαι	καυχωμένους	5:12	✓	✓	Ind. Ref.	✓	Sp. Act	✓
	κεκαύχημαι	7:14	✓	✓	Dyn.	✓	Sp. Act	✓
	καυχῶμαι	9:2	✓	✓	Ind. Ref.	✓	Sp. Act	✘
	καυχήσωμαι	10:8	✓	✓	Ind. Ref.	✓	Sp. Act. Ind. Ref.	✓
	καυχησόμεθα	10:13	✓	✓	Ind. Ref.	✓	Sp. Act	✓
	καυχώμενοι	10:15	✓	✓	Ind. Ref.	✓	Sp. Act	✓
	καυχήσασθαι	10:16	✓	✓	Ind. Ref.	✓	Sp. Act	✓
	καυχώμενος	10:17	✓	✓	Ind. Ref.	✓	Sp. Act	✓
	καυχάσθω	10:17	✓	✓	Dyn.	✓	M. Act.	✓
	καυχῶνται	11:12	✓	✓	Ind. Ref.	✓	Sp. Act Ind. Ref.	✓
	καυχήσωμαι	11:16	✓	✓	Ind. Ref.	✓	Sp. Act	✓
	καυχῶνται	11:18	✓	✓	Ind. Ref.	✓	Sp. Act	✓
	καυχήσομαι	11:18	✓	✓	Ind. Ref.	✓	Sp. Act	✓
	καυχᾶσθαι	11:30	✓	✓	Dir. Ref. Ind. Ref.	✓	Dir. Ref. Ind. Ref.	✓
	καυχήσομαι	11:30	✓	✓	Ind. Ref.	✓	Sp. Act	✓
	καυχᾶσθαι	12:1	✓	✓	Dir. Ref. Ind. Ref.	✓	Dir. Ref. Ind. Ref.	✓
	καυχήσομαι	12:5	✓	✓	Dyn.	✓	Sp. Act	✘
	καυχήσομαι	12:5	✓	✓	Ind. Ref.	✓	Sp. Act	✓
	καυχήσασθαι	12:6	✓	✓	Ind. Ref.	✓	Ind. Ref.	✓
	καυχήσομαι	12:9	✓	✓	Ind. Ref.	✓	Sp. Act	✓

Chapter 7
Exegetical Significance: Sample Studies from Galatians

In the previous chapters, the syntactic function of middle-form verbs (both oppositional and *media tantum*) in their context in 1 Thessalonians or 2 Corinthians was examined. This function was then compared to three descriptors of middle function.[1] These criteria are presented once more for reference:

1. The grammatical middle function in which the subject is essentially the direct or indirect object of the verb, acting on, for or by itself.
2. The linguistic notion of subject-affectedness with different manifestations as described by Rutger Allan.
3. The linguistic concept of internal *diathesis* posited by Benveniste and developed by Eberhard as medial function, indicating that the subject is actively engaged within the encompassing process of the verb.

Significant correlation was discovered between these descriptors and the function of the verbs examined, as indicated by the chapter summaries §3.1.10; §4.20; §5.11 above. The inter-dependence of a verb's lexical sense, its tense, literary context, and its voice function have been carefully examined throughout this investigation. In this synergistic relationship between all these components, it is in fact the context which

---

[1] This formulaic application of descriptors attempts to overcome the difficulty noted by Robertson, namely that the middle nuance is often difficult to discern, especially in the case of his "dynamic middle" category into which most of the *media tantum* verbs fall (*Grammar*, 811). Note that this dynamic middle is not the same as Cooper's dynamic middle which has been employed in the analysis of middle function in this study.

indicates the specific nuance with which the middle form is invested in each situation.² The results of this investigation indicate that middle morphology is indeed a signifier of middle function, whether the verb has a corresponding active form or not. Such an assertion challenges the traditionally held view noted in ch.2 above, which regarded verbs having middle but not active forms (*media tantum* verbs) as deponent. That is, they were previously construed as having middle form but active function.³

The postulate that all middle form verbs do have a distinctive middle voice function will now be applied to a sample of case studies from Paul's letter to the Galatians. As in previous chapters, extra-biblical texts may serve to illustrate the ways in which the verb was understood in Paul's day. This sheds light on the sense in which he used the middle verb under investigation and the way his readers may have interpreted his letter. In this epistle, Paul employs forty-six middle forms representing twenty-seven different verbs. Of these, there are thirteen that have not been previously studied in this investigation that appear in present or aorist forms in Galatians. These are listed in Table 7.1 below.

First, two in-depth studies of Gal 1:4 and 3:3 will explore the exegetical implications of reading the verbs in the middle voice according to the three criteria above. Moreover, the theological insights so conveyed will be examined for consistency with the wider corpus of Paul's writings. Second, a brief study of the lexical sense and general use of

---

² As noted by Robertson, *Grammar*, 804: "In the active voice the subject is merely acting; in the middle the subject is acting in relation to himself somehow. What this precise relation is the middle voice does not say. That must come out of the context or from the significance of the verb itself." This has been illustrated particularly in relation to verbs such as γίνομαι (§3.2) which have different types of middle function in different applications, indicating that a generic sub-type such as "spontaneous middle" is not applicable in all instances.

³ The true middle function of many *media tantum* verbs has been demonstrated above, e.g., λογίζομαι, "I consider" and ῥύομαι, "I rescue." See §5.10 & §4.2, respectively.

each remaining verb above is undertaken in order to explore the potential contribution of their middle form in specific contexts in Galatians.

Table 7.1 Further Present and Aorist Middle Verbs from Galatians

Lexical form	Inflected form	verse	Translation Context
ἐξαιρέω	ἐξέληται	1:4	...in order to <u>deliver</u> you from the present evil age.
προσανατίθημι	προσανεθέμην	1:16	I did not <u>confer</u> with any human person
	προσανέθεντο	2:6	they <u>contributed</u> nothing to me
ψεύδομαι	ψεύδομαι	1:20	before God, I do not <u>lie</u>
ἀνατίθημι	ἀνεθέμην	2:2	I <u>put before</u> them the gospel I proclaim
φοβέω	φοβούμενος	2:12	<u>fearing</u> the circumcision proponents
	φοβοῦμαι	4:11	I <u>fear</u> for you, lest I have toiled among you in vain
ἐνάρχομαι	ἐναρξάμενοι	3:3	<u>having begun</u> by the spirit ...
ἐπιτελέω	ἐπιτελεῖσθε	3:3	Are you now <u>trying to finish</u> with the flesh?
ἐπιδιατάσσομαι	ἐπιδιατάσσεται	3:15	no one <u>adds a condition</u> to an established covenant
παρατηρέω	παρατηρεῖσθε	4:10	you <u>carefully observe</u> special days, months, seasons
ἀπορέω	ἀποροῦμαι	4:20	I <u>am perplexed</u> about you
ἀπεκδέχομαι	ἀπεκδεχόμεθα	5:5	We <u>eagerly await</u> the hope of righteousness
ἀντίκειμαι	ἀντίκειται	5:17	Spirit and flesh are <u>in opposition</u> to each other
προκαλέω	προκαλούμενοι	5:26	<u>provoking</u> and envying one another

7.1 ἘΞΕΛΗΤΑΙ (ἘΞΑΙΡΕΩ) IN GALATIANS 1:4

The first middle verb to appear in Paul's letter to the Galatians is ἐξέληται, the 3rd singular aorist middle subjunctive form of ἐξαιρέω. It appears in the customary prescript of the letter, within the greetings expressed by Paul subsequent to the identification of himself as sender (1:1) and the Galatians as recipients (1:2).[4] The elements of the basic prescript have been significantly extended, providing a foundation for the theological issues addressed in the letter.[5] Noticeably absent is the commonly expressed thanksgiving of Paul's letters (see Rom 1:8; 1 Cor 1:4; Phil 1:3; Col 1:3; 1 Thess 1:2; 2 Thess 1:3). This is compatible with the general theme of reproach regarding the direction the Galatians were taking (e.g., Gal 1:6, 3:1, 3).[6] The text of Gal 1:3–5 is given below with English translation, ἐξέληται appearing in the purpose clause of v.4.

---

[4] Stowers observes the customary opening of several personal letters of the Hellenistic era, noting that basic elements are the identification of sender and recipient, followed by a greeting (*Letter Writing*, 20). His sample letters demonstrate that these elements may be concisely expressed as in P.Oxy. 42.3069 (201–400 CE): "Aquila to Sarapion, Greetings" (99), or expanded descriptively as in P.Harr. 1.107 (201–300 CE): "to my most precious mother Maria, from Besas, best greetings in God" (74). This custom is also noted by David E. Aune, *The New Testament in Its Literary Environment*, LEC 8 (Philadelphia: Westminster, 1989), 163 and Hans-Josef Klauck, *Ancient Letters and the New Testament: A Guide to Context and Exegesis*, trans. Daniel P. Bailey (Waco, TX: Baylor University Press, 2006), 18–20.

[5] As noted, e.g., by J. Louis Martyn, *Galatians: A New Translation with Introduction and Commentary*, AB 33A (New York: Doubleday, 1997), 87; F. F. Bruce, *The Epistle to the Galatians: A Commentary on the Greek Text*, NIGTC (Grand Rapids: Eerdmans, 1982), 71–75; Gordon D. Fee, *Galatians: A Pentecostal Commentary* (Dorset, U.K.: Deo, 2007), 18–19; and Frank J. Matera, *Galatians,* SP 9 (Collegeville, MN: The Liturgical Press, 1992), 42. Matera notes the emphasis on the nature of Christ's salvific work and the closing doxology as distinctive features of the salutation.

[6] See Martinus C. de Boer, *Galatians: A Commentary*, NTL (Louisville: Westminster John Knox, 2011), 37. Accordingly, de Boer not only comments on the absence of the thanksgiving prayer which usually follows the prescript but notes that a rebuke and imprecation take its place in 1:6–10, thus disclosing the point of the letter.

Gal 1:3 χάρις ὑμῖν καὶ εἰρήνη ἀπὸ θεοῦ πατρὸς ἡμῶν καὶ κυρίου Ἰησοῦ Χριστοῦ ⁴τοῦ δόντος ἑαυτὸν ὑπὲρ τῶν ἁμαρτιῶν ἡμῶν, ὅπως <u>ἐξέληται</u> ἡμᾶς ἐκ τοῦ αἰῶνος τοῦ ἐνεστῶτος πονηροῦ κατὰ τὸ θέλημα τοῦ θεοῦ καὶ πατρὸς ἡμῶν, ⁵ᾧ ἡ δόξα εἰς τοὺς αἰῶνας τῶν αἰώνων, ἀμήν

Grace and peace to you from God our father and the Lord Jesus Christ, ⁴who gave himself for our sins, in order that he may <u>deliver</u> us from the present evil age according to the will of our God and Father, ⁵to whom be the glory for ever and ever, amen.

Paul affirms that the grace and peace he wishes for the Galatians come specifically from God our father *and* the Lord Jesus Christ. The latter title is then qualified with the theologically replete statement: "who gave himself for our sins in order to deliver (ἐξέληται) us from the present evil age" (1:4). This signals from the outset Paul's emphasis on the coming of the new apocalyptic era in which Gentiles also may experience salvation (deliverance) directly through the gracious gift of Christ and the Spirit. (3:3–5, 26–29).

Galatians 1:4 contains the only instance of ἐξαιρέω in Paul's writings. This, together with the less characteristic use of sins (plural) rather than the singular sin in 1:4a has led to the suggestion that this could be a traditional kerygmatic summary, akin to that in 1 Cor 15:3. There Paul passes on the tradition he had received, that " Christ died for our sins [ὑπὲρ τῶν ἁμαρτιῶν ἡμῶν] in accordance with the scriptures" (NRSV).[7] Some scholars have noted intra-canonical threads also. Thus,

---

[7] As discussed by Martyn, *Galatians,* 89; also noted by, e.g., Douglas J. Moo, *Galatians* BECNT (Grand Rapids: Baker Academic, 2013), 72, and Bruce, *Galatians,* 75. Richard B. Hays, however, considers that the discussion of originality detracts from the fact that "as in every other Pauline Epistle, the opening lines highlight precisely the themes that lie theologically at the heart of the letter" ("Apocalyptic *Poiēsis* in Galatians: Paternity, Passion and Participation," in *Galatians and Christian Theology: Justification, the Gospel, and Ethics in Paul's Letter,* ed. Mark W. Elliott et al. [Grand Rapids:

Richard N. Longenecker considers 1:4a to be an "outcropping of one of the early confessions of the Christian church." He traces it back to Jesus' statement recorded in Mark 10:45 (the Son of Man came ... to give his life as a ransom for many) and in turn to the suffering servant in Isa 53:5–6, 12.[8]

Ultimately, however, whether dependent on traditional material or not, Paul chooses to employ this language[9] and in doing so he reminds the Galatians of the essence of the gospel message they received.[10] Thus 1:4a speaks of the sacrificial function of Christ's death for the forgiveness of sins,[11] while 4b speaks of the purpose and effect of this: existential deliverance of believers from the power of sin.[12] With this basic

---

Baker Academic, 2014], 201).

[8] Richard N. Longenecker, *Galatians*, WBC 41 (Dallas: Word, 1990) 7. Martyn mentions similar expressions in the epistles, e.g., παραδόντος ἑαυτὸν ὑπὲρ ἐμοῦ (Gal 2:20) and παρέδωκεν ἑαυτὸν ὑπὲρ ἡμῶν προσφορὰν καὶ θυσίαν (Eph 5:2) (*Galatians*, 89). Likewise, Betz comments that "Christ gave himself up for our sins" suggests "an old christology which understood Jesus' death as an expiatory self-sacrifice" and which "is likely to have originated in Judaism" (*Galatians: A Commentary on Paul's Letter to the Churches in Galatia*, Hermeneia [Philadelphia: Fortress, 1979], 41).

[9] Das comments: "Paul would not cite such material unless it expressed his own sentiments.... If Paul is paraphrasing an earlier Christian tradition, he has clearly placed his own, apocalyptic stamp on that material" (*Galatians*, 83–84).

[10] As J. B. Lightfoot points out, the Galatians appeared to have neglected the significance of the atoning death of Christ (see, e.g., 2:21; 5:4) (*Saint Paul's Epistle to the Galatians* [London: Macmillan, 1914; repr., Grand Rapids: Zondervan, 1957], 73).

[11] In the phrase ὑπὲρ τῶν ἁμαρτιῶν ἡμῶν (NA[28]), both ὑπὲρ and περί are attested in the manuscripts. This is discussed by Ernest De Witt Burton, who notes that Paul uses both prepositions to mean "concerning" or "on behalf of" but ὑπὲρ more commonly for the latter (*A Critical and Exegetical Commentary on The Epistle to the Galatians*, ICC [Edinburgh: T&T Clark, 1921; repr., 1968], 12, 13). Longenecker notes the use of ὑπὲρ in the similar expression in 1 Cor 15:3 (*Galatians*, 8). Matera remarks that the preposition (ὑπὲρ) "functions as a technical term when the Apostle speaks of Christ's death on our behalf" (*Galatians*, 39). See likewise Gal 2:20.

[12] This figuring of sin as a power that enslaves people is consistent with Paul's expression elsewhere, e.g., in Romans chapter 6 he speaks of the power of the resurrected Christ enabling believers to be no longer slaves to sin (6:6, 14) but to be set free from sin (6:18). Thus in 1:4b, Paul asserts that Christ delivers us from "the present evil age"

understanding of Paul's expression in 1:4, the wider use of ἐξαιρέω in both active and middle forms will now be explored before examining the significance of the middle voice of ἐξέληται in this verse.

7.1.1 Lexical Meaning and Use of ἐξαιρέω

The lexical definitions of ἐξαιρέω in LSJ and BDAG refer to the general sense of "taking out" or "removal" for the active and "choose for oneself," "set free" or "deliver" for the middle.[13] A further indication of the sense of this verb may also be gleaned from its application in the LXX and NT. In the active, ἐξαιρέω occurs only twice in the New Testament, these being parallel passages in Matthew referring to plucking out one's eye. Thus, we read: εἰ δὲ ὁ ὀφθαλμός σου ὁ δεξιὸς σκανδαλίζει σε, ἔξελε αὐτὸν καὶ βάλε ἀπὸ σοῦ: If your right eye causes you to stumble, pull it out and throw it away from you (Matt 5:29).[14] Similarly, in the LXX the relatively few uses of the active form refer to taking something (an impersonal grammatical object) out from a physical location.[15]

The middle form, on the contrary, is used widely in the LXX in the sense of delivering or rescuing *persons* from danger or an undesirable situation. Hence it is used in reference to deliverance of the Hebrews from slavery in Egypt: ἐξείλατο αὐτοὺς κύριος ἐκ χειρὸς Φαραω καὶ ἐκ χειρὸς τῶν Αἰγυπτίων: the Lord delivered them from the hand of Pharaoh and of the Egyptians, (Exod 18:8). Likewise, it appears in the record of the deliverance of Shadrach, Meshach, and Abednego from the fiery furnace (Dan 3:17) as below:

---

i.e., the power of sin. This power is evinced by sins committed (Gal 1:4a).

[13] LSJ, s.v. "ἐξαιρέω." BDAG, s.v. "ἐξαιρέω."

[14] Matthew 18:9 expresses the same thought but omits ὁ δεξιός. The parallel passage in Mark omits any reference to plucking out and simply states ἔκβαλε αὐτόν (throw it away).

[15] In the LXX the active form occurs four times. These are in in reference to taking out of a house any stones that are affected by disease (Lev 14:40), Samson taking honey from the mouth of a lion carcass, Judg 14:9 (twice), and taking the inner parts out of a fish before cooking and eating it (Tob 6:40).

Dan 3:17 ἔστι γὰρ θεὸς ἐν οὐρανοῖς εἷς κύριος ἡμῶν ὃν φοβούμεθα ὅς ἐστι δυνατὸς <u>ἐξελέσθαι</u> ἡμᾶς ἐκ τῆς καμίνου τοῦ πυρός καὶ ἐκ τῶν χειρῶν σου βασιλεῦ <u>ἐξελεῖται</u> ἡμᾶς

For there is one God in heaven, our Lord whom we fear, who is able to <u>deliver</u> us from the burning fiery furnace, and he will <u>deliver</u> us from your hands, O king.

In the Psalms, the middle form of ἐξαιρέω is used in reference to the divine deliverer in many prayers, for example, <u>ἐξελοῦ</u> με ἐκ τῶν ἐχθρῶν μου ὁ θεός: God, <u>deliver</u> me from my enemies (Ps 58:2).[16] Likewise it is found in promises of deliverance, for example, ἐπικάλεσαί με ἐν ἡμέρᾳ θλίψεως καὶ <u>ἐξελοῦμαί</u> σε καὶ δοξάσεις με: call on me in the day of trouble and I will <u>deliver</u> you, and you will glorify me (Ps 49:15).[17] Typically, the recipient of deliverance appears as the direct object of the verb (ἐξελοῦ **με**, ἐξελοῦμαί **σε**, respectively, above), and the situation or power from which one is delivered is expressed (when specified) as a phrase introduced by ἐκ (hence **ἐκ** τῶν ἐχθρῶν μου, above).[18]

The middle form of ἐξαιρέω is used in a similar sense in literary texts from the Hellenistic era. Hence, Philo employs ἐξέληται in conjunction with εἰς ἐλευθερίαν (into freedom) in reference to the cries of the children of Israel for deliverance from Egypt.[19] In alluding to their ill-treatment by their oppressors, he speaks of future justice when God "<u>brings forth</u> the one to full liberty" (καὶ τὸ μὲν εἰς ἐλευθερίαν <u>ἐξέληται</u> παντελῆ) but "renders recompense to the other for his

---

[16] Also, Ps 30:2,3; 58:2; 63:2; 70:2; 81:4; 118:153; 139:2,5; 142:9; 143:7; 143:11.

[17] So also, ἐπικαλέσεταί με καὶ εἰσακούσομαι αὐτοῦ μετ' αὐτοῦ εἰμι ἐν θλίψει καὶ ἐξελοῦμαι καὶ δοξάσω αὐτόν: "he will call to me, and I will listen to him; I am with him in trouble; I will deliver him and glorify him" (Ps 90:15, NETS).

[18] Likewise: ἐξελοῦ με κύριε ἐξ ἀνθρώπου πονηροῦ: Deliver me, Lord, from the evil person, (Ps 139:2); ἐξείλατο τὴν ψυχήν μου ἐκ θανάτου: he has delivered my soul from death (Ps 114:8).

[19] Philo, *Conf.* 94.1 (Colson, Whitaker, LCL 261:60–61).

misdeeds."[20] Similarly, Plutarch employs the middle form in reference to Demetrius being ambitious to rescue (ἐξελέσθαι) Aristides and Socrates from the evil of poverty.[21] This naturally implies that a new state of security (not poverty) would be reached and that the subject has a personal concern for this.

Middle forms of ἐξαιρέω likewise appear in the papyri, for example, ἐξαιρεῖται in P.Sorb. 3.109 (ca. 220 BCE) and ἐξελέσθαι in both PSI 4.357 (252 BCE) and P.Zen.Pestm. 27 (254 BCE). The imperative occurs in a letter from Paosis to Zenon (his guardian). Having been imprisoned to exact a payment he cannot supply, Paosis asks Zenon to secure his release (ἐξελοῦ με) so that he may contact his father for assistance (P.Cair.Zen. 3.59492 [275–226 BCE]).

Similarly, ἐξελοῦ appears in P.Zen.Pestm. 25 (257 BCE), a letter from Apollonios to Zenon instructing him to take excess oil out of the house to a warehouse (ἐξ [οἴ]κου ... εἰς Ἐμπόριον ἐξελοῦ, *l* 2–3) for safekeeping; to be guarded by servants. Thus, although it is removed from one place, it is not discarded, but transferred to a place of safety, with servants being appointed to guard it (κατάστησ[ον]τῶν παίδων τοὺς τηρήσοντας). This aligns with the literary and biblical uses discussed above, where someone or something is transferred from one 'place' (whether concrete or conceptual) to a better one, the middle form indicating the interest and involvement of the subject in such an outcome.

In the New Testament, apart from Galatians 1:4, the only other middle forms of ἐξαιρέω appear in Acts. Stephen speaks of the divine deliverance of Joseph: ἐξείλατο αὐτὸν ἐκ πασῶν τῶν θλίψεων (Acts 7:10) and of the Hebrew people: κατέβην ἐξελέσθαι αὐτούς (7:34). Peter is delivered from prison by an angel: ἐξαπέστειλεν [ὁ] κύριος τὸν ἄγγελον αὐτοῦ καὶ ἐξείλατό με ἐκ χειρὸς Ἡρώδου (Acts 12:11). Paul is rescued [ἐξειλάμην] from prison and transferred to safety in Caesarea (Acts 23:27) and recounts the promise of deliverance given to him by the risen Christ on the Damascus road: ἐξαιρούμενός σε ἐκ τοῦ λαοῦ καὶ ἐκ τῶν ἐθνῶν εἰς οὓς ἐγὼ ἀποστέλλω σε (26:17).

---

[20] Philo, *Her.* 271.4 (Colson, Whitaker, LCL 261:422–423).
[21] Plutarch, *Aristides* 1.9.3 (Perrin, LCL 47:214–215).

Each of these (as also the LXX references above) pertains to deliverance from a place of physical danger with the implication that the persons are transferred to a situation that enables their divine calling to be pursued. Notably, in each case above, the deliverance is attributed to God, whether explicitly or indirectly, as when working through an agent such as the angel in Acts 12:11.[22] As in the LXX, the recipients of deliverance are signified in the accusative as a direct object and the situation from which they are delivered (when identified) is introduced by ἐκ (from).

7.1.2 Exegetical Significance of ἐξέληται in Gal 1:4

Although appearing in similar syntax to many of the examples above, ἐξέληται in Galatians 1:4 does not refer to deliverance from immediate physical danger. Rather, it refers to deliverance of believers (ἡμᾶς, [accusative direct object]) from the spiritual dominion of the "present evil age" (ἐκ τοῦ αἰῶνος τοῦ ἐνεστῶτος πονηροῦ); that is, not from a physical place but from the conceptual place of slavery to sin.[23] This does not refer to a change of situation in space or time. Hence, Gerhard Ebeling states: "To be delivered from the present evil age means that a place has

---

[22] In Acts 23 Paul was previously visited by the risen Lord who assured him that he would go on to testify in Rome (23:11), indicating that the Lord himself was behind the rescue mission that the commander reports to Governor Felix (23:27).

[23] Bruce states that the apocalyptic backdrop to Paul's reference to αἰών πονηρός is "an age dominated by an ethically evil power" totally opposed to the will of God (*Galatians*, 76); similarly, Matera, *Galatians*, 43. Betz notes that while the concept of the present evil age and the notion of the age to come stem from Jewish apocalypticism, the deliverance to which Paul refers is "out of the evil aeon and not of the change of aeons themselves" (*Galatians*, 42). A helpful discussion of the forensic and cosmological types of apocalyptic eschatology which form a background to Paul's writings is also given by de Boer, *Galatians*, 31–35. He comments that "the present evil age" as used by Paul here "is an all-encompassing sphere of evil," equivalent to his frequent references elsewhere to "this age" (e.g., Rom 12:2. 1 Cor 1:20) or "this world" (e.g., 1 Cor 3:19, 5:10) (*Galatians*, 30).

been prepared through Jesus Christ, a place not subject to any power belonging to the world," that is, "the kingdom of his beloved Son."[24]

This notion is explicitly expressed in the parallel passage in Col 1:13–14 which speaks of being rescued (ἐρρύσατο) from the power of darkness and *transferred* to the kingdom of the beloved son in whom we have redemption.[25]. The apocalyptic concept of two realms is integral to Paul's argument of Galatians. He juxtaposes metaphors such as flesh and spirit (Gal 3:3; 5:17), law and faith (2:16; 3:23; 5:6), slave and child (4:1–7), and Mt. Sinai and the Jerusalem above (4:24–26) to develop the notion of deliverance from the present evil age expressed in the salutation. Therefore, the understanding of transfer out of one realm and into another when one receives the Spirit through hearing the gospel with faith (Gal 3:1) provides the theological backdrop against which to examine the syntactical function of ἐξέληται.

In Galatians 1:4 there are both active and middle verbs. The action by which Christ secured atonement for the believer is articulated using an active verb (the participle δόντος) with a reflexive pronoun. Thus, he writes: τοῦ <u>δόντος ἑαυτὸν</u> ὑπὲρ τῶν ἁμαρτιῶν ἡμῶν in reference to the one who <u>gave himself</u> for our sins.[26] This customary NT combination indicates the volitional action of a subject on itself, thus

---

[24] Gerhard Ebeling, *The Truth of the Gospel: An Exposition of Galatians*, trans. David Green (Philadelphia: Fortress, 1985), 39. Likewise Bruce states: "Christ's self-oblation not only procures for his people the forgiveness of their past sins; it delivers them from the realm in which sin is irresistible into the realm where he himself is Lord" (*Galatians*, 75).

[25] For concordant thought, see James D. G. Dunn, *The Theology of Paul the Apostle* (Grand Rapids: Eerdmans, 1998), 179–80. Dunn refers to "rescue from the present evil age" in Gal 1:4 in reference to "apocalyptic disjunction," i.e., an entirely different plane of existence in the "eschatological now."

[26] On Christ giving himself, Matera notes the distinction in language from that of the synoptic gospels which regularly employ passive forms of παραδίδωμι (hand over, betray) in relation to Christ's death, e.g., ὁ υἱὸς τοῦ ἀνθρώπου παραδίδοται εἰς χεῖρας ἀνθρώπων (Mark 9:31), similarly παραδίδοται εἰς τὸ σταυρωθῆναι (Matt 26:2) (*Galatians*, 43). Thus, attention is here drawn to Christ and his role in the process of redemption.

functioning as an alternative to a middle-form direct reflexive.[27] While it does speak of the involvement of the subject in the action (since he gave *himself*) it essentially tells us what happened and what was given, speaking of the event as a whole (aorist tense, perfective aspect). The *purpose and goal* of this self-sacrifice is then articulated by means of a middle verb in the clause that follows: ὅπως ἐξέληται ἡμᾶς ἐκ τοῦ αἰῶνος τοῦ ἐνεστῶτος πονηροῦ (so that he may deliver us out of this present evil age), again highlighting the involvement of the subject (Christ) in the action. Although this in itself is noteworthy, the particular type of involvement may be further considered by exploring the implications of each criterion under discussion. As noted early in this study, these are not incompatible; rather, each one provides a particular perspective on involvement of the subject in the middle-voiced situation.

The grammatical sense indicates that the subject (Jesus) is acting on, for, or with reference to himself in the process of deliverance. He is clearly not acting *on* himself (direct reflexive) for the verb takes the direct object ἡμᾶς (us); but he may well be acting *for* himself.[28] Such a reading would imply that we are not simply rescued, being plucked out and then left alone, but that it is in Christ's interest that we are delivered; he delivers us for himself. As per the lexical study, this verb is commonly used to refer to rescue from a place of danger to a place of safety. Hence, if we are to be delivered out of this present evil age, this reading suggests that we are to be delivered into another realm, a place of safety,

---

[27] Direct reflexive actions are more commonly expressed by an active and a reflexive pronoun in the NT; the middle is rarely used in this sense, as noted above. See also, Robertson, *Grammar*, 806–7 and Black, *New Testament Greek*, 88.

[28] This corresponds to the indirect reflexive middle and is a common gloss for the middle voice. See, for example, Peter Frick, *A Handbook of New Testament Greek Grammar* (Montreal: Laodamia, 2007), 52. Frick states: "When translating the middle voice, it is translated with "for" and a reflexive pronoun, for example, "I am reading for myself; she is speaking for herself"[.]" Similarly, Mounce comments that the notion of self-interest is one understanding of the middle voice, translating the middle voice of αἰτέω as "I ask (for myself)" as an example (*Basics*, 231). The notion of benefit to the subject in this case is discussed further below.

where Christ our deliverer rules.[29] This is consistent with the apocalyptic understandings of this verse noted above[30] It is also consistent with expressions of the unity of believers with Christ given elsewhere by Paul. For example, in the context of marriage imagery, he refers to Christians (ἀδελφοί μου) as those who *belong to him* who was raised from the dead (Rom 7:4).

The middle voice of ἐξέληται may also indicate that Jesus rescues us *by reference to* himself, drawing on, energizing, and applying his own resources, drawing us into his "sphere of control and effectiveness" as in Cooper's evocative description of the dynamic middle.[31] Such a reading implies that Jesus *himself* delivers us out of the sphere in which evil enslaves. Paul refers to this new freedom for which Christ has set us free (Gal 5:1) as "living by the Spirit" (πνεύματι περιπατεῖτε 5:16) and being "led by the Sprit" (πνεύματι ἄγεσθε, 5:18). In this vein Paul remarks in Romans: "You, however, are not in the realm of the flesh but are in the realm of the Spirit, if indeed the Spirit of God lives in you" (Rom 8:9, NIV). Notably, he employs πνεῦμα θεοῦ (Spirit of God) and πνεῦμα Χριστοῦ (Spirit of Christ) alternatively in the same verse to refer to the Spirit who indwells the Christian as the source of new life. Hence a middle reading of ἐξέληται to indicate that Christ delivers the believer through the application of his own resources, expressed in terms of the relationship between disciple and Savior through the indwelling Spirit, is clearly consistent with Paul's theology.[32]

---

[29] The Gospel of John carries a similar theme in different language. While Paul speaks of the present evil age, John speaks of "this world" as the realm from which we may be delivered, and which stands in contrast to the kingdom of God (e.g., John 18:36).

[30] See n25, 26, 27, above.

[31] Cooper, *Attic Greek Prose Syntax* vol. I, 589. See §1.6.10 above.

[32] Elsewhere Paul uses the expression "in Christ" to refer to this union, e.g., Rom 8:1; 1 Cor 1:30; John's gospel expresses this relationship in terms of the metaphor of the shepherd and his sheep (John 10). As seen in §4.4.18 the middle voice characteristically expresses the dynamics of relationship and interaction. In similar vein, Hays draws attention to such "participatory soteriology" as "the dominant paradigm in Galatians for understanding the way in which Christ rescues his people" ("Apocalyptic *Poiēsis* in Galatians," 214).

Applying the criterion of subject-affectedness indicates that Jesus, as grammatical subject of ἐξέληται is somehow impacted by the process of deliverance. Clearly Christ is also affected by giving himself over to death, but this effect is articulated by the reflexive ἑαυτὸν in 1:4a, whereas the middle verb under consideration (ἐξέληται) is in the purpose clause that follows. This clause explains the reason why Christ gave himself, and it is the middle voice of ἐξέληται that indicates Christ is affected. Allan does not include this particular verb among his examples but does include the near synonym ῥύομαι in his indirect reflexive category. He defines this as follows: "The indirect reflexive middle involves transitive events performed by a volitional subject (an agent). The subject is affected in that s/he derives benefit from the action performed, i.e., the subject has the semantic role of *beneficiary*."[33]

Thus, the criterion of subject affectedness points to the benefit that Christ desires and obtains through the process of deliverance, essentially akin to the manner discussed above for the grammatical sense of delivering us *for* himself. This notion is endorsed by Paul's identification of the church, the community of believers, as those called to be God's holy people (κλητοῖς ἁγίοις, e.g., Rom 1:7, 1 Cor 1:2). This inference of a new community participating in the life of God is consistent with Richard A. Young's comment that the basic notion of the middle voice "is that the subject intimately participates in the results of the action. It is the voice of personal involvement."[34]

The concept of personal involvement leads us also to consider the medial notion (internal *diathesis*) of the middle voice as described by Eberhard, which would indicate that Christ is internal to the process of deliverance. This conception of the middle points to the fact that Christ's death is not only a transaction to atone for sin (1:4a) but also facilitates (ὅπως: in order to) a process of mediation in which God, Christ and believer are all involved. That is, the deliverance expressed by ἐξέληται in 1:4b is equivalent to the redemption of which Paul

---

[33] Allan, *Polysemy*, 112, 114 (italics original).

[34] Richard A. Young, *Intermediate New Testament Greek: A Linguistic and Exegetical Approach* (Nashville: Broadman & Holman, 1994), 134.

speaks in 4:5–7. It is rescue not simply *out of* the present evil age but *into* a new situation, adopted as children into the family of God. As mediator, Christ brings two formerly hostile parties (God and human) together, facilitating a relationship which could not otherwise be obtained.[35]

These exegetical possibilities illustrate that the middle form of ἐξαιρέω has connotations which would not appear if the active form were used. As indicated above, the active is used in reference to the simple removal of something from somewhere, such as the diseased items from a house (Lev 14:40) or the offending eyes which need to be plucked out and thrown away (Matt 5:29). The middle form, however, is characteristically used when the objects removed are valued and need to be preserved, even in the case of the oil in P.Zen.Pestm. 25. The context and the voice function thus coalesce in this pericope to indicate that Christ is involved in the process of deliverance as the divine agent. He is not acting outside of himself, but is within the process (internal *diathesis*), not acting dispassionately but having a personal interest in the outcome of the action (indirect reflexive middle) and using his own resources (dynamic middle). Just as Paul himself was concerned to deliver the offering from the Gentile churches to Jerusalem (Rom 15:25–29) and escort it safely to its destination, this middle voice reading of Gal 1:4 likewise portrays Christ as inextricably bound to the believer in the process of deliverance. This process involves rescue, safe conduct and not only delivery to the desired *destination* but continued union, as the believer is now "in Christ" (Gal 3:13, 14, 26, 28) as a member of God's own people.[36] The middle voice is thus appropriately used, subtly yet evocatively affirming the theological assertions of the New Testament in respect to deliverance of the believer through union with Christ.

---

[35] This resonates with New Testament expressions that speak of Christ as the one who brings the redeemed person to God (1 Pet 3:18), as the mediator of the new covenant (Heb 9:15), and the one mediator between God and humankind (1 Tim 2:5).

[36] See also Rom 8:1 (those who are in Christ Jesus walk according to the Spirit, not the flesh) and John 14:20 (On that day you will know that I am in my Father and you in me and I in you).

7.2 Ἐναρξάμενοι (Ἐνάρχομαι) and Ἐπιτελεῖσθε (Ἐπιτελέω) in Galatians 3:3

Chapter 3 of the Epistle to the Galatians begins Paul's argument against those who insist on the need for the Galatian Christians to be circumcised (Gal 5:2, 6:12). Reasoning from the Galatian's own experience, Paul poses rhetorical questions to induce them to reflect on the fact that they have already received the Holy Spirit as a result of responding to the message of Christ crucified (3:2, 5). Essentially referring to beginning and completing a task or process, ἐνάρχομαι and ἐπιτελέω are used antithetically in Paul's argument as he attempts to persuade the Galatians of the folly involved in submitting to circumcision after already having received the gift of the Holy Spirit. This is not simply an unnecessary option in Paul's mind; it is a matter of vital theological importance, for it opposes his emphasis on the Holy Spirit as the source and sustenance of the Christian life (Gal 3:14, 5:16–18, 25, 6:8).[37] Thus Paul writes:

| Gal 3:3 οὕτως ἀνόητοί ἐστε, <u>ἐναρξάμενοι</u> πνεύματι νῦν σαρκὶ <u>ἐπιτελεῖσθε</u>; | Are you so foolish? Having <u>started</u> with the Spirit, are you now <u>trying to finish</u> with the flesh? |

The rhetorical question expressed in this verse distils the essence of Paul's argument. He is highlighting the absurdity of the position taken by those who seek to add to their Christian experience in some way by submitting to circumcision. Having entered into new life in Christ, they have already experienced the eschatological realm of the Holy Spirit. It is therefore impossible to continue their progress through circumcision, an initiation to Torah observance. Paul asserts (3:25) that the Law was a prelude to the gospel, a custodian for Israel until the time of fulfillment in Christ. Accordingly, Table 7.2 below summarizes the stages of

---

[37] The theological import is developed further below.

salvation history addressed by Paul in this section of discourse, illustrating his argument with respect to the Galatian converts.

Table 7.2 Stages of Salvation History in Galatians 3

A	B	C	D	E
Circumcision/Torah Pedagogue ⟶	Christ the τέλος (end) of the Law	Hearing the gospel with faith ⟶	Received Spirit, "In Christ" ⟶	Spiritual maturity
Gal 3:23–25	(Rom 10:4)	Gal 3:1, 2	Gal 3:2, 14, 26.	5:22–25

As new Christians, the Galatians who were previously pagan (Gal 4:3, 8, 9) have entered into fellowship with Christ directly at stage C and are now at stage D. How then, Paul argues, can going back to stage A help their progress towards spiritual maturity (stage E)? Such a notion conflates the two covenants; the first was specifically for Israel, but the new covenant is for all people (Gal 3:8, 14). Having begun on one path they would be now starting on another; Paul effectively asks, "how can this lead to progress and completion of the first?"[38] In his succinct positing of this question, he employs two middle form verbs: ἐναρξάμενοι and ἐπιτελεῖσθε which will now be examined more closely.[39]

7.2.1 Lexical Semantics and Use of ἐνάρχομαι

A middle-only verb, ἐνάρχομαι is a compound of ἄρχομαι that is used in the sense of beginning an action or process, for example, Καὶ ἤρξατο αὐτοῖς ἐν παραβολαῖς: So he <u>began</u> to speak to them in parables (Mark 12:1).[40] Although ἄρχομαι is used sixty-nine times in the New

---

[38] Accordingly, Frederic Rendall comments, "Conversion had brought about a spiritual change as its immediate result; it was folly to look for a consummation of this change from an ordinance of the flesh like circumcision" (*The Epistle to the Galatians*, vol. III of *The Expositors Greek Testament* [Grand Rapids: Eerdmans, 1967], 167.

[39] Being in the present tense, ἐπιτελεῖσθε could be middle or passive; see discussion below.

[40] The middle nuance of ἄρχομαι is discussed in §5.9 above

Testament, the compound ἐνάρχομαι occurs only twice, both being in the writings of Paul (Gal 3:3 and Phil 1:6).

Setting aside these New Testament uses for the moment, we see that the compound verb appears in the LXX in reference to beginning to engage in an action or procedure. For example, regarding the festival of unleavened bread we see: <u>ἐναρχόμενοι</u> τῇ τεσσαρεσκαιδεκάτῃ ἡμέρᾳ τοῦ μηνὸς τοῦ πρώτου ἀφ' ἑσπέρας ἔδεσθε ἄζυμα ἕως ἡμέρας μιᾶς καὶ εἰκάδος τοῦ μηνὸς ἕως ἑσπέρας: <u>beginning</u> on the fourteenth day of the first month at evening you shall eat unleavened bread until the evening of the twenty-first day of the month (Exod. 12:18).[41] Likewise the Israelites were told to begin (ἔναρχου) to inherit the land (Deut 2:24).

Similar instances appear in literary works, such as ἅμα δ' αὐτός τε λέγειν <u>ἐνήρχετο</u>: "at one and the same moment himself <u>began</u> to speak[.]";[42] Likewise: Ἅμα τε οὖν ἐπιτήδειος ἐδόκει ἡμέρα τέχνης <u>ἐνάρχεσθαι</u>: "So as soon as it seemed a suitable day <u>to begin</u> a trade[.]"[43] This general use of ἐνάρχομαι also appears among papyri documents. For example, in a letter written ca. 250 BC Aristeas and Pausanias send a request for wheat to Demeas, indicating that they will try to visit him in person when the *month of Mesore has <u>begun</u>* ([τ]οῦ δὲ Μεσορὴ <u>ἐναρχομένου</u>).[44]

There is also a more specific, though concordant use of ἐνάρχομαι in classical Greek in reference to ritual sacrifice.[45] Indeed, LSJ lists this use as the first entry: "*begin the offering* by taking the barley from the basket," before the general use: "*begin, make a beginning, engage in*[.]" Thus, when Iphigenia is about to sacrifice herself to Artemis in the hope of securing victory for Greece, she calls for someone to prepare the

---

[41] Similarly, ἤδη ἐνῆρκτο ἡ θραῦσις ἐν τῷ λαῳ: "already the plague had begun among the people" (Num 17:12, Brenton).

[42] Plutarch, *Sulla* 30.2.6 (Perrin, LCL 80:424–425).

[43] Lucian, *Somnium*, 3.2 (Harmon, LCL 130:216–217).

[44] P.Cair.Zen. 3.59396 *l* 4.

[45] MM, s.v. "ἐνάρχομαι." Also, Lightfoot, *Galatians*, 135; Betz, *Galatians*, 133.

sacrificial baskets (κανᾶ δ' ἐνάρχεσθω τις).⁴⁶ Consequently, some scholars suggest that these connotations may be evoked by Paul's expression in Galatians 3:3 (see further below for discussion).⁴⁷

7.2.2. Lexical Semantics and Use of ἐπιτελέω

The verb ἐπιτελέω is mainly used in the active and passive in reference to completing something begun or accomplishing something according to a plan or purpose.⁴⁸ There is little mention of the middle in the lexica. LSJ has "*get it completed*" and BDAG equates it to the active, while the examples given by MM are active or passive.

The middle form occurs only once in the LXX, at Esth 9:27, referring to the inauguration of the feast of Purim, the days specified <u>being observed</u> as a memorial (μνημόσυνον <u>ἐπιτελούμενον</u>). This exhibits the sense of performing or carrying out, rather than finishing.⁴⁹ It appears twice in the NT: ἐπιτελεῖσθε (Gal 3:3, discussed below) and ἐπιτελεῖσθαι in 1 Peter 5:9, where the verb is more generally understood as passive (e.g., NAS, NIV, NRSV, NJB) in reference to the sufferings accomplished or experienced by the believers.⁵⁰

---

⁴⁶ Euripides, *Iph. aul.* 1470. (Kovacs, LCL 495:328–329). Similarly, ἐνῆρκται μὲν τὰ κανᾶ δὲ τὰ θύματα τοῖς βωμοῖς: "the sacred baskets are prepared; the sacrificial victims stand ready at the altars." Aeschines, *Ctes.*, 120.7 (Adams, LCL 106:400–401).

⁴⁷ E.g., Betz, *Galatians*, 133 and Lightfoot, *Epistle to the Galatians*, 135.

⁴⁸ LSJ, s.v. "ἐπιτελέω." BDAG, s.v. "ἐπιτελέω." MM, s.v. "ἐπιτελέω."

⁴⁹ The active and passive are found more frequently, particularly in the Apocrypha, e.g., "and whatever you, along with your kindred, wish to do with gold and silver, discharge it [ἐπιτέλει] according to the will of your God" (1 Esd 8:16, NETS). This reflects the weaker sense of simply "doing" (i.e., performing a task).

⁵⁰ εἰδότες τὰ αὐτὰ τῶν παθημάτων τῇ ἐν κόσμῳ ὑμῶν ἀδελφότητι ἐπιτελεῖσθαι: knowing [that] the same sufferings are being accomplished by your fellow believers throughout the world (1 Pet 5:9). Some important manuscripts (ℵ, A, B*, 33) have the indicative ἐπιτελεῖσθε rather than the infinitive, indicating that those addressed are the ones undergoing the sufferings, as noted by J. Ramsey Michaels, *1 Peter*, WBC 49 (Waco, TX: Word, 1988), 293.

The active form of ἐπιτελέω is more frequently found, for example, αἱ χεῖρες Ζοροβαβελ ἐθεμελίωσαν τὸν οἶκον τοῦτον καὶ αἱ χεῖρες αὐτοῦ ἐπιτελέσουσιν: the hands of Zerubbabel have laid the foundations of this house and his hands <u>shall finish it</u> (Zech. 4:9). In similar vein, in reference to the offering he was collecting for the church in Jerusalem, Paul writes: νυνὶ δὲ καὶ τὸ ποιῆσαι ἐπιτελέσατε, ὅπως καθάπερ ἡ προθυμία τοῦ θέλειν, οὕτως καὶ τὸ ἐπιτελέσαι: Now <u>finish</u> the work, so that your eager willingness to do it may be matched by your <u>completion</u> of it, (2 Cor. 8:11, NIV).[51]

Notably, both verbs under consideration in Gal 3:3 viz., ἐνάρχομαι and ἐπιτελέω, are also juxtaposed in Phil 1:6. There Paul states: ὁ <u>ἐναρξάμενος</u> ἐν ὑμῖν ἔργον ἀγαθὸν <u>ἐπιτελέσει</u> ἄχρι ἡμέρας Χριστοῦ Ἰησοῦ: the one who <u>began</u> a good work in you will <u>carry it through</u> until the day of Christ Jesus. Although the same verbs are used, there are significant differences. In particular, the aorist participle ἐναρξάμενος is transitive in Phil 1:6, having God as the inferred subject and ἔργον ἀγαθὸν (good work) as the direct object. By contrast, the participle ἐναρξάμενοι in Gal 3:3 is intransitive, referring to what the Galatians are doing in reference to themselves. More pertinently, ἐπιτελέσει is active and transitive in Phil 1:6, referring to God completing a good work in others. God is not represented as being within the process; rather, the active form draws attention to the activity, with God as agent. In Gal 3:3, ἐπιτελεῖσθε is clearly middle or passive, with people as agents.

In the papyri, MM notes that ἐπιτελέω is used to refer to the performance of religious duties as well as to carrying out a function in general, giving several examples.[52] A further search reveals a similar reference to religious duties in the closing lines of UPZ 1.43 (161 BCE),

---

[51] Other NT instances of the active: Rom 15:28, 2 Cor 7:1, 8:6,11; Phil 1:6, Heb 8:5, 9:6.

[52] MM, s.v. "ἐπιτελέω." E.g., P.Par. 63 (= UPZ 1.110) *l* 16 (164 BCE): ἕκαστα δ' ἐπιτελεσθῆι κατὰ τὸν ὑπο-δεδειγμένον ἐν τῶι πεμφθέντι σοι παρ' ἡμῶν ὑπομνήματι τρόπον: that everything <u>be performed</u> in the manner laid down in the minute sent to you by us.

There we read: ὅπως δύνωνται τὰς ἐν τῶι ἱερῶι λειτουργίας ἐπιτελεῖν: so that they may be able to <u>perform</u> services in the temple. The active infinitive ἐπιτελεῖν may also be found frequently in a person's will, being used in regard to carrying out (executing) the specifications contained therein.[53] Although the active predominates, middle forms do appear, for instance, the infinitive ἐπιτελεῖσθαι is thought to be attested in BGU 4.1165 (20–19 BCE) and P.Fouad 16 (68 BCE), although these manuscripts are not entirely clear.

Active forms of ἐπιτελέω are again more common than the middle in ancient Greek literature. Notably, however, the aorist middle form ἐπετελέσατο is often seen in accounts of remarkable achievements, being particularly common in the historical library of Diodorus Siculus (first c. BCE). For example, Λεωνίδης μετὰ τῶν πολιτῶν ἡρωικὰς πράξεις καὶ παραδόξους <u>ἐπετελέσατο</u>: "Leonidas together with his fellow citizens <u>performed</u> heroic and astounding deeds[.]"[54] It is similarly used in earlier literature. Hence, Xenophon writes of Socrates: ἀλλ' ἱλαρῶς καὶ προσεδέχετο αὐτὸν καὶ <u>ἐπετελέσατο</u>: "but he was cheerful not only in the expectation of death but in <u>carrying it out</u>."[55]

The various examples above together illustrate the two senses of ἐπιτελέω listed in the lexica. That is, it is used both in regard to completing or finishing something begun, in a temporal sense, or performing or accomplishing something planned, on the conceptual plane. The latter would thus include the sense of putting an idea or desire into effect, bringing it to fruition, as in the execution of a person's will, noted above. This understanding should assist in the interpretation of Paul's expression in Gal 3:3 in which ἐπιτελέω appears as the present middle/passive indicative ἐπιτελεῖσθε in NA[28].[56] Thus, we must now consider the two possibilities for the voice of ἐπιτελεῖσθε.

---

[53] E.g., P.Oxy. 3.491, 3.492, 3.494, 3.495, all dated 2nd c. CE.

[54] Diodorus Siculus, *Bibl. Hist.* 11.9.2.3 (Oldfather, LCL 375:144–145).

[55] Xenophon, *Apologia Socratis* 34.1 (Marchant, Todd, Henderson, LCL 168:686–687).

[56] Some significant manuscripts attest the infinitive instead. Notably ℵ and 33 have

7.2.3 Ἐπιτελεῖσθε: Middle or Passive?

In the case of the present form ἐπιτελεῖσθε in Gal 3:3, it cannot simply be asserted that middle form equates to middle function, since the present form is ambiguous as to voice. That is, it could be middle or passive on the basis of morphology. Even if we were to adopt Allan's scheme in which the passive is a sub-set of middle, we would still need to decide if it was a passive-middle or some other class of middle. For the Koine (NT) Greek under discussion, it is customary to distinguish three voices: active, middle and passive. What is needed therefore, is to discern whether Paul is referring to the Galatians as recipients only of the completion or performance (passive) or whether they are acting voluntarily and being affected in the process (middle).

Some translations render ἐπιτελεῖσθε as passive. for example, "Are you so foolish? Having begun by the Spirit, are you now *being perfected* by the flesh?" (ESV). Other passive expressions for the second clause include "are ye now *made perfect* by the flesh?" (KJV), "are ye now *perfected* in the flesh?" (ERV), and "do you now look to the material to *make you perfect*?" (NEB). Such interpretations take ἐπιτελεῖσθε to indicate that something which is not yet perfect is completed or perfected, essentially understanding it in the temporal sense. A process has been started and it is added to in order to complete the task. The understanding would be that the Galatian Christians may now be perfected by undergoing circumcision and Torah obedience (5:2–4); the Galatians are the patients, the agent being the rite of circumcision.

ἐπιτελεῖσθαι whereas P[46] and B have ἐπιτελεῖσθε. These variants are identified in the CNTTS critical apparatus and discussed by Stephen C. Carlson, *The Text of Galatians and Its History*, WUNT 385 (Tübingen: Mohr Siebeck, 2015), 158. In agreement with NA[28], Carlson prefers the indicative since it is the harsher reading and has greater external support. Citing W. Sidney Allen, *Vox Graeca: The Pronunciation of Classical Greek* 3rd ed. (Cambridge: Cambridge University Press, 1987), 79, Carlson comments that the pronunciation was the same for both forms. Likewise, Horrocks notes that the pronunciation of αι and ε had become the same by 2nd c. BCE as confirmed by the papyri (*Greek*, 167–68).

One disadvantage of such a reading is that it implies the Galatians *themselves* are being completed (ἐπιτελεῖσθε being read as *you are completed*), yet it is unclear what this would actually mean. For instance, Matera adopts a passive reading and translates verse 3: "Are you so foolish [as to think] that having begun with the Spirit you are now made perfect by the flesh[.]"⁵⁷ However, he also comments that the broader sense of the letter indicates that the Galatians are seeking "to gain something by circumcision: to perfect *their faith*." This is not the same as perfecting themselves, as the translation infers.⁵⁸ Such an impasse illustrates the difficulty in rendering the asyndeton of Paul's pithy statement ἐναρξάμενοι πνεύματι νῦν σαρκὶ ἐπιτελεῖσθε; in another language.

Dunn achieves a more concise translation: "Having begun with the Spirit are you now made complete with the flesh?"⁵⁹ This maintains Paul's antithesis between Spirit and flesh, yet still portrays the Galatians as patients. It tends to place the emphasis on the initiation ritual and what it may achieve for those who submit to it, not on what the Galatians are choosing for themselves. Yet it is their choice of following this path that is the issue under contention. Further, such wording implies that the Galatians *themselves* may be completed, rather than the process of salvation.

On the other hand, as preferred by BDAG, ἐπιτελεῖσθε in Gal 3:3 may be read as a present indicative middle verb as in the NAB translation: "After beginning with the Spirit, are you now ending with the flesh?" ⁶⁰ This implies that the Galatians are the agents, and their full salvation is the inferred object they are now seeking to pursue by undergoing the rite of circumcision. This is an action performed literally "on the flesh" and metaphorically "in the flesh" (that is, by human effort, since circumcision entails submission to outward observances).⁶¹ The

---

⁵⁷ Matera, *Galatians*, 112.

⁵⁸ Matera, *Galatians*, 113 (italics added).

⁵⁹ James D. G. Dunn, *A Commentary on the Epistle to the Galatians*, BNTC (London: Black, 1993), 155.

⁶⁰ Likewise, CEB, NET, NIV, NRSV.

⁶¹ While other observances of Torah may also be in view (e.g., calendar observances, 4:10), the main issue Paul addresses is circumcision, being the entrance rite and

sense would then be as follows: having begun [your Christian life] by the Spirit are you now performing it by human effort? [62] That is, their faith is now being placed in what they can achieve by human means, by works of the law, rather than by God's grace (1:6, 5:4).

It is the folly of this change of approach that invokes Paul's invective. Reading both verbs in the middle voice generates a logical symmetry: *they* began one way, *they* are completing in another, pointing to the responsibility of the Galatians themselves in each case.[63] This serves to highlight the antithesis between the Spirit and flesh, substantiating Paul's vehement censure.[64] Hence, the middle reading, which interprets ἐπιτελεῖσθε as completing in the sense of carrying out or accomplishing rather than perfecting or finishing, is to be preferred.[65] The options for interpretation of ἐπιτελεῖσθε/ ἐπιτελεῖσθαι may be summarised as indicated in Table 7.3 below.

Table 7.3 Possible Translations of Galatians 3:3b

Middle	Infinitive		Are you now to complete [the process] by the flesh?
	Indicative	Present	Are you now completing [the process] by the flesh?
		Future	Are you now going to reach perfection through the flesh?

---

mark of identification for those submitting to Torah observance. See, e.g., 2:3, 12; 5:2, 3, 6, 11; 6:12, 13, 15.

[62] Similarly, CEB: "Are you so irrational? After you started with the Spirit, are you now finishing up with your own human effort?" It is also possible that the present verb here could have a future sense, as implied by Weymouth's translation: "Having begun by the Spirit, are you now going to reach perfection through what is external?" This futuristic use of the present tense form is noted by Wallace, *Exegetical Syntax*, 535–7.

[63] Betz asserts that "beginning in the Spirit" ought to lead to "finishing in the Spirit", hence "Paul formulates what he perceives as their self-contradiction in the form of a dilemma and a chiastic *antitheton*" juxtaposing the two pairs of opposites, "beginning and end" with "Spirit and flesh" (*Galatians*, 133).

[64] The variant reading is also tenable: Having begun in the Spirit are you so foolish [as] to pursue completion in the flesh?

[65] In agreement with, e.g., Betz, *Galatians*, 133´ Burton, *The Epistle to the Galatians*, 149´ and Longenecker, *Galatians*, 103. The middle is discussed and preferred also by Moo, *Galatians*, 184.

| Passive | Infinitive | | Are you now to be completed in the flesh? |
| | Indicative | | Are you now made complete with the flesh? (Dunn) |

7.2.4 Exegetical Insights

What is essentially at stake in interpreting ἐπιτελεῖσθε as either middle or passive is the question of whom or what is being completed or accomplished. Reading ἐπιτελεῖσθε as a transitive middle verb, the focus is on the *process* by which the Galatians carry out the new life in Christ that they have undoubtedly begun and experienced (3:4, 5).[66] That is, they are responsible for maintaining their dependence on the Spirit; having begun their spiritual life by faith, by the power of the Spirit (3:2) they must continue in the same manner. This is a major concern expressed by Paul in Galatians, for we see that he exhorts them to live by the Spirit (5:16), be led by the Spirit (5:18), and produce the fruit of the Spirit (5:22).

Notwithstanding that the Spirit is given as a gift (Acts 2:38; Gal 3:2, 14) the recipients are immersed in a process. They are experiencers and beneficiaries (to use Allan's terms) of the life and power of the Spirit which they must nevertheless engage volitionally (sowing to the Spirit, Gal 6:8). They are not passive recipients. Pursuing their life in the Spirit requires them to be led by the Spirit (Gal 5:25) yet this is an interactive process; it requires their involvement. Thus, Rendall comments: "The middle voice ἐπιτελεῖσθε is used here because the spiritual process is to be wrought by them upon themselves."[67] Likewise, understanding the middle voice as internal *diathesis* signifies that the Galatians are within the process of accomplishing and realizing this life in the Spirit, a process which has already begun and must be completed on the same continuum, in the same realm.[68]

---

[66] The translation by Bruce reflects this interpretation: "are you now *trying to obtain* completion by the flesh?" (*Galatians*, 147 [italics added]).

[67] Rendall, *Epistle to the Galatians*, 167.

[68] Likewise, "Just as you received Christ Jesus as Lord, so continue to walk in him, rooted in him and built upon him" (Col 2:6, 7).

Whether or not intended by Paul, the possible "cultic overtones" noted by Betz may have had some resonance for the Galatian readers.[69] In this regard, George Duncan notes the custom of an initiate into some of the ancient religions passing through different stages on the way to "spiritual completeness," so the analogy with circumcision as a further stage in the life of a disciple may have had some appeal.[70] However, while the two verbs ἐνάρχομαι and ἐπιτελέω are both used in relation to beginning and performing religious ceremonies, the above examples from the papyri and the literature illustrate that it is the active form of ἐπιτελέω that is employed in pagan contexts. This is consistent with carrying out rituals, for the participants act outside of themselves. Paul, on the other hand uses the middle, for according to his argument in this letter, the believers are *within the process* of dependence on the Spirit as they progress in the Christian life.[71] They are not performing an action externally. The middle voice therefore augments the antithesis in Galatians 3:3, for to act according to the flesh, that is, to depend on human effort, implies an active, external type of action. This is incompatible with the subject being internal to the process; hence σαρκὶ ἐπιτελεῖσθε is a logical contradiction in reference to the Christian life of faith.

Without mentioning the middle voice, Ebeling points to yet another irony in this extremely fecund verse. He notes that the ambiguity of ἐπιτελεῖν, meaning either bring to an end (finish) or bring to perfection, generates the impasse that in seeking to bring to perfection by the flesh that which was begun by the Spirit actually brings the latter to an end.[72] This insight may be illustrated by Figure 7.1 below, in which the corresponding voices are included to "complete" the picture and

---

[69] Betz, *Galatians*, 133.

[70] George S. Duncan, *The Epistle of Paul to the Galatians*, MNTC (London: Hodder & Stoughton, 1934, 1948), 80. Any such resonance, however, would fit more naturally with a passive reading of ἐπιτελεῖσθε.

[71] In addition to Gal 3:3, we see this in 4:6,7; 5: 16–18, 22–25; 6:8,

[72] Ebeling, *Truth of the Gospel*, 161.

illustrate the import of Paul's deceptively simple rhetorical question in Galatians 3:3.[73]

Figure 7.1 Conceptual Diagram of Galatians 3:3

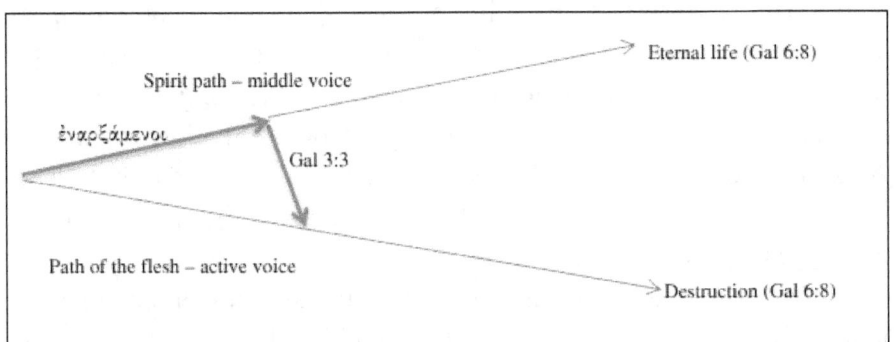

7.3 SUPPLEMENTARY EXAMPLES

This section of the study consists of brief comments on each of the remaining middle verbs identified in Table 7.1 with a view to discerning the potential significance of their middle form in context. Although brief, it is intended that these explorations should suffice to illustrate some of the implications of reading the middle forms as verbs exhibiting one or more of the characteristics outlined above.

7.3.1 Προσανατίθημι (προσανεθέμην 1:16; προσανέθεντο 2:6)

The relatively rare double compound verb προσανατίθημι occurs in the middle form in Gal 1:16 and 2:6, these being the only occurrences of this lemma in the NT or LXX. Therefore, examples of use in other writings are especially relevant. The active form is only sparsely attested, having the basic sense (in accord with its constituents) of putting

---

[73] As previously, circumcision is indicative and representative of dependence on human effort. Accordingly, Moo comments that "by the flesh" (σαρκί) is naturally associated with "works of the law" in Paul's discourse in Galatians (*Galatians*, 184).

something on in addition, hence: "offer or dedicate besides," and "ascribe, attribute," are examples given in the lexica.[74]

The middle form is more common and reflects the personal involvement of the subject. Thus, lexical definitions refer to taking something additional on oneself, contributing of oneself to another, or consulting with another.[75] This latter sense is common in the literature, being used in regard to referring a matter to someone or consulting a soothsayer. For example, in an historical account by Diodorus Siculus, when King Alexander found that a native had escaped from fetters and boldly assumed his throne, he <u>consulted</u> the seers about this (τοῖς μάντεσι <u>προσαναθέμενος</u> περὶ τοῦ σημείου τοῦτον), perceiving it to be a portent.[76] In his letter to the Galatians, after Paul has claimed that his revelation of the Gospel came from God alone (1:11–12, 15–16), in 1:16-17 he asserts that he did *not* consult with any other person: [77]

Gal 1:16–17 εὐθέως οὐ <u>προσανεθέμην</u> σαρκὶ καὶ αἵματι ¹⁷ οὐδὲ ἀνῆλθον εἰς Ἱεροσόλυμα πρὸς τοὺς πρὸ ἐμοῦ ἀποστόλους, ἀλλ' ἀπῆλθον εἰς Ἀραβίαν	straight away I did not <u>consult</u> flesh and blood, nor did I go up to Jerusalem to those being apostles before me, but I went away into Arabia

---

[74] LSJ, s.v. "προσανατίθημι"; GE, s.v. "προσανατίθημι," respectively. BDAG does not discuss the active, nor does MM. Among the few extant attestations of the active form in the relevant era, προσαναθεῖναι appears in Philo, *Legat.*, 137.3 (Colson, LCL 379:68–69) in the sense of *consecrating additional* precincts.

[75] See LSJ, s.v. "προσανατίθημι"; BDAG, s.v. "προσανατίθημι"; GE, s.v. "προσανατίθημι"; the latter stating "impose in addition" with Gal 2:6, as the example. However, since no other early references are cited, this may be a gloss for this context alone. See below for further discussion.

[76] Diodorus Siculus, *Bibl. Hist.* 17.116.4.2 (Welles, LCL 422:462–463). Similarly, "<u>confide</u> in me" (ἐμοὶ <u>προσανάθου</u>), Lucian, *Jupp. trag.*, 1.3 (Harmon, LCL 54:90–91).

[77] English translations typically translate προσανεθέμην here as "consult" (ESV, NAB, and NIV) or "confer" (NJB, NKJ, and RSV).

If this were a positive statement, the aorist middle indicative προσανεθέμην would indicate that he shared something with others from within himself; it could also indicate that he was acting in self-interest, seeking information or approval from others. In the consultative process he would be internal to the action of the verb, engaged in a relational process. Paul asserts that he did none of these. He did not place himself or his gospel into a position of vulnerability but guarded what had been entrusted to him and promptly began to preach the message he received.

Only after several years of proclaiming this gospel did Paul go to Jerusalem in response to a revelation, and then place it before the men of repute (2:1, 2). The verb used for this submission (ἀνεθέμην 2:2) has the sense of explaining rather than consulting (see §7.3.2 below). In essence, Paul asserts that in contrast to the contentious false brothers (2:4, 5), the leaders (the men of repute, 2;1, 2) affirmed his gospel.[78] They did not require Titus to be circumcised (2:3), they acknowledged that the grace of God was upon Paul for the mission to the Gentiles (2:7, 9), and they placed nothing extra upon him, as seen in 2:6 below.

Gal 2:6 Ἀπὸ δὲ τῶν δοκούντων εἶναί τι, —ὁποῖοί ποτε ἦσαν οὐδέν μοι διαφέρει· πρόσωπον [ὁ] θεὸς ἀνθρώπου οὐ λαμβάνει- ἐμοὶ γὰρ οἱ δοκοῦντες οὐδὲν προσανέθεντο	But from those who are held to be something (whatever they once were is of no difference to me; God is no respecter of persons)—the men of repute laid nothing else on me.

According to Dunn, προσανέθεντο here indicates that they "added nothing" to Paul *himself*, (ἐμοὶ, emphatic position), his standing as an apostle, or his gospel. Hence, no further claim (in particular, circumcision) could be made on Paul's converts on the authority of the Jerusalem apostles.[79] Paul had therefore succeeded in gaining their blessing but had

---

[78] For the purposes of this study, Paul's parenthetical remarks about the leaders do not require discussion.

[79] Dunn, *Epistle to the Galatians*, 103–4. Hence, Paul's opposition to those

himself conceded nothing in respect to his gospel of grace.[80] While this is a helpful and satisfying exegesis of the text it does not overtly account for the use of the middle, rather than the active, form of προσανατίθημι in this context. Similarly, most English versions translate προσανέθεντο in 2:6 in the sense of simply adding something. For example, "added nothing to me" (CJB, ESV, NKJ and RSV); "added nothing to my message" (NIV); "had nothing to add to my message" (NJB); "contributed nothing to me" (NRSV).[81] Apart from the NRSV to some extent, these expressions appear to focus on the outcome (for which the active form could equally be used), rather than on any interdependent process.[82]

Betz, however, refers to Galatians 2:6 as a statement of the results of a "conference," and translates it: "upon me these 'men of eminence' did not make any demand."[83] Such a demand necessarily implies that the leaders would be acting in their own interest, thus correlating with the use of the middle form. LSJ indicate that with accusative direct and dative indirect objects, the sense of the middle voice of προσανατίθημι is *"contribute of oneself* to another," and cite Gal 2:6 as an example.[84] This would imply that in the case under discussion, the leaders had nothing from within themselves, from their own resources (dynamic middle)

---

advocating circumcision of the Galatians is validated.

[80] Thus Betz translates τῶν δοκούντων εἶναί τι in 2:6 as "the men of eminence," and comments: "This expression, when used in an apologetic context, allows Paul both to acknowledge the fact that these men possess authority and power and to remain at a distance with regard to his own subservience to such authority" (*Galatians*, 92).

[81] Similarly, "added nothing to me" (de Boer, *Galatians*, 116); "contributed nothing" (Bruce, *Galatians*, 118); "did not add anything" (Martyn, *Galatians*, 199).

[82] As, e.g., the use of προσανατιθέντες in reference to adding an additional burden, Clement, *Quis dives salvetur*, 1.3.8 (Butterworth, LCL 92:272–273).

[83] Betz, *Galatians*, 95. Likewise, Maximillian Zerwick translates "add any provisos" (*Analysis of the Greek New Testament*, trans. and rev. Mary Grosvenor [Rome: Biblical Institute Press, 1981], 566).

[84] LSJ, s.v. "προσανατίθημι." Lightfoot comments that προσανατίθεσθαι refers to communication, impartation, whether for the purpose of giving (Gal 2:6) or of obtaining (Gal 1:16) instruction (*Galatians*, 83).

to add, or that they saw no need to add anything to Paul's message. In either case Paul's authority to preach the Torah-free gospel to the Gentiles is affirmed.

7.3.2 Ἀνατίθημι (ἀνεθέμην, 2:2)

Ἀνεθέμην occurs in Galatians within the same section of Paul's defence of his apostolic authority as the double compound προσανατίθημι (1:16, 2:6) discussed above. Literally having the sense of putting upon or setting forth, ἀνατίθημι has a variety of applications in active, passive and to a lesser extent, middle forms.[85] No active forms appear in the NT, but two different senses of ἀνατίθημι occur in the LXX. First, it is used in reference to setting in place physical objects such as the armor of the slain Saul (1 Sam 31:10) and the Ark of the Covenant (2 Sam 6:17). Second, it is used in the sense of dedicating or consecrating something to the Lord (Lev 27:28; Jdt 16:19; Mic 4:13), as also are passive forms (Lev 27:29; 2 Macc 5:16).

Middle forms appear twice in the LXX (2 Macc 3:9; Mic 7:5) in reference to communicating or disclosing a matter, and it is in this sense that the middle form is used in the NT. In Acts we read that Festus explained or <u>laid before</u> King Agrippa the matters regarding Paul: ὁ Φῆστος τῷ βασιλεῖ <u>ἀνέθετο</u> τὰ κατὰ τὸν Παῦλον (Acts 25:14). In writing to the Galatians, Paul mentions the visit he made to Jerusalem after fourteen years of preaching in Syria and Cilicia (1:21, 2:1), in 2:2 as below:

Gal 2:2 ἀνέβην δὲ κατὰ ἀποκάλυψιν· καὶ <u>ἀνεθέμην</u> αὐτοῖς τὸ εὐαγγέλιον ὃ κηρύσσω ἐν τοῖς ἔθνεσιν κατ'	I went up according to a revelation; and I <u>put before</u> them the gospel which I preach among the Gentiles (but privately with the

---

[85] Hence, e.g., lay upon, refer, attribute, set up as a votive gift, for the active; impart, communicate something one's own, refer, for the middle. LSJ, s.v. "ἀνατίθημι." Similarly, the middle sense of laying something before someone for consideration is noted by BDAG, s.v. "ἀνατίθημι."

ἰδίαν δὲ τοῖς δοκοῦσιν, μή πως	men of repute) lest I am running
εἰς κενὸν τρέχω ἢ ἔδραμον.	or have run in vain.

After his initial revelation of the gospel Paul did not *consult* (προσανεθέμην, 1:16) the leaders in Jerusalem. However, many years later, in response to another revelation, he did visit them and explain or put before them (ἀνεθέμην αὐτοῖς 2:2) the gospel he preached. Apparently, the question of circumcision of the Gentiles had become a point of contention at this stage. The middle voice of the verb ἀνεθέμην in 2:2 indicates that Paul did not simply place his gospel before the leaders and leave them to pronounce a verdict. Rather, it suggests that he would have been engaged in discussion with them, since the middle form implies an interactive process. This conforms to the tenor of the passage, for it appears that Paul is not so much seeking their approval (although this was an outcome of the meeting) but rather taking the opportunity to argue his case. It also implies that Paul was deeply concerned about the outcome of this presentation, clearly offering it from his own belief and experience, in accord with the description of this use of the middle form as *"impart, communicate* something *one's own*[.]"[86]

7.3.3 Ψεύδομαι (1:20)

Only the middle form is attested in the NT and refers to lying or deception by lying.[87] However, the less common active transitive ψεύδω is found in earlier literature in reference to falsifying something or to deception in a general sense (not always by an animate subject).[88] The middle form, on the other hand refers more specifically to deceiving

---

[86] LSJ, s.v. "ἀνατίθημι." (Only the middle is used in this sense).

[87] BDAG, s.v. "ψεύδομαι."

[88] LSJ, s.v. "ψεύδω." GE, s.v. "ψεύδω." Allan discusses both voice forms, giving an example of an inanimate subject: "ἀλλὰ πιστεύω (...) μὴ ψεύσειν με ταύτας τὰς ἀγαθὰς ἐλπίδας (Xen. *Cyr.* 1.5.13): But I feel confident, that these sanguine hopes will not deceive me" (*Polysemy*, 110, 111).

another person by lying or speaking falsely.[89] Allan therefore classifies ψεύδομαι as a speech act middle verb, the subject being both beneficiary and experiencer, since the subject would be mentally affected by the action.[90] In Galatians 1:20 Paul insists that he does not lie:

> Gal 1:20 ἃ δὲ γράφω   now what things I write
> ὑμῖν, ἰδοὺ ἐνώπιον τοῦ   to you, behold, before
> θεοῦ ὅτι <u>οὐ ψεύδομαι</u>   God, <u>I am not lying.</u>

Thus, Paul is affirming that he is not seeking any advantage for himself by making false claims; indeed, he is very specific about the source of his revelation (1:11–16) and about his lack of consultation with others (1:16–18). If he *were* lying, he would be acting in self-interest, trying to deceive by words. Here the lexical sense and the middle nuance of self-interest (grammatical middle) augment each other. Nevertheless, since the verb is negated, Paul indicates that he is *not* acting in self-interest.

As noted by Robertson (note 2 above) and corroborated by the previous investigations of the middle verbs in 1 Thessalonians and 2 Corinthians, the particular middle nuance of a verb depends on its context. It may therefore be pertinent to examine this matter more closely, to probe beneath the surface structure of the language to examine what is precisely being expressed. In this regard, James Dunn comments that while the expression οὐ ψεύδομαι in itself has the force of a formula of affirmation, it is given the force of an *oath* by the preceding expression ἐνώπιον τοῦ θεοῦ (before God).[91] Since Paul is defending the validity of his apostleship in this section of the text, he is effectively making an oath in his own defense as if on trial. J. Paul Sampley sees in this statement by Paul a clear allusion to Roman law and considers that any such

---

[89] These meanings are given by BDAG, noting that only the middle form appears in early Christian literature. BDAG, s.v. "ψεύδομαι."

[90] Allan, *Polysemy*, 105, 111.

[91] Dunn, *Epistle to the Galatians*, 77, 78; similarly, Hans Conzelmann, *TDNT* 9:601.

allusion would be understood by his Gentile audiences.[92] In the said law there is the provision for an oath given by a defendant in a court scenario to be a legitimate, even conclusive form of defense in the absence of other evidence.[93]

If, therefore, οὐ ψεύδομαι is considered to represent an oath or testimony in 1:20, it would also carry a dynamic middle function since Paul is investing his very self into the statement.[94] Paul considers the Galatians to have been bewitched (ἐβάσκανεν, 3:1) and drawn away from the truth (5:7) by those advocating circumcision out of self-interest (4:17, 6:13). He therefore seeks to regain their allegiance (4:14–16) and exhorts them not to be deceived (6:7). By emphatically stating οὐ ψεύδομαι (I do not lie) regarding his claim that his message came uniquely from God (1:11, 12, 17-19), he asserts that *he* is not acting in his own interest but is zealous to preserve the truth of the gospel (2:5).

As the appropriate vehicle for such an emphatic assertion, the Greek middle verb draws attention to the involvement of the subject in the action; hence, in contrast to the deceptiveness of the agitators, Paul is effectively stating on oath: "*I* do not lie," "*I* am not deceiving you by my speech."[95] The middle voice of ψεύδομαι in this instance does not essentially change the surface meaning of Paul's statement but enhances the intensity of his assertion and registers his soul-felt investment in the affirmation (dynamic middle).

7.3.4 Φοβέω (φοβούμενος, 2:12; φοβοῦμαι, 4:11)

While BDAG lists φοβέω in the active form, it states that only the "passive" form (φοβέομαι) occurs in the New Testament and early Christian

---

[92] J. Paul Sampley, "'Before God I do not lie' (Gal 1:20). Paul's Self-Defence in the Light of Roman Legal Praxis," *NTS* 23 (1977): 480.

[93] For discussion on this matter, see A. H. J. Greenidge, *The Legal Procedure of Cicero's Time* (Oxford: Clarendon, 1901), 259.

[94] As, similarly, διαμαρτύρομαι (solemnly testify) §3.1.5 above.

[95] Some English translations accommodate this emphasis, this dynamic force of the middle, by an exclamation mark in 1:20 (e.g., ESV, NET, NRSV).

literature.[96] Accordingly, since it appears active in English translation it is commonly referred to as a passive deponent, employing the -θη- form in the aorist (ἐφοβήθην).[97]

Curiously, the morphological data base used throughout this project identifies present and imperfect forms of φοβέομαι as middle verbs but aorist and future forms as passive. This is clearly a reference to form alone, since in terms of function, they are found to be used consonantly. Hence, both may occur with an accusative object, for example, φοβούμεθα τὸν ὄχλον: <u>we fear</u> the people (Matt 21:26) and ἐφοβήθη τὸν ὄχλον: <u>he feared</u> the people (Matt 14:5).[98] Likewise, both present and aorist forms are used as imperatives, for example, μὴ οὖν φοβεῖσθε: therefore, do not <u>fear</u> (Matt 10:31) and μὴ <u>φοβηθῆτε</u> do not <u>fear</u> (1 Pet 3:14). These inconsistencies arising from the database illustrate the frequent lack of clarity concerning middle verbs in the New Testament.

Allan profitably classifies φοβέομαι as a mental process middle, in which the subject experiences a change of state as a response to a (sometimes external) stimulus.[99] He notes that although verbs expressing a permanent state (such as δουλέω, I am a slave) tend to be active, the more transitory states are expressed by a middle verb, in deference to the change in state experienced.[100] Thus the various middle forms of φοβέομαι indicate a sense of *entering* a state of fear, *becoming* afraid.[101]

---

[96] BDAG, s.v. "φοβέω."

[97] It is identified as a passive deponent in Duff, *Elements*, 174; McLean, *NT Greek*, 151; Mounce, *Basics*, 221; and Young, *Intermediate NT Greek*, 136.

[98] Allan (*Polysemy*, 74) notes that for verbs of emotion such as φοβέομαι, such accusatives do not have the prototypical function of patient; rather, he suggests they designate the stimulus that produces the emotion.

[99] Allan, *Polysemy*, 64.

[100] Allan asserts that event types which do not involve subject-affectedness cannot be expressed by a middle verb; consequently, stative verbs are expressed in the unmarked active, while verbs which do involve a change of state are expressed by the middle form, thus marking the effect on the subject (*Polysemy*, 29).

[101] Allan does not discriminate between middle and passive forms of this verb since he views the passive as one instance of the middle. See §2.2.1 above.

This is the manner in which they are read here; that is, as middle verbs which exhibit the MP2 (-θη-) morphology in the aorist, as discussed in chapter 2 above.[102]

In Galatians, a present middle participle of φοβέω occurs in 2:12 as Paul speaks of Peter's duplicity in changing his eating habits for fear of the circumcision proponents.

| Gal. 2:12 πρὸ τοῦ γὰρ ἐλθεῖν τινας ἀπὸ Ἰακώβου μετὰ τῶν ἐθνῶν συνήσθιεν· ὅτε δὲ ἦλθον, ὑπέστελλεν καὶ ἀφώριζεν ἑαυτὸν <u>φοβούμενος</u> τοὺς ἐκ περιτομῆς. | For before certain men came from James, he [Peter] used to eat with the Gentiles; but when they came, he withdrew and separated himself, <u>fearing</u> the circumcision [party]. |

In terms of Allan's mental process middle, Peter enters a temporary state of fear in response to the presence of the circumcision party, the latter being the stimulus in Allan's model. The participle φοβούμενος appears to be causal, introducing the reason why Peter subsequently separated himself from the Gentiles when eating (because he feared those of the circumcision party). The middle voice signals to the reader that the subject is the focus of the verbal process; it refers to the change of mental state (becoming afraid) that Peter experienced. Hence the middle form is not redundant but is the appropriate means by which to refer to the subject-affectedness which subsequently led to Peter's change in behavior.

In Gal 4:11 Paul uses a present middle indicative to express his own fear that his work among the Galatians may have been for naught:

| Gal. 4:11 <u>φοβοῦμαι ὑμᾶς</u> μή πως εἰκῇ κεκοπίακα εἰς ὑμᾶς | <u>I am afraid</u> lest perhaps I have labored over you in vain |

---

[102] See §2.1.7.1 and §2.3.1.

In this expression we have an instance of prolepsis;[103] that is, Paul is not saying that he fears the Galatians, but rather he fears *for* them, lest his work among them may have been in vain. The middle/passive form thus speaks of Paul's mental or emotional affectedness as he considers the state of their faith. It points to the subject being the locale of the verbal action, being within and therefore experiencing the process. Therefore, both voice and lexical sense enhance each other in this instance, making it doubly clear to the reader that Paul is speaking of his personal feelings as a response to the situation he contemplates.

7.3.5 Ἐπιδιατάσσομαι (ἐπιδιατάσσεται, 3:15)

The verb ἐπιδιατάσσομαι appears nowhere in Scripture except Gal 3:15 where it is used in the sense of adding further instructions to a person's will (NRSV). This appears to be the first attestation of the verb, which does not appear in a search of ancient Greek pre-Christian literature, and subsequently is only used in Christian writings.[104] However, the related verb διατάσσομαι is used in regard to setting in order or making arrangements in general and to making testamentary dispositions, arrangements for inheritance, or burial.[105] The prefix ἐπί may then be understood to contribute the sense of "besides, in addition[.]"[106] thus

---

[103] This example is noted in BDF §476; BDAG, s.v. "φοβέω."

[104] E.g., Eusebius, *Historia ecclesiastica*, 5.16.3.7 (Lake, LCL 153:472–473) in expressing concern that he might be thought by some "to be adding to the writings or injunctions of the word of the new covenant" (ἐπισυγγράφειν ἢ ἐπιδιατάσσεσθαι τῷ τῆς τοῦ εὐαγγελίου καινῆς διαθήκης λόγῳ).

[105] Hence, e.g., Philo speaks of God's power by which ἔθηκε καὶ διετάξατο καὶ διεκόσμησε τὰ ὅλα: "He established and <u>ordered</u> and marshalled the whole realm of being" (*Migr.* 182.4 [Colson, Whitaker, LCL 261:238–239]). Similar uses are noted among the papyri (MM, s.v. "διατάσσω"). It is employed in Gal 3:19 in reference to the Law being "ordained" (KJV, NAS, NRSV) by angels (διαταγεὶς δι' ἀγγέλων) and in 1 Cor 7:17 Paul states: καὶ οὕτως ἐν ταῖς ἐκκλησίαις πάσαις διατάσσομαι: and so I <u>direct</u> in all the churches.

[106] GE, s.v. "ἐπί."

correlating with Paul's use of the term in Galatians, in reference to adding *further* instructions or arrangements to a person's will.[107]

Another term which requires clarification in 3:15 is the use of διαθήκη for will or testament. This is used in the LXX for covenant, for example, ἡ <u>διαθήκη</u> μου μετὰ σοῦ καὶ ἔσῃ πατὴρ πλήθους ἐθνῶν: "my <u>covenant</u> is with you and you will be the ancestor of a multitude of nations" (Gen. 17:4, NETS). In Hellenistic Greek it was widely used as the term for a person's testament (will).[108] While it is unclear which particular type of testament Paul has in mind (since Greek and Roman wills may be revoked), it is clear from the context that he is referring to one which is irrevocable.[109] According to MM, the term διαθήκη is consistently used among the papyri and inscriptions to refer to a person's will. Further, they note that: "διαθήκη is properly *dispositio*, an "arrangement" made by one party with plenary power, which the other party may accept or reject, but cannot alter."[110] It would therefore appear that it is this unilateral nature of the διαθήκη which Paul draws upon in his analogy. Hence, in Galatians 3:15 he states:

Gal 3:15 Ἀδελφοί, κατὰ   Brothers and sisters, I speak in
ἄνθρωπον λέγω· ὅμως   human terms: no one annuls
ἀνθρώπου κεκυρωμένην   or <u>adds a further condition</u> to

---

[107] Hence, "legal t.t. add a codicil to a will" (BDAG, s.v. "ἐπιδιατάσσομαι").

[108] As noted by de Boer, *Galatians*, 219. Martyn also remarks that the legal language indicates that the sense in 3:15 is clearly that of a person's last will (*Galatians*, 338). So also, Betz, *Galatians*, 155.

[109] There has been considerable discussion as to which type of legal testament Paul had in mind, since both Greek and Roman wills could be revoked by the testator. For a succinct discussion, see Betz, *Galatians*, 155 and Bruce, *Galatians*, 130–31. As an example of a second will which annuls the former one, P.Wash.Univ. 1.13 (161–169 CE) is discussed by S. R. Llewelyn, *A Review of the Greek Inscriptions and Papyri published in 1980–81*, vol.6 of *New Documents Illustrating Early Christianity* (North Ryde: Macquarie University Ancient History Documentary Research Centre, 1992), 41–42. Others have attempted to relate Paul's reference to certain types of irrevocable Jewish legal documents which may have been widely known. For a comprehensive discussion of possibilities, see Llewelyn, *New Documents*, 43–47.

[110] MM, s.v. "διαθήκη."

διαθήκην οὐδεὶς ἀθετεῖ	a human testament that has
ἢ <u>ἐπιδιατάσσεται</u>	been ratified

The middle voice of ἐπιδιατάσσεται implies that the modifications or additions (*if* they were made) to the διαθήκη, would be in the interest of the person making them, or would affect him/her in some way, or that he/she would be internal to the process. To apply Paul's analogy (3:15–18) would mean that, if God modified his διαθήκη he would be acting in his own interest. Because we are again dealing with a negative situation (the additions *cannot* be made) Paul is essentially saying that God does *not* add something which alters his διαθήκη (promise), nor is it added in his own interest or for his benefit. In fact, the Law is given for the benefit of the people according to Deut 10:13. Alternatively, οὐδεὶς may be taken to refer to "no-one else," meaning that no-one else can amend a person's will.[111] By analogy, this means that the Law, given by angels (3:19) four hundred and thirty years later (3:17) cannot annul or add conditions to God's promise.

It is recorded that God established an everlasting covenant (διαθήκην αἰώνιον, Gen 17:7) with Abraham and his offspring; it would not be revoked or altered. This is precisely what Paul argues in Gal 3, stating that the inheritance comes from the promise, the original Abrahamic διαθήκη. The Law was introduced not as a codicil to that promise but as a guardian (παιδαγωγὸς) for the people until the time for fulfilment of the promise, when the inheritance would become available through Christ (3:16, 22–29). While it is largely the flexibility of the term διαθήκη which permits Paul to reason as he does, the middle form of ἐπιδιατάσσεται serves to subtly enhance his argument: just as no human διαθήκη may be altered in one's own interest, neither may God's promise to Abraham.[112] That is, no-one, not even God himself, Paul argues, may nullify or change the promise he made.

---

[111] Thus, Martyn, *Galatians*, 338.

[112] Whereas Scripture does speak of a new covenant (e.g., Heb 9:15) this does not

7.3.6 Παρατηρέω (παρατηρεῖσθε, 4:10)

The use of a middle form of παρατηρέω in Galatians is the only occurrence of this verb in the writings of Paul. Elsewhere in the New Testament, it appears in Mark 3:2; Luke 6:7; 14:1; 20:20; and Acts 9:24, each of which applies the more general sense of "watch closely, observe carefully[.]"[113] Both active and middle forms are used in this sense in the parallel passages of Mark 3:2 and Luke 6:7. Mark employs the active (παρετήρουν) but Luke uses the middle (παρετηροῦντο) to indicate that the Scribes and Pharisees *were watching* Jesus to see if he would heal a man on the Sabbath in the hope of having a cause for accusation.[114] This demonstrates that the middle form is not obligatory, but is used to mark the self-affectedness or self-interest of the subject through the morphology of the verb;[115] the active may be used if the self-interest is apparent from the narrative context.[116]

This is not the manner, however, in which the middle form παρατηρεῖσθε is employed in Gal 4:10. Paul is not referring to watching someone or something from a distance; rather, the other sense of the

---

refer to an annulment of the Abrahamic promise, which is the sense in which Paul is using διαθήκη in Gal 3. Rather, what becomes obsolete is the priestly sacrificial system of the Mosaic Law (Heb 7:18, 19; 813; 9:9-14), the shadow of the reality to be fulfilled in Christ (Heb 10:1).

[113] BDAG, s.v. "παρατηρέω."

[114] BDAG notes this equivalence of active and middle (s.v. "παρατηρέω"); likewise, Robertson, *Gramma*r, 804–6.

[115] As noted by Allan, *Polysemy*, 25 and Robertson, *Grammar*, 804. Similarly, in the story of Susanna from the LXX, although the men were watching her out of self-interest, active forms of παρατηρέω are used (Sus 1:12, 15, 16); the narrative context makes clear their selfish motives.

[116] It is not surprising that Luke employs the middle, for as Figure 3.1 illustrates, Luke has the highest proportion of middle verbs among the gospels. However, one cannot assume that Mark is negligent with respect to middle forms, as his gospel has a significantly higher percentage than Matthew, using middle forms in some instances in which Matthew uses the active, e.g., ἐφυλαξάμην (Mark 10:20) cf. ἐφύλαξα (Matt 19:20); ὁ ἐμβαπτόμενος (Mark 14:20) cf. ὁ ἐμβάψας (Matt 26: 23), as noted by Moule, *Idiom Book*, 24.

verb applies, namely, "carefully observing a custom or tradition" used in the middle voice with an accusative object.[117] Paul is concerned that the Galatians are not fully appreciating the gospel of grace and are lapsing into the observance of customs or rituals, as below:[118]

Gal 4:10, 11 ἡμέρας παρατηρεῖσθε καὶ μῆνας καὶ καιροὺς καὶ ἐνιαυτούς; φοβοῦμαι ὑμᾶς μή πως εἰκῇ κεκοπίακα εἰς ὑμᾶς.	you observe days and months and seasons and years; I fear for you, lest my labor for you was in vain.

While this sense of the verb is not found elsewhere in Christian Scripture, there are occurrences in other writings. For example, παρατηρεῖσθε is used as an imperative in the *Roman History* of Dio Cassius: "pay strict heed [ἀκριβῶς παρατηρεῖσθε] to do whatever these laws enjoin upon you[.]"[119] Hence, the exhortation is to observe various laws by exhibiting the appropriate behavior. The active is also used to refer to the observance of customs, for example, "no one shall be prevented from keeping [παρατηρεῖν] the Sabbath days [.]"[120] Therefore, both active and middle may be used in this sense also.[121] The distinction, as for the previous sense of watching, is that although the middle form does not essentially change the lexical sense of the verb it does indicate personal participation in a process.

In Galatians, Paul is therefore indicating that his converts are personally participating in traditional religious activities such as

---

[117] BDAG, s.v. "παρατηρέω."

[118] Hence, "observe religiously" is cited for the middle in LSJ, s.v. "παρατηρέω."

[119] Cassius Dio, *Historiae Romanae*, 53.10.2.3 (Cary, Foster, LCL 83:214–215)

[120] Josephus, *A.J.*, 14.264.3, (Markus, Wikgren, LCL 489:144–145). Similarly, in a summary of the Decalogue: "the fourth to keep [παρατηρεῖν] every seventh day by resting from all work" (*A.J.*, 3.91.4 [Thackeray, LCL 242:360–361]).

[121] Contra LSJ which only lists this sense of observance for the middle. LSJ, s.v. "παρατηρέω" (3).

observances of Sabbaths, new moons and annual feasts.[122] Although not specific as to whether he is referring to Jewish or pagan observances, the context and argument of the letter would imply that the Galatians were adopting (or giving thought to adopting) Jewish calendrical observances.[123] Instead of this being a move forward, Paul sees it as a return to being enslaved, as when they did not know God and were being ruled by "those beings who by nature are not gods" (4:8).[124] This perception is implied in the preceding verse where Paul refers to turning *again* and being enslaved *again* to the elements of the universe (στοιχεῖα τοῦ κόσμου).[125] That is, whatever is meant specifically by the beings in v. 8 and the στοιχεῖα in vv. 3 and 9, Paul is stating that by observing special occasions as a religious duty, they are or would be effectively returning to a form of slavery.[126]

---

[122] Matera takes this verse to refer "undoubtedly" to such requirements of the Law (*Galatians*, 157).

[123] παρατηρεῖσθε may be taken as a conative present, as by de Boer, *Galatians*, 276. Burton (*Galatians*, 233) contends that the context indicates that it is Jewish festivals to which Paul refers, and possibly the Galatians had accepted these before being fully persuaded of circumcision. Alternatively, Betz argues that v.10 summarizes the activities in which the Galatians *would* be engaged if they adopted Torah and circumcision (*Galatians*, 217).

[124] As, e.g., Moo who states: "The religious observances that Paul mentions here are governed by the movements of the heavenly bodies: precisely those "elements" that Paul has mentioned in verse 9" (*Galatians*, 277). Likewise, de Boer comments that "the Jewish observances that the Galatians are wanting to observe are no different in kind from the observances linked to *ta stoicheia tou kosmou*" and contends that Paul deliberately uses non-specific terms for the calendrical observances to make them realize that by turning to the law they are essentially "going *back* to where they came from" (*Galatians*, 276).

[125] "Elements of the universe" rather than "elements of the world" is posited here as a broad translation of στοιχεῖα τοῦ κόσμου because of the allusions to heavenly bodies which govern the seasons in v.10.

[126] Discussion abounds as to what may be specifically meant by Paul's reference to "beings which are not gods" in v.8 and στοιχεῖα in vv.3 and 9. Betz considers the two expressions equivalent and provides a helpful discussion of possible sources (*Galatians*, 213–15). For a summary of viewpoints, see Moo, *Galatians*, 277–78. Harald Riesenfeld comments that Paul may be referring either to the observance of festivals ordained by

Matera contends that Paul sees these calendar observances as part of a wider pattern.[127] It is not the observance of special days *per se* that is at stake but the motivation of the participants and the value placed on such observances.[128] The implication is that they are observing the special days out of a conviction that such legal practices are a necessary part of their faith (see discussion on Gal 3:3 above); they are seeking to be "justified by the law" (5:4). Accordingly, Betz discerns in 4:10 an allusion to the behaviour of religiously scrupulous or superstitious people (δεισιδαίμων) portrayed in Greek writings of the period. They exhibit such fearful superstitions in regard to divinities that the associated mental and emotional damage so disables them in respect to everyday life that they are effectively enslaved by their superstitions.[129]

Such a powerful allusion may well be intended by Paul, given his serious concern that the Galatians, having received and experienced the power of the Spirit through faith in Christ (3:2) should not fall back into bondage (5:1) by returning to "the rudimentary form of religion from which they have so recently been converted."[130] This regression may be illustrated by Figure 7.2 below.[131]

Mosaic law or to "apocryphal Jewish speculations about lucky and unlucky days and seasons whose superstitious observance expresses inner bondage" ("παρατηρέω," *TDNT* 8:146–48).

[127] Matera, *Galatians*, 157.

[128] Paul's words elsewhere would imply that he is not against the observance of special days as such; e.g., Rom 14:5–6 indicates that he sees this as a matter of personal choice so long as the purpose is to honor God.

[129] Betz, *Galatians*, 217–18. Accordingly, see Plutarch, *Superst.*, 170 F. 3–5 (Babbitt, LCL 222:490–491): "The atheist thinks there are no gods; the superstitious man [ὁ δὲ δεισιδαίμων] wishes there were none, but believes in them against his will; for he is afraid not to believe."

[130] Matera, *Galatians*, 157.

[131] Paul uses a variety of metaphors in his arguments. Some of the key contrasts in this section of the epistle are indicated in this diagram, while not limiting these precisely to the subsequent allegory of 4:21–31.

Figure 7.2 Conceptual Diagram of Galatians 4:10–11

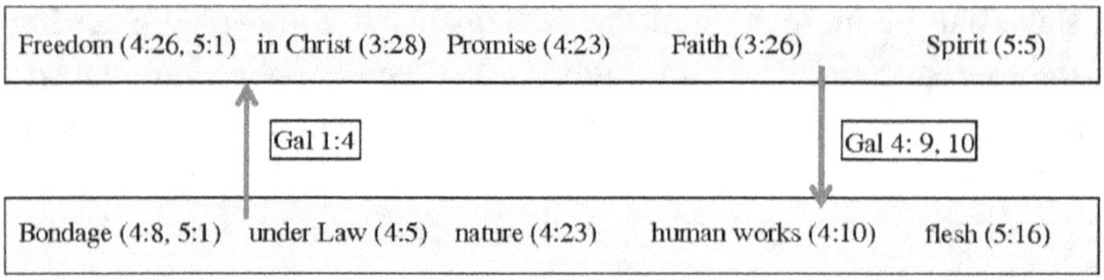

Freedom (4:26, 5:1) in Christ (3:28) Promise (4:23) Faith (3:26) Spirit (5:5)
↑ Gal 1:4 ↓ Gal 4: 9, 10
Bondage (4:8, 5:1) under Law (4:5) nature (4:23) human works (4:10) flesh (5:16)

The middle voice of παρατηρεῖσθε is integral to Paul's argument. In context, it indicates that the Galatians are (or are considering) not only personally engaging in questionable observances, but are doing so in their own interest, seeking to derive benefit from the ritual practices. This is Paul's concern precisely. Instead of looking to Christ alone and being led by the Spirit (5:18, 25), they are seeking to be justified, in addition, by legal observances. The middle form also marks the fact that they would be internal to the process as they personally engage and participate, and that the participants would be affected in the process. Such an effect may be positive (as they appear to seek) or negative (as per the description of superstitious observance by Betz above).

Paul evidently reasons that it can only be negative. He considers such observances to be a return to bondage (4:9), placing themselves on the wrong side of the apocalyptic divide which is so evident throughout the letter and which he proceeds to illustrate by the analogy of Hagar and Sarah.[132] Thus the middle form of παρατηρεῖσθε is one way in which Paul seeks to communicate the importance of being immersed in

---

[132] In this illustration, Hagar represents bondage and Sarah the promise (4:22, 24, 28). This allegory is amply discussed in commentaries. Dunn, for instance, emphasizes the apocalyptic contrasts between the two positions and itemizes the factors on each side (*Epistle to the Galatians*, 244). For a comprehensive analysis of Paul's exegetical argument, see Martyn, *Galatians*, 447–66.

the right salvific process, namely, life in the Spirit, as opposed to observance of rituals which are antithetical to this (5:2).[133]

7.3.7 Ἀπορέω (ἀποροῦμαι, 4:20)

The verb ἀπορέω is derived from πόρος, literally meaning a pathway through an obstruction, and metaphorically, (with genitive) a means of accomplishing or providing something.[134] The adjective ἄπορός may describe one who lacks means of any sort, while the verb ἀπορέω in general indicates that one is at a loss, in want, facing a difficulty.[135] The lemma therefore appears frequently in the documentary papyri in reference to financial matters. For example, P.Ryl. 2.75 / 5 (176–200 CE) is a record of judicial proceedings in which the advocate states that "Glycon has no revenue" (ἄπορός ἐστιν ὁ Γλύκων). Likewise, the verb ἀπορέω may be used to refer to people lacking resources. Hence, Plutarch's advice to one who has money is "[d]o not borrow, for you are not in need" (μὴ δανείσῃ, οὐ γὰρ ἀπορεῖς).[136] Similarly, in Proverbs 31:11, it is said that the husband of the woman being praised will have no lack (οὐκ ἀπορήσει) of fine spoils.[137] The middle may also be used in this manner, as when Josephus writes of Queen Helena who distributed grain to the needy (τοῖς ἀπορουμένοις).[138]

When, ἀπορέω is used in reference to being mentally at a loss, hence, uncertain or perplexed, both middle and active forms are found in literary works. For example, in a work by Philo, Gaius states: "You are perplexed, [ἀπορεῖς] Agrippa," employing the active.[139] However, Josephus uses the middle in speaking of the Romans who, "seeing none

---

[133] As the discussion on Gal 3:3 above.
[134] LSJ, s.v. "πόρος."
[135] LSJ, s.v. "ἀπορέω."
[136] Plutarch, *Vit. aere. al.* 829.F.5. (Fowler, LCL 321:326–327).
[137] Similarly, Sir 10:27, referring to one who walks about glorifying himself yet "lacks bread" (ἀπορῶν ἄρτων).
[138] Josephus, *A.J.*, 20.102.1 (Feldman, LCL 456:54–55).
[139] Philo, *Legat.* 263.3. (Colson, LCL 379:134–135).

to oppose them, were truly perplexed" (ἠπόρηντο).[140] In the LXX *only* the middle is used in this sense.[141] Hence, when Jacob saw Esau coming towards him with four hundred men, he was afraid and ἠπορεῖτο, that is, "perplexed" (Gen 32:8, NETS).

It is solely in this sense of mental paucity that ἀπορέω is used in the New Testament. Thus, in Mark 6:20, the active is used to indicate that Herod was greatly perplexed (πολλὰ ἠπόρει).[142] In Luke 24:4, the middle infinitive ἀπορεῖσθαι indicates that the disciples were perplexed at seeing the empty tomb. Similarly, in John 13:22, the disciples were uncertain (ἀπορούμενοι) of whom Jesus spoke when predicting that one of them would betray him. In Acts 25:20, Festus tells King Agrippa that he is at a loss (ἀπορούμενος δὲ ἐγὼ) as to how to investigate the Jews' charges against Paul. In 2 Cor 4:8, Paul refers to being perplexed (ἀπορούμενοι) but not in despair (ἐξαπορούμενοι).

In Gal 4:20, Paul exclaims that he is perplexed about the Galatians. This may be interpreted as a culmination of his escalating sense of frustration that is seen in various expressions in ch. 4. For example, we read, "how can you want to be enslaved again?" (4:9), "I fear I have labored over you in vain" (4:11), "I beg you" (4:12). In a transition from these exhortations to his next argument (4:21–31), Paul reminds the Galatians of their close relationship with him in the past (4:14, 15); then, after addressing them as "my little children" in 4:19, in the following verse (4:20) he exclaims:

---

[140] Josephus, *B.J.* 6.404.1 (Thackeray. LCL 210:294–295).

[141] Hence: ἠπορεῖτο (Gen 32:8); ἠπορεῖτο (1 Macc 3:31); ἀπορουμένων (2 Macc 8:20); ἀπορούμενοι (Isa 51:20) ἀπορουμένης (Jer 8:18).

[142] This is the only use of the active with the meaning "perplexed" in Christian Scripture. The Majority Text has πολλὰ ἐποίει rather than πολλὰ ἠπόρει. Hence KJV reads Herod "did many things," instead.

Gal 4:20 ἤθελον δὲ παρεῖναι
πρὸς ὑμᾶς ἄρτι καὶ ἀλλάξαι
τὴν φωνήν μου, ὅτι
ἀποροῦμαι ἐν ὑμῖν

Would that I were present with you right now and could change my tone, for I am at a loss in regard to you![143]

This expression of consternation *could* be seen as a rhetorical device; Paul may be stepping aside temporarily from his forceful arguments to allow the Galatians a moment to recover, presumably with the intention of making them more susceptible to his next strategy.[144] Nevertheless, it is apparent that Paul is deeply concerned, thus emotionally affected, as he pens his epistle. This is reflected in his use of the middle verb ἀποροῦμαι, indicating that he is "perplexed" (ESV, NAB, NIV, NRSV) or "in doubt" (KJV) or "at a loss" (NJB). If this were simply a detached statement of Paul's resources, his external assets (as in the papyri document noted above) the active form would suffice. Hence, as Lightfoot comments: "The idea of inward questioning is expressed more strongly by ἀπορεῖσθαι than by ἀπορεῖν."[145] That is, while the active *may* refer to a lack of *internal* resources (as in Mark 6:20, noted above) the middle, as the voice of personal involvement, *intrinsically* does.[146]

The following implications of the middle form may therefore be suggested: It may intensify the sense of personal involvement, so that

---

[143] The imperfect is taken here as conative as in Wallace, *Exegetical Syntax*, 552. Whether Paul's meaning is to change his tone to adapt to their personal response (hence, "change my tone," NIV; "find the right way of talking to you," NJB) or to exchange his letter for a personal visit (posited by Longenecker, *Galatians*, 196) does not affect the function of the verb under discussion. Further, the ambiguity of Paul's expression may be intentional.

[144] Thus, Betz claims that Paul employs the device known as *dubitatio*, only pretending to be "at the end of his wits" so that by "confessing his own perplexity in 4:20 Paul removes himself from the haughty position of one who has all the arguments and all the answers" (*Galatians*, 236, 237). See also Ben Witherington III, *Grace in Galatia: A Commentary on Paul's letter to the Galatians* (Grand Rapids: Eerdmans, 2006), 316. Witherington notes that Paul is nevertheless genuinely concerned about the Galatians.

[145] Lightfoot, *Epistle to the Galatians*, 179.

[146] Similarly, Longenecker notes that the middle voice of ἀπορέω "relates the action intimately and directly to the subject" (*Galatians*, 196).

one might read ἀποροῦμαι as "I *myself* am at a loss." According to the traditional paradigm, it could also be read as "I am at a loss *for myself*." This interpretation generates a subtle shift in the typical reading. Rather than focusing on the problem the Galatians are causing for Paul, it emphasizes Paul's inward state of perplexity, albeit one which is directly related to them. The notion of internal *diathesis* likewise accommodates this viewpoint well, as Paul is functioning within a process which encompasses him. The perplexity, the Galatians and Paul are all interactive participants in this process; a process by which Paul is affected as he agonizes over his "little children," envisaging them sliding back into bondage.

Thus, Paul is not simply at a loss concerning the Galatians and perplexed as to how to deal with them, he is so frustrated by their folly that he is effectively claiming to be at a loss with himself. He has not simply exhausted his arguments (for the remainder of the letter demonstrates that this is not the case), nor is he merely pausing to think of his next rhetorical strategy (for why then would he need to write anything at this point?). In essence, he is expressing his own mental and emotional anguish by his use of the middle voice, consonant with the tone of this section of the epistle.

7.3.8 Ἀπεκδέχομαι (ἀπεκδεχόμεθα, 5:5)

Being an intensified form of the more widely attested verb ἐκδέχομαι which refers to "waiting" in general, the middle-only verb ἀπεκδέχομαι characteristically means to "await eagerly," thus, to wait out a situation in anticipation.[147] This uncommon double compound does not appear in the LXX, nor does it appear in other Greek works before 2nd c. BCE, so it appears to be an innovation of the Hellenistic era.[148]

---

[147] LSJ, s.v. "ἀπεκδέχομαι." BDAG, s.v. "ἀπεκδέχομαι." LSJ also lists alternative uses: "misunderstand, misinterpret," and "understand a word from the context," but these clearly do not apply to Paul's use of the verb here.

[148] Hence the use by Hipparchus (2nd c. BCE) in the alternative sense of "misunderstanding" and by Sextus Empiricus (2nd– 3rd c. CE) in the sense of "await" is noted by Friedrich Büchsel, "ἀπεκδέχομαι," *TDNT* 2:56.

Paul employs it in Rom 8:19, 23, 25; 1 Cor 1:7; Gal 5:5, and Phil 3:20; elsewhere it appears in the NT only in Heb 9:28 and 1 Pet 3:20. In Paul's letters ἀπεκδέχομαι occurs in regard to awaiting the consummation of the believer's salvation, the particular matter to which he refers in each case being expressed as a direct object in the accusative. Hence, he speaks of awaiting the redemption (τὴν ἀπολύτρωσιν) of our bodies (Rom 8:23) and the revelation (τὴν ἀποκάλυψιν) of our Lord Jesus Christ (1 Cor 1:7). In his letter to the Galatians, Paul states:

Gal 5:5 ἡμεῖς γὰρ πνεύματι	for we, in the Spirit, by
ἐκ πίστεως ἐλπίδα	faith, <u>eagerly await</u> the
δικαιοσύνης <u>ἀπεκδεχόμεθα</u>	hope of righteousness

He consequently asserts that neither circumcision nor uncircumcision is of any avail, but only faith working through love (5:6). Therefore, again contrasting the two alternatives of grace and law, Paul admonishes the Galatians that by seeking any further salvific benefit through circumcision (and hence Law) they would be falling away from grace, the realm of the Spirit and faith (5:4). This is spoken in contrast to "we" (ἡμεῖς, emphatic) who in the Spirit, by faith, eagerly await the hope of righteousness (5:5).[149] Such ones do not yet experience the full realization of salvation, (the declaration of their righteousness at the final judgement), but are, by faith in response to grace, placing themselves in the appropriate realm; that is, in Christ. Circumcision and Law observance cannot do anything to bring their full salvation any closer;

---

[149] See Martin Luther, *A Commentary on Paul's Epistle to the Galatians*, rev. ed. (London: James Clarke, 1953), 457–58. Luther comments that while justification through the Spirit by faith has been mentioned before, waiting for the hope of righteousness is a new addition here. He contends that hope may be construed in two ways, either in reference to the thing hoped for, viz., the righteousness to be revealed at the appointed time, or the hope that one has as one waits. These two interpretations are reflected in translations such as "For through the Spirit, by faith, we eagerly wait for the hope of righteousness" (NRSV) and "We are led by the Spirit to wait in the confident hope of saving justice through faith (NJB)." In either case, there is a sense of futurity.

it cannot add anything to Spirit and faith, their means of entering into freedom and their means of preserving it.[150]

This dynamic aspect of waiting, of living in eschatological hope while nevertheless having the down payment of the Spirit,[151] leads into the consideration of the middle voice of ἀπεκδεχόμεθα in this context. That they are waiting in their own interest, for their own benefit, is evident from the lexical sense of the verb and the statement itself. The middle voice is not needed to herald this, although it does, of course, endorse it.

The more particular contribution of the middle voice may be discerned by contemplating the manner in which the subject is internal to the process. Being a recipient of grace, believers must remain attentive to the Spirit, to the new life within, awaiting with confidence the "full consummation of perfect righteousness in heaven."[152] Having been born of the Spirit, it is as if they are in a state of gestation as this new life is brought to maturity.[153] Nevertheless, they are not passively waiting for this to happen but are required to nurture this new life, to exercise faith to remain in this state of grace and not fall from it. They are thus manifestly acting within a situation which encompasses them. By drawing attention to the subject's role in the anticipation, the middle voice of ἀπεκδεχόμεθα both signals and reflects the dynamics of this medium.[154]

---

[150] For more comprehensive comments along these lines, see Dunn, *Epistle to the Galatians*, 269–70 and Betz, *Galatians*, 261–62.

[151] As discussed in reference to σφραγίζομαι, §5.4 above.

[152] Luther, *Galatians*, 458

[153] This imagery of gestation is employed by Karl Barth, *The Epistle to the Romans*, 6th ed., trans. Edwyn C. Hoskyns (London: Oxford University Press, 1950), 306. Translating Rom 8:19, he writes: "For the earnest expectation of the creature waiteth [ἀπεκδέχεται] for the manifestation of the sons of God," and states that "the time in which we live is the time of the divine 'Now', and that it bears in its womb the eternal, living, unborn Future."

[154] Eberhard asserts that the middle voice is the medium "in which and not only by which something takes place," comparing it to the medium in which a chemical reaction

7.3.9 Ἀντίκειμαι (ἀντίκειται, 5:17)

The middle-only verb ἀντίκειμαι conveys the sense of lying opposite, opposing, or resisting.[155] Occurring twenty-three times in the LXX and NT, only three of these uses are in the indicative; more commonly, the lemma appears as a participle, often being used as a substantive in reference to an opponent or adversary. For example, the Lord told Moses: ἀντικείσομαι τοῖς ἀντικειμένοις σοι: I will resist those who resist you (Exod. 23:22, NETS). Jesus' opponents in the synagogue are referred to as οἱ ἀντικείμενοι (Luke 13:17), and Paul tells the Philippians not to be frightened ὑπὸ τῶν ἀντικειμένων: by their opponents (Phil. 1:28). As these examples illustrate, ἀντίκειμαι is commonly used in reference to manifest opposition to God, his representatives, or his teaching. L&N indicates that ἀντίκειμαι involves "not only a psychological attitude but also a corresponding behaviour—to oppose, to be hostile toward, to show hostility."[156] In Gal 5:17 Paul employs the present indicative of ἀντίκειμαι in stating:

Gal 5:17 ἡ γὰρ σὰρξ ἐπιθυμεῖ κατὰ τοῦ πνεύματος, τὸ δὲ πνεῦμα κατὰ τῆς σαρκός, ταῦτα γὰρ ἀλλήλοις ἀντίκειται, ἵνα μὴ ἃ ἐὰν θέλητε ταῦτα ποιῆτε.	For the flesh yearns against the Spirit, and the Spirit against the flesh, indeed these are in opposition to one another, so that you do not do the things you want.

In the previous verse (5:16), Paul has declared that the Galatian Christians should walk by the Spirit and not fulfil the desires of the Flesh.[157] This indicates that they have a choice. In 5:17 Paul elaborates

---

occurs (*Middle Voice*, 8).

[155] BDAG, s.v. "ἀντίκειμαι." LSJ, s.v. "ἀντίκειμαι." GE, s.v. "ἀντίκειμαι."
[156] L&N, s.v. "ἀντίκειμαι." (39.1).
[157] The English noun is capitalized here (as in Bruce, *Galatians*, 243), since in this section of the epistle, σάρξ is used in reference to a power (Flesh) that can produce "works of the flesh" (5:19). Das refers to it as "a quasi-personified power that *opposes*

on the reason why (γάρ) they should do so, explaining that Flesh is in opposition to the Spirit they received, viz., the divine Spirit.[158] The Galatians are therefore portrayed as being in a spiritual battle, with both Spirit and Flesh vying for their allegiance, each pulling them in opposite directions.[159] That is, Paul speaks of them in the sense of opposing powers that, when submitted to, have the capacity to produce palpable effects. Thus, he refers to "the works of the Flesh" as a list of vices (5:19–21) and "the fruit of the Spirit" as a list of virtues (5:22–23).

How, then, does the middle verb ἀντίκειται contribute to the understanding of this verse? Paul does not state that the *works* of the flesh lay opposite (ἀντίκειται) those of the Spirit, in a sense of static orientation, but that Flesh and Spirit as personified powers are opposed. This evokes an interactive, dynamic situation. In grammatical terms, this is a reciprocal middle function, each power acting on the other, contending *for* itself. The internal *diathesis* of the middle form signals that the two subjects are agentive while being affected within the process of mutual interaction. They both experience the process of which they are active participants.

This understanding is supported by the imperfective aspect of ἀντίκειται, for there is ongoing reciprocal activity.[160] Further, the

---

and actively resists the Spirit" (*Galatians*, 592).

[158] That "Spirit" is a reference to the Spirit of God is clear from the letter as a whole, e.g., 3:5; 4:6, 29; and is widely acknowledged as such, e.g., Betz, *Galatians*, 279; Das, *Galatians* 591; and Longenecker, *Galatians*, 103.

[159] Betz comments that the origin of the dualism between Flesh and Spirit is not really known but is reflected in other Hellenistic writings and in the Gospel of John. He asserts that Paul depicts the human person as the "battlefield of these forces within" (*Galatians*, 279). Similarly, Witherington comments that Paul's reference to these powers is a "graphic way of speaking of the opposition between the leading of the Spirit and the desires of the flesh" (*Galatians*, 394).

[160] This reciprocity is not to suggest equal and opposite powers. Witherington argues plausibly that ἵνα in 5:17 indicates a purpose clause, the Spirit opposing the flesh and providing the power to enable believers to avoid acting on its desires (*Galatians*, 393, 395). Dunn argues for an even more dynamic situation, with Spirit restraining the desires of the flesh and the flesh opposing the desires of the Spirit (*Epistle to the Galatians*, 297–

lexical sense incorporates and mandates a medial situation, with the subjects being internal to the process of the verb. Not surprisingly therefore, ἀντίκειμαι is a *media tantum* verb. Thus, the middle form of ἀντίκειται underpins the lexical meaning of the verb in this context by emphasizing the dynamic nature of the opposition and therefore the significance of being led by the Spirit. The voice function, tense, and lexical semantics of the verb all work synergistically within the context in this regard.

7.3.10 Προκαλέω (προκαλούμενοι, 5:26)

Προκαλέω has the basic sense of "to call out to someone to come forward" and hence provoke, challenge, summons or invite.[161] It appears only once in the LXX, in reference to inviting (προκαλούμενος) people from coastal towns to buy Jewish slaves (2 Macc 8:11), and only once in the NT, in reference to challenging (προκαλούμενοι) one another (Gal 5:26) as discussed below. Notably, both these instances employ middle forms. The basic use of the active in calling people to come forward may be seen in the historical account of Caesar's assassins on the Capitol calling forth (προκαλοῦντες) those at the base of the hill to come within hearing distance.[162]

There are too few examples of the active to enable a clear distinction between active and middle use to be discerned. Nevertheless, as noted by LSJ, it is the middle form that is mainly used, being widely attested in Greek literature in reference to challenging someone to combat, as well as in the sense of invitation or summons.[163] Accordingly, Plutarch

---

300). This is not in the sense of cancelling each other but in the sense of inward contradiction, of ongoing conflict in which the Spirit-led Christian is the battleground; hence, there is the need to side with, or walk by, the Spirit. Similarly, Martyn asserts that whereas the agitators are proposing circumcision and Law as an antidote to the flesh, Paul argues for the Spirit (*Galatians*, 526–29).

[161] BDAG, s.v. "προκαλέω."
[162] Cassius Dio, *Historiae Romanae*, 44.34.2.4 (Cary, Foster, LCL 66:364–365).
[163] LSJ, s.v. "προκαλέω." Several examples are cited.

employs both senses of the verb in one work, *Lucullus*. The first is as follows: "Marius ... came out to meet him and challenged [προκαλουμένου] him to combat."[164] Later, we see: "Here he received an embassy from the king of the Parthians also, inviting [προκαλουμένου] him into friendly alliance."[165] The sense of self-interest is apparent in both instances, as is the potential engagement of both parties. In line with these uses, the middle participle προκαλούμενοι is employed in the sense of challenging or provoking in a hostile sense in Gal 5:26, thus:

Gal 5:26 μὴ γινώμεθα κενόδοξοι,	Let us not be conceited, <u>chal-</u>
ἀλλήλους <u>προκαλούμενοι</u>,	<u>lenging</u> one another, envying
ἀλλήλοις φθονοῦντες	one another[166]

This provides a contrast to the previous verse, in which Paul gives the exhortation: "Since we live by the Spirit, let us keep in step with the Spirit" (5:25, NIV).[167] Thus, keeping in step or walking in formation (στοιχῶμεν, 5:25) with the Spirit is the outward manifestation of having life through the Spirit.[168] To follow, in Gal 5:26, Paul is speaking of conduct which is *not* in accord with the Spirit, but reflects the works of the Flesh he previously listed, namely, rivalry, jealousy, dissension and envy (5:20, 21). Accordingly, the type of challenge or provocation in view here is most likely to be verbal hostility, such as boasting or arguing.[169]

---

[164] Plutarch, *Lucullus*, 8.5.6 (Perrin, LCL 47:494–495).

[165] Plutarch, *Lucullus*, 30.1.2 (Perrin, LCL 47:570–571).

[166] English translation by Betz, *Galatians*, 291.

[167] Accordingly, de Boer comments that Gal 5:25–6:10 is a discrete section, with positive and negative exhortations expressed as first-person plural subjunctives providing "discernible correspondence between beginning and end" (*Galatians*, 339); thus, Let us follow the Spirit (5:25); Let us not become conceited (5:26); Let us not grow weary (6:9); Let us accomplish good (6:10).

[168] As noted by Bruce, *Galatians*, 257.

[169] Betz comments that the verbs used in 5:26 are common in diatribes (*Galatians*, 295).

The dynamic middle sense of behavior emanating from one's own means is most pertinent in this context. It is consonant with Paul's language of Flesh and Spirit, for the works of the Flesh are produced, according to Paul's argument, when the power of the Flesh is given sway within a person. This aligns with what Jesus said about evil thoughts and deeds coming from the heart (Matt 15:18, 19). Therefore, in this portion of discourse the middle voice of προκαλούμενοι affirms that in provoking others to engage in competitive behavior, the Flesh-controlled self is asserted over others, acting in one's *own* interest and drawing others into one's *own* sphere, rather than loving one's neighbor. By seeking their *own* glory, they generate interpersonal conflict, the opposite of love and mutual service, which are the fruit of the Spirit.[170]

7.4 Concluding Comments

In this chapter I have explored the exegetical possibilities arising when the relevant nuances of the middle voice (as appropriate from the three main descriptors) are attributed to verbs with middle form in Galatians. In some instances, these generate potential theological significance, as the detailed studies of ἐξέληται in 1:4 and ἐπιτελεῖσθε in 3:3 reveal. At other times, the middle voice of the verb has been found to enhance the meaning derived from the overall context or generate a subtle shift in focus. On no occasion has the middle form been found simply extraneous.

In the case of *media tantum* verbs such as ἐνάρχομαι, the middle voice is interwoven with the lexical semantics of the verb, such that the self-affectedness, or self-interest, or self-origin, is virtually innate. For the oppositional middles, the middle voice has been shown to be appropriately employed in the context, evoking a sense of meaning that would not be derived from the active, by highlighting the involvement of the subject.

---

[170] As Luther comments, provoking and envying are "the effect and fruit of vainglory" (*Galatians*, 533).

There are of course, several other middle verbs in this Epistle. In order to provide the widest possible sample for the entire study, only those which were not previously investigated have been considered in this chapter. Of the remainder, ἐνεργουμένη in Gal 5:6 (previously explored in §4.9) could be of particular interest, due to the middle/passive form and the important motifs of faith and love to which the verb relates. This limited study has nevertheless demonstrated that an examination of the middle nuance of a verb draws one more closely into the text, contributing to the overall sense of that which is expressed. Since the author has expressed his thought in verbs of middle form, it behooves the reader to seek out the particular type and extent of subject involvement that is correspondingly coded.

CHAPTER 8
CONCLUSION

This investigation has sought to contribute to the understanding of a matter that has not received due recognition in exegetical discussion; namely, the use of the middle voice in the Greek New Testament. A survey of relevant literature revealed a number of traditional and recent understandings of the Greek middle voice from both grammatical and linguistic perspectives. These were distilled into three specific criteria against which to compare the function of middle form verbs in context to ascertain whether the middle form did in fact designate middle, not simply active, function.

From the grammars, the consensus notion of the subject acting on, for or with reference to itself was adopted as a descriptor of middle voice function. It was assumed that such a criterion inherently requires an animate, volitional subject. From the specific middle voice studies, the notion of subject-affectedness emerged as a currently accepted rationale of the middle voice, with various applications in different situation types, as outlined by Rutger Allan.[1] One further less well-known description of the middle voice as internal *diathesis* or mediality, was also adopted as a means of comparison. In this, the subject is perceived to be actively participating in, and encompassed by, the verbal process.

These three descriptors of the middle voice articulate different aspects of middle function. The grammatical descriptors focus on the subject as agent, that is, the distinct way it acts in reference to itself. The principle of subject-affectedness emphasizes the various ways the subject is impacted, while the medial notion is concerned with the location of the subject within a process of which it partakes. This does not require a specific type of effect to be articulated; rather it implies an interactive, interdependent experience, often pointing to relational situations. These

---

[1] While such a definition necessarily includes the passive within the scope of the middle, this study has been restricted to middle form verbs without external agents.

three perspectives are not mutually exclusive but rather complementary; they have been employed as precise articulations of the middle voice against which each middle form could be tested. Taken together, they have enabled the middle function of the middle verb forms in this investigation to be recognized.

8.1 RESULTS OF INVESTIGATIONS

In 1 Thessalonians and again in 2 Corinthians, the investigations strongly indicate that middle form correlates widely with middle function. In chs. 3 and 4, every aorist and present middle verb form in 1 Thessalonians was investigated, with the result that at least two of the three descriptors applied to 89 percent of all the forty-six middle forms examined (δύναμαι being a notable exception). In chapters five and six, another forty-seven middle verb forms from 2 Corinthians were studied with the result that 100 percent satisfied at least two criteria, and 96 percent satisfied all three. It is therefore evident that when verbs were examined in context, *middle morphology was found widely to indicate middle function*, with 95 percent of all the verbs examined satisfying at least two of the middle voice criteria employed.

The positive outcome of this stage of the investigation, namely, that middle form generally did signify middle function, was applied to a further sample of verbs from Galatians. The process was effectively inverted: by assuming a middle form to have some type of middle function, the possible implications for exegesis and interpretation of a text were explored. Two in-depth studies, one of ἐξέληται in Gal 1:4 and the other of both ἐναρξάμενοι and ἐπιτελεῖσθε in Gal 3:3 demonstrate that reading with due attention to the middle voice can evoke significant theological insights. In addition, several shorter studies reveal that the middle voice serves to complement or refine the sense carried by lexical and syntactical considerations of the text.

8.2 Further Outcomes

The findings above applied not only to oppositional middles but also to middle-only verbs, affirming that they also exhibit middle function and are not simply active as the traditional term "middle-deponent" would suggest. Further, the awkward notion of "passive deponents" has been de-mystified in the process of this study. These have been seen to be nothing more than middle verbs exhibiting the alternative MP2 (-θη-) morphology in the aorist. As middle voice verbs, they have agentive subjects and consequently appear active in English. They are neither passive, nor active, but middle; however, the middle force is generally lost in translation.

While it has not been the intention of this study to evaluate the efficacy of the three descriptors employed, it may be noted that the criterion of subject affectedness was the most widely applicable (91 of the 93 instances). Nevertheless, the grammatical and medial descriptors applied to a significant majority as well (grammatical, 78; medial, 85). Each has advantages and limitations. Allan's spontaneous category aptly describes certain event types whose middle function is not easily explained by the grammatical descriptor (notably when there is an inanimate subject). The medial notion is helpful in situations where there is clear engagement of the subject in a process of interdependence, but a particular type of affectedness may be difficult or unnecessary to identify. While the grammatical descriptor is less widely applicable, it is nevertheless clearly discernable and cogent in several cases.

Notably, many times the perceived grammatical function was Cooper's dynamic middle, referring to the personal investment of the subject in the action. This could account for the previous lack of recognition of the middle function of certain verbs in an era when grammar was dominant and linguistic insights were less widely adopted. Testament to the validity of this category, however, is that the dynamic middle function was not the sole descriptor to apply to any event. It was complemented often by Allan's speech act or mental activity middle as well as by the medial notion, each of these expressing a particular interpretation of the middle function.

It has also been demonstrated that a particular lexeme may exhibit a different type of middle function in different contexts, as may readily be seen in the studies on καυχάομαι. The use of this verb aligned with Allan's classifications of speech act, indirect, or direct reflexive middle on different occasions. This observation replicates that made by Robertson long ago, namely, that middle morphology indicates the subject is acting in reference to itself somehow, but the precise manner of such must be determined from the context in which it is employed.[2]

8.3 IMPLICATIONS

The findings of this project have implications for the study of the New Testament. As often acknowledged, it is difficult to accommodate the Greek middle voice in translation for it is necessarily rendered by an active in many modern languages. However, the exploration of different types of middle function in this study calls for more attention to be given to the nuance encoded by the middle form in any given context. Significantly, this difficulty of translation does not prevent the relevance of the middle voice being discussed in exegetical commentary; in fact, because it cannot be duly rendered, there is even more need for an exploration of possible interpretations.

Particularly important are the pedagogical implications for New Testament Greek. In the wake of the demise of deponency a clearer treatment of the middle voice has begun to appear in more recent grammars. These generally adopt the sense of subject-affectedness from linguistic studies, although terminology still varies. A genuine appreciation of the middle voice needs to be firmly adopted and developed in the classroom, beginning at the introductory level, if the middle voice is to be given due respect in the reading of the New Testament. There is no need for any mention of deponency; there is, on the other hand a need

---

[2] See §2.1.6.2 above.

for teachers to become confidently aware of the distinct function of the Greek middle voice.

8.4 Future Trajectories

In investigating the specific use of middle verbs in some of Paul's epistles, this study has uncovered similar uses of these verbs elsewhere in Christian Scripture. This suggests that similar or related studies of middle verbs in other Pauline epistles and throughout the whole New Testament corpus could generate further understanding and recognition of the Greek middle voice as a vehicle for deeper meaning beyond the active/passive mindset to which many modern western readers are accustomed. Studies of middle verbs in the gospels would be of particular interest, in order to explore the use of the middle voice in the narrative genre as well as to examine comparisons of synoptic parallels. Similar investigations could also be extended to non-biblical writings in Koine Greek.

The difficulty of classifying δύναμαι has already been raised as a possible area of future research. Yet another potential field of inquiry is the rationale for the future middle forms of certain otherwise active verbs. This could possibly interact with recent studies on aspect, for the Greek future tenses may not be time related as generally assumed. Since future events refer to a change of existing conditions (hence, state), the middle voice could well be the appropriate vehicle for such expressions.

8.5 Final Comment

This study of middle voice usage in sample texts of one author, namely, Paul, has demonstrated that the middle form of a verb generally does indicate middle function, and that such function may have considerable influence on the interpretation of a passage of Scripture. Often lacking recognition in commentaries, the function of the middle voice requires due consideration in exegesis alongside other factors such as lexical semantics, tense, mood, and aspect of a verb. To constrain the meaning of the Greek text to the limitations of its translated form is to render a disservice to both author and reader. Further investigation into the significance of the 3,726 middle verb forms in the Greek New Testament is therefore summoned.

APPENDIX
MIDDLE VERB FORMS IN 2 CORINTHIANS

Ch	Middle verb forms per chapter in order of occurrence.	Middle verbs	Middle forms
1	Δύνασθαι, ἐνεργουμένης, γενομένης, ἐρρύσατο, ῥύσεται x2, ἐπιγνώσεσθε, ἐβουλόμην, βουλόμενος, ἐχρησάμην, βουλεύομαι x2, ἐγένετο, σφραγισάμενος, ἐπικαλοῦμαι, φειδόμενος.	11	16
2	Χαρίσασθαι, χαρίζεσθε, κεχάρισμαι x2, ἀποταξάμενος.	2	5
3	ἀρχόμεθα, λογίσασθαι, δύνασθαι, ἔσται, χρώμεθα, κατοπτριζόμενοι.	6	6
4	ἀπειπάμεθα, ἀπορούμενοι, ἐξαπορούμενοι, ἐνεργεῖται, κατεργάζεται.	5	5
5	ἐπενδύσασθαι, ἐκδύσασθαι, ἐκδυσάμενοι, ἐπενδύσασθαι, κατεργασάμενος, φιλοτιμούμεθα, κομίσηται, καυχωμένους, λογιζόμενος, θέμενος, δεόμεθα, γενώμεθα.	10	12
6	δέξασθαι, γίνεσθε, ἔσομαι, ἔσονταί, ἅπτεσθε, εἰσδέξομαι, ἔσομαι, ἔσεσθέ	5	8
7	μεταμέλομαι, μετεμελόμην, ἐργάζεται, κατεργάζεται, κατειργάσατο, κεκαύχημαι, ἐδέξασθε.	5	7
8	δεόμενοι, προενήρξατο, προενήρξασθε, γένηται x2, ἐδέξατο, στελλόμενοι μωμήσηται, ἐνδεικνύμενοι.	7	9
9	καυχῶμαι, παρεσκεύασται, παρεσκευασμένοι, ἡγησάμην, προῄρηται, κατεργάζεται.	5	6
10	δέομαι, λογίζομαι, λογιζομένους, στρατευόμεθα, ἐπαιρόμενον, λογιζέσθω, καυχήσωμαι, λογιζέσθω, καυχησόμεθα, ἐφικέσθαι, ἐφικνούμενοι, καυχώμενοι, εὐαγγελίσασθαι, καυχήσασθαι, καυχώμενος, καυχάσθω.	7	16
11	ἀνείχεσθέ, ἀνέχεσθε, ἡρμοσάμην, φοβοῦμαι, ἐρχόμενος, ἐδέξασθε, ἀνέχεσθε, λογίζομαι, εὐηγγελισάμην, καυχῶνται, μετασχηματιζόμενοι, μετασχηματίζεται, μετασχηματίζονται, ἔσται, δέξασθέ, καυχήσωμαι, καυχῶνται, καυχήσωμαι, ἀνέχεσθε x2, ἐπαίρεται, καυχᾶσθαι, καυχήσομαι, ψεύδομαι.	12	24
12	Καυχᾶσθαι, ἐλεύσομαι, καυχήσομαι, καυχήσομαι, καυχήσασθαι, ἔσομαι, φείδομαι, λογίσηται, καυχήσομαι, χαρίσασθέ, ἀπολογούμεθα, φοβοῦμαι.	8	12
13	ἔρχομαι, φείσομαι, γνώσεσθε, εὐχόμεθα, δυνάμεθά, εὐχόμεθα, χρήσωμαι, ἔσται, Ἀσπάσασθε, Ἀσπάζονται.	8	10

BIBLIOGRAPHY

GENERAL

Allan, Rutger J. *The Middle Voice in Ancient Greek: A Study in Polysemy*. Amsterdam Studies in Classical Philology Vol. 11. Amsterdam: J.C. Gieben, 2003.

Allen, W. Sidney. *Vox Graeca: The Pronunciation of Classical Greek*. 3rd ed. Cambridge: Cambridge University Press, 1987.

Argyle, A. W. *An Introductory Grammar of New Testament Greek*. London: Hodder and Stoughton, 1965.

Aubrey, Rachel. "Motivated Categories, Middle Voice, and Passive Morphology." Pages 563–625 in *The Greek Verb Revisited: A Fresh Approach for Biblical Exegesis*. Edited by Steven E. Runge and Christopher J. Fresch. Bellingham: Lexham, 2016.

Aune, David E. *The New Testament in Its Literary Environment*. LEC 8. Philadelphia: Westminster, 1989.

———. *The Westminster Dictionary of New Testament and Early Christian Literature and Rhetoric*. Louisville: Westminster John Knox, 2003.

Bagnall, Roger S., Raffaella Cribiore, and Evie Ahtaridis. *Women's Letters from Ancient Egypt, 300 BC–AD 800*. Ann Arbor: University of Michigan Press, 2006.

Bakker, Egbert J. "Voice, Aspect and Aktionsart: Middle and Passive in Ancient Greek." Pages 23–47 in *Voice Form and Function*. Edited by Barbara Fox and Paul J. Hopper. TSL 27. Amsterdam: John Benjamins, 1994.

Barrett, C. K. *The Second Epistle to the Corinthians*. BNTC. London: Black, 1973.

Barth, Karl. *The Epistle to the Romans*. Translated by Edward C. Hoskyns. 6th ed. London: Oxford University Press, 1950.

Bechert, J. *Die Diathesen von ἰδεῖν und ὁρᾶν bei Homer*. Munich: Kitzinger 1964.

Benveniste, Emile. "Actif et Moyen Dans Le Verbe." Pages 168–175 in *Problèmes De Linguistigue Générale*. Paris: Gallimard, 1966.

———. "Active and Middle Voice in the Verb." Translated by Mary Elizabeth Meek. Pages 145–151 in *Problems in General Linguistics*. Coral Gables: University of Miami Press, 1971.

Best, Ernest. *A Commentary on the First and Second Epistles to the Thessalonians*. BNTC. London: Black, 1979.

Betz, Hans Dieter. *Galatians: A Commentary on Paul's Letter to the Churches in Galatia*. Hermeneia. Philadelphia: Fortress, 1979.

Black, David Alan. *Learn to Read New Testament Greek*. 3rd ed. Nashville: B&H Academic, 2009.

Boring, M. Eugene. *I & II Thessalonians*. NTL. Louisville: Westminster John Knox, 2015.

Bruce, F. F. *1 & 2 Thessalonians*. WBC 45. Waco, TX: Word, 1982.

———. *The Epistle to the Galatians: A Commentary on the Greek Text*. NIGTC. Grand Rapids: Eerdmans, 1982.

Burton, Ernest De Witt. *A Critical and Exegetical Commentary on the Epistle to the Galatians*. ICC. Edinburgh: T&T Clark, 1921.

Campbell, Constantine R. *Advances in the Study of Greek: New Insights for Reading the New Testament*. Grand Rapids: Zondervan, 2015.

Caragounis, Chrys C. *The Development of Greek and the New Testament: Morphology, Syntax, Phonology, and Textual Transmission*. WUNT 167. Tübingen: Mohr Siebeck, 2004.

———. *New Testament Language and Exegesis: A Diachronic Approach*. WUNT 323. Tübingen: Mohr Siebeck, 2014.

Carlson, Stephen C. *The Text of Galatians and Its History*. WUNT 385. Tübingen: Mohr Siebeck, 2015.

Chamberlain, William Douglas. *An Exegetical Grammar of the Greek New Testament*. New York: Macmillan, 1941.

Conrad, Carl W. "New Observations on Voice in the Ancient Greek Verb," 2002. https://cpb-us-w2.wpmucdn.com/sites.wustl.edu/dist/8/2865/files/2020/10/newobsancgrkvc.pdf

Cooper III, Guy L. *Attic Greek Prose Syntax*. 2 vols. Ann Arbor: University of Michigan Press, 1998.

Croy, N. Clayton. *A Primer of Biblical Greek*. Grand Rapids: Eerdmans, 1999.

Dana, H. E., and Julius R. Mantey. *A Manual Grammar of the Greek New Testament*. London: SPCK, 1928.

Das, A. Andrew. *Galatians*. Concordia Commentary: A Theological Expositon of Sacred Scripture. Saint Louis: Concordia, 2014.

Davidson, Thomas. *The Grammar of Dionysios Thrax*. St. Louis: R.P. Studley, 1874.

Davis, William Hersey. *Beginner's Grammar of the Greek New Testament*. San Francisco: Harper & Row, 1923.

de Boer, Martinus C. *Galatians: A Commentary*. NTL. Louisville: Westminster John Knox, 2011.

Decker, Rodney J. *Reading Koine Greek: An Introduction and Integrated Workbook*. Grand Rapids: Baker Academic, 2014.

Deissmann, Adolf. *Die neutestamentliche Formel "in Christo Jesu."* Marburg: N.G. Elwert'sche, 1892.

──── . *Light from the Ancient East: The New Testament Illustrated by Recently Discovered Texts of the Graeco-Roman World*. Translated by Lionel R.M. Strachan. Rev. ed. London: Hodder & Stoughton, 1927.

Deissmann, G. Adolf. *Bible Studies: Contributions Chiefly from Papyri and Inscriptions to the History of the Language, the Literature, and the Religion of Hellenistic Judaism and Primitive Christianity*. Translated by Alexander Grieve. Edinburgh: T&T Clark, 1901.

Donfried, Karl Paul. *Paul, Thessalonica and Early Christianity*. Grand Rapids: Eerdmans, 2002.

Duff, Jeremy. *The Elements of New Testament Greek*. 3rd ed. Cambridge: Cambridge University Press, 2005.

Duncan, George S. *The Epistle of Paul to the Galatians*. MNTC. London: Hodder & Stoughton, 1934.

Dunn, James D. G. *Romans 9–16*. WBC 38B. Dallas: Word, 1988.

──── . *A Commentary on the Epistle to the Galatians*. BNTC. London: Black, 1993.

_____. *The Theology of Paul the Apostle.* Grand Rapids: Eerdmans, 1998.

Durie, David. *Greek Grammar: A Concise Grammar of New Testament Greek.* 4th ed. Macquarie, A.C.T.: Zoe, 1989.

Ebeling, Gerhard. *The Truth of the Gospel: An Exposition of Galatians.* Translated by David Green. Philadelphia: Fortress, 1985.

Eberhard, Philippe. "The Mediality of Our Condition: A Christian Interpretation." *JAAR* 67 (1999): 411–34.

_____. *The Middle Voice in Gadamer's Hermeneutics: A Basic Interpretation with Some Theological Implications.* HUTh 45. Tübingen: Mohr Siebeck, 2004.

Fee, Gordon D. *God's Empowering Presence: The Holy Spirit in the Letters of Paul.* Peabody, MA: Hendrickson, 1994.

_____. *Galatians.* Pentecostal Commentary. Dorset, UK: Deo, 2007.

_____. *The First and Second Letters to the Thessalonians.* NICNT. Grand Rapids: Eerdmans, 2009.

Frame, James Everett. *A Critical and Exegetical Commentary on the Epistles of St. Paul to the Thessalonians.* ICC. Edinburgh: T&T Clark, 1912.

Frick, Peter. *A Handbook of New Testament Greek Grammar.* Montreal: Laodamia, 2007.

Funk, Robert W. *A Beginning-Intermediate Grammar of Hellenistic Greek.* 3rd ed. Salem, OR: Polebridge, 2013.

Furnish, Victor Paul. *II Corinthians: Translated with Introduction, Notes and Commentary.* AB 32A. Garden City, NY: Doubleday, 1984.

Furnish, Victor Paul, *1 Thessalonians, II Thessalonians*, ANTC Nashville: Abingdon, 2007.

Gadamer, Hans-Georg. *Truth and Method.* Rev. ed. London: Continuum, 2004.

Gignac, Francis Thomas. *Morphology.* Vol. II of *A Grammar of the Greek Papyri of the Roman and Byzantine Periods.* Testi E Documenti Per Lo Studio Dell'antichità. Milan: Cisalpino-La Goliardica, 1981.

Greenidge, A. H. J. *The Legal Procedure of Cicero's Time*. Oxford: Clarendon, 1901.
Guthrie, George H. *2 Corinthians*. BECNT. Grand Rapids: Baker Academic, 2015.
Hafemann, Scott. "'Self-Commendation' and Apostolic Legitimacy in 2 Corinthians: A Pauline Dialectic?" *NTS* 36 (1990): 66–88.
Harris, Murray J. *The Second Epistle to the Corinthians: A Commentary on the Greek Text*. NIGTC. Grand Rapids: Eerdmans, 2005.
Hays, Richard B. "Apocalyptic *Poiēsis* in Galatians: Paternity, Passion and Participation." Pages 200–219 in *Galatians and Christian Theology: Justification, the Gospel, and Ethics in Paul's Letter*. Edited by Mark W. Elliott et al. Grand Rapids: Baker Academic, 2014.
Horrocks, Geoffrey. *Greek: A History of the Language and Its Speakers*. 2nd ed. Maldon, MA: Wiley-Blackwell, 2014.
Hort, F. J. A. *The Epistle of St. James: The Greek Text*. London: Macmillan, 1909.
Householder, Fred W., ed. *The Syntax of Apollonius Dyscolus*. SiHoLS 23 Amsterdam: John Benjamins, 1981.
Hughes, Philip Edgcumbe. *Paul's Second Epistle to the Corinthians*. NICNT. Grand Rapids: Eerdmans, 1979.
Jannaris, A. N. *An Historical Greek Grammar Chiefly of the Attic Dialect*. London: Macmillan, 1897.
Jay, Eric G. *New Testament Greek: An Introductory Grammar*. London: SPCK, 1961.
Kemmer, Suzanne. *The Middle Voice*. TSL 23. Amsterdam: John Benjamins, 1993.
Klaiman, M. H. *Grammatical Voice*. CSL 59. Cambridge: Cambridge University Press, 1991.
Klauck, Hans-Josef. *Ancient Letters and the New Testament: A Guide to Context and Exegesis*. Translated by Daniel P. Bailey. Waco, TX: Baylor University Press, 2006.
Köstenberger, Andreas J., Benjamin L. Merkle, and Robert L. Plummer. *Going Deeper with New Testament Greek: An Intermediate*

Study of the Grammar and Syntax of the New Testament. Nashville: B&H Academic, 2016.

Kruse, Colin. *The Second Epistle of Paul to the Corinthians*. TNTC. Leicester: Inter-Varsity Press, 1987.

Ladewig, Stratton L. "Defining Deponency: An Investigation into Greek Deponency of the Middle and Passive Voices in the Koine Period." Dallas Theological Seminary, 2010.

Lambrecht, Jan. *Second Corinthians*. SP 8. Collegeville, MN: Liturgical Press, 1999.

Land, Christopher D. *The Integrity of 2 Corinthians and Paul's Aggravating Absence*. NTM 36. Sheffield: Sheffield Phoenix, 2015.

Langacker, R. W. *Foundations of Cognitive Grammar*. 2 vols. Stanford, CA: Stanford University Press, 1987.

Lavidas, Nikolaos. "Passives in the History of Greek: Evidence for the Role of the Passive Suffix." *Folia Linguistica Historica* 33 (2012): 87–121.

Lightfoot, J. B. *The Epistle of St. Paul to the Galatians*. London: Macmillan, 1914. Repr., Grand Rapids: Zondervan, 1957.

Llewelyn, S. R. *A Review of Greek Inscriptions and Papyri Published in 1980–1981*. Vol. 6 of *New Documents Illustrating Early Christianity*. North Ryde: Macquarie University Ancient History Documentary Research Centre, 1992.

Long, Fredrick J. *Koine Greek Grammar: A Beginning-Intermediate Exegetical and Pragmatic Handbook*. Accessible Greek Resources and Online Studies. Wilmore: GlossaHouse, 2015.

Longenecker, Richard N. *Galatians*. WBC 41. Dallas: Word, 1990.

Luther, Martin. *A Commentary on Paul's Epistle to the Galatians*. Rev. ed. London: James Clarke, 1953.

Lyons, John. *Introduction to Theoretical Linguistics*. Cambridge: Cambridge University Press, 1968.

Malherbe, Abraham J. "Exhortation in First Thessalonians." *NovT* 25 (1983): 238–56.

———. *The Letters to the Thessalonians*. AB 32B. New York: Doubleday, 2000.

Martin, Ralph P. *2 Corinthians*. 2nd ed. WBC 40. Waco, TX: Word, 2014.

Martyn, J. Louis. *Galatians: A New Translation with Introduction and Commentary*. AB 33A. New York: Doubleday, 1997.

Matera, Frank J. *Galatians*. SP 9. Collegeville, MN: Liturgical Press, 1992.

———. *II Corinthians: A Commentary*. NTL. Louisville: Westminster John Knox, 2003.

McLean, B. H. *New Testament Greek: An Introduction*. New York: Cambridge University Press, 2011.

Merkle, Benjamin L., and Robert L. Plummer, *Beginning with New Testament Greek: An Introductory Study of the Grammar and Syntax of the New Testament*. Nashville: B&H Academic, 2020.

Michaels, J. Ramsey. *1 Peter*. WBC 49. Waco, TX: Word, 1988.

Miller, Neva F. "A Theory of Deponent Verbs." Pages 423–30 in *Analytical Lexicon of the Greek New Testament*. Edited by Timothy Friberg, Barbara Friberg and Neva F. Miller. Victoria, BC: Trafford, 2005.

Milligan, George. *St. Paul's Epistles to the Thessalonians: The Greek Text with Introduction and Notes*. London: Macmillan,1908.

Mills, Watson E. *New Testament Greek: An Introductory Grammar*. Lewiston, NY: Mellen, 1985.

Monro, D. B. *A Grammar of the Homeric Dialect*. Oxford: Clarendon, 1882.

Moo, Douglas J. *Galatians*. BECNT. Grand Rapids: Baker Academic, 2013.

Morris, Leon. *The First and Second Epistles to the Thessalonians*. NICNT. Grand Rapids: Eerdmans, 1991.

Moule, C. F. D. *An Idiom Book of New Testament Greek*. 2nd ed. Cambridge: Cambridge University Press, 1960.

Moulton, James Hope. *Prolegomena*. Vol. 1 of *A Grammar of New Testament Greek*. 4 vols. Edinburgh: T&T Clark, 1906–1976.

Mounce, William D. *Basics of Biblical Greek Grammar*. 2nd ed. Grand Rapids: Zondervan, 2003.

_____. *Basics of Biblical Greek Grammar*. 4th ed. Grand Rapids: Zondervan, 2019.

Oates, John F. and William H. Willis, founding editors. *Checklist of Editions of Greek, Latin, Demotic, and Coptic Papyri, Ostraca, and Tablets*. http://papyri.info/docs/checklist

Pennington, Johnathan T. "Setting Aside 'Deponency': Rediscovering the Greek Middle Voice in New Testament Studies." Pages 181-203 in *The Linguist as Pedagogue: Trends in the Teaching and Linguistic Analysis of the Greek New Testament*. NTM. Edited by Stanley E. Porter and Matthew Brook O'Donnell. Sheffield: Sheffield Phoenix, 2009.

Plummer, Alfred. *A Critical and Exegetical Commentary on the Second Epistle of St. Paul to the Corinthians* ICC. Edinburgh: T&T Clark, 1915. Repr.,1966.

Porter, S. E. *Καταλλάσω in Ancient Greek Literature, with Reference to the Pauline Writings*. EFN 5. Córdoba, Spain: El Almendro, 1994.

Porter, Stanley E. *Idioms of the Greek New Testament*. 2nd ed. Sheffield: Sheffield Academic, 1992.

Porter, Stanley E., Jeffrey T. Reed, and Matthew Brook O'Donnell. *Fundamentals of New Testament Greek*. Grand Rapids: Eerdmans, 2010.

Rendall, Frederick. *The Epistle to the Galatians*. Vol. III of *The Expositor's Greek Testament*. Edited by Robertson W. Nicoll. Grand Rapids: Eerdmans, 1967.

Richard, Earl J. *First and Second Thessalonians*. SP 11. Collegeville, MN: Liturgical Press, 1995.

Rijksbaron, Albert. *The Syntax and Semantics of the Verb in Classical Greek: An Introduction*. 3rd ed. Amsterdam: J.C. Gieben, 2002.

Robertson, A. T. *A Grammar of the Greek New Testament in the Light of Historical Research*. London: Hodder & Stoughton, 1914.

Robins, R. H. *The Byzantine Grammarians: Their Place in History*. TiLSM 70. New York: Mouton de Gruyter, 1993.

Sampley, J. Paul. "'Before God I Do Not Lie' (Gal 1:20). Paul's Self-Defence in the Light of Roman Legal Praxis." *NTS* 23 (1977): 477–82.

Savage, Timothy B. *Power through Weakness: Paul's Understanding of the Christian Ministry in 2 Corinthians*. SNTSMS 86. Cambridge: Cambridge University Press, 1996.

Schmidhauser, Andreas U. "The Birth of Grammar in Greece." Pages 499–511 in *A Companion to the Ancient Greek Language*. Edited by Egbert J. Bekker. Chichester: Wiley-Blackwell, 2010.

Seifrid, Mark A. *The Second Letter to the Corinthians*. PNTC. Grand Rapids: Eerdmans, 2014.

Signes-Codoñer, Juan. "The Definitions of the Greek Middle Voice between Apollonius Dyscolus and Constantinus Lascaris." *Historiographia Linguistica* 32 (2005): 1–33.

Smyth, Herbert Weir. *Greek Grammar*. Revised by Gordon M. Messing. Cambridge: Harvard University Press, 1956.

———. *Greek Grammar for Colleges*. New York: American Book Company, 1920.

Stowers, Stanley K. *Letter Writing in Greco-Roman Antiquity*. LEC 5. Philadelphia: Westminster, 1989.

Strachan, R. H. *The Second Epistle to the Corinthians*. MNTC. London: Hodder & Stoughton, 1935. Repr.,1954.

Taylor, Bernard A. "Deponency and Greek Lexicography." Pages 167–176 in *Biblical Greek Language and Lexicography: Essays in Honor of Frederick W. Danker*. Edited by Bernard A. Taylor. Grand Rapids: Eerdmans, 2004.

———. "Greek Deponency: The Historical Perspective." Pages 177–90 in *Biblical Greek in Context: Essays in Honor of John A. L. Lee*. Edited by James K. Aitken and Trevor V. Evans. BTS. Leuven: Peeters, 2015.

Thrall, Margaret E. *A Critical and Exegetical Commentary on the Second Epistle to the Corinthians* ICC. 2 vols. Edinburgh: T&T Clark, 1994.

Turner, Nigel. *Syntax*. Vol. 3 of *A Grammar of New Testament Greek*. By James Hope Moulton. 4 vols. Edinburgh: T&T Clark, 1908–1976.

Vandorpe, Katelijn. "Seals in and on the Papyri of Graeco-Roman and Byzantine Egypt." Pages 231–291 in *Archives et sceaux du monde Hellénistique*. Volume 29 of *Bulletin de correspondance hellénique: Supplément*. Edited by M. F. Bousacc and A. Invernizzi. Athens: École Française d'Athènes, 1996.

Wallace, Daniel B. *Greek Grammar Beyond the Basics: An Exegetical Syntax of the New Testament*. Grand Rapids: Zondervan, 1996.

Wanamaker, Charles A. *The Epistles to the Thessalonians: A Commentary on the Greek Text*. NIGTC. Grand Rapids: Eerdmans; Carlisle, UK: Paternoster, 1990.

Weima, Jeffrey A. D. *1–2 Thessalonians*. BECNT. Grand Rapids: Baker Academic, 2014.

Wenham, J. W. *The Elements of New Testament Greek*. Cambridge: Cambridge University Press, 1965. Repr., 1970.

White, John L. *Light from Ancient Letters*. Foundations and Facets. Philadelphia: Fortress, 1986.

Wifstrand, Albert. "Language and Style of the New Testament." Translated by Denis Searby. Pages 71–77 in *Epochs and Styles: Selected Writings on the New Testament, Greek Language and Greek Culture in the Post-Classical Era*. Edited by Lars Rydbeck and Stanley E. Porter. Translated by Denis Searby. WUNT I. Tübingen: Mohr Siebeck, 2005.

Winter, John Garrett. *Life and Letters in the Papyri: The Jerome Lectures*. Ann Arbor: University of Michigan Press, 1933.

Witherington III, Ben. *1 and 2 Thessalonians: A Socio-Rhetorical Commentary*. Grand Rapids: Eerdmans, 2006.

_____. *Grace in Galatia: A Commentary on Paul's Letter to the Galatians*. Grand Rapids: Eerdmans, 1998.

Woodhouse, S. C. *English-Greek Dictionary: A Vocabulary of the Attic Language*. London: Routledge, 1910.

Young, Richard A. *Intermediate New Testament Greek: A Linguistic and Exegetical Approach*. Nashville: Broadman & Holman, 1994.
Zerwick, Maximillian. *Biblical Greek Illustrated by Examples*. 4th ed. Translated by Joseph Smith. Rome: Pontificii Instituti Biblici, 1963.

ANCIENT GREEK WORKS

Aeschines. *The Speeches of Aeschines,* Translated by C. D. Adams. LCL 106. Cambridge, MA: Harvard University Press, 1919.
Apollonius Dyscolus. *De constructione*, 1–497 in G. Uhlig, *Grammatici Graeci*, vol. 2.2. Leipzig: Teubner, 1910. Repr., Hildesheim: Olms, 1965.
Babbitt, F.C., ed. *Plutarch's moralia*, vol. 1. Cambridge, MA: Harvard University Press, 1927. Repr., 1969.
Babbitt, F.C., ed. *Plutarch's moralia*, vol. 2. Cambridge, MA: Harvard University Press, 1928. Repr., 1962.
Bardy, G., ed. *Eusèbe de Césarée. Histoire ecclésiastique.* 3 vols. [*Sources chrétiennes* 31, 41, 55. Paris: Éditions du Cerf, 1:1952; 2:1955; 3:1958. Repr., 3:1967]
Boissevain, U.P., ed. *Cassii Dionis Cocceiani historiarum Romanarum quae supersunt*, 3 vols. Berlin: Weidmann, 1:1895; 2:1898; 3:1901. Repr., 1955.
Burnet, J., ed. *Platonis opera*, vol. 3. Oxford: Clarendon Press, 1903. Repr., 1968.
Clement of Alexandria. *The Exhortation to the Greeks. The Rich Man's Salvation. To the Newly Baptized.* Translated by G. W. Butterworth. LCL 92. Cambridge, MA: Harvard University Press, 1919.
Cohn, L., ed. *Philonis Alexandrini opera quae supersunt*, vol. 1. Berlin: Reimer, 1896. Repr. Berlin: De Gruyter, 1962.
———, ed. *Philonis Alexandrini opera quae supersunt*, vol. 4. Berlin: Reimer, 1902. Repr. Berlin: De Gruyter, 1962.

Cohn, L. and S. Reiter, eds. *Philonis Alexandrini opera quae supersunt*, vol. 6. Berlin: Reimer, 1915. Repr., Berlin: De Gruyter, 1962.

Diggle, J., ed. *Euripidis fabulae*, vol. 3. Oxford: Clarendon Press, 1994.

Dio Cassius. *Roman History, Volume IV: Books 41–45*. Translated by Earnest Cary, Herbert B. Foster. LCL 66. Cambridge, MA: Harvard University Press, 1916.

———. *Roman History, Volume VI: Books 51–55*. Translated by Earnest Cary, Herbert B. Foster. LCL 83. Cambridge, MA: Harvard University Press, 1917.

Dio Chrysostom. *Discourses 61–80. Fragments. Letters*. Translated by H. Lamar Crosby. LCL 385. Cambridge, MA: Harvard University Press, 1951.

Diodorus Siculus. *Library of History, Volume IV: Books 9–12.40*. Translated by C. H. Oldfather. LCL 375. Cambridge, MA: Harvard University Press, 1946.

———. *Library of History, Volume VI: Books 14–15.19*. Translated by C. H. Oldfather. LCL 399. Cambridge, MA: Harvard University Press, 1954.

———. *Library of History, Volume VII: Books 15.20–16.65*. Translated by Charles L. Sherman. LCL 389. Cambridge, MA: Harvard University Press, 1952.

———. *Library of History, Volume VIII: Books 16.66–17*. Translated by C. Bradford Welles. LCL 422. Cambridge, MA: Harvard University Press, 1963.

Diogenes Laertius. *Lives of Eminent Philosophers, Volume I: Books 1–5*. Translated by R. D. Hicks. LCL 184. Cambridge, MA: Harvard University Press, 1925.

Dionysius Thrax, *Ars grammatica*. 5–100 in G. Uhlig, *Grammatici Graeci*, vol. 1.1. Leipzig: Teubner, 1883. Repr. Hildesheim: Olms, 1965.

Epictetus. *Discourses, Books 3–4. Fragments. The Encheiridion*. Translated by W. A. Oldfather. LCL 218. Cambridge, MA: Harvard University Press, 1928.

Euripides. *Bacchae. Iphigenia at Aulis. Rhesus.* Edited and translated by David Kovacs. LCL 495. Cambridge, MA: Harvard University Press, 2003.

Eusebius. *Ecclesiastical History, Volume I: Books 1–5.* Translated by Kirsopp Lake. LCL 153. Cambridge, MA: Harvard University Press, 1926.

Farquharson, A.S.L., ed. *The meditations of the emperor Marcus Aurelius*, vol. 1. Oxford: Clarendon Press, 1944. Repr., 1968.

Fischer, K.T., (post I. Bekker & L. Dindorf) and F. Vogel, eds. *Diodori bibliotheca historica*, 5 vols. 3rd ed. Leipzig: Teubner, 1:1888; 2:1890; 3:1893; 4–5:1906. Repr., 1964.

Fowler, H.N., ed. *Plutarch's moralia*, vol. 10. Cambridge, MA: Harvard University Press, 1936. Repr., 1969.

Früchtel, L., O. Stählin, and U. Treu, eds., *Clemens Alexandrinus*, vol. 3. 2nd ed. [*Die griechischen christlichen Schriftsteller* 17. Berlin: Akademie Verlag, 1970].

Harmon, A.M., ed. *Lucian*, vol. 2. Cambridge, MA.: Harvard University Press, 1915. Repr., 1960.

———, ed. *Lucian*, vol. 3. Cambridge, MA.: Harvard University Press, 1921. Repr., 1969.

Homer. *Odyssey, Volume I: Books 1–12.* Translated by A. T. Murray. Revised by George E. Dimock. LCL 104. Cambridge, MA: Harvard University Press, 1919.

Homer. *Odyssey, Volume II: Books 13–24.* Translated by A. T. Murray. Revised by George E. Dimock. LCL 105. Cambridge, MA: Harvard University Press, 1919.

Josephus. *Jewish Antiquities, Volume I: Books 1–3.* Translated by H. St. J. Thackeray. LCL 242. Cambridge, MA: Harvard University Press, 1930.

———. *Jewish Antiquities, Volume II: Books 4–6.* Translated by H. St. J. Thackeray, Ralph Marcus. LCL 490. Cambridge, MA: Harvard University Press, 1930.

———. *Jewish Antiquities, Volume III: Books 7–8.* Translated by Ralph Marcus. LCL 281. Cambridge, MA: Harvard University Press, 1934.

_____. *Jewish Antiquities, Volume IV: Books 9–11*. Translated by Ralph Marcus. LCL 326. Cambridge, MA: Harvard University Press, 1937.

_____. *Jewish Antiquities, Volume V: Books 12–13*. Translated by Ralph Marcus. LCL 365. Cambridge, MA: Harvard University Press, 1943.

_____. *Jewish Antiquities, Volume VI: Books 14–15*. Translated by Ralph Marcus, Allen Wikgren. LCL 489. Cambridge, MA: Harvard University Press, 1943.

_____. *Jewish Antiquities, Volume VII: Books 16–17*. Translated by Ralph Marcus, Allen Wikgren. LCL 410. Cambridge, MA: Harvard University Press, 1963.

_____. *Jewish Antiquities, Volume IX: Book 20*. Translated by Louis H. Feldman. LCL 456. Cambridge, MA: Harvard University Press, 1965.

_____. *The Jewish War, Volume I: Books 1–2*. Translated by H. St. J. Thackeray. LCL 203. Cambridge, MA: Harvard University Press, 1927.

_____. *The Jewish War, Volume III: Books 5–7*. Translated by H. St. J. Thackeray. LCL 210. Cambridge, MA: Harvard University Press, 1928.

_____. *The Life. Against Apion*. Translated by H. St. J. Thackeray. LCL 186. Cambridge, MA: Harvard University Press, 1926.

Latte, K., ed. *Hesychii Alexandrini lexicon*, 2 vols. Copenhagen: Munksgaard, 1:1953; 2:1966.

Long, H. S., ed. *Diogenis Laertii vitae philosophorum*, 2 vols. Oxford: Clarendon Press, 1964 Repr., 1966.

Lucian. *The Downward Journey or The Tyrant. Zeus Catechized. Zeus Rants. The Dream or The Cock. Prometheus. Icaromenippus or The Sky-man. Timon or The Misanthrope. Charon or The Inspectors. Philosophies for Sale*. Translated by A. M. Harmon. LCL 54. Cambridge, MA: Harvard University Press, 1915.

_____. *The Dead Come to Life or The Fisherman. The Double Indictment or Trials by Jury. On Sacrifices. The Ignorant Book Collector. The Dream or Lucian's Career. The Parasite. The Lover of Lies. The Judgement of the Goddesses. On Salaried Posts in Great Houses.* Translated by A. M. Harmon. LCL 130. Cambridge, MA: Harvard University Press, 1921.

Marcus Aurelius. *Marcus Aurelius.* Edited and translated by C. R. Haines. LCL 58. Cambridge, MA: Harvard University Press, 1916.

Marchant, E.C., ed. *Xenophontis opera omnia,* vol. 2, 2nd ed. Oxford: Clarendon Press, 1921. Repr., 1971.

Martin V. and G. de Budé, eds. *Eschine. Discours,* vol. 2. Paris: Les Belles Lettres, 1928. Repr., 1962.

Mau, J., ed. *Plutarchi moralia,* vol. 5.2.1. Leipzig: Teubner, 1971.

Niese, B., ed. *Flavii Iosephi opera,* vols. 1–4. Berlin: Weidmann, 1:1887; 2:1885: 3:1892; 4:1890; Repr., 1955.

———, ed., *Flavii Iosephi opera,* vol. 5. Berlin: Weidmann, 1889 Repr., 1955.

———, ed., *Flavii Iosephi opera,* vol. 6. Berlin: Weidmann, 1895. Repr., 1955.

Perrin, B., ed. *Plutarch's lives,* vol. 4. Cambridge, MA.: Harvard University Press, 1916. Repr., 1968.

Philo. *On Abraham. On Joseph. On Moses.* Translated by F. H. Colson. LCL 289 Cambridge, MA: Harvard University Press, 1935.

_____. *On the Cherubim. The Sacrifices of Abel and Cain. The Worse Attacks the Better. On the Posterity and Exile of Cain. On the Giants.* Translated by F. H. Colson, G. H. Whitaker. LCL 227. Cambridge, MA: Harvard University Press, 1929.

_____. *On the Creation. Allegorical Interpretation of Genesis 2 and 3.* Translated by F. H. Colson, G. H. Whitaker. LCL 226. Cambridge, MA: Harvard University Press, 1929.

_____. *On the Confusion of Tongues. On the Migration of Abraham. Who Is the Heir of Divine Things? On Mating with the Preliminary Studies.* Translated by F. H. Colson, G. H. Whitaker. LCL 261. Cambridge, MA: Harvard University Press, 1932.

_____. *On the Embassy to Gaius. General Indexes.* Translated by F. H. Colson. Index by J. W. Earp. LCL 379. Cambridge, MA: Harvard University Press, 1962.

Plato. *Lysis. Symposium. Gorgias*. Translated by W. R. M. Lamb. LCL 166. Cambridge, MA: Harvard University Press, 1925.

Plutarch. *Lives, Volume I: Theseus and Romulus. Lycurgus and Numa. Solon and Publicola*. Translated by Bernadotte Perrin. LCL 46. Cambridge, MA: Harvard University Press, 1914.

———. *Lives, Volume II: Themistocles and Camillus. Aristides and Cato Major. Cimon and Lucullus*. Translated by Bernadotte Perrin. LCL 47. Cambridge, MA: Harvard University Press, 1914.

———. *Lives, Volume IV: Alcibiades and Coriolanus. Lysander and Sulla*. Translated by Bernadotte Perrin. LCL 80. Cambridge, MA: Harvard University Press, 1916.

———. *Lives, Volume VI: Dion and Brutus. Timoleon and Aemilius Paulus*. Translated by Bernadotte Perrin. LCL 98. Cambridge, MA: Harvard University Press, 1918.

———. *Lives, Volume VII: Demosthenes and Cicero. Alexander and Caesar*. Translated by Bernadotte Perrin. LCL 99. Cambridge, MA: Harvard University Press, 1919.

———. *Lives, Volume VIII: Sertorius and Eumenes. Phocion and Cato the Younger*. Translated by Bernadotte Perrin. LCL 100. Cambridge, MA: Harvard University Press, 1919.

———. *Moralia, Volume I: The Education of Children. How the Young Man Should Study Poetry. On Listening to Lectures. How to Tell a Flatterer from a Friend. How a Man May Become Aware of His Progress in Virtue*. Translated by Frank Cole Babbitt. LCL 197. Cambridge, MA: Harvard University Press, 1927.

———. *Moralia, Volume II: How to Profit by One's Enemies. On Having Many Friends. Chance. Virtue and Vice. Letter of Condolence to Apollonius. Advice About Keeping Well. Advice to Bride and Groom. The Dinner of the Seven Wise Men. Superstition*. Translated by Frank Cole Babbitt. LCL 222. Cambridge, MA: Harvard University Press, 1928.

———. *Moralia, Volume VII: On Love of Wealth. On Compliancy. On Envy and Hate. On Praising Oneself Inoffensively. On the Delays of the Divine Vengeance. On Fate. On the Sign of Socrates. On Exile. Consolation to His Wife*. Translated by Phillip H. De

Lacy, Benedict Einarson. LCL 405. Cambridge, MA: Harvard University Press, 1959.

———. *Moralia, Volume X: Love Stories. That a Philosopher Ought to Converse Especially with Men in Power. To an Uneducated Ruler. Whether an Old Man Should Engage in Public Affairs. Precepts of Statecraft. On Monarchy, Democracy, and Oligarchy. That We Ought Not to Borrow. Lives of the Ten Orators. Summary of a Comparison Between Aristophanes and Menander*. Translated by Harold North Fowler. LCL 321. Cambridge, MA: Harvard University Press, 1936.

Pohlenz, M., ed. *Plutarchi moralia*, vol. 3. Leipzig: Teubner, 1929. Repr., 1972.

Schenkl, H., ed. *Epicteti dissertationes ab Arriano digestae*. Leipzig: Teubner, 1916.

von Arnim, J., ed. *Dionis Prusaensis quem vocant Chrysostomum quae exstant omnia*. 2 vols., 2nd ed. Berlin: Weidmann, 1:1893; 2:1896. Repr., 1962.

von der Mühll, P., ed. *Homeri Odyssea*. Basel: Helbing & Lichtenhahn, 1962.

Wendland, P., ed. *Philonis Alexandrini opera quae supersunt*, vol. 2. Berlin: Reimer, 1897. Repr., Berlin: De Gruyter, 1962.

———, ed. *Philonis Alexandrini opera quae supersunt*, vol. 3. Berlin: Reimer, 1898. Repr. Berlin: De Gruyter, 1962.

Xenophon. *Memorabilia. Oeconomicus. Symposium. Apology*. Translated by E. C. Marchant, O. J. Todd. Revised by Jeffrey Henderson. LCL 168. Cambridge, MA: Harvard University Press, 2013.

Ziegler, K., ed., *Plutarchi vitae parallelae*, vol. 1.1, 4th ed. Leipzig: Teubner, 1969.

———,. ed., *Plutarchi vitae parallelae*, vol. 1.2, 3rd ed. Leipzig: Teubner, 1964.

———, ed., *Plutarchi vitae parallelae*, vol. 2.1, 2nd ed. Leipzig: Teubner, 1964.

INDICES

AUTHOR INDEX

Allan, Rutger J., 5, 43, 44, 45, 46, 47, 48, 49, 50, 51, 52, 53, 54, 55, 57, 58, 59, 60, 62, 63, 64, 65, 66, 67, 68, 73, 77, 78, 82, 86, 87, 88, 89, 90, 92, 93, 94, 96, 97, 98, 100, 101, 103, 105, 108, 110, 113, 115, 116, 120, 122, 124, 126, 131, 133, 135, 137, 140, 141, 145, 146, 147, 150, 152, 153, 154, 156, 159, 162, 163, 166, 167, 169, 174, 177, 179, 183, 185, 188, 191, 194, 195, 196, 197, 204, 205, 206, 213, 215, 216, 217, 227, 228, 229, 230, 231, 233, 234, 236, 237, 238, 239, 240, 241, 242, 243, 245, 258, 266, 269, 276, 277, 279, 280, 284, 301, 303, 304, 309

Allen, W. Sidney, 266, 309, 322

Argyle, A. W., 15, 309

Aubrey, Rachel, 64, 65, 309

Aune, David E., 220, 222, 224, 248, 309

Bagnall, Roger S., Raffaella Cribiore, and Evie Ahtaridis, xx, 121, 122, 142, 309

Bakker, Egbert J., 10, 40, 309, 317

Barrett, C. K., 237, 238, 309

Barth, Karl, 294, 309

Bechert, J., 51, 309

Benveniste, Emile, 5, 65, 66, 67, 68, 69, 73, 87, 116, 144, 245, 310

Best, Ernest, 92, 144, 310

Betz, Hans Dieter, 250, 254, 262, 263, 268, 270, 274, 282, 286, 287, 288, 291, 294, 296, 298, 310

Black, David Alan, xv, 37, 92, 237, 256, 267, 309, 310, 311

Boring, M. Eugene, 78, 103, 108, 110, 115, 134, 136, 140, 154, 161, 165, 310

Burton, Ernest De Witt, 250, 268, 286, 310

Campbell, Constantine R., 2, 35, 63, 310

Caragounis, Chrys C., 3, 4, 310

Carlson, Stephen C., 4, 266, 310

Chamberlain, William Douglas, 23, 310

Conrad, Carl W., 34, 35, 36, 37, 38, 40, 41, 53, 59, 63, 84, 89, 161, 310
Cooper III, Guy L., 32, 33, 34, 38, 55, 72, 73, 77, 82, 88, 117, 120, 137, 166, 229, 245, 257, 303, 310
Croy, N. Clayton, 7, 14, 311
Dana, H. E., and Julius R. Mantey, 24, 25, 29, 31, 178, 197, 311
Das, A. Andrew, 75, 250, 295, 296, 311
Davis, William Hersey, 15, 311
de Boer, Martinus C., 248, 254, 274, 282, 286, 298, 311
Decker, Rodney J., 34, 39, 40, 41, 42, 43, 68, 311
Deissmann, Adolf/Deissmann, G. Adolf, 3, 75, 76, 148, 226, 311
Donfried, Karl Paul, 81, 94, 311
Duff, Jeremy, 14, 18, 39, 48, 195, 279, 311
Duncan, George S., 270, 311
Dunn, James D. G., 182, 255, 267, 269, 273, 277, 288, 294, 296, 311
Durie, David, 14, 15, 312
Ebeling, Gerhard, 254, 255, 270, 312
Eberhard, Philippe, 5, 65, 68, 69, 70, 71, 73, 87, 88, 96, 109, 115, 116, 125, 127, 133, 144, 148, 152, 156, 159, 162, 168, 175, 191, 196, 212, 236, 237, 245, 258, 294, 312
Fee, Gordon D., 83, 103, 108, 124, 128, 152, 154, 156, 161, 181, 183, 248, 312
Frame, James Everett, 83, 86, 90, 107, 108, 125, 131, 140, 312
Frick, Peter, 256, 312
Funk, Robert W., xv, 4, 7, 77, 312
Furnish, Victor Paul, 78, 88, 201, 209, 211, 215, 226, 240, 312
Gadamer, Hans-Georg, 5, 68, 69, 70, 71, 312
Gignac, Francis Thomas, 3, 30, 31, 312
Greenidge, A. H. J., 278, 313
Guthrie, George, 224, 233, 234, 313
Hafemann, Scott, 224, 313
Harris, Murray J., xxi, 175, 182, 183, 184, 185, 190, 200, 201, 202, 203, 205, 209, 213, 226, 229, 230, 232, 234, 237, 313
Hays, Richard B., 249, 257, 313
Horrocks, Geoffrey, 3, 4, 8, 66, 160, 266, 313
Hort, F. J. A., xix, 172, 313
Hughes, Philip Edgcumbe, 209, 313
Jannaris, A. N., 3, 7, 8, 13, 14, 16, 17, 20, 23, 33, 53, 313
Jay, Eric G., 14, 15, 195, 313

Kemmer, Suzanne, 43, 45, 60, 65, 90, 204, 313
Klaiman, M. H., 60, 313
Klauck, Hans-Josef, 248, 313
Köstenberger, Andreas J., Benjamin L. Merkle, and Robert L. Plummer, 42, 182, 184, 216, 226, 232, 313, 315, 316
Kruse, Colin, 231, 314
Ladewig, Stratton L., 61, 62, 63, 314
Lambrecht, Jan, 209, 314
Land, Christopher D., 225, 239, 314
Langacker, R. W., 43, 46, 314
Lavidas, Nikolaos, 7, 314
Lightfoot, J. B., 250, 262, 263, 274, 291, 314
Llewelyn, S. R., 282, 314
Long, Fredrick J., iv, vi, 42, 314, 322
Longenecker, Richard N., 250, 268, 291, 296, 314
Luther, Martin, 293, 294, 299, 314
Lyons, John, 8, 43, 44, 45, 66, 217, 314
Malherbe, Abraham J., 78, 82, 83, 91, 95, 100, 103, 108, 110, 114, 115, 120, 136, 144, 145, 314
Martin, Ralph P., xxiii, 185, 202, 237, 240, 293, 314, 315, 323

Martyn, J. Louis, 248, 249, 250, 274, 282, 283, 288, 297, 315
Matera, Frank J., 182, 248, 250, 254, 255, 267, 286, 287, 315
McLean, B. H., 39, 279, 315
Michaels, J. Ramsey, 263, 315
Miller, Neva F., xv, 55, 56, 57, 58, 59, 62, 63, 77, 115, 125, 162, 315
Milligan, George, xvi, 85, 92, 103, 107, 108, 112, 139, 145, 156, 161, 315
Mills, Watson E., 14, 315
Monro, D. B., 12, 18, 315
Moo, Douglas J., 249, 268, 271, 286, 315
Morris, Leon, 127, 315
Moule, C. F. D., 7, 29, 31, 39, 284, 315
Moulton, James Hope, xvi, 3, 10, 16, 17, 18, 26, 27, 29, 31, 63, 315, 318
Mounce, William D., 2, 14, 15, 18, 42, 48, 256, 279, 315
Oates, John F. and William H. Willis, xx, 316
Plummer, Alfred, 42, 182, 184, 216, 226, 232, 313, 315, 316
Porter, S. E./ Porter, Stanley E., 3, 29, 30, 38, 39, 59, 63, 72, 205, 316, 318
Porter, Stanley E., Jeffrey T. Reed, and Matthew Brook O'Donnell, 3, 29, 30, 38, 39, 59, 63, 72, 205, 316, 318

Rendall, Frederick, 261, 269, 316
Rijksbaron, Albert, 43, 316
Robertson, A. T., 3, 12, 15, 18, 19, 20, 21, 22, 26, 29, 30, 31, 38, 56, 63, 72, 124, 152, 173, 217, 245, 246, 256, 277, 284, 304, 316
Robins, R. H., 8, 9, 10, 316
Sampley, J. Paul, 277, 278, 317
Savage, Timothy B., 237, 317
Schmidhauser, Andreas U., 10, 317
Seifrid, Mark A., 209, 214, 234, 317
Signes-Codoñer, Juan, 11, 317
Smyth, Herbert Weir, 22, 23, 24, 25, 31, 317
Stowers, Stanley K., 221, 248, 317
Strachan, R. H., 76, 215, 311, 317
Taylor, Bernard A., 11, 58, 59, 60, 62, 63, 317
Thrall, Margaret E., 174, 202, 209, 216, 317

Thrax, Dionysius, 8, 9, 10, 58, 311, 320
Turner, Nigel, xxiii, 187, 318
Vandorpe, Katelijn, 318
Wallace, Daniel B., 7, 8, 18, 31, 32, 61, 90, 142, 149, 167, 195, 268, 291, 318
Wanamaker, Charles A., 83, 88, 89, 103, 110, 121, 124, 127, 158, 165, 318
Weima, Jeffrey A. D., 83, 94, 103, 110, 112, 144, 318
Wenham, J. W., 13, 14, 39, 318
White, John L., 104, 114, 129, 157, 318
Wifstrand, Albert, 3, 318
Winter, John Garrett, xxii, 222, 318
Witherington III, Ben, 152, 291, 296, 318
Woodhouse, S. C., 227, 318
Young, Richard A., 258, 279, 319, 324
Zerwick, Maximillian, 27, 28, 29, 31, 32, 274, 319

SUBJECT INDEX

Active Verbs
  As distinct from middle and passive, 14, 34, 37, 38, 39, 40, 44, 62, 71, 205, 246
  As situation focused, 40
  With middle future forms, 18, 27
Defective Verbs, 15, 18, 25, 56
Deponency, 2, 11, 13, 14, 15, 16, 18, 19, 22, 23, 24, 25, 30, 32, 34, 38, 39, 41, 42, 48, 55, 56, 57, 58, 59, 60, 61, 62, 63, 72, 101, 116, 117, 122, 124, 127, 129, 146, 167, 170, 173, 177, 186, 188, 189, 195, 206, 211, 219, 243, 246, 279, 303, 304, 314, 315, 316, 317
Diathesis, see also Voice, 5, 66, 67, 76, 83
Greek Language
  Attic/Classical, xvi, xxi, 3, 4, 5, 7, 8, 13, 15, 17, 22, 26, 27, 28, 30, 32, 33, 34, 39, 43, 46, 54, 64, 82, 84, 101, 111, 137, 167, 197, 227, 257, 262, 266, 309, 310, 313, 316, 318
  Evolution/Continuity of, 3, 4, 8
  Koine, 1, 2, 3, 4, 5, 7, 8, 28, 30, 31, 32, 34, 35, 36, 39, 40, 41, 42, 54, 61, 62, 64, 78, 111, 146, 152, 266, 305, 311, 314
Linguistic Terms
  Agent, 5, 11, 12, 16, 22, 24, 36, 39, 40, 41, 44, 46, 47, 48, 49, 51, 52, 54, 64, 67, 68, 71, 73, 77, 86, 88, 89, 90, 93, 96, 97, 110, 119, 123, 127, 133, 144, 145, 147, 159, 160, 161, 204, 213, 215, 216, 217, 227, 254, 258, 259, 264, 266, 301
  Beneficiary, 44, 51, 52, 53, 62, 82, 101, 124, 135, 152, 162, 166, 179, 183, 185, 196, 227, 236, 258, 269, 277
  Experiencer, 44, 51, 52, 101, 108, 141, 147, 154, 196, 204, 213, 227, 237, 269, 277
  Markedness, 7, 35, 44, 45, 46, 51, 66, 116, 182, 279
  Patient, 44, 45, 46, 47, 54, 64, 266, 267, 279
  Media Tantum, 1, 2, 45, 48, 50, 53, 55, 62, 66, 73, 78, 79, 84, 99, 101, 104, 114, 116, 122, 125, 127, 129, 131, 133, 135,

146, 150, 153, 162, 166, 170, 172, 177, 186, 189, 195, 197, 206, 218, 245, 246, 297, 299
Medial Event, 70, 71, 87, 98, 101, 110, 115, 116, 144, 177
Middle Verbs
  Morphology, 35, 47
  Oppositional, 1, 2, 45, 67, 73, 110, 175, 177, 243, 245, 299, 303
  Translated as active, 1, 10, 13, 14, 15, 30, 35, 39, 49, 58, 217
Middle Voice
  As Internal diathesis, 67, 68, 69, 73, 92, 144, 237, 245, 258, 259, 269, 292, 296, 301
  As voice of personal interest, 15, 18, 23, 141, 145, 147, 259
  Categories
    Allan's Subcategories (Situation Types)
      Body Motion Middle, 48, 54, 58, 77, 126, 127, 150, 213
      Collective Motion Middle, 49, 54, 77
      Direct Reflexive Middle, 20, 23, 50, 77, 215, 304
      Indirect Reflexive Middle, 23, 53, 78, 82, 115, 122, 124, 125, 135, 147, 152, 162, 166, 183, 185, 188, 191, 228, 230, 237, 256, 258, 259
      Mental Activity Middle, 51, 78, 154, 175, 177, 303
      Mental Process Middle, 47, 77, 88, 94, 108, 156, 279, 280
      Perception Middle, 51, 58, 77, 197
      Reciprocal Middle, 19, 23, 49, 77
      Speech Act Middle, 52, 78, 92, 103, 105, 122, 137, 140, 147, 194, 227, 229, 230, 231, 236, 239, 240, 277
      Spontaneous Process middle, 47, 77, 94, 97
  Cateogies
    Dynamic Middle, 16, 33, 38, 55, 72, 73, 77, 82, 84, 88, 93, 94, 101, 104, 106, 120, 122, 133, 135, 137, 141, 145, 154, 164, 166, 167, 169, 177, 180, 183, 185, 187, 188, 192, 196, 204, 205, 206, 216, 229, 233, 234, 241, 243, 245, 257, 259, 274, 278, 299, 303
  Criteria used for middle function, 73

Criteria utilized, 73, 245, 301, 302
Form indicating function, 22, 48, 124, 184, 212, 253
Theta aorist morphology, 35, 36, 41, 53, 64, 79, 108
Transitivity, 10, 11, 12, 16, 19, 35, 36, 38, 40, 44, 47, 48, 49, 59, 64, 65, 67, 68, 71, 72, 103, 107, 109, 113, 124, 126, 158, 190, 199, 201, 213, 214, 229, 258, 264, 269, 276
New Testament (Language of), 2, 4, 46
Passive Voice
   As a subcategory of middle, 46, 47, 73, 77, 217, 266
   Compared to active middle, 35, 217
Prototypical Transitive Event, 44, 64, 71, 96, 116, 126, 136, 243, 279

Index of Exegetical Case Studies

Gal 1:4 (ἐξέληται)	248–259
Gal 1:16 (προσανεθέμην)	271–275
Gal 1:20 (ψεύδομαι)	276–278
Gal 2:2 (ἀνεθέμην)	275–276
Gal 2:6 (προσανέθεντο)	271–275
Gal 2:12 (φοβούμενος)	278–281
Gal 3:3 (ἐναρξάμενοι, ἐπιτελεῖσθε)	260–271
Gal 3:15 (ἐπιδιατάσσεται)	281–283
Gal 4:10 (παρατηρεῖσθε)	284–289
Gal 4:11 (φοβοῦμαι)	278–281
Gal 4:20 (ἀποροῦμαι)	289–292
Gal 5:5 (ἀπεκδεχόμεθα)	292–294
Gal 5:17 (ἀντίκειται)	294–297
Gal 5:26 (προκαλούμενοι)	297–299

INDEX OF MIDDLE VERBS EXAMINED

ἀντέχομαι	164–166
ἀπέχομαι	148–150
ἀποτάσσομαι	192–195
ἄρχομαι	195–197
ἀσπάζομαι	114–115
βουλεύομαι	175–177
βούλομαι	172–175
γίνομαι	84–99
δέομαι	146–148
δέχομαι	79–84
διαμαρτύρομαι	104–106
δύναμαι	129–131
ἐνδύομαι	109–111
ἐνεργέομαι	141–146
ἐπαίρομαι	213–218
ἐπικαλοῦμαι	183–186
ἐργάζομαι	133–135
ἔρχομαι	125–128
εὐαγγελίζομαι	101–104
ἐφίσταμαι	157–159
ἡγέομαι	162–164
καυχάομαι	218–243
κοιμάομαι	106–109, 155–157
κτάομαι	150–153
λογίζομαι	197–205
μαρτύρομαι	138–141
ὁμείρομαι	131–133
παραμυθέομαι	135–138

παρρησιάζομαι	99–101
ποιοῦμαι	120–122
προΐσταμαι	160–162
προσεύχομαι	166–168
ῥύομαι	122–125
στρατεύομαι	211–213
σφραγίζομαι	180–183
τίθεμαι	111–113
φείδομαι	186–189
φιλοτιμέομαι	153–154
χαρίζομαι	189–192
χράομαι	177–180

www.ingramcontent.com/pod-product-compliance
Lightning Source LLC
Chambersburg PA
CBHW071811230426
43670CB00013B/2424